IMPERIAL BROTHERHOOD

A volume in the series Culture, Politics, and the Cold War

EDITED BY CHRISTIAN G. APPY

GENDER

AND THE MAKING OF

COLD WAR FOREIGN POLICY

IMPERIAL
BROTHERHOOD

Robert D. Dean

University of Massachusetts Press   *Amherst*

LC 2001005553
ISBN 1-55849-312-3 (cloth); ISBN 1-55849-414-6 (paper)

Designed by Milenda Nan Ok Lee
Set in Adobe Garamond and Castellar MT by Graphic Composition, Inc.
Printed and bound by Thomson-Shore, Inc.

Library of Congress Cataloging-in-Publication Data

Dean, Robert D., 1956–
    Imperial brotherhood : gender and the making of Cold War foreign policy /
Robert D. Dean.
    p. cm. — (Culture, politics, and the cold war)
Includes bibliographical references and index.
    ISBN 1-55849-312-3
    1. United States—Foreign relations—1945–1989—Social aspects. 2. Masculinity—Political
aspects—United States—History—20th century. 3. Sex role—Political aspects—United
States—History—20th century. I. Title. II. Series.
E744 .D43 2001
327.73'009'045—dc21

                    2001005553

British Library Cataloguing in Publication data are available.

In Memory of Jack L. Dean (1925–2001)

CONTENTS

ACKNOWLEDGMENTS

I owe thanks to many who helped make this book possible. Michael Schaller, Karen Anderson, and Laura Tabili deserve thanks for the examples they set as productive and engaged scholars and for the intellectual stimulation, support, and valuable criticism they provided. At several critical junctures Frank Costigliola, Emily Rosenberg, and Geoff Smith provided much-needed encouragement and practical support. I am also indebted to each of them for suggestions (and clues) that made this a better book. For several years Rob Buffington heard more about this project than anyone else, and our extended conversation on gender, culture, class, and race generated much that improved the book. The comments and suggestions of many other scholars, on conference panels and in conversation, have also helped me. Special thanks go to David L. Anderson, Elaine Tyler May, Andy Rotter, Michael Sherry, Anders Stephanson, and Marilyn Young. In a more general sense I thank Michael Hogan for his openness to cultural approaches to the history of international relations during his tenure as editor of *Diplomatic History*, providing a forum for much new and interesting work.

This project depended heavily on the skill and cooperation of many librarians and archivists. I was ably assisted by staff at the Truman, Eisenhower, Kennedy, and Johnson Presidential Libraries; the National Archives in College Park and Washington; the Seely G. Mudd Manuscript Library, Princeton University; the Hoover Institution Archives; the Library of Congress; Special Collections at the University of Massachusetts Amherst; University of Nevada Reno; the University of Arizona Library; the Nebraska Historical Society; the Nevada Historical Society. I particularly want to thank Chris Wilhelm of the National Archives, Randy Sowell of the Truman Library, Linda Hanson of the LBJ Library, Susan Searcy of the University of Nevada Reno, and Nancy Young and Susan Illis of the Seely G. Mudd Library. I also appreciate the provision of support for a portion of the research by a John F. Kennedy Library Foundation grant. I wish I could be as enthusiastic in my endorsement of the FBI FOIA office, but an institutional culture of secrecy and a systematic underfunding of the office made obtaining needed documents a slow and frustrating undertaking.

Chris Appy, general editor of the series *Culture, Politics, and the Cold War,* deserves special mention. His suggestions have made this a better book. His patience and support during the longer-than-expected completion of the manuscript are greatly appreciated. Clark Dougan, senior editor, and the excellent staff of University of Massachusetts Press also deserve thanks for making the publication process a painless experience.

This book would not have been possible without the support of my family. Riva, Ben, and Hannah provided love and a sense of purpose even when the practical wisdom of a scholarly career was not entirely apparent. The most heartfelt thanks go to my parents, Jack and Norma Dean, whose unflagging encouragement and generosity underpin the very existence of this book.

R. D. D.

IMPERIAL BROTHERHOOD

•INTRODUCTION•

CULTURE, GENDER,

AND FOREIGN POLICY REASON

I BEGAN this book seeking to answer a riddle presented by the American military intervention in Southeast Asia during the Kennedy and Johnson years. It has since grown into a more extensive and discursive meditation on the ramifications of culture, class, and gender as factors in U.S. Cold War foreign policy. Nonetheless, the central puzzle remains at the heart of the project: how did highly educated men, who prided themselves on their hard-headed pragmatism, men who shunned "fuzzy-minded" idealism, lead the United States into a prolonged, futile, and destructive war in Vietnam and Southeast Asia? The magnitude of the disaster—the disproportion between any measure of United States "interests" in Vietnam, whether strategic or economic, and the economic and social costs of the war—raises questions about reason and decision making among the elite men who made policy. These questions have not yet been fully answered by historians.[1]

Such questions still bedevil even those who made the decisions, as demonstrated by Robert S. McNamara's memoirs of Vietnam decision making.[2] The account by the former secretary of defense under Presidents Kennedy and Johnson has provoked acrimonious responses from commentators at both ends and at the center of the political spectrum. The book has been scorned by conservatives and some veterans' groups for calling into question the justice and wisdom of the American intervention itself, and scorned by the left for the long delay between the events described and McNamara's confession of error. Nor have historians embraced McNamara's account.

Many seem angry and baffled by the seeming inadequacy or incompleteness of his explanations for the Vietnam war.[3]

The usefulness of the book has been overlooked in a rush to condemn. Many fault the former secretary of defense for his apparent failure to reveal a "smoking gun" that would lay bare the logic of the otherwise seemingly irrational and egregious decisions made by American policymakers. "This memoir could have been a veritable treasure trove of information and knowledge," one scholar asserts. "Instead it merely rehashes familiar themes and seems like a last minute confession to clear his conscience."[4]

However unsatisfactory it may be as a complete account of the war, McNamara does grapple with the failure of reason among policymakers. Perhaps one reason critics find his memoirs frustrating is that he identified many occasions where the policymakers failed to ask truly significant questions about the costs and benefits of their decisions. He argues that had such fundamental questions arisen, rational assessment of the contradictions between means and ends would have precluded the U.S. intervention. Instead, he draws a picture of men whom he describes as bright, brave, dedicated public servants, acting blindly, with the best of intentions, never questioning the assumptions that led them and the United States into folly and disaster. But his account never provides a satisfying analysis that can explain this failure of individual and collective reason. McNamara's story of the tragedy of Vietnam conveys pathos as well. He reveals the inadequacy of the anointed to manage U.S. imperial interests according to the standards of the imperial administrators themselves: "I had spent twenty years as manager identifying problems and forcing organizations—often against their will—to think deeply and realistically about alternative courses of action and their consequences. I doubt I will ever fully understand why I did not do so here [in July 1965]."[5]

This, perhaps, helps explain the disdain and resentment his book has evoked. The magnitude of the tragedy demands a more heroic narrative; closure demands the revelation of conscious malevolence, conspiracy, evil, greed, or, alternately, the tragic striving of heroic men against inevitable circumstance. Others may prefer the story of a noble endeavor betrayed by the cowardice of peace protesters and civilian bureaucrats who "tied the hands" of those who fought the war. Whatever one's narrative preference, few are satisfied with the puzzled confessions of error and inadequacy by one of the "best and the brightest." Perhaps they believe that McNamara's account can be interpreted as effectively diminishing the sacrifice of those who believed and fought, or as reducing the moral significance of resistance to the war by those who opposed McNamara's policy.

Nonetheless, analyzing and understanding the historical failure of foreign policy reason is an important task. McNamara's memoirs offer important clues toward rethinking the history of elite foreign policy decision making: "I want to put Vietnam in context. We of the Kennedy and Johnson administrations who participated in the decisions on Vietnam acted according to what we thought were the principles and traditions of this nation. We made our decisions in light of those values. Yet we were wrong, terribly wrong."[6]

A central premise underlying this book is that all meaning is dependent on context. McNamara invokes the "principles and traditions of this nation" as the operative context that gave meaning to perceived threats, and in which the benefits and costs of possible responses to those threats were analyzed. He fails, however, to analyze the nature of those principles and traditions, or to articulate the context that made the perception of threat meaningful; thus even now, he cannot completely explain his former lapses from an idealized operational reason.

This book attempts to provide a much broader context for understanding the actions and reasoning of the small and strikingly homogenous group of men who made the decisions to intervene in Vietnam. It assumes that the process of foreign policy decision does not and cannot exist in an abstract realm of reasoned calculation of "national interest." Instead it assumes that the men who make the decisions are complex, socially constructed beings, who act from a repertoire of possibilities that are a product of their experience. Foreign policy reason too, is thus culturally constructed and reproduced; a full analysis demands an account of the formative patterns of class and gender among the policymakers.

While the Vietnam decision makers employed a formally rational procedure for making cost-benefit decisions about intervention, the costs and benefits discussed often emphasized abstractions such as "prestige," "credibility," "national honor," or "tests of resolve." As Robert McNamara now confesses, these formally rational procedures resulted in policy of "substantive irrationality," to borrow from Max Weber. Scholarship on the intervention reveals a pattern of repeated incremental escalations of military force, accompanied by a pessimism about the real chances of success for the ostensible goal of the intervention, "nation building."[7]

This demands a more satisfactory account of apparent paradoxes of ends and means, costs and benefits, pessimistic prediction and interventionist policy.[8] Other literature about the Kennedy and Johnson administrations—biographies, memoirs, and tales of political culture—contain innumerable anecdotes that reveal an obsession with "toughness" and the use of a sexualized language of competition and dominance among men who contended for power within the American electoral system and within the foreign policy bureaucracy. In spite of twenty years of feminist scholarship, this evidence of "gendered" policy has never been systematically explored. Writers such as Richard Barnet and David Halberstam acknowledged the significance of masculine competition and language but did not pursue the implications of their insights. Most others simply used such anecdotes to add color to otherwise conventional narratives about the lives of great men.[9]

Halberstam, Barnet, and others did, however, point to significant patterns in the construction of masculinity among foreign policy elites. They argued that the postwar "containment" doctrine and U.S. policy toward Vietnam were the product of a foreign policy "establishment," dominated by civilian national security bureaucrats—Wall Street lawyers, investment bankers, academics, and other elite men—who, "regarding service as an honor, and imbued with a sense of noblesse oblige, . . . glided easily between public and private careers." The "establishment" that dominated U.S. foreign policy between 1947 and 1968 was made of men who shared strikingly similar patterns of education, socialization, and, in many cases, class background.[10]

Understanding "masculinity" as a factor in the foreign policy reasoning of the Kennedy and Johnson national security bureaucrats demands a shift of emphasis toward the construction of particular kinds of elite masculinities; at the same time it requires consideration of the historical milieu that produced such men. The foreign policy decision makers of the two administrations incarnated an imperial masculinity tied to patterns of class and education; they embodied one legacy of twentieth-century U.S. imperial expansion. Their reflexive preference for policy "toughness" was also linked to the history of domestic political conflicts between "internationalist" elites and provincial conservatives as they played out in the sexualized political discourse and bureaucratic purges of the postwar Red Scare.[11] The vision of political manhood held by the policymakers of the 1960s had its origins in the late nineteenth century and was shaped by the imperial expansion and domestic politics of the twentieth century. Thus the book explores both the formation and the foreign policy implications of a "masculine" political identity.[12]

As biographers of "establishment" figures have indicated, but not analyzed, the actions and attitudes of foreign policy decision makers were grounded in prescriptive lessons learned in a series of exclusive male-only institutions—boarding schools, Ivy League fraternities and secret societies, elite military service, metropolitan men's clubs—where imperial traditions of "service" and "sacrifice" were invented and bequeathed to those that followed. One aspect of this book is founded on the assumption that these institutions served to imbue men with a particular kind of "manhood," that one of the crucial experiences of individuals in such institutions is an indoctrination in an "ideology of masculinity" and the ritual creation of a fictive brotherhood of privilege and power.

The term "ideology of masculinity" refers to the cultural system of prescription and proscription that organizes the "performance" of an individual's role in society, that draws boundaries around the social category of manhood, and that can be used to legitimate power and privilege. Because the roles men play in society and the powers they wield are linked to social class, ideologies of masculinity are inseparable from class experience. An ideology of masculinity in its *prescriptive* aspect provides the raw material needed to imagine and construct a narrative identity—the internal story that lends coherence to the self. In its *proscriptive* aspect, it rules out certain ways of imagining and acting in the world.[13] An ideology of masculinity is, in this sense, a subset of a larger "gender discourse"—a symbolic system of meaning by which social relations of power and privilege are rendered "natural" and transparent by reference to sexual biology, a supposedly fundamental and unquestionable set of relationships.

These ideas are, of course, tied to a number of related premises that underlie the whole book. One of the most fundamental is now a commonplace of feminist and postmodernist scholarship: the attributes of men and women as social actors are not simply functions of innate biological differences. Instead, those attributes are constructed and reproduced by cultural practice. "Gender" is the term that refers to this social organization of the relationship between the sexes, the cultural reproduction of "roles" for sexed individuals. Further, gender operates as a "symbolic system, a central organizing discourse of culture, one that not only shapes how we experience ourselves as men and women, but that also interweaves with other discourses and shapes them." As Joan Scott argued in an influential essay, political discourse is permeated by this structure of symbolic meanings: "gender is a primary way of signifying relationships of power. . . . politics constructs gender, and gender constructs politics."[14]

Another premise of this book is the assumption that the ideals of "manhood" or "womanhood" held by a society (or, more specifically, by classes within modern societies) are circulated through the culture and, to a large extent, are individually internalized in the form of narratives. As Graham Dawson has argued, "masculinities are lived out in the flesh, but fashioned in the imagination." These cultural narratives work in a reciprocal or circular way, providing "a range of possible selves" for individuals to use to "compose" the narrative(s) of their own life.[15]

The narrative possibilities from which individuals construct gendered identities are constrained by culture and class. The stories one tells oneself and others about personal identity are part of an "inescapably social process." Social recognition is necessary to confirm that the narrative of self corresponds to "the experience of others, as shared, collective identities and realities." To be recognized socially (as an affirmation of "masculinity" or "femininity"), the individual must deploy a narrative (or narratives) that fall within a range of culturally accepted types. "The narrative resource of a culture—its repertoire of shared and recognized forms—therefore functions as a currency of recognizable social identities."[16] One aim of this book is to explore the reciprocal relation between elite identity narratives and social and political practice.

While culture offers individuals some latitude in the choice of socially recognized and accepted masculinities, social systems of inclusion and exclusion operate to favor "hegemonic" ideologies of masculinity. Nonetheless, such narratives often create contradictions within individuals. Men may wish and strive to become the man they imagine they might be. Their need for the recognition of others may compel them to identify with particular forms of masculinity. Since the demands of social life are not uniform but multifaceted and contradictory, the achievement of an absolutely unified and coherent gendered social identity, for masculinity as well as femininity, is an impossibility.[17]

There is always a tension between the lived experience of individual masculinities and cultural ideals of manhood. The social "self" is a complex, divided entity. The roots of this division inhere in the complexities of the social world, divided as it is by sex/gender, race/ethnicity, and class; these are further complicated by contradictions in the narratives of gender ideals and in the social relations and practices of gender socialization.[18] In this book I emphasize the collective and "hegemonic" aspects of cultural ideologies of masculinity and their ramifications in foreign policy decision making and politics. Nonetheless, the patterns I describe emerged from an examination of the stories of individuals whose lives often contradicted the ideals of elite masculinity to which they were exposed during their formative years.

The narrative identity of the men under study here intertwined with ideals of "public service" and the maintenance of positions of power in the competitive and heavily scrutinized realm of national politics. In such a context, men faced great pressures toward conformity to dominant ideologies of masculinity. For many, the composition of serviceable identity narratives required erasing, repressing, or explaining away deviations from ideal master narratives. The stories constructed depended on the audience addressed. For example, men whose bodies did not match the ideal of athletic and warrior strength could employ a variety of strategies. One might use the story of bodybuilding through force of will (Teddy Roosevelt is the narrative archetype), while others concealed or denied their debility, or created fictions of athletic and war injuries to explain away or even glorify visible defects. Sexuality carried highly charged meaning in narratives of masculine political power. A few elite men in positions of power or influence whose sexuality deviated from publicly sanctioned norms constructed public personas to deny and conceal aspects of themselves (e.g., homosexuality) that left them vulnerable to attack by political rivals, while living a "private" sexual narrative that contradicted dominant ideologies of masculinity.

A word on the structure of the book is in order. The early chapters discuss the historical creation of an "imperial brotherhood" and institutions central to perpetuating a particular kind of political and foreign policy elite. They focus on the role of elite boarding schools and volunteer military service in the imagination of imperial manhood and in the construction of networks of patronage across generations. This material emphasizes the prescriptive dimension of elite socialization. The middle three chapters of the book center on the political and personal effects of a state-sanctioned sexual inquisition—the McCarthy-era purge of homosexuals in the State Department and other government agencies. Because of its significance to the bitter battle between right-wing countersubversives and the imperial brotherhood of the establishment, I have provided the first empirically detailed account of the workings of the inquisition, focused on its effects as "proscriptive" lessons for then current and future policymakers. While John D'Emilio's pioneering work on gay history places the purge in the context of the creation of a self-conscious "sexual community" through "the bonds of oppression," my intent is to show how the subterranean sexual politics of slander, blackmail, and purge were an integral part of the "high politics" of Congress and the executive during the Cold War, and central to struggles over political inclusion and exclusion within foreign policy bureaucracies. The final chapters address the ways that this cultural legacy of prescription and proscription took form as an "ideology of masculinity" under President John F. Kennedy, and how the politics of gender shaped the chain of decisions leading Presidents Kennedy and Johnson into war in Vietnam.[19]

•ONE•

THE FOREIGN POLICY "ESTABLISHMENT"

Between 1940 and 1967, when I stopped counting, all the first and second level posts in a huge national security bureaucracy were held by fewer than four hundred individuals who rotate through a variety of key posts. The temporary civilian managers who come to Washington to run America's wars and preparations for wars, the national security managers, were so like one another in occupation, religion, style, and social status . . . it was possible to locate the offices of all of them within fifteen city blocks in New York, Boston, and Detroit. Most of their biographies in *Who's Who* read like minor variations on a single theme—wealthy parents, Ivy-League education, leading law firm or bank (or entrepreneur in a war industry), introduction to government in World War II.

The two qualities these men prize in themselves and in others are loyalty and duty. Loyalty is the supreme bureaucratic virtue. In the foreign policy establishment, it is far more forgivable to do something incompetent or dangerous inside than to talk about it on the outside.

Richard J. Barnet, *Roots of War*

IN MID-October 1962, as the first photographic confirmation of Soviet ballistic missiles in Cuba reached the White House, President Kennedy began secretly to assemble an executive committee of the National Security Council (or "ExComm") to advise him on possible responses to the emerging crisis. Kennedy faced a grave situation that seemingly threatened the balance of power upon which U.S. leadership of the Western coalition was founded. Even if the Soviet nuclear missiles didn't increase the real military danger facing the United States, as some around him argued, Kennedy and his advisers believed that the public revelation of their presence would be a crushing blow to American prestige worldwide and might severely damage the U.S.-led system of global alliances.

Kennedy turned his attention to the new Soviet threat with the awareness that after the failure of the Bay of Pigs invasion the preceding year, his presidency could ill afford another Cuban fiasco. In the weeks before the U-2 spy plane photographs arrived, right-wing Republican senators had already castigated the administration for weakness, publicizing unconfirmed rumors of Russian missile installations. Kennedy foresaw heavy domestic political damage during the midterm elections in November. The stakes were high enough for the president, with the counsel of a small group of powerful national security managers, to embark on a course that led the United States and the Soviet Union to the brink of nuclear war.[1]

The ExComm included most of the high-level national security managers of the Kennedy administration, but Kennedy also summoned three elder statesmen from their private business concerns as prominent international corporate lawyers and investment bankers: Dean G. Acheson, former secretary of state under Truman; John J. McCloy, former assistant secretary of war during World War II and former high commissioner of occupied Germany; and Robert A. Lovett, who had served FDR as assistant secretary of war and Truman as undersecretary of state and secretary of defense. The president reached Lovett by telephone and requested that the New York investment banker depart for Washington immediately. Lovett promptly left the meeting he was attending and rushed to the White House.

While receiving his first briefing on the missile emplacements with national security adviser McGeorge Bundy, in Bundy's White House office, Lovett noticed a portrait of Henry L. Stimson, his old mentor in the War Department. Lovett later recounted that during his conversation with Bundy, he felt that "the old Colonel seemed to me to be staring me straight in the face." Lovett was moved by Stimson's resolute visage, "so powerful a reminder" of duty and service, while he was briefed on a situation with the potential for a superpower confrontation that could end in nuclear holocaust. When the conversation progressed to other advisers' attitudes concerning possible responses to the Soviet missiles in Cuba, Lovett counseled Bundy, "Mac, I think the best service we can do to President Kennedy is to try to approach this as Colonel Stimson would." Bundy "fully agreed" that this would be the "benchmark" to aim for during the crisis.[2]

As Lovett later declared, this ritual invocation of Stimson's name had a "special meaning" to Bundy. Stimson's career represented a legacy of heroic statesmanship under three different presidential administrations. Stimson symbolized the ideal of masculine leadership for men within the government who shared his vision of American imperial destiny. "The Colonel" had played a significant role in the emergence of the activist, engaged, foreign policy of "liberal internationalism" that Bundy exemplified. Stimson helped fulfill the imperial ambitions of his friends and patrons, Theodore Roosevelt and Elihu Root. He helped move the United States from the periphery of world power to the center of a "Western coalition holding the world in balance against the infidel," replacing the British empire as "the economic and military guarantor and moral leader of the world."[3] Stimson's legacy, however, surely had a personal meaning to Bundy deeper than this précis of his career suggests. Stimson, Lovett, and Bundy were connected across generations by institutional ties of patronage, class tradition, education, and fraternalism; they were bound together by a common conception of patrician "manliness" and heroism. To Bundy, Stimson was an exemplary man, a stoic servant of the state, and a bridge linking the heroic foreign policy of Roosevelt and Root with his own ascension to power in the Kennedy foreign policy bureaucracy.

Henry Stimson's heroic service represented to Bundy, almost literally, a family legacy. Bundy's father, Harvey, had been another protégé of "the Colonel." A corporate and trust lawyer who had married into a prominent Boston "Brahmin" family, the elder Bundy faithfully served Stimson during the latter's tenure as secretary of state and as FDR's secretary of war. McGeorge was, through his father, intimately acquainted with the triumphs of Stimson's leadership during the ultimately victorious struggle against "international aggression" during World War II. McGeorge Bundy himself had played the role of Stimson's protégé. As a junior fellow at Harvard after the war, he spent eighteen months living on Stimson's Long Island estate researching and writing the former secretary's memoirs of life in public service.[4] Out of months of conversation with Stimson, Bundy created a narrative of masculine heroism--a tale of prescient statesmanship, of unwavering rejection of "appeasement," of resolute patrician service and sacrifice as both soldier and statesman.

Lovett invoked Stimson's name at a moment when the U.S. position as the military guarantor of the global balance of power (and America's preeminent imperial power) that Lovett had helped create seemed gravely threatened. As they looked "down the gun barrel of nuclear disaster," Lovett conjured up an emblem of tradition and brotherhood, an elite brotherhood of manly engagement in struggle to defend cultural, social, political, and territorial boundaries. Lovett invoked not only the image of Henry Stimson but also a self-identifying narrative of elite power: a story that granted legitimacy and self-assurance to a small group of privileged men empowered to make life or death decisions affecting not only the United States or the "West" but all humanity.[5] Bundy, of course, was intimately familiar with that heroic narrative through his youthful literary labors on behalf of bipartisan U.S. imperial "internationalism." Bundy had, in 1952, also produced a tome celebrating Dean Acheson's heroic leadership of the imperial coalition, defending the former secretary of state from charges that he was "either soft or pink."[6] The texts that made up the strands of a larger cultural narrative of elite masculine leadership were woven through the lives and histories of the men of Kennedy's ExComm. Stimson's life history provided an idealized version of a larger pattern of upper-class masculine socialization shared by most members of what came to be known as the "foreign policy establishment." The narrative of Stimson's career revealed the potential for self-realization inherent in that social pattern. For establishment elites, Stimson provided a model of masculine virtue, of ambition and power sanctified by service and sacrifice.[7]

John J. McCloy, an ExComm participant and himself a central figure in the U.S. foreign policy establishment, later celebrated the outcome of the Missile Crisis as the latest of Cold War triumphs orchestrated by great men of the national security state.

> The fight against the tyranny of the Nazis and the Japanese militarists *was* won, and in the aftermath of that war, the Marshall Plan was conceived and put into operation; the Bretton Woods institutions were erected; Berlin was defended, and so was Greece; the re-orientation of both Germany and Japan was effected; NATO was conceived, and so were the Coal and Steel community and the Common Market; the Cuban nuclear missile crisis was confronted and passed. Some might say that this was statesmanship in a rather heroic mold—and most of it was primarily motivated by Americans.[8]

U.S. hegemony over the "free world" required the cultivation of imperial masculinity. Containing communism demanded the manly patrician stoicism of the brotherhood, of men like Stimson. Only such men could "prevent the expansion of forces that, as has been demonstrated in the past, lead to the permanent suppression of all liberties." McCloy proudly described a central aspect of the elite identity narrative, a neo-stoic masculinity:

> The Romans would have understood what I am trying to say. They had a word for it—"gravitas"—and the one who possessed it had the respect and regard of his countrymen, whether he was in the forum or on the farm. "Gravitas" did not imply age nor brilliance, and, least of all a style or school of thought—it means a core, a weight of judgment and honest appraisal. . . . I had the great good fortune to be rather closely associated, in the course of my life, with a number of famous statesmen—Franklin Roosevelt, Winston Churchill, George Marshall. I could name a number of others who are en-

titled to be called statesmen, but my hero statesman, perhaps because I was most closely associated with him, was Henry L. Stimson, once Secretary of State, twice Secretary of War, and advisor to a number of Presidents; —a man of rugged integrity, force, and courage. He possessed "gravitas" in solid measure.[9]

The notion of a brotherhood of privilege, power, "service," and "sacrifice" was central to the identity narrative of Kennedy's foreign policy elite. This is not simply a metaphorical use of language; it refers to a ritual pattern enacted in the course of an individual's life in a sequence of sex-segregated institutions. Within the government, linked to socially constructed brotherhoods, older powerful men used mechanisms of patronage to approve the inclusion of younger men into the circles of power. After 1940, a patrician class (by birth or assimilation of values) of civilian national security managers became increasingly important to U.S. foreign policy. Conceiving themselves as aristocratic (in the sense of "the rule of the best") warrior-intellectuals, many gravitated to the newly powerful national security bureaucracies of the executive branch, where they exercised power and "responsibility" with a degree of isolation from the capricious demands of the electorate.

Membership in a series of overlapping exclusive male-only institutions provided such men with set a of credentials demonstrating that they met the criteria of masculine success required for inclusion. Boarding schools taught an ideology of "manly character" and patrician service and sacrifice. University fraternal secret societies were important to the construction of a sense of upper-class masculine privilege and power. Metropolitan men's clubs, evidence suggests, served to maintain elite male solidarity both socially and professionally. Another kind of experience, elite voluntary military service during war, provided a lifelong validation of membership in a brotherhood with life-and-death power over others.

Stimson, Lovett, and Bundy illustrate this overlapping membership in male "solidarity groups." All three had received their secondary education at elite eastern boarding schools designed to instill "manly character" and muscular Christianity, modeled more or less explicitly on the British public schools.[10] Stimson graduated from Phillips Andover Academy in 1883, Lovett from the Hill School in 1914, and Bundy from Groton School in 1936. All three were graduates of Yale. Equally significant to the construction of elite "brotherhood," each had been elected to the secret senior society Skull and Bones, Yale's most prestigious men's club. Stimson on occasion referred to Skull and Bones as "the most important educational experience of his life," and he had shown a distinct preference for "Bonesmen" and alumni of Harvard Law School when staffing the War Department in 1940. Later, McGeorge Bundy similarly assessed the significance of the secret society: "It was and is an important part of my life," he told a biographer, because of its "focus around the intense experience of learning to trust your colleagues." The pattern of elite fraternalism continued in their later professional life; each of the three men was (or had been) a member of Washington's Metropolitan Club, among others.[11]

The other men of ExComm were linked by the personal bonds of membership in such institutions and by the ideology of imperial stoic masculinity that pervaded their upbringing. Even when they were not born into the American upper class, the men recruited into the establishment had experienced a similar ideological indoctrination in manliness in less socially exalted but functionally comparable sex-segregated institutions. The aura of social inferiority attached to the "second rate" schools may well have spurred ambitious upwardly mobile young men to strive harder to meet ideals of imperial manhood and to reap the rewards of power implicitly promised by such ideals.

John J. McCloy, another central establishment figure (sometimes half-jokingly called the "chairman" of the establishment), provides a good example. McCloy was of "respectable" working-class background, but through the untiring efforts of his widowed mother and his own doggedness, he received a gentleman's education at a second or third-tier boy's boarding school modeled on Groton, the Peddie Institute, where he also belonged to a prep-school fraternity, Alpha Phi. From Peddie, McCloy went to Amherst College (joining Beta Theta Phi fraternity) and then to Harvard Law School. Three summers at the Plattsburg, N.Y., military "preparedness" officer-training camp run by Grenville Clark and General Leonard Wood helped indoctrinate McCloy in the imperial destiny of the United States as foretold by the erstwhile Rough Riders, General Wood, and Theodore Roosevelt. There, McCloy's contact with martial Wall Street millionaires and their sons initiated him into yet another brotherhood of power and privilege. Other men of middle- and working-class origins who rose to positions of power in the foreign policy bureaucracy of the 1960s such as Dean Rusk or Robert McNamara followed similar paths. They, too, were trained to stoic manly brotherhood in school and university (another credential of gentlemanly meritocracy, the Rhodes Scholarship, was frequently important in the recruitment of middle-class talent), served in the military during wartime, and were certified for office by powerful older patrons.[12]

President Kennedy was an admirer of the elite narrative of vigor, physical and moral courage, service, and sacrifice that permeated the self-conception of the foreign policy establishment. Despite the suspicion with which the

JOHN FITZGERALD KENNEDY

Born May 29, 1917, in Brookline, Massachusetts. Prepared at The Choate School. Home Address: 294 Pondfield Road, Bronxville, New York. Winthrop House. *Crimson* (2–4); Chairman Smoker Committee (1); St. Paul's Catholic Club (1–4). Football (1), Junior Varsity (2); Swimming (1). Squad (2). Golf (1). House Hockey (3, 4); House Swimming (2); House Softball (4). Hasty Pudding-Institute of 1770; Spee Club. Permanent Class Committee. Field of Concentration: Government. Intended Vocation: Law.

John F. Kennedy, Harvard Yearbook, June 1940. Courtesy John Fitzgerald Kennedy Library.

establishment initially regarded him because of his father's isolationism and unorthodox financial dealings, Kennedy actively courted the bearers of Stimson's legacy. Kennedy possessed, according to an influential friend and admirer, the Washington columnist Joseph Alsop (of Groton, Harvard, and the Porcellian Club), "a strong respect for what may be called 'WASP Establishment opinion.'"[13] As a beneficiary of a large trust fund that made his parvenu father's new money old, Kennedy had been cultivated for the exercise of power by immersion in the institutions that conferred legitimacy upon aspirants to the establishment. The Choate School, Harvard, and the Spee Club trained him to the code of the patrician gentleman and lifted the social burden of his Boston-Irish Catholic ancestry. His heroic volunteer military service in an elite unit during World War II conferred additional legitimacy, not only with the electorate in general, but with the "old-money" upper class, among whom such volunteer service had long functioned as an important totem of manhood.[14]

The conformity to patrician ideals represented by Kennedy's upbringing, and his espousal of a vigorous and activist foreign policy, made his patronage congenial to men with strong ties to the legacy of U.S. imperial expansion. Kennedy had taken great pains to assemble a bipartisan foreign policy apparatus. He had offered the cabinet posts of Treasury and Defense to both Lovett and McCloy; Lovett also refused the top State Department job. After consultations with Lovett, McCloy, and Dean Acheson, Kennedy "passed the torch to a new generation" of establishment recruits, the patrician banker Douglas Dillon (Groton, Harvard, and the Spee Club) and the automobile executive Robert McNamara, both Republicans, and Dean Rusk, the good soldier of Acheson's State Department and protégé of George C. Marshall. Kennedy and his appointees staffed the cabinet-level national security bureaucracy and the White House office of the National Security Council with exemplars of patrician and meritocratic "toughness": men who knew the code and fit the mold of the establishment.[15] Joseph Alsop, a resolute cold warrior and propagandist of patrician statesmanly heroism, expressed a representative opinion held by "Stimsonian" internationalists toward Kennedy's staffing choices:

> The competence of Doug Dillon at the treasury, the toughness that Bobby Kennedy soon began to show at the Justice Department, and the brilliance of McGeorge Bundy, serving as what amounted to the president's in-house secretary of state with authority like that of Harry Hopkins during Roosevelt's time, were all beyond contest. Furthermore, I found myself excited both in their company and, more importantly, by their presence in Washington. Indeed, I often thought, during those first months of the Kennedy administration, that in McNamara, Bundy, and all the others this country had at last found successors to the "Wise Men": civil servants as able, as tough-minded, as national minded, and as self denying as those men had been— and as courageous too.[16]

Alsop's breathless enthusiasm for the hard-boiled cold warriors of the Kennedy administration amounted to self-congratulation. Alsop as well as the "wise men" and Kennedy's foreign policy advisers were members of a small but powerful social world rooted in a particular construction of class and gender. His celebratory list of virtues obscured much: how this vision of "courage" and "tough-mindedness" meant conformity to a blinkered Cold War orthodoxy; how inclusion in the brotherhood hinged on an array of surface appearances and mannerisms, a way of talking, a set of memberships and associations, the right contacts and connections; and how the exercise of privilege, self-aggrandizement, and power seeking were construed as "self-denial" and "sacrifice."

·TWO·

THE REPRODUCTION OF

IMPERIAL MANHOOD

There was no duplication of fagging, the English custom of allowing the big boys to use the smaller ones as servants, but the rector kept the idea that the senior boys should discipline the junior ones. If a boy met an older boy on the narrow boardwalk between Brooks and Hundred House on a winter morning, he was expected to step off into the snow. If a boy was fresh, or did not have the Groton tone, he was boot boxed (crammed doubled up into a footlocker), or pumped (removed to a lavatory where water was poured over and into him). The pumpings were brutal—it happened that boys nearly drowned and had to be resuscitated. The rector saw a moral value in this sort of hazing. It also had the practical advantage of enforcing conventional behavior without his interference, by peer-group pressure.

Groton was a Darwinian training ground for power. You started at the bottom with small humiliations and you rose to a position of seniority and, in some cases, eminence.

Ted Morgan, *FDR*

THE MEN who made American foreign policy during the 1960s were products of a cultural milieu and a system of education that took form in the late nineteenth century. A pattern of upper-class masculine socialization that solidified between roughly 1885 and World War I retained its central attributes at least until the onset of World War II. In many respects its assumptions went largely unchallenged until the upheavals of the 1960s spread to all-male boarding schools, Ivy League universities, and racially segregated elite metropolitan men's clubs. Central to this pattern was a concatenation of sex-segregated institutions that prepared and certified elite men for inclusion in the establishment. This preparation began in boyhood with attendance at elite boarding schools. It continued in Ivy League universities and the exclusive fraternities, clubs, and senior societies attached to them. During times of war, volunteer service in an elite military unit became part of the pattern. Adult membership in one or more exclusive urban men's clubs provided a final step in the sequence of male secret societies that certified a man as worthy of membership in a brotherhood of powerful men—a masculine aristocracy, or "rule by the best," as the members of the brotherhood saw it. This "curriculum" instructed men in class values and the gentlemanly code necessary to function as an insider. Of equal significance, and inseparable from class indoctrination, the curriculum inculcated men with an ideology of elite masculinity.[1]

This curriculum was a part of a late-nineteenth-century "upper-class enclosure movement," a period of boundary marking through the creation of a range of institutions that defined and delimited a group of insiders. The publication of the first *Social Register* (1888), the foundation of the first country clubs (1882), the social dominance of the fraternal clubs and secret societies at Harvard, Yale, and Princeton, and the emergence of a network of exclusive metropolitan men's clubs represented one aspect of old-stock patrician efforts to create and maintain class solidarity in the face of threatening new developments. This was the "private" aspect of the "progressive" upperclass campaign to pass immigration restriction laws, wrest political control of the cities from urban ethnic/immigrant political machines through civil service reform, and protect their professional privileges with new licensing laws controlling medicine, surgery, architecture, and engineering. Through such a process of "social closure," an old-stock WASP upper class attempted to "restrict access to rewards and opportunities to a limited circle of eligibles" and promote national networks of the privileged and the powerful. Elite American boarding schools represent one important legacy of this period.[2]

The American boarding school, modeled more or less explicitly upon the British public school, trained the adolescent sons of a moneyed elite in the stoic virtues of manliness and service to the state. An "invented tradition," this culture helped to create, reproduce, and validate a self-conscious ruling class. Animated by fears of the corrupting influence of the city with its immigrant hordes, Anglophile patrician old-stock Americans patronized newly founded or recently reconfigured boarding schools in rural New England, such as Groton, St. Paul's, Choate, Phillips Exeter and Andover, and others.[3]

Like British ones, American boarding schools provided indoctrination in manliness to strengthen character and harden bodies. The all-male schools were intentionally designed to provide a toughening ordeal for privileged sons of the upper class, otherwise thought to be at risk of regressing into weightless lives of indolence, luxury, and enervation. The upper class of the era was gripped by anxieties about Darwinian fitness and "race suicide," worries about struggles between nations for global empire, and by apprehension about U.S. "national efficiency" in global competition. Old-stock WASP elites feared the erosion of their political power and of protective cultural boundaries in the tide of immigration sweeping the cities. They feared, too, the waning of their social power with the emergence of large-scale industrial capitalism and the huge fortunes newly amassed by entrepreneurial parvenus.[4]

Partly in response to such fears, American boarding schools inculcated a masculine code of strength, loyalty, stoic service, and engagement in struggle. This code served to systematically create and reproduce a serviceable manhood, one that could answer the perceived threats to the Anglo-Saxon upper class. The boarding schools were "total institutions" designed to produce a stoic, boundary-defending masculinity in elite young men. Boys were taken from their homes and families in early adolescence and sent off to remote rural schools, an innovation that replaced the private tutors and private day schools previously employed by wealthy American families to educate their sons. One object of such an extreme solution to the problem of child rearing was to strip away a boy's personal identity and replace it with an understanding that "the collective identity of the group must take precedence over individual identities." "These boys were meant to become soldiers for their class and to become 'combat ready.' They had to be made tough, loyal to each other, and ready to take command without self-doubt. Boarding schools were not founded to produce Hamlets, but Dukes of Wellington who could stand above the carnage with a clear head and an unflinching will to win."[5]

The highest ambitions, and loftiest rhetoric, of the schoolmasters centered on the goal of promoting public service to the state. Rigor, ordeals, and sermonizing taught boys that it was the responsibility of men with a legitimate claim to social power to harden their bodies, discipline their minds, and realize their destiny in service to the state. "If some Groton boys do not enter political life and do something for our land it won't be because they have not been urged," asserted Endicott Peabody, headmaster of Groton School. A friend and relative of Theodore Roosevelt, Peabody repeatedly invited Roosevelt, Alfred Thayer Mahan, and other advocates of empire, duty, and martial virtue to visit the school. There they set about "drilling into the minds of such boys as are many of yours that they must use aright the gifts given to them and that they must render service to the State," as Roosevelt described the task to Peabody.[6] Students were reminded of the manliness and republican virtue of famous predecessors. Some bore "names great in American history"; thus they were exhorted to "follow nobly where their ancestors led so well, and to be prepared for their turn to lead."[7]

Many graduates, of course, largely rejected the model of the Platonic Guardian pressed upon them, eschewing government office or political careers. Instead, they exercised the privilege and power bestowed by birth and upbringing through lucrative careers in finance, law, and business, and in patrician philanthropic pursuits. Nonetheless, enough did develop an ambition to serve the state that alumni of Groton and other elite boarding schools wielded an extraordinary influence in government. Most often, of course, this meant combining a career as an investment banker or Wall Street lawyer with that of cabinet officer, diplomat, or White House aide.[8] But Groton also produced imperial leaders—who returned to the school to tout the rewards of public life and service to the state. Dean Acheson, who as Harry Truman's secretary of state could claim as much credit as anyone for promoting America's post–World War II global preeminence, demonstrated the durability of the tradition begun by Peabody and Theodore Roosevelt. He symbolized the realization of the dual aspiration of men like Peabody— the imperial hegemony of the United States under the leadership of the WASP upper class. Delivering the Groton School Prize Day address of 1966, Acheson, class of 1911, mapped the route to "happiness" for his youthful audience. Personal fulfillment came from pursuit of the "old Greek" ideal: "The exercise of vital powers in the direction of excellence, in a life affording them scope." Acheson asserted that no other career offered such "scope" as did imperial leadership, given the global power and reach of the United States:

> The prestige of public life waxes and wanes with the scope it offers. It was high in the period of Athens's greatness, the fifth century B.C. and at its nadir in the next century after defeat and humiliation. Today in the United States, its pull upon the able, the eager, and the ambitious is great. For the prize of the general, as Justice Holmes observed, is not a bigger tent but command. The managers of industry and finance have the bigger tents, but command rests with government. Command, or if one prefers, supreme leadership, gives scope for the exercise of vital powers in the direction of excellence.[9]

Acheson admonished his audience with the "stoic doctrine" he had absorbed during his own (unhappy) career at Groton. Their duty lay in self-realization through the aggrandizement of the power of the state—his vision of the individual in harmony with Logos. Railing against injustice was futile, he asserted: "remember that Aeschylus, Terence, and Jesus have all warned that it is hard and unwise to kick against the pricks. It is worse than unwise; it is disintegrating. Much in life cannot be affected or mitigated, and, hence must be borne; borne without complaint because complaint undermines the serenity essential to endurance." Referring to the escalating and increasingly problematic U.S. imperial intervention in Vietnam, Acheson warned his young listeners against "protest marches and burned draft cards." Instead, they should accept the inevitability and propriety of officials' decisions to wage war; their energy should go toward claiming their own commanding place in "public life." The former secretary of state's prescription for conformity highlights the narrow and particular definition of the "courage" and "toughness" so exalted by the imperial brotherhood.[10]

Acheson's vision of self-realization through command was consonant with the vision of empire advanced at Groton sixty years earlier. American patricians of the Edwardian era suffered from a pronounced imperial envy—an admiration for, and desire to emulate, the British Empire. Progressive headmasters exhorted their charges to take up the "civilizing" and "Christianizing" imperial burden. Just as the British elite conceived of their public schools as training grounds for the soldiers and administrators of empire, so too, around the turn of the century, headmasters and patrons imagined an expanded role for American boarding schools. In mid-August 1898, elated by the outcome of the "splendid little war" against Spain, Henry Cabot Lodge expressed his triumphant enthusiasm for the new overseas empire by encouraging the headmaster of Groton school to produce "a class of men precisely like those employed by England in India" to manage the new American colonial possessions. As it happened, the scale and nature of the American empire never demanded a "class of men" precisely like that of the British colonial service envisioned by turn-of-the-century American imperialists. Yet the boarding schools were premised on the economic and political power of "internationally minded" elites tied to international financial markets and concerned with the management of their interests abroad, which they identified with the national interest. Headmasters and patrons of the eastern boarding schools came to believe in an American imperial destiny surpassing the much-admired British one.[11]

Insiders understood and acknowledged that the imperial boarding-school narrative operated to create and perpetuate a privileged class. They also assumed that the inheritance of this tradition—which amounted to the creation and perpetuation of a ruling caste—was also a good thing. In this view, the "Anglophile element" associated with elite eastern boarding schools served as a bulwark against the forces arrayed against "civilization" and its values. Civilization, of course, was intimately connected to empire. This explicit justification for the boarding schools as creators of a warrior-aristocratic caste was remarkably durable. As late as 1960, when American leaders had realized their dream of inheriting the legacy of the British Empire, a Groton old boy (class of 1930) writing for the benefit of his peers identified the school and its famous statesmen with "chivalry, tolerance, and civilization":

> I believe that the Anglophile element, which looks seaward and is cosmopolitan, should keep free to lead the country, as needed, into new stages of foreign policy. Of course it will be objected that this element is biased too—in the direction of England or, more broadly, Western Europe. The bias is there, all right, but I maintain it is good. I think that the safeguarding of Christian culture is all-important now; that this means the saving of the Atlantic community; and that our country should work toward that end. Groton boys can help lead in the effort, and they should; and more of them should be produced all the time. Nor is it a question of leading by force. . . . The Brahmin caste led India centuries ago, and is leading India today, not by force, but by moral and intellectual superiority, which is maintained by dedication and by rigorous schooling of the Brahmin boys.[12]

Boarding-School Masculinity

Boarding schools separated adolescent boys from their mothers and the indulgences of feminized luxury. The schools were a first step in a sequence of ritual ordeals that constructed masculine privilege and social power by inducting boys and young men into a "purified male social order."[13] The boarding schools provided explicit lessons in the ideology of upper-class masculinity backed up by a variety of inescapable sanctions. In isolated and spartan settings, the daily lives of the students were closely supervised and regimented. Boys quickly learned to repudiate feminine characteristics and attributes, to conform, to compete physically and intellectually (although a genuine intellectual curiosity and love of learning was not stressed), and to penalize, through hazing, those that were different. "The result," as Joseph Alsop described his own experience at Groton, "was a fiercely rarefied and homogenous environment in which obedience and conformity were commended by one's teachers as well as by one's peers. Independence, in almost any form, was punished."[14]

Groton can be seen as the ideal type of an elite American boarding school. Founded in 1884 by the socially well-connected, British educated, Episcopal clergyman Endicott Peabody, Groton was advertised to its clientele as an in-

Endicott Peabody, Headmaster of Groton School from 1884 to 1940.

stitution meant to "cultivate manly, Christian character, having regard to moral and physical as well as intellectual development."[15] Peabody espoused the cult of manliness he had learned at the English public school Cheltenham and at Cambridge University. Charles Kingsley, propagandist of muscular

Christianity, profoundly influenced Peabody's conception of manhood, while his ideas about the education of boys were significantly shaped by two legendary English public-school headmasters, Thomas Arnold of Rugby and Edward Thring of Uppingham.[16] Peabody shared Thring's assessment of the indispensability of elite boarding schools in the construction of a stoic imperial masculinity among the sons of the upper class: "There is no point on which my convictions are stronger than on the power of boarding schools in forming the national character. . . . The learning to be responsible and independent, to bear pain, to play the game, to drop rank and wealth, and home luxury, is a priceless boon. I think myself that it is this which has made the English such an adventurous race; and that with all their faults . . . the public schools are the cause of this 'manliness.'"[17]

Peabody was a central figure in the emergence of an American imperial brotherhood, and Groton school was an immediate success with its upper-class clientele. Peabody employed the rhetoric of the Christian gentleman, while striving to "masculinize" patrician sons as preparation for the exercise of power. Peabody's credentials of stoic manliness included his own upper-class ordeal of imperial adventure, American-style, with a youthful stint as rector of the Episcopal church in Tombstone, Arizona Territory. There, in 1882, Peabody experienced his version of the eastern patrician's western adventure of strenuous manliness in the tradition established by R. H. Dana and Francis Parkman, and later elaborated by Theodore Roosevelt, Owen Wister, and Henry L. Stimson, among others. At roughly the same time that Roosevelt dressed himself in buckskins and chased bad men through the Dakotas, Peabody saddled up and explored the wild Sonoran Desert wearing "a broad brimmed white felt hat, a grey flannel shirt, riding breeches with yellow gaiters; and blankets strapped on behind and a gun hung on the pommel of the saddle." After his ministry in the frontier West "inhabited by roughs and Chinese," cowboys, gamblers, miners, and Indians ("perfect brutes," Peabody reported), he returned to the East to marry his cousin and founded Groton School.[18]

Boys at Groton and other boarding schools were systematically taught how to imagine manhood. Failure to adhere to an explicit ideal resulted in painful consequences: social, psychological, and, frequently, physical. Many boys, of course, had great difficulty conforming and, while craving the approval that came with conformity, resented the constricting and oppressive pattern used to mold them. As Groton alumnus Oliver La Farge recalled:

> At Groton it was important to be regular. . . . The collection of negatives and
> positives which governed our behaviour, the many precepts expressed to us,

all served to sketch out a fairly explicit and detailed ideal—The Groton Boy. The Groton Boy was a concept and a goal, it is the key to and influence of terrific power, yet so subtle that it took years for me to perceive it. This Boy was perfect according to the standards of the school, which meant that intellectual capacity was of secondary importance but he should not be stupid, and any strong aesthetic leanings were out of the question unless they could be so controlled as to have no influence upon daily behavior. He was the boy who fitted easily into every routine and institution of the school, a conformist, manly, honorable, courageous.[19]

The "stripping away of the private self" was enforced not only by the schoolmasters but by the collective, by the peer group following the example of hierarchy, privilege, and power held before it. Conformity to the standards of the brotherhood was compulsory; and the penalty for any conspicuous deviation was becoming the target of ostracism, ridicule, and ritual physical abuse.

Older, larger, stronger boys compelled the deference of the younger, smaller, weaker boys. With the unspoken sanction of Peabody (or headmasters at other schools), those whom the peer group selected for punishment were often subjected to brutal hazing. John F. Kennedy learned these lessons during his first term at Choate School in the fall of 1931. In a letter home reporting on the experiences of his older brother and rival, Joseph Jr., the fourteen-year-old John described the beating Joe received at the hands of a group of older boys. "Manly Youth. . . . He was roughhousing in the hall a sixth former caught him, he led him in and all the sixth formers had a swat or two. Did the sixth formers lick him. O Man he was all blisters, they almost paddled the life out of him. What I wouldn't have given to be a sixth former. They have some pretty strong fellows up there if blisters have anything to do with it."[20] Kennedy's invocation of "manly youth" to describe his brother's beating by older schoolmates hints at the schools' inculcation of the ideology of "character building" through group violence. While professing to identify with the attackers, the young JFK also recognizes that the humiliation and pain suffered by his older brother was designed to produce a particular kind of manliness in students.

Learning to conform, to adopt the ethos, manner, and morality of the group, was a matter of survival. The "total" nature of the institution, the absence of any escape from quasi-officially approved group punishment, led some to consider suicide. "A Groton winter term is grim under the best of circumstances," Joseph Alsop remembered: "A Groton winter term without human company was grim beyond imagining. So those few months were a desolate and lonely period; indeed, it was the only time I'd ever thought seriously about taking my own life."[21]

The example of those selected for persecution served as warning to all the boys that success and safety lay in the public display of conformity to the code of the brotherhood. Individual "bullies" were subdued when they threatened the bonds of the brotherhood or violated its code of stoic manliness, but the group also targeted manifestations of independence or individuality:

> The description comes back over and over again to conformity and insecurity, two major controls of our behavior, with the figure of the Groton Boy looming above. The Groton Boy and the Groton code cracked down on bullies swiftly, effectively; I've seen it happen. But they gave extra impetus to the mass-bullying which exists in most places where boys are confined together in numbers. Oddity was inferiority, and with most of any given Form suffering from a bad conscience, life was made much more comfortable by tagging a few members as definitely inferior, either because of real oddities or imaginary ones insistently ascribed to them. The middle mass of the Form, each individually harassed by his failure to conform perfectly, to reach the ideal, was quick to clamour the dreadful offenses of the chosen victims.[22]

Hazing assumed ritual forms. It became the school's mission to toughen boys and transform them, by stages, from imputedly weak, feminized "mother's boys" into full members of the brotherhood. At Groton one ritual was known as "pumping." "With the Rector's tacit acquiescence, the offender would be dragged from study hall by older boys and thrust headfirst into a lavatory sink" where water was "sprayed on his face until he was jerked to his feet, coughing, choking, retching." Another form was to "boot-box" a victim—to imprison him doubled-up in a footlocker. At other schools ritual hazing took different forms, but the underlying pattern was constant.[23]

According to his biographers, Dean Acheson was subjected to pumping because of his independence and "cheekiness." Perhaps even more scarring to the psyche, the spindly thirteen-year-old adolescent was forced to "stand like a Maypole while a circle of mocking students danced around calling him a 'fairy.'" Acheson later remarked that at Groton he had "bucked the Establishment and the system. . . . The result was predictable, painful, and clear." One immediate result was Endicott Peabody's conviction that because he could not make a "Groton boy" of his student, Acheson should leave the school at the end of his first year. Only the intervention of his mother, who believed that the psychic "scars of dismissal" would be worse for her son than the "authoritarianism" of the institution, prevented Acheson's ejection by the headmaster.[24]

The toughening regime of the boarding schools trained boys in the operations of social power. Some scholars have argued that the schools were designed to maintain an "innocence" throughout adolescence by removing boys from the temptations of city life and carefully supervising them. Despite "'official' guilt-producing pressure applied by the school" concerning sexual and moral conventions, it is more accurate to argue that the boarding schools represented a system by which boys were systematically stripped of their innocence of power.[25] Boys faced two linked systems of social power that often made contradictory demands. One was the official rule of the schoolmasters; the other was the peer-group pecking order. Students were forced to "fit in" to the group to protect themselves from the ritual hazing of the peer brotherhood. The brotherhood, however, shielded its own from the schoolmasters when it could. "Survival required different virtues from those desired by the masters," as one former Groton student put it, and the code of loyalty to the brotherhood often required transgressing the officially promoted codes of gentlemanly behavior. "The School as a whole was a closed organization against the masters when it came to real penetration into its society," another former Groton boy remembers. "The boys, victim and persecutors alike, shut up and covered up the instant a master appeared upon the scene."[26]

Because school officials valued group loyalty, they tacitly sanctioned the ostracism and abuse of those that did not fit into the brotherhood. "The boys who never did fit in and finally had to leave were more often expelled by their form-mates than by the faculty," one Groton alumnus recalled. Contradictions between "officially" taught ideals and values and the actual practice of the institution made up an important component of the toughening ordeal; according to one father such contradictions offered their sons pragmatic lessons in the workings of power: "Not to mince words, Groton pushes many a boy to become something of a hypocrite: or perhaps we should say, to acquire a certain protective coloration. Not so easy for a boy of spirit, and yet a useful lesson in many cases, an early experience of the problem of 'sophistication' and realism."[27]

The ordeals of the elite boarding schools typically succeeded in replacing the weak feminized child with a new subjectivity of male privilege and power. Membership in the brotherhood carried compensations for the brutalizing initiation ordeals. "Sacrifices must be made, and upper-class fathers, in particular, have been willing to sacrifice their sons' inner lives for the sake of their class."[28] For those who survived the system, the typical response has been a judgment later in life that whatever the pain inflicted on the individ-

ual, the advantages and privilege that accrued to members of the brotherhood justified the ordeals to which boys were subjected.

Dean Acheson, a target of hazing and ritual abuse at Groton, alluded to
his unhappiness at boarding school in his memoirs, but could not bring himself to name the school. Nonetheless, he sent his son David to Groton. Joseph
Alsop, who contemplated suicide during his time at Groton, spent much
effort during his adult career using his influence to have the sons of his
friends and associates accepted into the "right" schools. Occasionally he
wrote to console the unhappy boys themselves. Urging a stoic acceptance of
their situation, he referred to his own experience in boarding school: "It was
sheer hell to go away from home. . . . but the great point to remember is that
it always comes right in the end, and after it comes right, one somehow
forgets all about the bad part." Even Oliver La Farge, an ethnologist and
novelist (career choices *not* typical of Groton alumni) whose memoirs offer an articulate dissection of the alienating possibilities inherent in the
boarding-school culture, confessed with dismay "the incredible dishonesty of
registering my own son for Groton as soon as he was born."[29]

The culture of American patrician society is in some sense "patriarchal,"
as insiders like E. Digby Baltzell and Nelson W. Aldrich Jr. have noted. The
system of patriarchy operated by proxy, however, since fathers initiated the
process by placing their sons in institutions like boarding schools. Sons went
on to join their fathers' university clubs and other brotherhoods that, in life
sequence, created and controlled hierarchies of status and power.[30]

A few alumni, particularly those of an artistic bent, looked back on their
experience with dismay and a sense that the brutalities of boarding school
had damaged them (and their classmates) or had interfered with healthy adjustment to life.[31] More common reactions were expressions of a soldier's
pride—or, more specifically, a warrior-aristocrat's pride—tested and tough-
ened by war and thus prepared for further battle. John De Koven Alsop,
Groton class of 1933, and brother of the Washington columnists Joseph and
Stewart Alsop, made the parallel explicit, equating the ordeal of boarding
school with the ordeal of battle:

> Fifteen years ago, as a result of a series of rather improbable circumstances,
> the writer found himself, armed to the teeth, in occupied France as a repre-
> sentative of the Office of Strategic Services. The group which received him
> one moonlit night consisted largely of Spaniards, most of whom had been en-
> gaged in dog-eat-dog guerrilla warfare for eight years. They were tough. Any
> one of them could blow a bridge, stab a sentry in the back, and survive un-
> der almost any conditions. They were the last remnants of thousands. I re-

member feeling that I had been part of a group somewhere before, a tough, dedicated, lean and hungry group of survivors like them, and suddenly realized that I was thinking of graduation day, 1933, when the hardened remnants of our class were receiving their diplomas and were preparing to plunge into further battles of college and life.[32]

School traditions of hazing and ritual abuse represented the proscriptive aspect of the creation of loyalty and conformity in the brotherhood. Prescriptive aspects of the cultural identity narrative were equally important in the formation of individual masculine identities. Just as a boy's body could be the site of disciplinary ritual and pain during his early initiation into the brotherhood, it could be the focus of approbation and social rewards. Accordingly, boarding-school heroism was largely constructed around feats of athletic prowess.[33]

Dramas of risk, sacrifice, and pain enacted on the playing field had a central metaphorical significance to the construction of elite manliness. The imagination of male bodies in action and struggle became central to the imagination of manhood. Perhaps as a consequence of cultural anxieties (about "degeneracy," "race suicide," imperial rivalry) surrounding the pervasive trope of Darwinian competition, the conception of the ideal male body evolved from a slender lithe fitness to a massive muscularity, epitomized by the famous bodybuilder Eugen Sandow. As several scholars have noted, beginning in the late nineteenth century and continuing well into the twentieth, manly muscularity came to carry a heavy baggage of cultural meaning. The muscular male body symbolized the aggressive defense of boundaries; for the patricians, it stood for a resurgent defense of class, race, empire, and Christianity.[34]

Strenuousness and the games cult played a big part in the education of boarding-school boys. Upper-class fathers came to believe that athletic competition was crucial to the hardening of their sons. A growing emphasis on sport was not unique to American patricians; the tendency spread widely through the United States and the industrial world.[35] Nonetheless, the boarding schools offered a particularly focused and intense indoctrination in the moral and physical purpose inherent in athletic competition. Such trials were needed to restore manly legitimacy to a class beset by external threats and by the internal danger of an emasculating wealth and luxury. "Early Groton parents," wrote Peabody's biographer, "were privately disgusted with the bringing up of well-to-do American boys of that period. They thought them spoiled ladies' men tied to women's apron strings, and heartily welcomed the chance to send their sons to a place where the boys had to stand on their own feet and play rough-and-tumble games."[36] By 1902 it was clear to Theodore Roosevelt, a friend and relation of Endicott Peabody, that this trend had been reversed. He lauded the masculinizing benefits that a compulsory immersion in the boarding-school cult of games brought to the youth of his class:

> But during the last few decades there certainly have been some notable changes for the good in boy life. The great growth in the love of athletic sports, for instance, while fraught with danger if it becomes one-sided and unhealthy, has beyond all question had an excellent effect in increased manliness. Forty or fifty years ago the writer on American morals was sure to deplore the effeminacy and luxury of young Americans who were born of rich parents. The boy who was well off then, especially in the big Eastern cities, lived too luxuriously, took to billiards as his chief innocent recreation, and felt small shame in his inability to take part in rough pastimes and field-sports. Nowadays, whatever other faults the son of rich parents may tend to develop, he is at least forced by the opinion of all his associates of his own age to bear himself well in manly exercises and to develop his body—and therefore, to a certain extent, his character—in the rough sports which call for pluck, endurance, and physical address.[37]

The recurrent ritual drama of team athletics provided a powerful aid to the "bonding" of the brotherhood. Sports like football, crew, or hockey played crucial roles in the construction of individual and collective identity narratives. They functioned too, as another part of the initiation into manhood and its attendant privileges and rewards. Team sports provided an emotionally charged setting where boys ritually learned and tested courage, comradeship, and muscles. The emotionally charged exertion and controlled violence of the games may also have worked to increase the players' receptivity to the cultural meanings imbedded in the athletic drama. As some scholars have argued, ritual is primarily a "manipulation of consciousness, of, by and for actors, through symbolic objects, constructions and arrangements." An "alteration of consciousness" is the result—in this case another step in the construction of masculine power and privilege.[38] The drama of stoic sacrifice, risk, and heroism occupied a large part in the imaginative life of the elite boarding schools:

> I'll die for Dear Old Podunk. It isn't entirely tripe, certainly not in a preparatory school. Football is violent, in its periods of action it is the use of everything you have to the limit of your capacity directly against the bodies of your opponents. For the linemen it is pure physical conflict, formalized, disci-

plined to serve an objective, but nonetheless violent, and it is comradeship. These are strong things, part of the juice of life, they reach into the very origins of man. Call them forth, add the pure single-mindedness of your schoolboy, and you get something between ecstasy and a crusade. . . . As to dying, actually it's not usual for anyone to be killed in schoolboy football and we didn't think about it much, but we certainly were prepared to be severely injured.[39]

Whatever the "private" rewards of athletic accomplishment, the boarding-school culture offered tangible social rewards of status and prestige to the heroes of the playing field. The "big men" of the schools were often the athletic stars. The *agon* of athletic competition was metaphorically linked to the experience of war, with analogous opportunities to achieve a kind of immortality, a "homosocial rebirth."[40] Risk taking, physical prowess, and earned honors conferred fame and, in some cases, an aura of grace and immortality upon the athletic heroes of the peer group. Institutional privileges and power often followed athletic success, too. Athletic accomplishment was associated with "leadership" by the masters; positions of authority over other boys often went to those who excelled at sports.

The Imagination of Heroism

Muscular Christianity, as interpreted by boarding-school headmasters, took on a markedly stoic and militant cast. A cult of martial masculine virtue surrounded Endicott Peabody, described by one alumnus as "half warrior, half priest." Peabody agreed with his friend Theodore Roosevelt that athletic ordeals were indispensable to the development of manly character and *gravitas*. Contact sports represented the moral equivalent of war: "In my work at Groton I am convinced that foot ball is of profound importance for the moral even more than for the physical development of the boys. In these days of exceeding comfort, the boys need an opportunity to endure hardness and, it may be, suffering. Foot ball has in it the element which goes to make a soldier; and we must have it or some similar advantages, especially now when we are working for peace and hoping for the cessation of wars."[41]

Many in Peabody's eastern patrician milieu celebrated the risk and pain associated with violent competition. "I rejoice at every dangerous sport which I see pursued," boasted Oliver Wendell Holmes Jr. to a Harvard audience in 1895. Other patrician ideologues of manliness and America's imperial destiny asserted that the violence of football both justified and enabled the domination of lesser "races." Henry Cabot Lodge touted the benefits of team sports to his audience at the Harvard commencement of 1896: "The time given to athletic contests, and the injuries incurred on the playing field are part of the price which the English-speaking race has paid for being world conquerors." The very real chance of death on the football field helped forge "the spirit of victory," necessary in men destined to lead the state in coming global struggles.[42] The possession of inherited privilege, power, and material ease could be justified by men who also possessed deeply ingrained and re-flexive boundary-defending responses to dangers confronting country and class. In a competitive, militarized culture, men who had voluntarily taken risks and suffered for the good of all seemed to acquire a weight in the world denied to those who had not. Important aspects of the patrician ideal of manhood were embodied in men who were both athletic and war heroes, providing examples to those who followed them in school and university.

Legend attached a special heroic immortality to those volunteers who fought and died. Hobey Baker was one such icon who emerged from World War I.[43] Hobart Amory Hare Baker, even more than the average boarding-school alumnus, was a product of his school, St. Paul's, of Concord, New Hampshire. Sent there to board after the divorce of his wealthy parents, Baker lived at the school for seven years, from age eleven to eighteen. He even spent his summers in the care of a St. Paul's master. "St. Paul's," his bi-ographer notes, "was not just a surrogate family, to Hobey, but a real one." It was there that Baker's legend began. His phenomenal athletic talent made him a "hero of the school, the best all-round athlete, and the president of the athletic association." At Princeton, Baker's exploits at hockey and football made him famous. He was held up as an exemplar of gentlemanly amateur sportsmanship—a physical and moral prodigy who summed up the best of his world.[44]

In 1916, a few years out of Princeton, Baker began using the morning hours for training as a military pilot, "before taking the Wall Street train" to his banking job in New York. "Convinced that America's entry into the war was only a matter of time," Baker eagerly pursued adventure in service to duty and honor: "For him here was the ultimate excitement, a game more dangerous, more satisfying even, than hockey or football. To his natural love of danger and excitement, coordination and control was added the knowl-edge that the end for which he was training was mortal combat, between sportsmen playing aerial knights but with the result not defeat but death."[45] When the United States declared war, Baker went to France to fight. He joined an elite fighter squadron, the famous Lafayette Escadrille, officially, by then, the 103d Aero Squadron of the U.S. Army, but still known by its former name. The Lafayette, "probably the most thoroughly photographed, written about, and filmed fighting unit in history," was the glamorous volunteer squadron formed in 1915 by American patricians and their French counterparts. The press closely identified the squadron with the American aristocracy and depicted its actions as the modern equivalent of knightly single combat. Baker's reputation as an Ivy League athletic hero drew the attention of newspaper reporters, who consistently inflated his score of German planes shot down. When he was killed in a crash shortly after the armistice, the narrative achieved closure: the exemplar of patrician manhood, athlete, and decorated warrior, cut down in the prime of youth, gained heroic immortality through his sacrifice to duty.[46]

The institutional brotherhoods of school and university rushed to embrace the fallen hero. The president of Princeton University argued that "the spirit of this place [Princeton] was incarnate in him, the spirit of manly vigor, of honor, of fair play and the clean game."[47] A Hobey Baker hero cult sprang up. Memorials to Baker depicted him as akin to the gods in his physical and moral perfection, and as akin to the tragic Greek heroes in his fate. As late as 1952 Baker was remembered by the *New York Herald Tribune* in such terms:

> Hobey Baker was for American youth a hero in the truest sense, godlike almost in his stature. It was as though the gods had fashioned one shining symbol in their own image towards which boys should strive in the future. He was a sort of legendary hero like Sir Galahad, Richard the Lion-Hearted and even Paul Bunyan, for his athletic feats were legendary too. It is impossible to think of him as a man of 60. He is youth personified and represents an ideal of American youth for all time. If it is possible to say of any man that he is beautiful, it may be said of Hobey Baker, for he was beautiful of body as of soul and spirit. . . . The gods who fashioned him could not, it seemed, permit him to grow old. His destiny and his mission . . . already were complete. And so they took him back but left his great personality still shining as an example of what we should all strive to be.[48]

Immediately after his death the members of Baker's overlapping school, university, and military brotherhoods erected shrines and monuments immortalizing him, including a memorial hockey rink at Princeton, a memorial scholarship, and a gymnasium in France. The hero cult even included a fetish object as the center of one of its rituals, "an annual St. Paul's School–Princeton freshman hockey game in Madison Square Garden, played for the possession of Hobey's stick." Baker's name was inscribed under the Angel of Death in the St. Paul's school chapel, along with the names of the other forty-seven alumni who died during World War I. Samuel S. Drury, headmaster of St. Paul's from 1911 to 1936, saw the sacrifice of his alumni's lives in war as a redemption and justification for the school itself. St. Paul's "was not to be a dispensary for cripples, but an armory for soldiers—a place all glistening and clanging with breastplates of righteousness, swords of the spirit, and helmets of salvation."[49]

Hobey Baker's legend of patriotic redemption was just one of many narratives of patrician warrior heroism learned by succeeding cohorts of boarding-school and university boys. The Lafayette Escadrille was replete with products of Groton, St. Paul's, Yale, and Harvard, several of whom received the adulatory attention of the press and passed into legend with their death in battle.[50] Quentin Roosevelt, the son of the erstwhile Rough Rider and president of the United States, volunteered as a fighter pilot and served in France in the 94th Aero Squadron. Soon after his first aerial "victory" against a German aircraft he was shot down and killed by a member of "the Ritchthofen Circus." One hero, Tommy Hitchcock, joined the Lafayette Flying Corps at age seventeen directly out of St. Paul's school, through the auspices of Theodore Roosevelt. Hitchcock survived the war to become a member of the Porcellian club at Harvard, Wall Street investment banker, and renowned polo-player, only to be killed during World War II as an air-attaché in England voluntarily test-flying an experimental P-51 fighter aircraft. In 1916, still an undergraduate at Yale, Robert Lovett helped form another elite volunteer unit composed of the flower of patrician manhood, the Yale Unit of the Naval Reserve Flying Corps; it was inspired by and modeled on the Lafayette Escadrille.[51]

Boarding-school headmasters and wealthy, powerful alumni actively promoted the creation of a community of Spartan warrior-heroes as part of the Plattsburg preparedness movement of 1913–17. Henry Stimson, a Phillips Academy Andover alumnus and trustee and former secretary of war, became a participant and enthusiast of General Leonard Wood's officer's training camp at Plattsburg, New York. The Plattsburg movement strove to harden and prepare for battle both college boys and businessmen, while promising individual and collective redemption from the effeminate temptations of materialism.[52] In 1914, Stimson brought General Wood to Andover to help begin a program of military drill, rifle practice, and volunteer overseas ambulance service; the next summer Andover sent a delegation of twenty-two trainees to Plattsburg. Dr. Samuel Drury of St. Paul's School was another early enthusiast of martial training for schoolboys. He too consulted with Wood about military drill for his charges. In concert with Stimson and the wealthy Groton alumnus Horace Stebbins, Drury organized a military training camp specifically for boarding school boys. In 1916 a "Junior Plattsburg" opened at Ft. Terry (Plum Island), New York, under the command of a U.S. Army lieutenant colonel. Boys from St. Paul's, Groton, St. Mark's, and other elite schools were trained to take up the mantle of the stoic citizen-soldier as had their fathers and older brothers, buttressing claims to leadership by a privileged class.[53]

Like the Lafayette Escadrille, or the Plattsburg preparedness movement or, for that matter, Groton School, the First Yale Unit began as a project subsidized by the fortunes of patrician bankers and lawyers. Partners in the House of Morgan, for instance, were instrumental to the creation of all three. A network of patrician clubmen closed ranks to mobilize the sons of their class for redemptive engagement in battle. Voluntary sacrifice to duty would demonstrate to the citizens of a democracy the legitimacy of patrician claims to leadership. The boarding-school model of masculine virtue and heroic sacrifice could receive its most significant and visible test in battle.[54]

The pattern of elite volunteer military service as a credential of political manhood continued through the next world war; many of the men of the Kennedy administration foreign policy apparatus possessed such credentials. Motor Torpedo Boats, the naval unit in which Kennedy served, functioned as a publicly visible seagoing cavalry, much as the Lafayette Escadrille had functioned as the knighthood of the air.[55] Other venues for heroic action were popular, too. Wartime service in commando detachments, aviation, submarines, even elite intelligence and code-breaking units helped position members of the imperial brotherhood to take power in the postwar world. Elite military service helped ambitious and talented men not born to the upper class claim places in the postwar establishment. The next chapter examines these legacies of World War II.

· THREE ·

HEROISM, BODIES, AND THE CONSTRUCTION

OF ELITE MASCULINITY

We had all seen, in one context or another, what tactical defeat looked like during the Second World War. (In my case, it was the dangerous and frustrating days of 1942–1943 when it appeared quite likely that daylight bombers, in which America had invested vast resources, would fail to penetrate German anti-aircraft and fighter defenses without unacceptable losses.) We had known what it is to take stock, make new dispositions, and get on with the job. My wife caught this mood one night. I came home at three in the morning. She was sitting up in bed and said: "I've not seen you for years more cheerful or effective. You're not politicians or intellectuals. You're the junior officers of the Second World War come to responsibility." It remains not a bad characterization of the Kennedy administration.

Walt Whitman Rostow, 1972

HEROISM in war occupied a central place in the imagination of manhood for the men of the high-level national security bureaucracy under Presidents Kennedy and Johnson. Most of the men who filled the high-level posts were veterans of World War II who had served in elite volunteer military units of one kind or another. Both Kennedy and Johnson were themselves decorated for service during World War II, and according to biographers, both considered courage to be the virtue that takes precedence over all others.[1]

Arthur Schlesinger Jr., court historian of the Kennedy administration and longtime advocate of "heroic leadership," noted a deep "preoccupation" with "courage and death" by President Kennedy. This preoccupation came from his upbringing, including "his reading about the death of kings," his "illness" (as a youth), and finally, his brush with death in the waters of the South Pacific after the sinking of PT-109. The culturally sanctioned narrative of a youthful aristocratic hero going "to his fate, cool, poised, resolute, matter-of-fact, debonair," fascinated Kennedy. The idea of eternal youth, preserved forever through a brave death in battle recorded by history, appealed to him.[2]

The experience of war, and the creation of heroic wartime narratives both public and private, carry a multiplicity of meanings. Immersed in the traditions of republicanism, Kennedy, Johnson, and their bureaucrats took for granted the proposition that martial virtue was inseparable from masculine civic and political virtue; one was predicated on the other. But evidence suggests that other patterns of psychological meaning can inhere in participation in war. One potentially useful interpretation suggests that going "face to face with death" in battle can offer elite males a kind of immortality, a "homosocial rebirth" into a world of male heroes through memory and the retelling of the heroic stories in works of history (or oral tradition).[3] By deliberately confronting the risk of death (or by dying heroically) in a "zero-sum competition for honor," men separate themselves from the world of women, from "daily life, necessity, and production," thereby overcoming the obscurity of death that is otherwise the destiny of all mortal men born to women. As a reward for performing great deeds in battle with other men, the male actor overcomes the mortality of his body. The hero lives on, honored in history or tradition. Participation in war has, in the Western tradition, been a basic constituent of ideologies of elite masculinity and of male citizenship and political power.[4] War and heroic action can thus be implicated in the most fundamental "existential" anxieties confronting individual men; they are also part of the social creation of elite male dominance, the process of inclusion within or exclusion from political power.

For the men of the Kennedy and Johnson national security bureaucracy, participation in war helped to legitimate their later claim to the privilege of power and command in government. They regarded themselves as members of a patriotic brotherhood of warrior-intellectuals. These war veterans in the foreign policy establishment believed that they had proven their courage and effectiveness in battle and in the military and executive bureaucracies that defeated the Axis powers. Their efforts and sacrifice had successfully defended the nation from its gravest danger in this century.

In the United States, a reputation as a patriotic warrior has always proved politically useful. Since George Washington, the ranks of presidents have been replete with war heroes. For men like the young John Kennedy and Congressman Lyndon Johnson, who embodied family or personal ambitions for a career in electoral politics, the construction of a narrative of heroic wartime service became, at least in part, a calculated undertaking, designed to reap the rewards of political power that a militarized postwar society might bestow on its public heroes. Wartime service did so by creating a larger cultural manhood script of patriotic engagement in the defense of society, a willing self-sacrifice for the good of the nation.[5]

Service during World War II offered elite men of different class backgrounds means to elide class differences through a fictive kinship, a brotherhood of patriotic deeds. It offered many ambitious and talented middle-class men the chance for early command and responsibility. Their resourcefulness, ability, and courage was recognized by older, powerful men who later became their patrons in the national security bureaucracy. For patricians, volunteering for war served as a patterned ritual ordeal to reconnect them with American democracy (albeit as officers and gentlemen). The sons of privilege saw themselves as subjected to the same risk of defeat and death, or honor and glory, as the humblest citizen-soldier or self-made man. At the beginning of the century, with *The Rough Riders*, Theodore Roosevelt popularized this narrative of the old-stock, polo-playing aristocrat fighting and dying beside a panoply of democratic American manhood:

> We drew recruits from Harvard, Yale, Princeton, and many another colleges: from clubs like the Somerset, of Boston, and the Knickerbocker, of New York; and from among the men who belonged neither to club nor to college, but in whose veins the blood stirred with the same impulse which once sent the Vikings overseas. . . . All—Easterners and Westerners, Northerners and Southerners, officers and men, cowboys and college graduates, wherever they came from, and whatever their social position—possessed in common the traits of hardihood and thirst for adventure.[6]

The cultural narrative of individual volunteer heroism persisted. The Rough Rider model of strenuous manliness colored the imagination of martial heroism for future statesmen from backgrounds as diverse as Lyndon Johnson, Dean Acheson, and John Kennedy.[7] The industrialized mass butchery in the trenches of World War I reinforced a particular emphasis in the larger cultural narrative of warrior heroism, an emphasis already visible in Roosevelt's story of the First U.S. Volunteer Cavalry. Scope for individual initiative, command, and heroic deeds ideally demanded service in "irregular" or elite units rather than as cannon fodder in the regular infantry. This explains, for example, the journalistic emphasis on the World War I–era Lafayette Flying Corps as a "knighthood of the air." The "democratization" of trench warfare, and the "proletarianization" of officers and men in the mass slaughter of the Western Front,[8] meant that "after 1916, it was the 'irregular' soldier, rather than the regular army who would prove capable of sustaining adventure interest. The guerrilla, the commando, the Special Operations forces, the spies and saboteurs who operate in the margins, 'behind enemy lines,' in 'occupied territory,' or in peripheral colonial theatres of war: these are the characteristic heroes of military adventure in the twentieth century."[9] During World War II, Kennedy's national security bureaucrats and his favored career military officers had been disproportionately represented in elite volunteer units. PT boats, submarines, Marine assault battalions, paratroopers, and especially Office of Strategic Services (OSS) commando and intelligence operations all contributed alumni to the Kennedy, and later Johnson, foreign policy apparatuses.

Networks of elite men in positions of power in the wartime "establishment" promoted the pattern of upper-class voluntarism, just as the statesmen/investment banker/clubmen had done during World War I.[10] This network became institutionalized in the government war bureaucracy before the attack on Pearl Harbor in a way that had not been the case between 1914 and the U.S. declaration of war in 1917. In June 1940 President Franklin Roosevelt appointed Colonel Henry L. Stimson as secretary of war. For secretary of the navy he named "the old Rough-Rider and Theodore Roosevelt-adherent, publisher of the *Chicago Daily News,* and a considerable power in the Republican Party, Colonel Frank Knox."[11] Stimson and Knox staffed their departments with martial corporate lawyers and investment bankers, many of whom went on to become the future architects of the U.S.-led postwar imperial coalition in the early years of the Cold War. Knox brought in James V. Forrestal, a former Dillon Read partner, as undersecretary of the navy. Stimson surrounded himself with John J. McCloy, Robert Lovett, Harvey Bundy, and Robert Patterson. Other future "wise men" took up service in different government bureaucracies.

The patrician manhood script demanded volunteer service, even if one had to go to great lengths to take it up. The experience of the brothers Joseph, Stewart, and John DeKoven Alsop illustrates several aspects of a larger pattern. In his memoirs, Joseph Alsop remarked that he "had some sort of family connection with an actual majority" of the elite men who came to Washington with Stimson and Knox. This proudly asserted family connection also bound him to the traditions of wartime service of his class: "My father and, indeed, both my brothers held to the notion that when their country was at war, gentlemen tried their best to go out and shoot at the enemy, a process that generally entailed some risk. Johnny, Stew and I had all enlisted well before Pearl Harbor."[12]

Each of the Alsop brothers had a hereditary physical condition that would have, without special effort on their part, disqualified them from active service in the military.[13] Nonetheless, duty called the brothers. Joseph, already an influential Washington newspaperman, got a special "waiver" from Vice Admiral Alan G. Kirk, allowing him to enlist in the U.S. Navy despite his physical disability. Alsop soon learned that the navy intended to exploit his enlistment mainly for publicity purposes, however. His assignment as an intelligence officer in Bombay, India, would primarily entail "dining out" and other ceremonial duties. "This seemed," Alsop relates, "a poor way to do what I conceived to be my wartime duty." He searched for a fitter way to serve, seeking help and advice directly from two friends: Robert Lovett, serving as chief of the Air Corps for Stimson, and James Forrestal in the Department of the Navy.[14]

Both Lovett and Forrestal counseled Alsop to attach himself to former U.S. Air Corps "Colonel" Claire L. Chennault, then forming the American Volunteer Group to fight the Japanese in China. The AVG, later dubbed the "Flying Tigers," was an American-equipped fighter squadron financed by U.S. loans to the Kuomintang government. By staffing the squadron with American volunteer aviators, Chennault's band of adventurer/mercenaries harked back to the model of the Lafayette Escadrille.[15] Alsop, eager to escape the "ludicrous and unwarlike" assignment in Bombay, took the advice of Lovett and Forrestal. He used their influence to find Chennault and begin "the single greatest adventure" of his life. He took a position as Chennault's chief aide and de facto liaison with Washington. Alsop was captured and interned under the guise of civilian journalist by the Japanese during the fall of Hong Kong at the end of 1941. The Japanese released him several months later, and Alsop made his way back to China and Chennault's operation, by then incorporated into the U.S. Army air force. Through the intervention of his "cousin" FDR, Alsop eventually received a presidential commission in the army Air Corps, over the objections of military leaders General "Hap" Arnold and General George C. Marshall. He spent the war immersed in the political intrigue between the court of Chiang Kai Shek, General Joseph Stillwell, and Claire Chennault.[16]

Despite the many "adventures" and risks Joseph Alsop faced during World War II, he never directly experienced combat. This nagged at him for some years afterward, especially in comparison with his two younger brothers. Both Stewart and John Alsop suffered from a form of high blood pressure that disqualified them from combat duty in the U.S. military.[17] Nonetheless, they persisted in attempts to find roles in fighting units. After appealing his 4-F draft classification thirteen times, John Alsop served a brief stint with the Military Police. He then managed to join the OSS and parachuted first into France behind enemy lines to "join the French resistance" and later into "a disputed part of China's Kwangtung province, where his small guerrilla group had to fight both the Japanese and the Communists." Stewart was initially turned down for U.S. military service, so he enlisted in the British Army, 60th Regiment, King's Royal Rifle Corps, reaching the rank of captain by 1943. He also managed a transfer to the U.S. OSS, and then made a daring solo parachute jump into occupied France.[18]

Joseph Alsop "envied Stew and Johnny their fighting experience." He made the decision to join the AVG "because staff work with the Flying Tigers was nearer to being in combat than dining out in Bombay."[19] Nonetheless, Alsop's wartime service did not fully meet the demands of his internalized ideology of masculinity; he had not been tested by the ordeal of battle, a requisite credential of full manhood. With the outbreak of the Korean War in the summer of 1950, Alsop found an opportunity to try his courage under fire. He resolved to provide firsthand coverage of the infantry war in his nationally syndicated newspaper column.[20]

At age forty, as an influential establishment journalist, socially and professionally connected to the highest levels of government in Washington, Alsop went to Korea and put himself in the way of harm in battle.[21] A night "huddled fitfully" in an exposed position under mortar fire "shook" him "a great deal."

> The truth is, I had never been so frightened before in that sort of way. I had been a fat child, both physically incompetent and timid. Physical timidity is much more important in the makeup of character than people suppose, for cowardice spoils most other human attributes in the same way that courage adds to them. I have always observed that courage in and of itself is not a particularly attractive personal quality, but that its absence, like the absence of salt in cookery, can be devastating in total effect. Every major gain in my life, from adolescence on, has involved the conquering of some childish fear— whether of horses or people or unruly explosions—and in each case the remedy has been direct experience.[22]

Alsop rid himself of his childish fear and acquired the credentials of manly courage by immediately accompanying other U.S. units into the battle for the Pusan perimeter, and then going ashore with MacArthur's invasion at Inchon. He described his experience of battle as the culmination of a lifelong series of character-building ordeals that began in childhood when he had been "unceremoniously packed off to Groton."[23]

Just as Joseph Alsop's undergraduate initiation into the brotherhood of the Porcellian Club at Harvard had been a social "liberation" from "crippling doubts and petty inferiorities," his initiation under fire in Korea provided a symbolic rebirth into the brotherhood of male warriors. During the experience of battle his physical "apprehension gave way to a robust fatalism"; he discarded a feminized bodily cowardice for the tested masculine courage demanded by the manhood script of his class.[24] War provided a way to symbolically liberate himself from the perceived weakness and "incompetence" of his body, characteristics associated with women and children.

Alsop's trial by fire inspired him to write newspaper columns celebrating the courage, heroism, and resolution of the "everyday Americans" on the front lines, fighting for a "good life and a good society" against the communist enemy. Friends, colleagues, and his newspaper audience congratulated Alsop on the epic quality of his war reportage. Lincoln Kirstein saw in the work the makings of a larger piece comparable to T. E. Lawrence's *Seven Pillars of Wisdom;* George F. Kennan thought the Korean reports were "like Tolstoy's passages from *War and Peace.*" For Alsop, the brief Korean adventure and the positive response to his heroic narratives celebrating the defense of imperial boundaries confirmed the correctness of his hard-line geostrategic opinions; in late September 1950, he urged approval of General MacArthur's proposed "bold course" of invasion of North Korea to reunify the peninsula and roll back Communism.[25]

John F. Kennedy and the Story of PT-109

The case of the Alsop brothers provides just one example of a recurrent motif in upper-class volunteer wartime service. The U.S. military had an extensive medical system in place to examine and assess the fitness of men's bodies for the rigors of war. Yet the ordeal of battle was so critical to the patrician masculine ideology that many elite men who did not meet the physical standards of the military did whatever they could to join a "proper" fighting unit. This often involved tapping the influence wielded by the network of powerful men with whom they were connected. Others used subterfuge to defeat the screening process. Many employed both methods. For those who did not meet the minimum physical standards of the warrior ideal, service in elite military units worked to "erase" the defects of the body and to provide public proof of capacity for masculine action.

John F. Kennedy provides a well-known, and in some respects, extreme example of this pattern of upper-class military voluntarism. Kennedy had a history of severe, recurrent congenital illnesses. Had his true medical history been revealed to the military physicians screening the recruits, Kennedy would never have been assigned to combat duty. During his wartime career, however, Kennedy consistently misled navy doctors about his history of re-

John F. Kennedy (far right) with his crew on the deck of PT-109, Solomon Islands, 1943. Courtesy John Fitzgerald Kennedy Library.

current physical breakdowns, despite frequent interruptions in his duties due to back problems, "spastic colitis," and ulcers.[26] Nonetheless, with the intervention of his father, probably through James Forrestal, and through his own contact with David I. Walsh, senator from Massachusetts and chairman of the Senate Naval Affairs Committee, Kennedy managed a series of transfers leading from limited duty in the Office of Naval Intelligence into South Pacific combat duty in Motor Torpedo Boats.[27]

Complex motives and circumstances led John Kennedy into the war in the Pacific. One proximate cause was his sexual involvement with Inga Arvad, a slightly older married woman working as a gossip columnist for a Washington newspaper. Arvad, a Dane, had interviewed Goering, Goebbels, and even Hitler during a stint on a Copenhagen newspaper in the mid-thirties. Because of her past, and suspicions about her estranged husband, Arvad became a target of FBI surveillance and wiretapping during her affair with John Kennedy. As Kennedy's liaison with a suspected spy became known to the Office of Naval Intelligence, he was transferred from Washington to a routine desk job in Charleston, South Carolina, where he briefly continued his affair with Arvad. His father, Joseph Kennedy, was aware of the affair and feared a possible marriage that would damage his son's future political prospects. He put pressure on Kennedy to quit the relationship. Arvad too, understood that

Kennedy had ambitions to be a "White House man," and that a future with the son of the former ambassador was unlikely. Kennedy's awareness of FBI surveillance, his inchoate political ambitions, and his boredom and frustration with trivial military duties led him to seek a transfer to combat duty.[28]

Regardless of the "private" and immediate causes of Kennedy's transfer, cultural narratives of military heroism and the examples of his elite peers impelled him into duty in a dangerous, physically punishing, but seemingly glamorous service with the torpedo boats, despite his frailty. His favorite books celebrated manly military heroism and aristocratic power. The linked themes of heroism in war, masculine power, and the immortality conferred by history were present from his childhood reading of "King Arthur, *Scottish Chiefs, The White Company,* Cooper, and later Churchill's *Marlborough,*" to his later preference for John Buchan's descriptions of warrior and aristocratic heroes like T. E. Lawrence and Raymond Asquith in *Pilgrim's Way,* or for the heroic figures in Churchill's *Great Contemporaries.*[29]

The warrior narrative, however, was also deeply imbedded in Kennedy's social world. The one adult figure whom Kennedy admired from his boarding-school experience at Choate School had a reputation as a war hero. His housemaster, "Cap" Leinbach, had served as an intelligence officer during World War I. Captured behind German lines, and condemned to be shot, "he disarmed his captors and escaped," according to Choate legend.[30]

Kennedy's decision to volunteer for sea duty was also linked to the actions of friends and peers from boarding school and university who sought and found service in elite units. Perhaps his closest lifelong friend, a schoolmate at Choate, Lemoyne Billings, had been rejected for the U.S. military because of severely defective eyesight. Yet he managed to get a role as an ambulance driver accompanying the British Eighth Army campaign in North Africa against Rommel's forces. Kennedy's brother, Joe Jr., had been accepted into naval aviation. Other friends volunteered for the marines, as naval fighter pilots, and for service in armored cavalry under General George S. Patton.[31]

During the first two years of World War II, the press glamorized the Motor Torpedo Boats, just as the Lafayette Flying Corps had been singled out during World War I. Fame first came to the torpedo boat service with the dramatic rescue of the besieged General Douglas MacArthur, plucked from his Philippine redoubt and spirited to safety by a squadron of PT boats shortly before the final Japanese defeat of the American forces. In 1942, PT boats offered the press satisfyingly uplifting narratives of American triumph over superior enemy force during the otherwise discouraging months after Pearl Harbor and the surrender of the U.S. armies defending the Philippines. The leader of the torpedo boat squadron, Lieutenant John D. Bulkeley, became a national hero when he returned to the United States on a recruiting drive for volunteers to man the dangerous craft. With ticker-tape parades on Broadway, speeches at bond-drive and recruiting rallies, and even a popular book, *They Were Expendable*, Bulkeley and the torpedo boat enthusiasts of the press spread the heroic story of men who fought in the high-powered "mosquito" boats.[32]

The PT propagandists made vastly exaggerated claims about the effectiveness of the boats against the Japanese, just as the press had exaggerated the exploits of the Lafayette flyers more than twenty years earlier. *They Were Expendable* depicted Bulkeley and his small flotilla of outnumbered and outgunned torpedo boats repeatedly sinking Japanese destroyers, cruisers, tankers, even an "auxiliary aircraft carrier." The popular military adventure tale fabricated a legend of awesome proportions. Bulkeley claimed in the pages of the book that by February 1942 "we had probably sunk a hundred times our own combined tonnage in enemy warships." Facing severe shortages of supplies and arms, the desperately embattled heroes continued to devastate the Japanese Navy for several more months, before a last-minute evacuation of the remaining survivors.[33]

In reality PT boats were fragile wooden craft, powered by temperamental motors, devoid of armor, filled with inflammable aviation gasoline, and equipped with obsolete and often defective torpedoes. The boats never managed to sink full-sized Japanese warships. Despite their nearly complete uselessness as weapons of war, the heroic aura surrounding the boats ensured a large supply of volunteers for the hazardous units. Professional warriors, graduates of the Naval Academy, shunned the PT boats in the knowledge that career advancement would come with service on full-size ships. But Bulkeley had great success at the Naval Officers School in Chicago, where college-trained reservists became "ninety-day wonders" after a short course in gunnery, navigation, and seamanship. So many volunteered that Bulkeley had a problem selecting fifty future PT officers from a pool of over a thousand volunteers at the school at Northwestern University in Chicago. He favored college athletes, and the PT boats were also especially popular with Ivy League graduates with yachting experience who wanted to quickly get command of their own vessels. Kennedy soon found himself training and fighting alongside football stars and other exemplars of athletic masculinity.[34]

Kennedy's experience of torpedo boat service carried both public and personal meanings. Whatever his personal experience of the chaos, futility, and horrors of battle, Kennedy emerged from the navy a decorated war hero. The sickly son of the former ambassador to the Court of St. James (known as an appeaser) had proven his capacity for dramatic exploits in dangerous circum-

John F. Kennedy receiving the Navy and Marine Corps Medal, after family friend James Forrestal signed the citation on his first day in office as Secretary of the Navy. Courtesy John Fitzgerald Kennedy Library.

stances. The destruction of his PT boat, rammed by a Japanese destroyer (the only one of the fast, maneuverable craft to be lost that way during the war), and Kennedy's heroic if largely ineffectual efforts on behalf of the surviving members of his crew, provided the raw material for a widely disseminated war-hero narrative.[35]

Kennedy became a celebrated member of the warrior brotherhood of the junior combat officers of World War II. Having passed the test of courage in war, he generally showed a high regard for others who had performed well in battle. His experience in the South Pacific helped him form lasting bonds with many of his fellow warriors. Later, as president, he favored a few of these men for government positions in executive branch departments and in the military. One, Byron White, a football hero, PT veteran, and Rhodes Scholar, he appointed to the Supreme Court as the "ideal New Frontier judge." Likewise, he challenged journalists to examine the war records of his political rivals who might be vulnerable to charges of "shirking" military service during World War II.[36]

The narrative of warrior heroism surrounding Kennedy's South Pacific naval service profoundly shaped his political persona and his political career. Both he and his father deployed the story of his exploits in battle as proof of moral and physical courage, stamina, and self-sacrifice in patriotic defense of the nation. The dramatic story of PT-109 provided him with his single greatest political asset during his campaigns for public office.[37]

The tale of volunteer heroism in the torpedo boat became a central part of Kennedy's political iconography. It gave him a place in American cultural narratives of citizen-soldier-statesman heroism. While in the hospital awaiting back surgery, Kennedy recounted the tale of his ordeal in the South Pacific to journalist John Hersey. Although rejected by *Life,* the PT-109 story, entitled "Survival," appeared in the *New Yorker* on June 17, 1944. Through the efforts and influence of Joseph Kennedy, Hersey's heroic tale reached a mass-market audience when it was condensed in the August 1944 issue of *Reader's Digest.* In Kennedy's campaigns for office, from his first race for the House of Representatives in 1946, the Hersey article provided proof of his warrior manhood. Ten thousand copies of the *Reader's Digest* version were mailed to voters before the primary election in the 1946 campaign. Hundreds of thousands went out during his 1952 senatorial race.[38]

Kennedy regularly enlisted his former PT mates to appear on his behalf during his political campaigns. Paul B. Fay, Byron (Whizzer) White, Barney Ross, and other torpedo boat alumni helped Kennedy to his electoral success. The PT boat story supplied fetish objects for the cult of heroism surrounding Kennedy. These included PT-109 tie clasps for campaign workers, the carved coconut shell on Kennedy's desk, and a PT-109 float in the inaugural parade. This reached a culmination of sorts in the Hollywood film production of *PT-109,* with a script personally approved by Kennedy, starring Cliff Robertson in the role of JFK.[39]

Long after he left the House of Representatives, first for the Senate and then the presidency, the war story provided a plausible, though false, explanation for the physical debility that plagued Kennedy throughout his life. It transformed the weakness and failure of his body into a badge of honor. The hero narrative supplied a useful validation of masculinity in the militarized political culture of the Cold War. It also helped him stake a claim to the immortality that comes from doing great deeds in battle, risking all for a place in the warrior brotherhood.

Lyndon Johnson Goes to War

Since the founding of the republic, the image of military heroism has been a path to political power for men of diverse backgrounds. Lyndon Johnson, descended from pioneer Texans, was, from childhood, indoctrinated in the myths and the ethos of patriotic frontier masculinity. One of his biographers has demonstrated the links between specific narratives of frontier military adventure, Johnson family history, and the central place of manly courage in LBJ's imagination of self.[40]

Johnson repeatedly used the Texas Rangers as examples of the way "manly" men reacted to the external threats facing their community or nation. Roosevelt's Rough Rider narrative also shaped Johnson's conceptions of masculinity, patriotism, political power, and U.S. imperial destiny. The "western" and "frontier" manliness and heroism Roosevelt celebrated in his own quest for political power and recognition offered Johnson an opportunity to reshape the story of imperial masculine leadership to his political ends. Texas Rangers, after all, fought on Kettle Hill alongside the polo players, eastern clubmen, miners, cowhands, and other representatives of courageous American manhood.[41]

Johnson commonly employed a metaphorical language, ubiquitous in the writings of TR, that equated the character and actions of individual men with those of nations. The "coward and the bully" engaged in forms of behavior that, left unchecked, endangered individuals, society, and even the world order. In the manhood script of the Texas Hill Country, it was the "duty of the strong" to protect "the weak." For a man to perform his ordained social role as "the producer, the provider, the protector," meant that "bullies" must be faced down at the first sign of threat. Appeasement only leads to further aggression against self, kin, community, or country. To Lyndon Johnson the defense of boundaries demanded strong, resolute men: "the one thing a bully understands is force and the one thing he fears is courage." For the Hill Country democrat, traditions of frontier courage, force of will, and productive pragmatism on behalf of "the people" legitimated a paternal leadership. For a politically ambitious self-made man, the ordeals and ritual tests of manhood were less rigidly patterned and more contingent upon self-direction that those of the patrician; nonetheless, a demonstration of military valor was just as crucial. Johnson did differ from his patrician political rivals in his willingness to boast about his courage and aggressiveness; Ivy League manners demanded a reticence about heroic deeds, while Texas-style manliness sanctioned an open display of aggressive pride.[42]

With the outbreak of World War II, Johnson took immediate steps to establish his credentials as a military man. He obtained a leave of absence from the U.S. House of Representatives and took up a commission as a Naval Reserve officer at the rank of Lieutenant Commander; he was the first congressman in uniform. Since Johnson had served on the House Naval Affairs Committee, his political patron, President Roosevelt, assigned him to do staff work for Undersecretary of the Navy James Forrestal. But Johnson and his close political advisers soon decided that exposure to danger in battle would provide a bigger boost to his career than staff work in the United States. Comparison with other congressmen already fighting cast Johnson's stateside naval career in a politically dubious light. "Get your ass out of this country at once to where there is danger, and then get back as soon as you can to real work," one associate counseled. Johnson responded with alacrity. "I was ready to go and whip the Indians," asserted the Hill Country Texan, metaphorically reshaping the global imperial war as part of American frontier mythology, with racial and expansionist overtones.[43]

Johnson's chance came with an assignment from FDR and Forrestal to go on an overseas trip to investigate friction between General Douglas MacArthur and other branches of the military operating in the Pacific theater. In early June 1942, after visiting MacArthur's Australian headquarters, Johnson toured military installations in Australia and New Guinea. Resolving to put himself in harm's way, Lieutenant Commander Johnson demanded a place as an "observer" on a B-26 bombing mission to hit a Japanese base at Lae, New Guinea. He overcame the objections of escorting generals by invoking his role as the eyes and ears of FDR, with a need to "see personally for the president just what conditions were like."[44]

As a passenger on this single bombing mission Johnson found the validating exposure to death that he sought, and then received a medal for his risky ride. The bombers came under attack by Japanese Zero fighter planes. One B-26, carrying an army colonel who had been accompanying Johnson on the same inspection tour, was destroyed, killing all aboard. Zeros pursued and damaged the aircraft carrying Johnson with cannon fire, but the American pilot's hair-raising evasive maneuvers allowed escape and a limping return

U.S. Navy Lieutenant Commander Lyndon B. Johnson, while on leave of absence from Congress, examines a map of military activity in the South Pacific. LBJ Library / Photo by unknown.

Lieutenant Commander Lyndon B. Johnson poses next to a downed Japanese Zero during his inspection tour of the South Pacific, June 1942. LBJ Library / Photo by unknown.

to Port Moresby, New Guinea. While Johnson reportedly maintained his composure and curiosity even while "bullets and shells were hitting the plane," he took no active role in the aerial battle. Upon Johnson's return to army headquarters, General MacArthur informed him that Colonel Stevens, the colonel killed in the raid, would receive the Distinguished Service Cross. MacArthur then bestowed the Silver Star upon Johnson and the third member of the inspection tour, an Air Corps officer who had also flown the mission as an observer. None of the surviving combatants were decorated, and the aviators who died in the raid received only posthumous Purple Hearts.[45]

For the rest of his life, Johnson displayed the battle ribbon of his Silver Star on his lapel as proof of trial by fire. Soon after the interview with MacArthur, President Roosevelt issued a directive recalling members of Congress serving in the military. Johnson left the navy and returned to the House on July 17, 1942. Yet his brief exposure to battle became part of his identity narrative. On his return to Texas he arranged for several ceremonies at public appearances where the Silver Star was pinned to his lapel (on each occasion as if for the first time). With public retellings, Johnson exaggerated and embellished the tale for maximum political impact, until he sincerely came to believe in his own heroism.[46]

As president, LBJ trotted out his war story to help persuade congressional leaders to support his foreign aid spending and his policy toward Vietnam. Encountering resistance to his proposals, LBJ invoked his own experience of patriotic exposure to danger to spur House leaders toward greater efforts: "This is bad for our country. You still don't have ammunition in Vietnam right now. . . . I know foreign aid is unpopular. But I didn't want to go to the Pacific in '41 after Pearl Harbor, but I did. And I didn't want to let those Japs shoot at me in a Zero, but I did."[47]

"Tex" Hilsman and the Narrative of the Guerrilla Hero

The example of Roger Hilsman illustrates important links between the experience of war, the construction of narrative and self, and the rewards of social mobility and power that American society bestows on its warrior-heroes. Hilsman was, for a time, a significant foreign policy figure in the Kennedy administration. First as the director of the State Department Bureau of Intelligence and Research, then as assistant secretary of state for Far Eastern affairs, Hilsman helped construct "counterinsurgency" as the hoped-for solution to problems of American policy in Vietnam. He was one of the architects of the "strategic hamlet" program under the Ngo Dinh Diem regime and a proponent of the U.S.-sponsored coup that overthrew Diem in late 1963.[48]

A career in the military, in the intelligence bureaucracies, and in the civilian national security state offered Hilsman the rewards of inclusion in a powerful elite. He got high-level posts in the Kennedy administration in part through his reputation in combat duty with the OSS during World War II. Hilsman understood his military experience during World War II as a central element in his career trajectory. He has subsequently argued that the foreign policy of the Kennedy administration was deeply influenced by the experiences of its architects as "part of a generation" that "came to adulthood just in time to fight as ordinary soldiers and junior officers in World War II." This heroic legacy took form in the "Kennedy thesis": "We thought one man could make a difference. . . . We believed that the individual effort could change the world. . . . Pragmatic, idealistic, activist. This was an interventionist administration."[49]

An unintended irony resides in the leap from the experience of "an ordinary soldier or junior officer" during the global, industrialized, mass warfare of 1939–45 to the conclusion that "individual effort could change the world." To reconcile the contradiction required that fundamental aspects of modern warfare be denied, repressed, or erased and replaced with a more satisfactory narrative. The industrialized warfare of the twentieth century has been typified by the dehumanization of the individual warrior and by his sense of helplessness in the midst of battle with anonymous, faceless enemies who rained down death in the form of long-range artillery, bombs, mines and other impersonal technologies of destruction and dismemberment.[50] A distinctive feature of battle for most modern soldiers has been the necessity to tolerate long periods of enforced passivity while under assault by unseen or distant enemies. This contradicts the masculine warrior ideal of honorable conduct on the battlefield: aggression, face-to-face engagement, and defeat of foes. Modern warfare has often made it impossible for soldiers to experience themselves as "powerful and effective agents."[51]

Roger Hilsman faced this dilemma during military service in the Second World War. He resolved it by resort to a role as an "irregular," fighting "behind the lines" in a peripheral colonial theater of war. Hilsman's experience was shaped by the "manhood scripts" of his culture, and, in turn, his experience profoundly shaped his actions as a powerful political actor during the early 1960s.

Hilsman did not come from a patrician family. Nonetheless, his background and upbringing contained elements that helped socialize him to a

career of stoic service to the state; he was able to acquire credentials of masculine virtue and merit that later gave him credibility with patrician statesmen
and national security bureaucrats. Hilsman was the son of a career army
officer. He spent several years of his late childhood living in that outpost and
emblem of American Empire, the Philippines, while his father served as a
company commander and then commandant of a Philippine military academy. He attended public high school in Sacramento, California, during the
late 1930s, participating in the ROTC and rising to the rank of cadet colonel.
While Hilsman believed that his talents were more suited to a career as a
lawyer than a soldier, the looming threat of European fascism inclined him
toward the service academy at West Point. The glamour of the officer's persona also appealed to him: "In the final year, when seniors began asking each
other what they were going to do next, I answered that I might go to West
Point. West Point was far from Sacramento. It was a romantic place. Girls
would ooh and aah, and their reaction no doubt encouraged me as much as
the menace of Hitler."[52]

Hilsman did not experience West Point as a romantic interlude. He found
himself subjected to an extreme and institutionally formalized regime of ritual hazing during his "plebe" year. Like many victims of prep-school hazing,
Hilsman resented being the target of systematic abuse and humiliation. In
later years, however, he touted the benefits of the ordeal. Much like Joseph
Alsop or Dean Acheson, who later justified the abuse they suffered at Groton,
Hilsman formulated a functionalist argument to explain the advantages of
the brutalizing rituals. He incorporated the explanation as a part of his own
identity narrative. He has speculated that hazing is not, as "orthodox" explanations would have it, primarily useful as a means of "bonding" a group of
men or inculcating unthinking obedience in future soldiers. Instead, Hilsman argues, constant, seemingly arbitrary abuse taught men to cope with
the sensation of panic, a skill particularly useful to men in battle.[53]

As a graduate of the West Point class of 1943, Hilsman soon faced the need
to control panic on the battlefield. Hilsman chose the infantry, and then
volunteered for duty in a special "jungle unit." His wartime actions, and the
motivations that prompted them, present examples of several narrative
threads connected to culturally defined ordeals of manhood. For Hilsman
particularly, as the son of an army officer, masculine cultural ideals of stoicism, bravery, defense of boundaries, and service to the state were closely
intertwined with problems of personal autonomy and the achievement of
full manhood. While Hilsman attended West Point, his father had served as
an officer under General Douglas MacArthur in the Philippines. With the

fall of the archipelago and the surrender of American forces in 1942, Colonel Roger Hilsman Sr. was taken as a prisoner of war by the Japanese.[54]

According to his memoir, the young Lieutenant Hilsman sought service in the Pacific because his father was imprisoned by the Japanese. He was sent to Burma with Merrill's Marauders, arriving in May 1944 as part of a second (replacement) regiment attempting to take and hold the town of Myitkyina and its airfield. There Hilsman was quickly introduced to the horrors and frustrations of modern infantry warfare. Hilsman's company suffered 90 percent casualties among the enlisted men, and all six officers were either killed or wounded, as were the next two sets of six sent in to replace them. Hilsman himself lasted only two weeks in battle. He volunteered to lead a reconnaissance patrol to determine Japanese positions. During the patrol he was severely wounded by an enemy machine gunner. He attributed his survival to his ability "to handle feelings of panic" learned during the hazing rituals at West Point. This self-possession during the ordeal allowed him to make his way back to the American lines for medical treatment.[55]

Hilsman concluded that the realities of mass warfare in the industrial age left little scope for the kind of action that brought honor and satisfaction to individual warriors:[56]

> At least since World War I, infantryman has been synonymous with cannon fodder. Infantrymen cower in their trenches or foxholes, battered by artillery shells of an enemy they often never see before they die or are wounded. In the Marauders, the only Japanese I had seen were those sticking their bayonets in the bushes looking for me. The rest of the time the enemy consisted of shells exploding around me or bullets flying past me. What is so unnerving about the role of an infantryman in modern war is his utter helplessness, his inability to do anything about his situation.[57]

A state of "helplessness" contradicts a soldier's functionally necessary self-conception as an active, powerful agent. Such a sense of ineffectuality prevented the individual soldier from using the ordeal of war to compose a useable identity narrative of warrior masculinity. Perhaps unconsciously, Hilsman realized that the actual experience of modern war did not resemble its representation in popular stories of adventure, heroism, sacrifice, and imperial glory that valorized war and military service, and which, presumably, had helped shape his own imagination of battle.[58]

During an extended convalescence in army field hospitals, Hilsman had time to ponder what lay in store for him after his body healed. He was torn between a desire to escape future combat duty with its attendant risks of death, mutilation, and dismemberment, and an internalized ideology of manhood that dictated a return to battle. To imagine himself as a man of honor meant that only under special circumstances could he, as a soldier, avoid repeatedly putting his body in harm's way. Cultural scripts of warrior manliness left one costly escape from this double bind. Soldiers hoped for injury in battle as the lesser of evils. Hilsman received such a wound, and safety was possible: "Most of us dreaded the prospect of going back into combat, speculating privately about how we might escape it. But usually we felt guilty about those speculations. What men in combat long for is a wound that will get them out of battle but not be maiming—an honorable way out. I had imagined an ideal wound would be one on my left side that didn't perforate the intestines. The only difference between the one I had prayed for and the one I got was that mine was on the right."[59]

Despite a way to avoid battle sanctioned as "honorable" by society, Hilsman returned to combat. He did not return to the regular infantry, however. Instead, he joined the OSS, and soon volunteered to lead a guerrilla battalion operating behind enemy lines. This choice helped Hilsman to resolve the contradiction between his desire to avoid the "dangerous" "job of infantry platoon leader attacking pillboxes in Myitkyina" and his desire to earn the rewards of honor in battle. He knew that a "safe job . . . wouldn't do much for [his] future career."[60] His calculated assessment of the warrior culture and its bureaucracy led to the conclusion that it would favor those who demonstrated an unwavering willingness to fight. In Hilsman's mind heroism in battle was also linked with adult status and masculine autonomy, preconditions for legitimacy as a political actor. In his memoirs Hilsman retrospectively interprets his wartime voluntarism as "compulsive," psychologically motivated by the desire to escape the "domination" of his father, to "free" himself "from the guilt of that rebellion" and earn his father's "respect" by his acts of courage in combat. While this after-the-fact explanation is no doubt true for Hilsman—that is to say, it conforms to popular patterns of psychological explanation and forms an individually meaningful narrative resolution of part of his life story—it fails to address other strands that tie Hilsman's wartime actions to larger ideological constructions of masculinity. Hilsman's compulsions were not only products of family drama and individual psychology; he was also compelled by pervasive cultural prescription and proscription. His father represented but one example of normative masculinity, albeit one with a powerful influence sometimes resented by the young Roger Hilsman.[61]

The solution to the contradictions facing Hilsman lay in a military adven-

ture that gave him scope for heroic action away from the utterly dehumanizing industrialized battlefield. After his wounds healed, he first did a brief
stint in a relatively safe job as a liaison officer between the Burma OSS command, the Fourteenth Army headquarters, and the British in Burma. But
nagged by fears that he might be "less brave than the others," Hilsman sought
command of a guerrilla battalion of partisans and mercenaries operating behind Japanese lines, organized and supplied by Colonel Ray Peers's OSS Detachment 101. Colonel Peers assigned him to lead three hundred men—an
exotic mix of ethnically diverse indigenous people including "one Chinese
company, a company of Karens, and a scout platoon of Shans." News of the
combat command had a pronounced effect on Hilsman: "I felt much, much
better about myself."[62]

Not only could Hilsman stop worrying whether he was as brave as his
fellow soldiers, but the new assignment offered opportunities missing in the
regular army:

> Visiting guerrilla groups made me think that, dangerous though it was to be
> in a situation with no friendly troops nearby, at least a guerrilla leader could
> use his brains. At Myitkyina the Marauders had to attack on a hundred-yard
> front straight into machine-gun fire and hope that one or two men would
> still be on their feet to throw grenades. It wasn't brains that mattered—only
> luck. A guerrilla leader, on the other hand, could keep constantly on the
> move. He could engage in deception. Since joining Detachment 101 I had
> thought a lot about how a guerrilla group should fight, the tactics it might
> use, and ways it could operate effectively with as little risk as possible to the
> lives of its men. As a liaison officer I had heard bullets again, and it made me
> realize that though they frightened me as much as before, I could manage
> combat because there was a chance that I would be able to affect the
> outcome.[63]

Hilsman's new situation presented the chance to act out a role as a truly
potent warrior in full manhood, testing his courage, intelligence, stamina,
skill, and luck against the fortunes of war. Further, it contained many of the
elements of modern imperial adventure narrative.[64]

Hilsman led a troop of "native" soldiers with the assistance of three white
sergeants. Two of them might have sprung from the pages of an imperial
adventure tale. One was a former English pacifist, driven to volunteer to fight
after witnessing Japanese atrocities during his service with a Quaker medical
unit in China. Another was an American, an unreflective but heroic man of
violence, a former merchant seaman who helped organize a militia to fight

the Japanese at the fall of Singapore, then enlisted in the British Army, and finally wound up with the OSS in Burma. There the American noncom was

> a great favorite with the Chinese guerrillas. He wore a pair of camouflage pants with suspenders and no shirt, only a khaki towel around his neck to wipe away the sweat. He carried one of the fancy 9-millimeter submachine guns that the OSS had obtained from the Dutch, and a Chinese orderly trailed behind him with a high-powered sniper's rifle that had telescopic sights. [He] used both weapons with such enthusiasm that . . . I had to keep special watch to see that he didn't start firing before the order was given.[65]

Although Hilsman and his Asian guerrillas fought Japanese imperial forces on a territory still claimed as a part of the British Empire, the precedents that shaped his own conception of his role were taken from American history and frontier myth. Hilsman took the code name "Tex," evocative of Indian fighters and gunslingers. (Born in Texas, he had lived there for only a brief period as an infant.) Hilsman's "theory of guerrilla warfare" as he developed it then, and later in the national security bureaucracy, drew upon American traditions of the frontiersman, the minuteman, and the lessons of the Indian wars.[66] America's first overseas imperial conquest also provided valuable historical lessons for those willing to embrace them. The U.S. Army finally succeeded in defeating the Philippine insurgency on Mindanao, Hilsman argued, when the army realized "that the way to fight the guerrilla was to adopt the tactics of the guerrilla." By recruiting "native Filipinos—men wise to jungle ways" and by placing a "trained American officer—a bold and determined leader" over each patrol, the United States defeated the insurgents. This American military tradition he invoked prefigured and by implication glorified Hilsman's efforts in Burma and, later, his counterinsurgency policy for Vietnam.[67]

In the mountains of Burma, Hilsman first formulated and tested his theory of guerrilla war. The apparent success of his exploits buttressed his subsequent belief that his experience especially qualified him to provide advice on counterinsurgency theory and doctrine. His men traveled lightly, using hit-and-run tactics. When pursued by the Japanese they vanished deep into the forests, heading away from the front lines and Allied forces. Under Hilsman's leadership the guerrilla band ambushed and killed Japanese troops, destroyed a bridge to prevent Japanese reinforcements from engaging Allied main force units, and "kept a whole Japanese regiment of 3,000 men marching and countermarching over the mountains far away from the front lines" in pursuit of his elusive irregulars.[68]

Hilsman's adventure of a few months as a guerrilla leader required not only that he test his own strength, stamina and courage as a soldier, but that he make life or death decisions for many others. "Americans who commanded guerrilla battalions wielded enormous power," Hilsman remembers. "They were little kings." This power extended to the indigenous population in areas where the partisans operated. Hilsman on one occasion ordered the court-martial and execution of a Shan man evidently in the employ of the Japanese secret police; on another, a Karen villager who collaborated with the Japanese received the same treatment. The kingly power of the American guerrilla leaders sometimes led to abuses. Hilsman encountered an OSS leader who had "gone native" in the fashion of Conrad's character Kurtz, and who from his position of power commanded the sexual services of indigenous women as well as the goods and labor of the villages.[69]

The abuse of power by the American commando and the resulting resentment by the native population reinforced an axiom of Hilsman's theory of guerrilla war: the absolute necessity to maintain at least the neutrality of the indigenous population of the territory contested by the armies of the opposing empires. This meant, for Hilsman, scrupulous payment for supplies and for services rendered, as when Hilsman employed villagers as porters. Hilsman's efforts to avoid alienating the local populace were greatly aided by the lavish logistical support of the U.S. military. The OSS units did not operate as did frontier fighters in American myth, living off the land. Instead, by radio, they called in parachute drops of food, ammunition, medical supplies, and raw opium for some of the Chinese mercenaries. They could summon fighter aircraft to provide close air support in battle. The bounty of the U.S. government allowed Hilsman and his band to purchase the goodwill of the local villagers. Hilsman's understanding of the "political" aspect of subsequent anticolonial nationalism and revolutionary movements was always colored by this fundamentally tactical emphasis on the efficacy of well-planned and lavishly supplied antiguerrilla military operations.[70]

Hilsman's war experience ultimately provided him with the ingredients to construct a meaningful and satisfying identity narrative. It became a "useable past"; he could later deploy his credentials of warrior manhood to legitimate and to expedite his rise to power in the national security bureaucracy. His war experience also helped create the self-confidence necessary to make life or death decisions on a global scale. Roger Hilsman was one of many young warriors who emerged from World War II with an understandable belief that their effort and sacrifice played a significant part in the successful defense of their society and its material and political underpinnings.

Hilsman later argued that the responsibility and command exercised by the young officers of the Second World War was comparable to the kinds of experience that shaped the young patriarchs who were the founding fathers of the Republic. He called attention to the youth of the "men who ran the American Revolution." The comparison flattered the erstwhile junior officers of the Kennedy administration, while repressing the racial and imperial subtext that structured it:

> The oldest man was Washington, and he only was, what, forty-three. And he was oldest by far of the whole group. And how they got the experience, you know, to do this at so young an age—and of course it's the plantation system. The plantation system is everything: the blacksmith's shop, carriage makers, its all one economic unit. And because it's feudal and family run, the sixteen-year-old boy is sort of deputy administrator of the whole economic complex, a very large scale operation, you see. And by the time he's twenty-one or twenty-two he's had enormous experience. . . . in a mild way this happened to the men of my generation because—you know, I was a battalion commander at the age of twenty-five, commanded several hundred men. A PT boat is a very small thing, but you are the boss, you know. You get a hell of a lot of experience when you are very young in handling men and dealing with interacting matters, you know. You see, I was responsible, for example, for feeding these guys, finding them a place to sleep, fighting them, doing everything.[71]

Hilsman's personal war story achieved a special closure. After the Japanese surrender, he managed to get an assignment with an OSS detachment that parachuted into the Japanese prisoner-of-war camp at Mukden, Manchuria, where his father was imprisoned after the 1942 surrender in the Philippines. Hilsman liberated his father from the now-defeated Japanese captors; he understood that act as a completion of his symbolic passage into a culturally defined full manhood. He had been wounded in battle, had proven his courage, stamina, and competence as a guerrilla leader. By rescuing his formerly "dominating" father, Hilsman gained his approval and even deference, which marked his own maturity and inclusion in the world of male power and privilege.[72]

Hilsman used his OSS command to launch a career in the national security bureaucracy. He made a career in military intelligence working with the OSS and then the CIA, also earning a Ph.D. in political science at Yale by 1951. He resigned from the army after the Korean war and became chief of the foreign affairs division of the Legislative Research Service, Library of Congress. There he met Senator Kennedy and other members of Congress

"interested in defense and foreign affairs." When President Kennedy appointed Hilsman to head the State Department Bureau of Intelligence and
Research, the ex-guerrilla found his reputation as a warrior-intellectual particularly useful: "I had a lot going for me politically. You see, here I am, a
West Point graduate, wounded in the war, all of this military record, which
protects me from the right. In fact, guys like [Sen. Thomas J.] Dodd and
[Sen. Karl] Mundt thought I was great. On the other hand, my intellectual
activities made me welcome to the left. So I had no problem with Capitol
Hill at all, unlike say Walt Rostow, who had very severe problems."[73]

As a part of the Kennedy administration, Hilsman became a player in
Vietnam decision making by trading on his reputation as an expert on guerrilla war. Sent to Vietnam in early 1962 by the president, Hilsman returned
with a "strategic concept" for counterinsurgency operations that promised to
defeat the communist guerrillas without a huge, costly, direct U.S. intervention. President Kennedy responded enthusiastically to Hilsman's briefing.
The president and his brother Robert, attorney general and adviser on foreign policy and counterinsurgency, both gave special credence to men with
reputations as heroic warriors. The president sent Hilsman "all over Washington giving the same thing [the counterinsurgency briefing] to everybody,
and one of them was Bobby [Kennedy]." Hilsman's emphasis on the prowess
and brains of the individual warrior—outsmarting and outfighting communist enemies on their terms—appealed to the president's pugnacious brother:
"So I go out to Hickory Hill, and Bobby and I spend about two or three
hours. And when I got through, he put his arm around me, you know, and
he said, 'Great stuff.' He says 'Terrific.' And from that time on, I think, we
both regarded each other as—there was a personal intimacy here that developed after that."[74]

As Hilsman himself asserted, the experience of command and victory during World War II was a formative experience for the men of the Kennedy
and Johnson administrations. The luster of their military service helped their
rise to prominence in the postwar government. Their experience as elite junior officers in a global imperial war, however, provided lessons inappropriate
to the intensely nationalist upheavals in Vietnam fifteen and twenty years
later. Hilsman, the Kennedys, and others were seduced by a romantic image
of American jungle fighters successfully combating popular nationalist upris-
ings led by intensely committed indigenous revolutionaries. The illusion that
their own experience of war had taught them how to defeat such an insurgency, that it was essentially a matter of skill, technique, and will, proved
enormously destructive. Hilsman, after all, had fought in the OSS as a commando using some guerrilla tactics; he was never a true guerrilla with a com-

mitment to an indigenous political organization. The conviction that Americans could successfully shape the political future of postcolonial societies by supplying and directing the military operations of local counterrevolutionary proxies was part of the mind-set that produced the Bay of Pigs and the Vietnam debacle.[75]

The individual experiences of the erstwhile warriors of the Kennedy and Johnson administrations varied. The net result was, as Walt Whitman Rostow put it, to make them "not so scared of big decisions." Rostow, chairman of the State Department Planning Council under Kennedy, and national security adviser to Lyndon Johnson between 1966 and 1969, agreed with Hilsman that such an effect was part of "a generational phenomenon."[76] They "had all seen, in one context or another, what tactical defeat looked like during the Second World War." Despite setbacks, the United States emerged victorious. When the junior officers of the Second World War came to power, their experience of the Cold War was strongly colored by their earlier experience of the hot war. A predisposition for the use of force colored the "big decisions."[77]

Rostow, an exponent of the use of American air power to subdue the Vietnamese "insurgents," had served with the OSS during World War II, picking strategic bombing targets. He found satisfaction in the replication of a culture of "fraternal small units" of elite officers and men within the national security bureaucracy where he served two presidents. He later described that period of power and service as "taking my tour on the line."[78] Such a comment suggests that the warrior ethos of elite combat played a central role in the self-identification of the national security bureaucrats, even as they embarked on the U.S. intervention in Vietnam.

·FOUR·

"LAVENDER LADS" AND THE

FOREIGN POLICY ESTABLISHMENT

It is the opinion of this subcommittee that those who engage in acts of homosexuality and other perverted sex activities are unsuitable for employment in the Federal Government. This conclusion is based upon the fact that persons who indulge in such degraded activity are committing not only illegal and immoral acts, but they also constitute security risks in positions of public trust.

Senate, *Employment of Homosexuals and
Other Sex Perverts in Government,* 1950

Lieutenant Blick has been a member of the police vice squad for 18 years. . . . He estimated that there are 5,000 homosexuals in the District of Columbia and that three-fourths of them, 3,750, work for the Government. He also testified that he has in his possession the names of between 300 and 400 Department of State employees suspected or allegedly homosexuals.

Senator Kenneth Wherry, 1950

V ICTORIOUS over the Axis powers, the imperial brotherhood of the Truman foreign policy bureaucracy undertook the next heroic task. Men such as Robert Lovett, Dean Acheson, James Forrestal, Averell Harriman, John J. McCloy, George Kennan, Charles Bohlen, Paul Nitze, and others began forming a new global imperial alliance under U.S. leadership, in opposition to the Soviet Union. They helped create a "national security state" dedicated to the containment of communism and the expansion of a corporate capitalist world economic order. To mobilize domestic support for expensive foreign policy and military initiatives, Truman's policymakers used alarmist rhetoric to persuade the American public that the

Members of the imperial brotherhood "present at the creation": President Truman confers with (*left to right*) Undersecretary of State Robert Lovett, George F. Kennan, and Charles E. Bohlen. Courtesy Harry S. Truman Library.

Soviets posed an immediate and direct threat to U.S. interests and to world peace. Using newly constructed secret intelligence and covert action bureaucracies, the professional functionaries of the imperial brotherhood including Kennan, Bohlen, Frank Wisner, Charles Thayer, and others conducted a secret foreign policy directed at Soviet and European communism, outside the scrutiny of Congress or the public.[1]

Soon, however, the foreign policy ascendance of the imperial brotherhood came under assault. Conservative politicians, searching for a means to regain power after the long years of the New Deal, wartime "internationalism," and Democratic rule, helped spark a second Red Scare. Republican congressmen especially, covertly abetted by right-wing allies in the FBI and other federal agencies, attacked President Truman's leadership. They accused the Democratic administration of treason in its conduct of foreign policy and in its failure to root out suspected subversives in government. Many conservative midwestern legislators resented the pretensions to imperial leadership of the eastern, patrician, liberal internationalists so clearly dominant in the Truman foreign policy apparatus. Elite diplomats of privileged and cosmopolitan background, seemingly contaminated by exposure to foreign ideas, morality, and practices, provided attractive targets of opportunity for right-wing politicians. Many congressional conservatives explained setbacks to U.S. foreign policy as a result of "weakness" introduced by the treachery of concealed communists or of enfeebled "dupes" in high places.[2]

The Department of State became a target of relentless attack and vilification by isolationist critics of Truman's "containment" doctrine, unhappy with the expensive international entanglements and the apparent constraints on the unilateral use of U.S. force inherent in containment strategy. Driven by a sense of their own political impotence, conservatives depicted the foreign service as a bureaucracy staffed by effete "cookie-pushing" Ivy League internationalist homosexuals and "pinks." After 1949 Secretary of State Acheson, "the Red Dean of Washington" who sported aristocratic airs and a cultivated arrogance, supplied a convenient and symbolically resonant target for their political invective. Revulsion toward the State Department often transcended party affiliation; right-wing Democrats and Republicans alike identified the State Department as the epicenter of conspiratorial subversion and perversion. They conflated fears of domestic political subversion and foreign aggression with anxieties about the maintenance of domestic social and sexual order.[3]

The result was a Lavender Scare, a partly subterranean purge linked to the anticommunist crusade and mirroring its form, but not subsumed by it. The homosexual purge, too, came complete with congressional investigations, inquisitorial panels, executive branch "security" doctrine, guilt by association, threat of punitive exposure, ritual confession, the naming of names, and blacklisting. The Lavender Scare has often been treated in passing as a peripheral absurdity stemming from the "sheer primitive ferocity" and irrational cultural prejudices of the congressional far Right. This misses the significance of the purge. Gender, sexuality, and the production and control of sexual secrets played a central role in many political struggles of the Red Scare era. Just as the anticommunist inquisition has been blamed for the unwarranted dismissal of the "China hands" John Stewart Service, John Carter Vincent, O. Edmund Clubb, and John Paton Davies, with regrettable effects on U.S. Far Eastern policy in the subsequent decades, the sexual inquisition resulted in the purge of several high-level members of the imperial brotherhood including Russian and European experts such as Charles Thayer and Samuel Reber, among many others. Countersubversives managed to link appeasement and subversion to homosexuality. By destroying the careers of prominent diplomats they showed the establishment the dan-

gers of becoming vulnerable to accusations of "softness," lessons that profoundly shaped the subsequent calculation of personal and political costs and
benefits of policy decisions these men later faced.[4]

The State Department became a prime focus of a state-sanctioned sexual
inquisition, designed to certify normative masculinity and sexual orthodoxy
as a condition for employment in the foreign policy bureaucracy. Under Truman's administration between January 1947 and January 1953, more than four
hundred State Department employees, from ambassadors and senior foreign
service officers to clerks and secretaries, were fired or forced to resign for real
or imagined homosexuality—a rate approaching twice that of those dismissed for communist "sympathy" or other offenses. After the Republicans
took office in 1953, the "pervert" hunt resumed with renewed vigor, and hundreds more were dismissed. Perhaps because of the chronic shortage of genuine communists in the high offices of the Department of State, the homosexual security issue became one of the mainstays of the far Right's attempt to
wrest control of U.S. foreign policy from the eastern establishment architects
of containment. A homosexual panic exploited by ultraconservatives peaked
with the 1953 controversy surrounding the nomination of Charles E. Bohlen
as ambassador to the Soviet Union.

Constructions of Gender, Sexuality, and the Political Order

Previous scholarship has stressed anticommunism as the central ideology of
the Red Scare. But this focus has neglected the extent to which "McCarthyism" was also driven by related and equally deep-rooted concerns about
sexual and gender order. In this conservative vision of politics and society,
effective resistance to communism or other threats to "100 percent Americanism" demanded that citizens adhere to a traditional, patriarchal sexual
order. The public performance of "respectable" masculinity became increasingly crucial as a test of political legitimacy for men in public life. Unmasking
secret sexual behavior, thus revealing a "true" but concealed identity that
belied a man's public pose of conformity to social norms, became a weapon
wielded against political enemies, linked in form and function to the unmasking of "secret communists" that formed the more visible dimension of
the Red Scare purges.

In the political and ideological struggle subsumed under the labels "Red
Scare" or "McCarthyism," contesting groups of elites attempted to portray
their opponents as threats to the "natural" order and proper functioning of
American society. Because sex and gender roles are fundamental elements of

social order, Cold War contests over political inclusion placed a strong emphasis on sexuality and on the "perversion" of sexual norms. Countersubversive rhetoric linked behavior that subverted the "natural" relations between the sexes with behavior that subverted the proper political relations of American society.[5]

The full-blown emergence of a national security state dedicated to the production and control of secrets, codified in the National Security Act of 1947 (and the creation of the CIA), contributed to public fears of secret conspiracies fomented by men or women of concealed or unstable political and sexual identities. Congress endorsed the growth of covert policy and espionage bureaucracies whose actions were protected from public scrutiny. This official culture of secrecy increased worries that "deviant" or subversive men could infiltrate the bureaucracy and injure the national interest. Fears of secret and socially destabilizing sexuality were reinforced with the 1948 publication of Alfred C. Kinsey's widely publicized *Sexual Behavior in the Human Male.* Its startling but apparently "scientific" statistical assertions that 37 percent of American men had some "overt homosexual experience to orgasm" or that "10 percent of the males are more or less exclusively homosexual for at least three years between the ages of 16 and 55" served to magnify the threat of homosexual "infiltration" of the state in the eyes of many conservative politicians and administrators.[6]

Communism, depicted as an implacable, expansionist, militarily threatening enemy in its external imperial incarnation, was portrayed domestically as an "infection"; a conspiratorial, protean invasion of the boundaries of state and society, undermining national strength from within. According to this demonology, homosexuals provided one vector for infection. Homosexuals were depicted as "moral weaklings," vulnerable to both the blandishments and to the blackmail of communist agents because of their "softness," their "instability," and their inability to deny themselves the pleasures of their "perverted" sexuality.[7]

Homosexuality put men outside the pattern of republican "engendered" civic virtue taken as the basis for individual political legitimacy by both Cold War conservatives and left-centrists. Both groups believed that homosexuals lay outside the anchoring interests of the patriarchal nuclear family, and thus outside the moral order of rational political discourse. Homosexuals were by definition not legitimate political actors in a republic, for they lived in a conspiratorial "world all to themselves associating and consorting with other homosexuals." Driven by their appetites, they lacked the ability to sublimate their passions to the requirements of civic duty and political life, "seeking sexual gratification from one person one night and from another person the next, in a paltry and endless gesture at a happiness they never realize," as one government official asserted.[8]

Anticommunist conservatives and anticommunist liberals alike deplored the "lavender" threat just as they deplored the red menace. Each used the rhetoric of red-blooded masculinity to establish their credentials as legitimate defenders of a truly American social and political order. Such language also distanced them from suspicion of sympathy with the political and sexual "other" during a period when guilt by association supplied the favored instrument of countersubversive inquisitors.

Commentators and political rivals from both the Right and the Center-Left detected danger in the analogy they perceived between the underground communities of communism and homosexuality. Both were closeted, secretive, conspiratorial, and the activities of each were proscribed by law. Both insidiously infiltrated government and society because those outside the group could not easily recognize either a communist or a homosexual by any set of "outward characteristics or physical traits." The presence of either presented a danger of further infection. "One homosexual can pollute a government office," warned a Senate investigative report. "If a homosexual attains a position in Government where he can influence the hiring of personnel, it is almost inevitable that he will attempt to place other homosexuals in Government jobs." For those eager to believe, a series of highly publicized spy scandals also seemed to provide concrete proof of the intimate connection between "underground" communism, and "underground" homosexuality.[9]

Despite their ability to "pass" in "normal" society, each group had subtle and secret means of identifying their own members. Arthur Schlesinger made the analogy explicit with a literary allusion to homosexuality in his 1949 polemic extolling "vital center" liberalism. The "underground arm of the Party works through secret members and through fellow travelers," Schlesinger revealed: "They can identify each other . . . on casual meeting by the use of certain phrases, the names of certain friends, by certain enthusiasms and certain silences. It is reminiscent of nothing so much as the famous scene in Proust where the Baron Charlus and the tailor Jupien suddenly recognize their common corruption."[10] The young ideologue of liberalism explained the nature of contemporary politics by using a metaphorical language of sexual vice and virtue. Flirtation with "totalitarianism," warned Schlesinger, led away from the path of true political manhood. "It perverts politics into something secret, sweaty and furtive like nothing so much, in the phrase of one wise observer of modern Russia, as homosexuality in a boys' school." Schlesinger's sexual similes instructed his audience that communism lay outside the boundaries of legitimate politics, just as homosexuality lay outside legitimate boundaries of gender and sexuality; both were infantilizing subcultures of "deviance."[11]

While a Cold War liberal like Schlesinger might link countersubversion and counterperversion by urbane allusion to fictional homosexuals of European literature, midwestern Republicans exploiting the issue framed the threat more urgently, although with some sacrifice of clarity and elegance of prose. Conservatives warned of active conspiracies that connected homosexuality to communist subversion. Senator Kenneth Wherry of Nebraska, the Republican floor leader, admonished the Senate: "Only the most naive could believe that the Communists' fifth column in the United States would neglect to propagate and use homosexuals to gain their treacherous ends in view of the resort to every conceivable form of sabotage revealed in every country infiltrated and finally taken over by the ruthless Communists."[12] In this view, homosexuality represented more than a way to metaphorically depict the distasteful conspiratorial politics of communism to the Cold War audience; it posed a clear and present danger to the integrity of the state.

Schlesinger and Wherry differed considerably in their politics. They disagreed on the precise nature of the threat posed by domestic communism and on the question of what boundaries should be defended and what methods should be used to defend disputed boundaries. Senator Wherry fought communism hoping to "save the American way of life" from the tightening grip of the "socialistic welfare state." Arthur Schlesinger fought communism hoping to save the tradition of "radical democracy" exemplified by Andrew Jackson and Franklin Roosevelt, threatened, he believed, by "soft," "doughface progressives." "The sentimentalists, the utopians, the wailers," with their sympathy for communism and their fellow traveling, undermined the political legitimacy of "hard" pragmatic liberals, Schlesinger asserted. Nonetheless, the Harvard propagandist of virile cosmopolitan liberalism and the midwestern anti–New Deal, isolationist, and self-described conservative "fundamentalist" agreed that sexual, social, and political maladjustment were intertwined.[13] "The party fills the lives of lonely and frustrated people, providing them with social, intellectual, even sexual fulfillment they cannot obtain in existing society," averred Schlesinger.[14]

This vision of communism relentlessly exploiting sexual weaknesses to undermine American society pervaded public discourse. Even heterosexual sexuality could provide a vector for the "infection," according to popular depictions stigmatizing domestic communism. In a 1948 scenario portrayed by *Life* magazine, "party girls" helped entrap maladjusted young men. The

CPUSA preyed upon intellectually precocious but sexually inadequate men by flattering their vanity and providing sexual gratification otherwise unobtainable. Communist Party operatives identified a potential recruit and invited him to communist "parties": "Each time he was welcomed as a fine fellow by these suave intellectuals, pretty girls appeared and responded generously to his clumsy lovemaking. What more could a boy want than this?"[15] In the *Life* fantasy, a young woman's political commitment to the party meant giving up control of her own sexuality to party leaders, becoming, in effect, a prostitute in thrall to the communist procurer: "These party girls were wonderful. They could talk with the best of the law students, they carried placards and fought policemen, they danced and went to bed. He didn't appreciate, at the time, that they went to bed in much the same way they carried placards: as a service to the party."[16]

Communist Party officials used women's sexuality in the deliberate transgression of racial boundaries, too. They "assigned" "party girls" to "enfold likely Negroes," arranging interracial marriages in accordance with the official communist line. When the line changed, the party expelled the interracial couples, a cruel and cynical act of political opportunism.[17]

Lest readers feel a twinge of regret at being left out of the sexual revels of the "party," *Life* hastened to show that the initial seduction of the recruit led quickly to years of "hard work, boredom and grim discipline." Vulnerability to sexual temptation, the failure to resist communist seductresses, led inexorably to a regimented, joyless underground life that excluded one from the potential rewards open to members of mainstream American society. First the party compelled the recruit to break social ties that connected the recruit to family and noncommunist friends. Soon the erstwhile idealist became a kind of automaton forced to submit his individuality to the brutal and demeaning dictates of the party. Ultimately, in this scenario, the CPUSA demanded one's manhood in exchange for a party card.[18]

"Perversion" and the Security Purges

By early 1950, the sexualized Cold War discourse linking subversion and perversion became much more than a rhetorical ploy. Gender and the politics of sexuality and "deviance" were not peripheral issues; they were central to the operations of power within the state. Cold War boundary-marking contests between elites saw competing groups striving to eliminate ideological opponents from positions of power. The rhetoric of sexual virtue and vice became a weapon, along with subterranean campaigns of sexual surveillance,

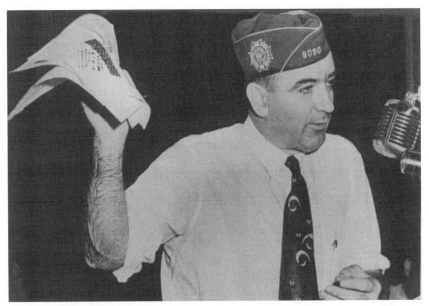

Senator Joseph R. McCarthy, speaking before the Veterans of Foreign Wars in August 1950, alleges the presence of "Communists and stooges of the Kremlin" in the State Department. Courtesy Cleveland Public Library / © Bettmann/CORBIS.

smear, and blackmail. These stratagems were central to the high-stakes contests to defeat political and bureaucratic rivals.

Soon after Senator Joseph McCarthy's February 9 speech in Wheeling, West Virginia, where he brandished his "list" of 205 "active members of the Communist party and members of a spy ring" working in the State Department, McCarthy and his right-wing allies in the Senate launched a full-blown crusade to unearth and purge the "commies and queers" from their hiding places in the foreign service and other executive branch agencies.[19] McCarthy and his right-wing congressional colleagues systematically struck at the patrician, bipartisan "establishment" figures of the Truman foreign policy and national security apparatuses. The attacks damaged or ended the careers of a few internationalist figures of some prominence. The inquisitors purged many less powerful establishment functionaries. Senatorial countersubversives called the campaign a "purge of the perverts." State Department and other government employees understood it as a campaign of political terror and exclusion.[20]

Conservative countersubversives managed to control the terms of the discourse, using homophobia and gay-baiting as a tool against the imperial brotherhood and its functionaries. The congressional right wing struck where they believed their rivals to be most vulnerable, at the perceived homoerotic tendencies of many establishment patricians. Earlier homosexual scandals and current rumors confirmed their belief that a conspiratorial sexual subculture of deviance controlled institutions such as the State Department. "These charges have been rumored around here for the last 10 years," complained Representative Clare E. Hoffman, a Republican from Michigan, before Congress, "and from time to time various committees have uncovered it, but [homosexuals] still continue on the pay roll." Many anti–New Deal countersubversives embraced the proposition "that the foreign policy of the U.S., even before World War II, was dominated by an all-powerful, supersecret inner circle of highly educated, socially highly-placed sexual misfits in the State Department, all easy to blackmail, all susceptible to blandishments by homosexuals in foreign nations."[21]

Most notorious was the 1943 case of the aristocratic Sumner Welles, Groton old boy and Franklin Roosevelt's assistant secretary of state. Former ambassador William Bullitt, out of favor with President Roosevelt during World War II and resentful of the power and prestige held by Undersecretary of State Sumner Welles, spread gossip on Capitol Hill about an episode involving Welles's drunken sexual propositions to black Pullman porters during a rail trip in 1940. In 1943, with the help of Cordell Hull and the assistance of the conservative anti–New Deal senator Ralph Owen Brewster, Bullitt managed to get his fellow patrician Sumner Welles fired from the State Department. Prefiguring his expanded Cold War role as keeper and careful purveyor of voluminous "sex-deviates" files, J. Edgar Hoover investigated Welles and certified the Bullitt-Hull charges to Senator Brewster. Because Bullitt and Hull engaged in widespread subterranean publicity of Welles's transgressions, the reasons for Welles's departure became widely known in Washington, although not officially acknowledged. Welles became an archetype of the patrician, effete, "cookie-pushing," subversive homosexual diplomat sheltered by the State Department.[22]

Liberal establishment countersubversive rhetoric condemning "perversion" created an apparent public consensus about sexuality and political manliness. It allowed the Right to exploit the apparently ambiguous sexuality of many within the patrician establishment and to purge the targeted victims. This ostensible consensus masked a deeper political struggle and made establishment men more defensive and protective of their masculinity as an element of political legitimacy.

Between 1945 and 1950 a series of highly publicized espionage cases lent credence to the idea that domestic communism, its agents and sympathizers, might be responsible for a worrisome sequence of setbacks to U.S. foreign policy.[23] The perjury conviction of Alger Hiss, two weeks before McCarthy's Wheeling speech, seemed to confirm conservative Republican accusations of treason in high places and to demonstrate the inadequacy of the Truman loyalty program. Senator Homer Capehart of Indiana summed up the rage and frustration of the conservative countersubversives: "How much more are we going to have to take? Fuchs and Acheson and Hiss and hydrogen bombs threatening outside and New Dealism eating away at the vitals of the nation! In the name of Heaven, is this the best we can do?"[24]

Because of his background and career, Hiss provided a target of great symbolic resonance. Of genteel eastern origin, graduate of Johns Hopkins and Harvard Law School, he studied with Felix Frankfurter and clerked for Supreme Court Justice Oliver Wendell Holmes. Employed early in the New Deal by the Agricultural Adjustment Administration, Hiss acted as counsel for the Nye Committee in the fall of 1934 and the spring of 1935. He then worked briefly as a lawyer for the solicitor general, and finally moved to the State Department, in which capacity he attended the Yalta Conference as a minor functionary. Hiss's credentials as an establishment internationalist were completed by his role as executive secretary at the Dumbarton Oaks conference, by his work as principal adviser to the American delegation at the San Francisco Charter Conference of the United Nations, and by his appointment, in 1947, to the presidency of the Carnegie Endowment for World Peace.

Hiss served conservative Republicans as an emblem of the corruption and betrayal of the New Deal and the "sellout" at Yalta. He represented the entire liberal "internationalist eastern establishment" in the minds of many conservative countersubversives.[25] This impression was strengthened as many of the imperial brotherhood followed the dictates of their upbringing and offered support to the embattled Hiss. When Dean Acheson willingly asserted his friendship with Alger Hiss during hearings in 1949 on Acheson's confirmation as secretary of state, the young McGeorge Bundy admired his display of manliness under political pressure. "Your statement today as a friend about a friend is one of the two or three really clear things that have been said by any one at any time in the Chambers affair," wrote the young protégé of Henry Stimson. "I know that hundreds who have watched men hedge will cheer—and I hope that millions will now think twice before they judge by headlines. Anyhow, they will know that the new Secretary of State is a man." During the perjury trial a parade of eminent establishment character witnesses testified on behalf of Hiss, including Supreme Court Justice Felix Frankfurter, intensifying the perception that Hiss was part of a larger "conspiracy of the gentlemen." The conviction of Hiss seemed to puncture the pretensions of his class; conservative countersubversives resented and deplored the failure of many prominent liberal patricians to repudiate Hiss and took it as further evidence that the patriotic loyalty of the class as a whole was questionable.[26]

In his Wheeling speech, McCarthy erupted in a denunciation of the "traitorous actions of those men who have been treated so well by this Nation. . . . The bright young men [in the State Department] who are born with silver spoons in their mouths are the ones who have been the most traitorous." McCarthy expressed the resentment harbored by the conservative countersubversives toward the unearned privilege symbolized by Hiss, "important not as an individual any more, but rather because he is so representative of a group in the State Department," one of a class "who have had all the benefits that the wealthiest nation on earth has to offer—the finest homes, the finest college education, and the finest jobs in government we can give." The masculinity of men of this class was questionable too, implied McCarthy, weakened as it was by access to luxury and ease denied to hardier entrepreneurial midwestern isolationists.[27]

As with most contestants in the countersubversive inquisitions, whispered rumors of homosexuality and other sexual scandal surrounded Alger Hiss and his accuser, Whittaker Chambers. Chambers, a bisexual and a repentant ex-communist, had led a confessedly dissolute and sexually unorthodox life during the period before he repudiated the party. Chambers's life in the depression-era communist "underground" seemingly offered confirmation of inevitable links between political and sexual conspiracy and crime. In his chosen role as informer-martyr, Chambers self-consciously created a narrative of intertwined political and sexual sin and redemption. As the lawyers on each side prepared the perjury case, he preemptively confessed his homosexuality to the FBI—a gesture that completed the ritual self-abasement so central to obtaining absolution from the purge tribunals of the Red Scare. Soon after he had gone "underground" as part of a communist espionage "apparatus," the married man had his "first homosexual experience." "It was a revelation to me," Chambers told his confessors in the bureau. "As a matter of fact it set off a chain reaction in me which was almost impossible to control." True to contemporary stereotypes of homosexual men as promiscuous slaves to their sexual appetites, Chambers described his life as a communist in thrall to "perversion": "At first I would engage in these activities whenever by accident the opportunity presented itself. However, after a while the desire became greater and I actively sought out the opportunities for homosexual relationships. . . . I never had a prolonged affair with any one man. . . . I generally went to parks or other parts of town where these people were likely to be found." But the former red provided an uplifting moral closure to the narrative; when he repudiated communism he regained control of his sexual life, rigidly repressing his homosexual "tendencies" despite remaining not "completely immune to such stimuli." Chambers became an exemplary property-owning American patriarch when he discovered "religion and God," purchased land and a home, got a regular job, and "lived a blameless and devoted life as husband and father."[28]

While not privy to the accuser's FBI confession, Hiss, his lawyers, and his partisans gathered evidence of Chambers's disordered sexual, political, and moral career as proof of "psychopathology." Joseph Alsop, the patrician Washington columnist and strident establishment cold warrior, himself a closeted homosexual, helped provide evidence to discredit Chambers. Alsop directed Hiss's legal team to homoerotic themes in Chambers's poetry and in his translations of German texts. Psychiatric expert witnesses called during Hiss's second trial testified to Chambers's psychopathology, including "sexual abnormality." But Hiss and his defense team did not fully exploit the issue of Chambers's homosexuality, fearing that Hiss, himself a target of sexual rumor, would be damaged by the tactic. Hiss's own theory, according to his son, was that Chambers sought "fairy revenge" for unreciprocated attraction. Others, countersubversives convinced of Hiss's guilt, were eager to believe that the ex-communist and the elite State Department diplomat had been lovers.[29]

In late February and early March 1950, the "attack of the primitives," as Dean Acheson later called it, upon the State Department as a haven for communists, homosexuals, and other "bad security risks" got fully underway. Secretary of State Acheson's avowal at a press conference on January 25, that he did "not intend to turn [his] back on Alger Hiss," infuriated conservative congressmen and provoked widespread condemnation in the press. McCarthy denounced the secretary of state as a "pompous diplomat in striped pants, with a phony British accent," who had "endorsed communism, high treason, and betrayal of a sacred trust."[30]

Alger Hiss was, if not especially close to Acheson personally, certainly a member of the imperial brotherhood of the foreign policy establishment. However, his brother Donald Hiss, also named by Chambers as a member of the underground communist "apparatus," had been professionally and personally close to Acheson. Donald Hiss had served as Assistant Secretary of State Acheson's assistant, and later became a partner in Acheson's law firm. A mixture of class and family allegiances, a personal "fondness" for his long-time associate, and his distaste for the unsavory ex-communist accuser made

Acheson resent the "outrage" perpetrated against Donald, whom he regarded as "a fortuitous victim of Chambers's vindictiveness against Alger." The patrician secretary of state, trained since childhood and his days at Groton School in the neo-stoic/Christian code of the gentleman, regarded a statement of loyalty to Alger Hiss as a matter of personal honor. The plight of Hiss had great symbolic resonance for the eastern establishment, too. He stood as an example of the grim fate that could await patrician "statesmen" who ran afoul of the unreasoning countersubversive conservatives.[31]

Summoning him before a Senate appropriations subcommittee on February 28, Republican Senators Styles Bridges (New Hampshire), Homer Ferguson (Michigan), and William Knowland (California), along with conservative Democrat Pat McCarran (Nevada), badgered Acheson about his relationship with Hiss, his former subordinate in the State Department. During the two-hour grilling about security measures in the State Department, Deputy Undersecretary of State John Peurifoy (in charge of department security) who accompanied Acheson, revealed that since 1947, ninety-one employees "in the shady category, most of them homosexuals," had been allowed to resign after security investigations cast them in shadow. Press reports later disclosed that Peurifoy "made it clear that all 91 were homosexuals." Conservative newspapers interpreted Peurifoy's revelation as shocking confirmation of "common rumor here for years that there were homosexuals in the State Department," and sounded an alarm warning of dangerous "cells" of "abnormal persons" threatening the security of the state.[32]

The Hoey Subcommittee, Blacklists, and Scandal

The senatorial countersubversives smelled blood. They exploited Peurifoy's testimony in a campaign to force Acheson's resignation. Styles Bridges urged a "manhunt for the master spy" who "moves the puppets" in the State Department. "Homosexuals and subversive agents" were deliberately placed in the department "because Russia wanted them there" proclaimed the New Hampshire red-hunter, demanding an answer to the question "who put the 91 homosexuals in the State Department?" Senators McCarthy and Wherry also seized upon this public evidence of further perfidy in the State Department to make strident attacks on Truman and Acheson.[33]

Kenneth Wherry considered himself the Senate expert on "homosexualism." He boasted of his attempts to eliminate "from the Department of State pro-communists, subversives, and other alien-minded radicals with low standards of morality," efforts dating from his 1943 election to the Senate. Wherry, joined by Senator Lister Hill, a Democrat from Alabama, conducted his own investigation into homosexual "infiltration of the government." Wherry's inquiry fueled the panic. House conservatives, perhaps reluctant to be upstaged by their senatorial colleagues, rose to denounce the homosexual threat to U.S. security. Arthur L. Miller, a Republican congressman from Nebraska, gave voice to the widely circulated myth positing the existence of a master list of homosexuals first compiled by the Nazis, then passed to the Soviets:

> Within the last 10 days a gentleman from the CIA told me that Mr. Goering of Germany and others had a complete list of all the homosexuals in the State Department, the Department of Commerce, and the Department of Defense and that they knew who to contact when they came over here on espionage missions. The danger of spies, the danger of blackmail, their fear of blackmail, has caused those people to sabotage our government. . . . the Russians rather glory in the accomplishments resulting from homosexuality and they undoubtedly have the same list of homosexuals who were in key positions in Government in this country, so they knew who to contact when they came here.[34]

The Hill-Wherry subcommittee of two began digging in the arrest records of the Metropolitan Police vice squad and the U.S. Park Service for evidence of sexual malfeasance among government workers. An official "Pervert Elimination Campaign" conducted since November 1947 by the Park Police offered the counterperversion inquisitors a possible means to obtain a list of 817 names of those either arrested (196) or "apprehended under suspicious circumstances" (621). Hill and Wherry demanded the list, but sensing danger, the Truman White House temporized for months before finally authorizing the release only of the names of those actually arrested.[35]

The testimony of Lieutenant Roy Blick of the Metropolitan Police vice squad proved more helpful to Wherry. Emboldened by the "evidence" he uncovered, the conservative senator called for an official Senate subcommittee inquiry and report. He asserted that his star witness, Lieutenant Blick, had "in his possession the names of between 300 and 400 Department of State employees suspected or allegedly homosexuals," out of an "estimated" 3,750 working for the government in the District of Columbia. On the basis of his professional expertise, Blick claimed that the city harbored a total of five thousand homosexual men; the figures soon appeared widely in the press. Much as in the case of Joe McCarthy's purported list of communists working in the State Department, there was less substance to Blick's list than Wherry professed.[36]

In meetings with State Department security officers, Blick was quizzed again about "how many perverts he would estimate [were] employed in the Department of State." Using a curious chain of reasoning and loose arithmetic, the vice squad cop explained that although it was "not based upon factual knowledge," he reached the figure of three to four hundred, because "the U.S. Public Health Bureau estimates that only $\frac{1}{10}$ of the people who have Venereal Disease report such Venereal Diseases to the Health authorities and on the premise that since 86 known perverts have been discharged from the Department of State ten times that number would be 800, and he cut his estimation in half, which would mean between 300 and 400 people of such a nature in the Department of State." Confronted directly, Blick assured the security officers "that he did not have any list of State Department employees tending to show that anyone in the Department of State [was] a pervert," but promised to forward any information to the "proper authorities" in the department.[37]

Lieutenant Blick, of course, did have a list of sorts; four full-time vice detectives spent their working hours hounding the Washington gay community. Frequenting the city's popular cruising spots, including Lafayette Park across from the White House, the vice squad cops offered themselves as sexual bait. Ben Bradlee, then a junior reporter whose duties included covering the vice squad for the *Washington Post,* later described the squad's tactics: "Blick specialized in young apple-cheeked police recruits who did the worst things in the world. They hung around in the cans in Lafayette Square and in first-run movie theaters. They'd hang out in the john and wave their tally-whackers around and see if anybody was interested." When gay men responded with propositions, the officers arrested them on charges of "disorderly conduct (pervert)."[38]

Interviewed by a liberal journalist, the "ungrammatical" but "tough" Lieutenant Blick boasted of his success extracting names for his list. The process mirrored the ritual naming of names in communist-hunting inquisitions: "Every one of these fellows has five or six friends. Take Smith. We bring him in. We say to him, 'Who are your friends?' He says, 'I have none.' I say, 'Oh come on Smith. We know you fellows go around in gangs. We know you go to rug parties. Who are your friends?' Then he tells us—Jones, Robinson."[39] But when pressed to reveal the method he used to produce his numerical "estimates" of homosexuals in the District, Blick embarked upon yet another "adventure in higher mathematics" illustrating the arbitrary and capricious origins of his "statistics." He haltingly explained that he began with the list of those arrested and added the named "friends." He then took a number corresponding to 40 percent of the arrest list, "multiplied by five," and added the product to the total number of names to arrive at his final figure.[40]

The Washington, D.C., sexual policemen specialized in the creation of blacklists to discipline "deviant" groups, just as did the congressional countersubversive committees. Their tools were the same: the threat of punitive exposure, public humiliation, and loss of livelihood. Victims of vice squad homosexual roundups were almost never convicted of a crime. Instead, the ritual pattern included the station-house naming of names, followed by the forfeiture of bond and failure to appear in court. Forfeiture was universally regarded as tantamount to confession of guilt by the vice squad and security men throughout Washington. Those arrested faced a formidable double bind. "If they chose to fight the charge," one journalist reported, "they might win acquittal, but they would never live down the publicity and whisperings."[41]

In the new climate of counterperversion and countersubversion, Blick found many eager customers for his homosexual blacklist. First in line after Wherry was J. Edgar Hoover, who soon began retailing Blick's list to other federal agencies under the official imprimatur of the FBI. Responding with alacrity to the new demand for lists of "perverts," Hoover streamlined record-keeping procedures for the sexual surveillance of federal employees. In April 1950, the FBI demanded that the Metropolitan Police Department specially flag the fingerprint card of any government workers arrested for homosexual offenses before sending it to the Bureau's central fingerprint file.[42]

Kenneth Wherry was eager to believe the vice squad lieutenant's "evidence" of conspiratorial sexual mischief at Foggy Bottom, but revelations about the handling of the purge initiated by the State Department in 1947 added fuel to the Nebraska senator's crusading zeal. Deputy Undersecretary John Peurifoy testified to Senators Wherry and Hill that the State Department maintained its own blacklist, accumulated since January 1947, "of about 3,000 names of persons in this country and abroad who are homosexuals or alleged homosexuals." Wherry tried to get the list to check names against Blick's roster, but Peurifoy denied the request, invoking Truman's executive order closing personnel files to the congressional branch. Peurifoy, however, assured the counterperversion crusader that "applicants for positions in the State Department as well as the 23,000 employees of the Department in this country and abroad are checked against this list."[43]

Wherry's demands for an investigation of homosexuals in government spurred the formation of the Hoey subcommittee of the Senate Committee on Expenditures to investigate the "alleged employment by the departments and agencies of government of homosexuals and other moral perverts."[44] As the Senate began its inquiry in the summer of 1950, the Truman White House and the Department of State sought to limit political damage. Press reports revealed that out of the "first 2,500 letters McCarthy got out of his campaign against the State Department," three-quarters expressed "shocked indignation at the evidence of sex depravity." Only one in four was "excited" about "red infiltration" of the government. Truman's advisers feared that the administration's enemies had found an issue likely to alienate working-class voters: "The charges about homosexuality have struck home with far greater effect, in certain quarters, than the Communist allegations. This has nothing to do with the alleged security risks involved in sexual aberrations. I believe, furthermore, that intolerance of this kind of deviation increases substantially as you go down the income scale. This investigation, therefore, represents a political problem of considerable magnitude."[45]

Truman's aides worried that the Democratic chairman of the subcommittee, Senator Clyde Hoey of North Carolina, might be a "dupe of the Republicans." In either case, they strongly suspected that "the Republican group is working up a very sordid smear campaign to the effect that the President is protecting the homos." Members of the White House staff warned him that even if the June 1950 outbreak of the Korean War had temporarily "driven McCarthy off the front pages," the investigation of "sex perversion in Government" still threatened the administration. They cautioned that a former HUAC committee countersubversive, Karl Mundt, the Republican senator from South Dakota then serving on the Hoey subcommittee, might use the issue to "step into McCarthy's shoes" with a "hue and cry" about loyalty and security.[46]

White House staff members successfully pressured Senator Hoey to conduct the investigative hearings in executive session not open to the public. They hoped to prevent "the McCarthys" from staging a "Roman Circus" at the expense of Truman and the State Department. "Any public discussion . . . of sex perversion at this time will result in giving the public the impression, no matter how mistaken, that government rolls are replete with sex perverts," counseled one adviser. "Without open hearings," predicted another, "there is a good chance at this juncture that the investigation won't get much press."[47]

Despite such hopes, lurid headlines appeared in opposition newspapers. "Perverts Fleeing State Dept. Under Probe Pressure" began one story trumpeting the news that "moral degenerates are fleeing the State Department at the rate of one or two each week." McCarthy's allies in the press blamed the secretary of state for harboring security risks and praised the purge of homosexuals. "The group's inquiry has finally stimulated State Department heads to put pressure upon the several hundreds of suspected degenerates who now hold office under Secretary Acheson." Lieutenant Blick's figures reappeared, accompanied by spurious claims that they came from a vice squad "list of all persons convicted of sex crimes": "A Washington police official testified that 300 to 400 persons arrested in such cases, most of whom forfeited bond, were in the State Department."[48]

The news from Korea failed to mute right-wing indignation about weak and treasonous homosexuals endangering the state. Walter Winchell scornfully remarked that "the State Department's 91 pansies are exempt from active duty. . . . But their dirty diplomatic linen is being washed in American blood." Such news and commentary prompted conservative voters to urge the investigating senators to root out the offenders and those officials who would "whitewash" the inquiry. "The Sodemites [sic] are a greater danger to the government and nation than the Communists," wrote one agitated supporter of Senator Wherry. "When the men of a nation become 'sissies' . . . then that nation is overthrown."[49]

Set against the outpouring of condemnation and alarm about "perverts" in government, one mass circulation paper sympathetic to the Truman administration spoke out against the purges. With a series of columns in the anti-McCarthy *New York Post,* columnist Max Lerner promised to bring the voice of liberal reason to the debate, "to tell the facts without snigger or smirk." He hoped to remove the issue from the Republicans' arsenal of political weapons by a thorough, "scientific," and dispassionate report. Underlying Lerner's extensive public discussion of the issue was an attempt to redraw the boundaries of political inclusion by recourse to scientific and medical expertise. Rather than accepting the ostensible consensus that any homosexual experience marked a man as part of a real or potential conspiracy, the journalist described hypothetical targets of the purge as harmless victims of an unjust and unreasoning political panic:

> He isn't a spy, and he isn't a Communist or a fellow-traveler, and he probably has no radical associations in the past. He has been doing a good job, is known to be able, lives quietly. But somewhere in his record, perhaps recently or perhaps 20 years ago, perhaps habitually or perhaps only on one or two occasions, he has had some kind of homosexual relations. . . . When the security officer confronts him with it, there is only one course for him to take. To fight the charge would be worse than futile.[50]

Lerner argued that the private sexual preferences of men were relevant to their fitness for public life only in cases of pathological "compulsion." Thus the automatic equation of "subversion" and "perversion" by countersubversives was an example of benighted anxiety or cynical political opportunism. Lerner implied that contrary to the overwhelming and quasi-official public consensus, some homosexual men could control their sexual passions, behave prudently, and thus act as legitimate participants in the political life of the republic.

The liberal journalist expressed alarm at the "wild Indian scalping yells" Wherry and his "desperate" Republican colleagues uttered as they began to politically exploit the scandal. He wondered if fear of "twisted sex" would "lead to some twisted politics in the Congressional elections" of 1950. Lerner worried about the recurrent public expressions of derision that undermined the morale and legitimacy of the U.S. foreign policy bureaucracy: "The State Dept. 'scandal' has become a joke good for a laugh on almost any occasion. The Washington Post has commented editorially about the laughter that greeted a man in a ticket-line who admitted that he worked at the State Dept. Then there is the *New Yorker* cartoon, by Alan Dunn, of the man applying for a job and assuring the personnel manager, 'It's true, sir, that the State Dept. let me go, but that was solely because of incompetence.'"[51]

Lerner, though, argued that the "homosexual panic" sweeping Washington political circles was no laughing matter. He deplored the ignorance and opportunism propelling the purges, and their damaging effects on the operations of the government: "Every Washington agency is combing their lists of employees for sexual deviations. The agency officers too have become frightened and panicky, and when men get that way they become cruel." Lerner used Alfred C. Kinsey's statistics from *Sexual Behavior in the Human Male* (1948) on the frequency and kind of homosexual experience among men in the general population to argue that the purges were both irrational *and* impractical. Because of the sheer numbers potentially involved, the purge would cripple the government, including Congress, if carried to its logical conclusion.[52]

Lerner, armed with Kinsey's report, argued that large numbers of men (37 percent) had some homosexual experience during their lifetime, while much smaller numbers were "exclusively" homosexual (4 percent). He cited medical experts to buttress his assertion that only "compulsive homosexuals" presented a genuine security risk. Lerner implied that the attempt to find and purge everyone who had ever had a homosexual experience was a practical impossibility driven by the ignorant obsessions of provincial yahoos in Congress. If Kinsey's numbers were applied to males on the federal civil service rolls, it "would mean 525,279 to be fired." Furthermore, Kinsey's figures held a lesson for the congressional pervert-hunters. Lerner pointed out that statistical probability indicated that 192 members of the House and Senate were likely to be "security risks" if held to Senator Wherry's standards. He cautioned Congress "before waving the purge sword too wildly, to ask how deep it will cut, and whether it may not cut both ways." Homosexuality, in his view, was primarily a medical problem best left to experts. The government should put the "problem in the hands of the scientists, rather than ignorant politicians or vice-squad cops or frightened Intelligence and security officers." An impartial scientific commission, he recommended, could distinguish between the small number of "compulsive homosexuals" who represented a genuine security threat and those individuals who simply offered conservative opponents of Truman a means to discredit the administration.[53]

Despite pervasive rumors of blackmail by foreign powers spread by security police and countersubversive congressmen, Lerner's research uncovered no concrete evidence that homosexuals represented a genuine threat of espionage or subversion, just as the Hoey subcommittee failed to document such a threat.[54] But he did turn up a fallback explanation to justify the purge in the absence of more tangible motivation: "One was offered to me by a Harvard professor with considerable government experience. It is a theory of the relation between virility and the needs of diplomacy in the age of the atombomb. It takes a virile man, he said, to be able to meet Russian diplomacy today. It requires the kind of toughness that an effeminate man simply would not have."[55]

Despite Lerner's calls to employ science to defuse the issue, the slightest hint of tolerance for homosexuals in *any* government post, even by casting the issue as a medical problem, appeared too politically dangerous for the Truman White House to accept. Truman's advisers quickly squelched one aide's suggestion that the administration attempt to minimize the security issue with expert medical testimony in public hearings before the Hoey subcommittee.[56] Instead, the White House and executive branch agency administrators embraced the purge, hoping to defuse political criticism, while struggling with congressional countersubversives over control of the process. In this way, Truman's public handling of the homosexuals-in-government issue mirrored the earlier handling of the communists-in-government issue with the establishment of the Loyalty-Security Program in 1947. The State Department began hunting for "sex perverts" in January 1947 at the instigation of Undersecretary Peurifoy, with one "expert assigned to homosexual matters" who "maintained close liaison with the District Police." This campaign actually predated Truman's Loyalty-Security Program by a couple of months, although a formal "policy of considering homosexuals security risks" did not completely "jell" until 1949. It was the seemingly inadvertent revelation of the purges during testimony before Congress that provided the opening for the congressional counterperversion crusade. The issue of "sexual deviance" subsequently enabled McCarthy and his countersubversive colleagues to attack and even destroy the careers of several important members of the foreign policy establishment and hundreds of less prominent employees of the State Department.[57]

The White House, the State Department, and other agencies intended to continue to quietly purge homosexuals. They tried to keep the whole process closeted, away from the prying eyes of rampaging senatorial countersubversives and their henchmen. They knew that the administration's enemies wanted lists with names of suspected "perverts" employed in the State Department and elsewhere to be used against Acheson and Truman as concrete evidence of treason and weakness. Although the embattled State Department officially closed ranks to deny files to the Senate inquisitors, the agency was internally divided. The security division, full of ex-FBI agents and policemen, zealously pursued the purges against lower-level employees. But McCarthy and his allies also received files leaked from within the department accusing high-level officials of sexual and political crimes, and of conspiring with each other to halt investigations that threatened to reveal such malfeasance. Much to the dismay of professional diplomats, the security division held the conviction that "the Foreign Service is especially attractive to homosexuals as an escape from a society which frowns upon them both from the point of view of 'getting far away from home' and 'getting to a foreign country where moral standards are not as high as in the United States.'"[58]

The Hoey subcommittee began with its own ambitious plan to purge the federal government. Ex-FBI agent and subcommittee counsel Francis Flanagan outlined a plan to create a central blacklist of "known and suspected homosexuals employed in government." He wanted to collect lists of such names from the Metropolitan Police Department, the Park Police, the Office of Naval Intelligence (in possession, it was reported, of a list naming exactly 7,859 homosexuals both "in and out of the military forces"),[59] the FBI, the Secret Service, the CIA, and the Army G-2 (intelligence). The lists were to be "used to prepare a central card index," then "checked against Civil Service files" and "those agencies where the homosexual is believed to be employed." The subcommittee then planned to forward the names of suspects to the employing agency, for "investigation or other appropriate action." After the subcommittee finished its investigation, the master blacklist was to be turned over to authorities in the FBI or the Civil Service Commission to coordinate the ongoing purge. Following in the footsteps of the crusading Senator Wherry, Flanagan also used blacklists and the investigative power of the sub-

committee to hunt down and root out homosexuals who had been fired by
one federal agency but had found work in another.[60]

The White House and the State Department resisted attempts by the
Hoey subcommittee to comb through personnel files, "investigative files,"
and FBI records. The administration walked a fine line, furnishing statistical
data to the committee about the operations of the purges throughout the
federal government, but refusing direct access to names and uncensored personnel files. At the same time, the State Department and the Civil Service
Commission assiduously compiled their own lists from FBI, vice squad, U.S.
Park Police, and internal investigation records.[61]

By 1950 the State Department security division had assigned two investigators as full-time "expert" homosexual-hunters. Perhaps spurred by the knowledge that an outside investigator had given the Hoey subcommittee the
names of two "top officials" of the Department as suspected homosexuals,
the agency created a new policy on the "Problem of Homosexuals and Sex
Perverts in the Department of State." It outlined procedure designed to arm
the agency against interference by the Hoey subcommittee or other congressional "security" crusaders. Carlisle Humelsine, named to replace Peurifoy as
deputy undersecretary of state for administration, assured the members of
the Hoey subcommittee that the State Department sleuths had become com-
mendably vigilant in their efforts to root out homosexuals. He told the law-
makers that investigators were alert to seemingly casual remarks obtained
from character references, formerly "meaningless . . . from the standpoint of
the investigation" but by then fraught with significance as code words indicating homosexual proclivities. For instance, an informant's testimony that
the subject of a security check, although a "fine person," nonetheless had
"prissy habits" now marked the subject for special scrutiny concerning his
sexual life, Humelsine reported. To guard against hiring homosexuals, covert
security officer "experts" in the detection of homosexuality interviewed all
unmarried male applicants for positions in the State Department or foreign
service. When "information or other evidence" such as an accusation of effeminacy put an employee under suspicion, the security investigators swung
into action with fearsome thoroughness:

> The investigation entails inquiries at all places of employment, all residences
> and habitats. The investigation also attempts to determine with whom the
> person associates and whether any of his friends or associates is homosexual.
> All available records, including school, credit, police and other investigative
> agency records are checked. All character references and other people who
> may know the subject of the investigation are interviewed personally. If the

circumstances warrant it, he may be placed under surveillance to determine whether he frequents known homosexual places or associates with other known homosexuals. . . . If the person is determined to be a homosexual through investigation or admission, he is promptly separated from the Department.[62]

This profoundly intrusive and humiliating inquisition with its presumption of guilt by association was justified on the grounds that "most homosexuals are weak, unstable and fickle people who fear detection and who are therefore susceptible to the wanton designs of others." The security inquisitors, however, found "no evidence that these designs of others have caused a breach of security." But they too, professed fear that the presence of homosexuals in the foreign policy bureaucracy threatened the sexual and gender order presumed to underpin the strength of the state. "Some experts hold that where the mores of a people have condoned homosexuality through apathy, the vigor and virility of that people have been emasculated," warned Deputy Undersecretary Humelsine. History provided ominous evidence, he argued, which "relate[d] the strong rise of homosexuality [to] the accompanying decline of the Egyptian, Greek, and Roman Empires."[63]

In executive session hearings during the summer of 1950, Francis Flanagan, Hoey subcommittee counsel, orchestrated a parade of "expert" witnesses—Hoover's assistant Milton Ladd of the FBI, the head of the CIA, the ubiquitous Lieutenant Blick, military psychiatrists, and others—to confirm the existence of a homosexual threat and to justify the pervasive, systematic purges already underway. The senators heard testimony that homosexuals made prized targets of foreign espionage agencies, who used blackmail to compel their victim's cooperation. But the only specific case cited to substantiate the risk posed by "perverts" was the story of the Austrian homosexual Captain Raedl, offered to the subcommittee by Admiral Roscoe Hillenkoetter, director of the CIA. Raedl, according to the tale, was the head of the Hapsburg imperial intelligence service who in 1913 was blackmailed by agents of the Russian Tsar and betrayed the Austrian war mobilization plans to prevent the public revelation of his own dark sexual secrets. Such evidence, Hillenkoetter argued, left "no doubt as to the fact that perversion present[ed] a very definite security risk." Leaked to the press, the story of the unfortunate Captain Raedl soon appeared in national newsmagazines and daily newspapers.[64]

Hillenkoetter and other subcommittee witnesses recited lists of stereotyped traits that supposedly made homosexuals dangerous to the republic. The CIA director assured the Hoey subcommittee that passivity, "psychological susceptibility," "physical cowardice," promiscuity, "general instability," indiscretion, and inability to control their sexual passions made homosexuals "vulnerable to seduction by another pervert employed for that purpose by a foreign power." Most worrisome, testified the head of the secret agency, was the potential for homosexual conspiracy within the state bureaucracy: "Perverts in key positions lead to the concept of a government within a government. . . . They belong to the lodge, the fraternity. One pervert brings other perverts into an agency, they move from position to position and advance them usually in the interest of furthering the romance of the moment."[65]

The subcommittee members assented to Hillenkoetter's conclusion that such unnatural but apparently inevitable sexual conspiracies followed as a "result of the strong bonds and loyalties which exist between homosexuals, and which makes them seek out, congregate with and support others of the same type." Senator Karl Mundt took pains to establish for the record the potential danger of conspiratorial groups of homosexuals in Washington. Mundt worried that homosexual "representatives of foreign governments" used their diplomatic immunity to avoid arrest and prosecution by Lieutenant Blick's vice cops even when "picked up" for "acts of perversion." Danger lay in the fact that without a formal arrest, record of their sexual crime never found its way into FBI records. Given the bonds between homosexuals that presumably compelled them to find others of their "type," the senator from South Dakota fretted that homosexuals of foreign embassies might escape notice and seek out "parallel homosexual clubs in our government," thereby posing a "serious" security risk.[66]

The testimony of psychiatric experts threatened to complicate the equation of homosexual with "security risk," earlier established by the assertions of secret policemen before the Hoey subcommittee. The psychiatrists argued that even drawing a meaningful distinction between "homosexual" and "heterosexual" was not a clear-cut task. Sexual identity was an unstable category complicated by a bewildering variety of sexual practices among American men, they testified, demonstrated by Kinsey's recent findings. The expert testimony of Captain George Raines, a navy psychiatrist, offered little support for the purges: "This matter of blackmail, when it first came up, I said, of course, homosexuals are more subject to blackmail, it has to be. Then I went back through my experience and I find I do not have a single fact on which to base that. . . . I do not think you could any more pick out the homosexual as a person who is a bad security risk, as such, . . . than you could say all people with size nine shoes were." Karl Mundt and the other members of the subcommittee ignored testimony that contradicted their fixed conviction that homosexuality posed "the worst conceivable security risk." Instead they pressed Captain Raines to instruct them on the best techniques for identifying "whether a suspect is actually a homosexual." Mundt seized the suggestion that "the lie detector would be the best judge" despite the navy psychiatrist's strong reservations about the ethical issues surrounding use of the polygraph. It offered the South Dakota senator a means to eliminate the uncertainty surrounding the purges; some men exhibited signs interpreted as markers of homosexuality but were not homosexual. "Like detecting a Communist by his vocabulary," opined Mundt, "you cannot be positive." The polygraph could help root out the true conspiracies while sparing the unjustly accused, undercutting objections of injustice against the purges. If a wrongly incriminated suspect "seem[ed] to fit the pattern" of homosexuality, he argued, "unquestionably the lie detector test would disclose that innocence."[67]

Fears of sexual conspirators undermining the empire sufficed to justify extensive purges in the absence of tangible evidence of a security threat to the United States posed by homosexuals. In December 1950 the Hoey subcommittee issued a report that served as a public declaration of the assumptions and understandings arrived at by congressional countersubversives and Federal agency security officials in the course of planning and executing the purge. In the years following the Hoey subcommittee's investigation, the State Department devoted ever greater effort to identifying and firing homosexuals in an attempt to raise the "prestige of the Department in the eyes" of Congress and the public. Nearly three hundred employees were fired or forced to resign for sexual "deviance" between mid-1950 and the beginning of 1953. Using the homosexual purge as a strategy to raise the "prestige" of the State Department extracted a heavy toll. Its most benign result was widespread demoralization in the ranks of the foreign service and among other department employees; its most malign consequence was the suicide of some victims of the purge. "It is a difficult thing . . . to handle," remarked Carlisle Humelsine to the Foreign Relations Committee, "because we have had several of them [i.e., homosexuals] that have done away with their lives after we have discharged them."[68]

While State Department security men found no real evidence that homosexual employees had succumbed to the blackmail or blandishments of foreign agents, six months after the Hoey subcommittee finished its work another widely publicized spy scandal again offered an apparent corroboration of the presumed connections between aristocratic "perversion," communism, treason, conspiracy, and espionage. In late May 1951, two British Foreign Office officials, Guy Burgess and Donald MacLean, vanished from London and were assumed to have fled to the Soviet Union to avoid capture as spies. Both had recently worked in the British embassy in Washington and had extensive contacts with their American diplomatic counterparts. Guy Burgess, a product of Eton and Cambridge, was an "admitted homosexual," as news reports later described him. MacLean, also recruited for espionage at Cambridge, also reputedly "showed homosexual tendencies when he was drinking." Burgess was "notorious" in Washington, for his reckless drinking, driving, and his apparently flagrant openness about his sexual preferences. Pat McCarran and his associates on the Senate Internal Security Subcommittee (SISS) found the case deeply alarming, and opened a file on the two spies.[69]

The Assault on Dean Acheson

In the spring of 1950, Joe McCarthy, worried that he was himself vulnerable to rumors about his own sexual "deviance," did not fully exploit the public dimension of the congressional inquiries into homosexuality in government; instead he left the heavy lifting to Senator Wherry.[70] But McCarthy strategically deployed sexual slander and smear to buttress his claims of subversive conspiracy permeating the Truman administration. The U.S. "loss" of China was the outcome of machinations by a dark and treasonous cabal, the embattled red-hunter announced. He recycled the conspiracy theories of Alfred Kohlberg and other right-wing China lobbyists, and improved upon them. He named Owen Lattimore (an academic with only tenuous connections to the State Department or U.S. Asia policy) as the "top Russian spy," "the boss of Alger Hiss." Lattimore, McCarthy asserted, was "a principal architect" of U.S. Far Eastern policy. In a series of inflammatory public statements McCarthy identified Lattimore as the head agent of a Kremlin conspiracy that made tools of Secretary of State Dean Acheson, Ambassador-at-Large Philip C. Jessup, and foreign service officers and China hands John Stewart Service and John Carter Vincent. The Truman administration, McCarthy asserted, was in thrall to the "disastrous Hiss-Acheson-Jessup-Lattimore-Vincent plan" to "turn all of Asia over to the Communists."[71]

Angry congressional countersubversives tirelessly worked to find evidence firmly linking the secretary of state to the international communist conspiracy. Grasping at straws, they obsessively traced his connections to Alger Hiss and other demonized figures fingered by Whittaker Chambers and Elizabeth Bentley. Their investigators discovered, for instance, that the Harvard alumni directory of 1937 contained the names of Dean Gooderham Acheson, Alger Hiss, Donald Hiss, Harry Dexter White, Lee Pressman, Nathan Witt, and Lauchlin B. Currie, among other suspect characters. They found Acheson's name, along with the Hisses and Harry Dexter White, on a list of "supporters or potential supporters" of the Washington Committee for Democratic Action, "listed as subversive" by the attorney general in 1947. Pat McCarran had an SISS staffer clip newspaper society columns that mentioned Acheson or his family, evidently hoping to track his after-hours contacts with other potential conspirators. Newspaper accounts of Acheson's regular morning walk to work with his friend and former mentor, Supreme Court Justice Felix Frankfurter, also alarmed McCarran and other anti–New Dealers. Countersubversive committee investigators compiled lists of "policies followed by Dean Acheson which either parallel the line of Moscow or cater to Soviet interests."[72]

Acheson was subjected to relentless vituperation by his political enemies. Countersubversive senators began a concerted and ongoing campaign to force his resignation. Their repeated accusations and demands for the secretary's removal received wide play in the press. A month after McCarthy's Wheeling speech, Kenneth Wherry labeled Acheson a "bad security risk" and blamed him for the international loss of American "prestige." "Even little countries like Bulgaria and Hungary trample upon our rights" but the State Department responded only with the "ignominy of futile daily protests," Wherry fumed. "State Department Prestige at Lowest Ebb in History," blared other headlines. Conservative newspaper editors, commentators, and cartoonists joined the fray. While no one overtly accused the secretary of state of homosexuality, many were infuriated by his aloof and supercilious demeanor and his apparent upper-class anglophilia; these were interpreted as signs of the enervating privilege and weakness that riddled the State Department. One political cartoon neatly encapsulated the countersubversives' denigration of Acheson's masculinity. Bearing the caption "Attack," it depicted the secretary as a mincing, limp-wristed fop in striped pants and morning coat, pinkie extended and handkerchief tucked into his sleeve, gently tossing "Acheson & Co. Cream Puffs" at Joseph Stalin. (See accompanying illustration.) Other right-wing tabloid journalists were even less restrained in their use of sexual and scatological innuendo—they profoundly despised Acheson and were little constrained by conventions of journalistic good taste, as one "investigation" of the political life of Washington demonstrated: "One of the queerest sights visible anywhere is the one from a window on the second floor of Dean Acheson's quaint home at 2805 P Street. It faces the 28th Street side over a back yard. The Secretary's personal lavatory faces that way. His mind apparently weighted by cosmos-shaking affairs of state, the secretary forgets to draw down the shade." Those few supporters of Acheson willing to speak up complained that he was subjected to a campaign of personal and political vilification manifesting a "virulence and shameless mendacity quite

Cal Alley cartoon

Cal Alley—Memphis Commercial Appeal
"ATTACK!!"

unequaled" in their memory. One warned that a dangerous opportunism propelled the Republicans, who had discovered "that it is less profitable, politically, to say you believe your opponents are mistaken than to call them Communists and perverts."[73]

The incessant attacks soon led even establishment journalists like Walter Lippmann and Joseph and Stewart Alsop to suggest that Truman should replace Acheson to "restore a measure of confidence and some national unity in the conduct of foreign affairs." "No human being can think clearly and effectively under such virulent and persistent personal attack," Lippmann warned. By late summer 1950, conservative newspapers reported that "responsible elements" from "coast to coast" united in a call for "the ouster of Secretary Acheson." In December, Republican Party caucuses in both houses of Congress formally demanded his resignation. Not a single legislator came to his defense. But, supported by Truman, Acheson soldiered on. Thwarted in their objective of forcing the hated secretary of state to resign, the following year enraged House Republicans attached an amendment to the appropriations bill to cut off Acheson's salary. In the other chamber, California's

Senator Tenney introduced a resolution calling for the impeachment of the secretary of state bearing "charges transmitted" from the "Senate and the Assembly of the State of California."[74]

Acheson publicly presented a picture of aloof aristocratic disdain for McCarthy and the attacking congressional ultraconservatives, but their loathing for him was fully reciprocated. His attitude was frequently remarked by journalists. "He has a deep contempt for 'stupid, narrow-minded people,' and frequently places most members of Congress in that category," stated a typical commentary. John Duncan Miller of the London *Times* summarized the attitude of the imperial brotherhood toward the countersubversive crusaders, coining a phrase subsequently adopted by Acheson. It was, he declared, "a revolt of the primitives against intelligence." Acheson strove to maintain his much noted public self-control. According to his internalized identity narrative, his display of the reasoned stoicism inculcated at Groton demonstrated his superior claims to power. For establishment liberals, this provided a telling contrast to the loutish and unreasoning congressional "primitives." But the cumulative effect of the senators' belligerence actually did provoke Acheson to physical violence on one occasion in August 1950. A confrontation with Kenneth Wherry before the Senate Committee on Appropriations escalated into a shouting match, Acheson later recounted. "The unhappy Wherry leaned across the table and shook his finger" in Acheson's face. Acheson rose and bellowed at Wherry: "Don't you dare shake your dirty finger in my face." Wherry persisted, and as Acheson "experienced the purging sensation of fighting rage," he "aimed and executed [a] swing" at the senator. Restrained by an aide (a former Princeton football player), Acheson did not succeed in coming to blows with Wherry. However, he later claimed a victory for violent confrontation instead of appeasement: "Curiously enough, my relations with Senator Wherry became much easier." Perhaps Acheson's willingness to brawl helped persuade the prairie senator that the secretary of state's waxed mustache and anglophile airs were not, after all, markers of "perversion."[75]

McCarthy, McCarran, Wherry, and their countersubversive associates never found sufficient leverage to pry Dean Acheson from the State Department. They did, however, get Acheson to turn his back on John S. Service. The China hand was subjected to a series of lengthy loyalty board investigations, but none ever found evidence of "disloyalty." Whispered allegations of homosexuality and other sexual indiscretions made by countersubversives appeared in Service's FBI files, further undermining his position. Service was finally blamed for bad judgment in the 1945 *Amerasia* case.[76] Beleaguered by the Right with front-page accusations such as Senator Wherry's that "the blood of our boys in Korea is on his shoulders, and no one else," Acheson decided to cut his losses where possible. In December 1951, Acheson decided the China hand was dispensable, and fired Service.[77]

Joseph Alsop, syndicated columnist and self-appointed voice of anticommunist establishment foreign policy, deeply resented the crude attacks impugning the patriotism and vigilance of the imperial brotherhood. Although he was a closeted homosexual, Alsop shared a version of the statesman-warrior identity narrative with his friends and club mates in the Truman foreign policy bureaucracies. Alsop led a "double life": establishment columnist by day, "homosexual adventurer by night." His close friends of the imperial brotherhood knew of or suspected his homosexuality, but an elite consensus about private sexual privilege and the spirit of a shared global mission within his Georgetown set gave cover of silence. Alsop's dress and effete manner were noted by professional associates and in the press. A sympathetic journalist of the time commented on his "reputation for having tastes somewhat out of the ordinary. His sartorial elegance is unquestioned, if at times slightly bizarre."[78]

To Alsop and his office-holding patrician friends the real threat facing the United States came from Soviet military capacity and from subversion of weakened regimes abroad, not from tiny sects of domestic political or sexual "deviants."[79] For the aristocrats and patricians who already held a place of preeminence at home, domestic subversion seemed a minor and easily dismissed issue. The possibilities for heroic self-realization came with the course already embarked upon: the creation and maintenance of a global imperial alliance with the United States replacing Britain as the leading power.

Alsop was more outspoken than those within the government. On July 29, 1950, he used the column he shared with his brother Stewart in the *Saturday Evening Post* to deplore the "miasma of fear" that hung over Washington in the wake of the renewed countersubversive inquisition. He declared that the "notion loudly proclaimed in Chicago and points West, that the Government is now in the hands of perverts and traitors," was "twaddle." In another column Alsop ridiculed the "vulgar folly" of Senator Wherry's attempt to discredit the State Department by elevating "the subject of homosexuality to the level of a serious political issue on the ground that sexual perversion represents a clear and present danger to the security of the United States." Instead, Alsop asserted, the domestic red-hunting of the isolationist bloc in Congress merely provided an excuse to cut defense spending and foreign aid, weakening the United States in its struggle with the genuine foreign threat.[80]

McCarthy responded by reading a letter to Alsop's editor into the *Congressional Record*, which, of course, lavender-baited the columnist. In so doing, the Wisconsin senator played upon his supporters' suspicious resentment of the class privilege Alsop embodied. Likening Alsop to a member of the "morally perverted and degenerate" ruling class during the decline of the Roman Empire, he insinuated that Alsop was himself homosexual. "McCarthyism" was not simply a rhetorical construction but a struggle among elites to redraw boundaries of privilege and politics. It was an attempt by the "primitives" to destroy the power and influence of the vulnerable members of the imperial brotherhood. So the senator took aim at the places where his enemies were weakest. In his "private" letter to the editor of the *Post,* McCarthy warned that the "phony anti-Communist" Alsop, "or anyone else who gets in the way of cleaning the Communists out of government may well get injured." For the next four years the editor of the *Post* refused to run another Alsop column attacking McCarthy or congressional countersubversion. Joseph and Stewart Alsop continued to oppose McCarthy in their syndicated newspaper column, but their stance resulted in the loss of twenty client newspapers.[81]

Joseph Alsop was a committed anticommunist, who held what appear in retrospect to be wildly alarmist ideas about the threat posed by the Soviet Union. After the fall of the French Army at Dien Bien Phu in 1954, for instance, Alsop warned that the Eisenhower administration had "decided on a Munich at all costs." "The geographical-strategic balance between the Soviet and free halves of the world is about to break down for good in Indochina," he lamented to Arthur Schlesinger Jr., predicting that the demonstration of "Soviet strength" would be to "discourage our friends, enflame our enemies, and bring the doubters down on the other side." Alsop foresaw the disintegration of the imperial alliance as the inevitable result; the process, he feared, would go "very far" and be "very terrible." In his column, and in conversation with his fellows of the imperial brotherhood, Alsop suggested a solution to the impending crisis. The U.S. military should swiftly use its "decisive superiority in . . . air-atomic striking power" to conduct a "preventive war" against the Soviet Union, before the "weapons-balance turn[ed] against us."[82]

Driven by his sense of foreign threat, Alsop fought the domestic conspiracy theorists and countersubversives who tried to besmirch the reputation of the "heroic" patrician statesmen who constructed the bulwark of containment against the red tide. He devoted his considerable powers as a journalist and Washington insider on behalf of containment and American imperial power. Armed with his anticommunist credentials, his relative professional autonomy, and his internalized patrician identity narrative, Alsop tried to offer support to some of those targeted by McCarthy and McCarran.

Beginning with his May 1950 testimony before the Tydings committee's investigation of McCarthy's charges, and continuing with appearances before McCarran's Senate Internal Security Subcommittee in 1951, Alsop invoked his own World War II involvement in the high politics of the Chinese Nationalist regime to deny the charges against Owen Lattimore, John S. Service, John Carter Vincent, and former vice president Henry Wallace. Alsop argued that while he had often disagreed with them over China policy, all had acted with "loyalty" and "courage and fidelity" during their wartime service. Alsop declared that an investigation of "Senators McCarthy, Wherry and Taft" would reveal that they had voted the Communist Party line on "the great post-war measures of foreign policy."[83]

In October 1951, testifying before an "enraged" and "insulting" Senator McCarran in hearings on the loss of China, Alsop challenged the credibility of the subcommittee's star witness, Louis Budenz. He subsequently accused the SISS counsel, Robert Morris, of taking "demonstrably false" evidence, and of conducting the examination with the "whole aim" of "protect[ing] his professional informer, Mr. Budenz." The combative journalist pressed Pat McCarran to submit Budenz's testimony to the Justice Department for investigation of perjury, asserting that the ex-communist's memory was shaped by the imperative to "give color of decency to the clamor of Senator McCarthy." His establishment friends celebrated his "magnificent performance" before the witch-hunters. Alsop also went to great lengths to find counsel for "the wretched Henry Wallace," to prevent the ex-VP from being "slaughtered" in an appearance before McCarran's inquisition. He was turned down by more than thirty Washington lawyers before George Ball, future undersecretary of state for Kennedy and Johnson, accepted the task. While Alsop was a certified anticommunist, in the climate of the purges his concealed homosexuality left him potentially vulnerable to the vengeance of the "primitives." Perhaps his head-on confrontations with the Senate bully-boys of countersubversion and counterperversion served as another of the character-building exercises in manliness to which he periodically subjected himself.[84]

Alsop could do little, though, to assist his admired imperial brothers in the State Department who became targets of the sexual inquisition as the homosexual "panic on the Potomac" gained momentum. The Truman administration, worried that the Republican Right would successfully exploit the proposition that the president was "protecting the homos," embraced and institutionalized the purge, while struggling for control of the blacklists compiled by executive branch agencies and congressional lavender-hunters. This concession to political expediency, justified by an ostensible ideological consensus on the necessity of "virility" as an attribute of Cold War diplomacy, masked a bitter contest over institutional power fought on the terrain of gender and sexuality. By institutionalizing the sexual inquisition and authorizing the array of secret police and intelligence agencies to root out homosexual "security risks," the Truman administration conceded enormous leverage over personnel matters to a subterranean network of ultraconservative inquisitors and informers in Congress, the FBI, the CIA, the State Department security division, and other government bureaucracies.

The "purge of the perverts" mirrored the form and methods of the anticommunist witch-hunt. There was no open court where defendants met their accusers with the protections of due process, leading to a final judgment. Instead the sexual inquisitors provided the cloak of anonymity to accusers often motivated by spite, resentment, professional rivalry, political opportunism, bureaucratic ambition, or other ends unrelated to genuine threats to "national security." They relied on gossip, hearsay, the presumption of guilt by association, and character assassination. Most significantly, no mechanism existed to truly "clear" a subject of the inquisition, regardless of the judgment issued by various "loyalty-security" tribunals. Even if one loyalty board dismissed "evidence" as unreliable, the "derogatory material" stayed in the files of the red- and lavender-hunting secret policemen, to be dredged up later when opportunity arose and deployed against the targeted individual. For several high-level members of the imperial brotherhood who ran afoul of the inquisition, this pattern proved fatal or damaging to their careers. The next chapter offers a detailed case study of two such figures, the patrician diplomats and Russian experts Charles Thayer and his brother-in-law, Charles Bohlen.

·FIVE·

THE SEXUAL INQUISITION AND THE
IMPERIAL BROTHERHOOD

The case of Charles W. Thayer is one of grave concern to ranking officials in the State Department, although the officials handling security
claim they are in the clear. Thayer is the brother-in-law of Charles Bohlen who went to Robert Lovett and had one investigation of Thayer's
homosexual proclivities stopped.

Anonymous letter received by Senator Styles Bridges, February 1950

EISENHOWER'S new Republican administration, despite the presence of many foreign policy "internationalists," failed for a long
while to do anything to check McCarthy. Despite an apparently
reckless and scatter-shot quality to his charges, Joe McCarthy waged a systematic campaign against the eastern patrician foreign policy establishment.
McCarthy, always willing to operate as the front man for more cautious Republican conservatives, also raised the specter of the lavender threat in the
spring of 1950. He and his allies fulminated in public about "moral perverts"
infesting the government; behind the scenes they tracked down every rumor
of "perversion" and sexual malfeasance that time and resources allowed, to
be later deployed in a campaign of political blackmail. As Lattimore and old
China hands like John S. Service, John Carter Vincent, and John Paton Davies became objects of new or revived security investigations, Senators Mc-
Carthy, McCarran, Wherry, Karl Mundt, Styles Bridges, William Jenner, and
others used allegations of homosexuality often originating in FBI files covertly provided by J. Edgar Hoover as ammunition against targets in the
foreign policy bureaucracy. But as early as mid-February 1950 McCarthy,
Styles Bridges, and their ideological allies in the Senate began receiving anonymous letters denouncing various high-level State Department and other
federal employees for homosexuality and communist sympathy. Some of the
letters were highly detailed and demonstrated a degree of knowledge that

could have only come from informants within the agencies. The accusations reinforced the countersubversives' conviction that a cabal of high-level establishment figures in the State Department conspired to block the legitimate security investigations of the FBI and of the State Department security office itself.[1]

Several such letters named Charles W. Thayer (St. Paul's School, West Point), a Philadelphia patrician and brother-in-law of Charles E. Bohlen (St. Paul's School, Harvard, Porcellian Club). Thayer was a respected, high-level foreign service officer with extensive credentials as a Soviet and Eastern European expert dating from his service with Charles Bohlen and George Kennan in Ambassador William C. Bullitt's first Moscow mission of 1934–35. Thayer conformed to the image of the aristocratic sportsman and soldier: he claimed credit for introducing polo to the Red Army in 1934; he was an avid hunter; and between 1944–46 he served with the U.S. Army and in the glamorous OSS in Yugoslavia and Austria during a hiatus in his foreign service career, earning the Legion of Merit. Thayer directed the State Department's International Broadcasting Division (Voice of America) from 1947 to 1949, "upon the recommendation of Mr. George Kennan, Mr. Charles Bohlen, and other top policy officers," according to Carlisle Humelsine's official account.[2]

The McCarthy-McCarran countersubversives regarded Thayer as a "key figure in State as of Feb. 1950." By the time the congressional red-hunters began tracking him, the establishment diplomat had a new assignment as political liaison officer in the Office of Political Affairs at Bonn, Germany. McCarthy's anonymous informer spewed forth a detailed list of accusations impeaching Thayer's political reliability and his sexual morality, directing the senator's gumshoes toward incriminating associates or toward witnesses who would testify against the patrician. "The case of Charles Wheeler Thayer constitutes one of the most scandalous abuses of personnel administration in the entire State Department," complained the informer, "and has been the subject of considerable rumor and gossip in the Department." The details of the scandal were contained in secret department files, but the dossier was "closely guarded since Thayer is the brother-in-law of Chip Bohlen," the letter asserted. After a brief and reasonably accurate résumé of Thayer's career came the indictment for political crimes: "He *had two political advisers both communists* and both employed by the state department," referring to the diplomat's wartime career in the OSS as liaison to Tito's Yugoslav partisans. "Their names—Alexander Vucinigh and Mike or Michael Petrovich." Even worse, "*Thayer was the man who swung the state department to Tito and laid the ground work for the assassination of the Slav patriot Mihailovich*," the missive accused. Accusations of corruption connected to the patrician's OSS career

Charles W. Thayer. Courtesy National Archives and Records Administration.

in Yugoslavia followed: black market profits in diamonds, official currency manipulations that cost the United States "over a million dollars." But it was his disreputable secret sexual practice that made the diplomat most contemptible and most vulnerable, the informer advised:

> Thayer is reported to *be a high class homosexual* and this information is known to State department officials and should be in the files. Check on Michael Petrovich he once lived with Thayer and once lived at the International house in New York and it is known that he has had relations with Thayer. Check on Col Ira Porter who was ousted from the State Department? Why? Was he a queer? Check on Carmel Offie. Was he queer? Did he play with Thayer? *Maybe the D.C. Police can help because they arrested Carmel a few years ago.*[3]

Not only had Thayer worked to advance the cause of international Communism in Eastern Europe, not only was he a homosexual "security risk," he was also the beneficiary of an elite conspiracy to cover up his subversive deviance, warned the agitated informer: "Find out the name of the State Department investigators who investigated Thayer they will tell you plenty as they were burned for their investigation, and had the goods on Thayer. If they will talk they will tell you that Thayer got Chip Bohlen to interced[e] by going to Bob Lovett who order[ed] John Peurifoy to stop the investigation."[4] These accusations were, the informer assured McCarthy, "only the beginning." The patrician diplomat could be linked to heterosexual immorality too. "Check on Olga Philipoff who worked in Voice of America," he urged:

> But before talking to her check up on Dr. J. M. Rowe who is on the payroll of the Soviet Consulate in New York. . . . And check hard because you will find out that Rowe is a Russian. Then go check birth records and see if Olga did not give birth to a child in March 1948 at the Manhatten [*sic*] General Hospital. If you can get the facts you can prove Thayer was the father, he took her to Rowe, and even if it was an innocent accident isn't this something for a high state department official who is open to blackmail and pressures from the Russians.[5]

Others, too, used the cloak of anonymity to impugn Thayer. One was clearly a lower-ranking employee of the State Department itself, probably connected to the security division. He, too, claimed that the diplomat had "shown communist leanings" in addition to possessing a "long record of perversion and degenerate practices" known to the State Department. Another suggested that Thayer had also had a male lover among his office staff while head of the VOA and that McCarthy should unearth the "inside story."[6]

The flood of denunciations against the patrician diplomat in the spring of 1950 was the product of political and bureaucratic animosities grounded in the secret workings of the purge during the preceding two years. Thayer's conduct as director of the Voice of America had provoked the lasting, although concealed, enmity of J. Edgar Hoover and the FBI. The diplomat ran afoul of the bureau through Hoover's incessant policing of its public image and its support in Congress. In 1948 Congress had passed a law mandating security investigations for all VOA employees and job applicants. Thayer enraged the bureau director when an October 1948 *New York Herald Tribune* article reported his complaint that the International Broadcasting Division's "search for able staff workers who know Russia and Central Europe . . . is handicapped since the FBI takes from three to six months to clear an applicant." Other reports of Thayer's complaints that the security investigations were "hamstringing" the VOA further angered Hoover and his minions. By January 1949, after a State Department spokesman testified before a congressional committee that Public Law 402, mandating FBI investigations of all employees, "understandably resulted in a slowing up of the recruitment process," Hoover decided to strike at the source of the bad publicity.[7]

Thayer was vulnerable, Hoover's subordinates revealed. Employees of the Voice of America were "the most disreputable group of individuals that this Bureau has ever been called upon to investigate," a senior agent reported. "Our files are replete with instances of individuals who were totally unfit for employment, either for loyalty, security, or moral reasons. One of the classic examples of these people is Charles W. Thayer." Although Thayer himself had been exempted from a security investigation by a provision of Public Law 402, which made exception for personnel appointed by the president and confirmed by the Senate (as a foreign service officer he technically fit the category), the mandated investigation of Olga Philipoff, Thayer's secretary, revealed that the diplomat had fathered her illegitimate child. Hoover directed his agents to "keep on top of this. Make a most thorough investigation of Thayer."[8]

Hoover's gumshoes began a "discreet" probe of Thayer's sexual life and political sympathies, "to avoid any possibility of criticism of the Bureau by Thayer." "All interviews were conducted in a most circumspect manner," Assistant Director D. M. Ladd reported to his boss, "in view . . . of his position and connections within the State Department in order to protect the Bureau's interest in this matter." The initial "security" investigation turned up allegations of "communist sympathy" during the subject's OSS years as liaison to Tito and the Yugoslav communists. FBI agents reported enough sexual rumor to lead Ladd to assert that Thayer was "undoubtedly a homosexual." Taken together, evidence of the diplomat's subversive political beliefs and of his sexual "perversion" confirmed the need for a second "loyalty" inquiry. "He should have no place in gov[ernmen]t," the bureau director instructed his underlings. The "bulk of the information obtained" came from John Finlator of the State Department security branch, who had investigated Thayer's alleged "homosexual proclivities" before the inquiry was halted by John Peurifoy on orders from Undersecretary of State Robert Lovett. Finlator had secretly "written up and maintained" the report on Thayer in defiance of Peurifoy's instructions. The lavender-hunting security cop kept the dossier in his possession, without making it a part of the "official files of the State Department." Chock-full of lurid but highly questionable testimony, Finlator's report formed the bedrock of the subsequent persecution of Charles Thayer by congressional pervert-hunters, the FBI, and the State Department under Eisenhower. Armed with "derogatory material" from Finlator's report, the bureau director authorized a nationwide FBI effort to impeach the loyalty and sexual orthodoxy of the patrician diplomat.[9]

As soon as the investigations were completed, Hoover moved to destroy Charles Thayer's career. But the imperative to protect FBI spies in other government agencies demanded caution. "[Finlator's] identity must be protected by all means, in view of the fact that his making the information available places his position in the State Department in jeopardy and would ruin an excellent source of information for the Washington Field Office," argued Assistant Director Ladd. Hoover was reluctant to openly challenge Thayer so long as Lovett and Bohlen of Acheson's State Department provided bureaucratic protection, but he took steps to oust the diplomat. In late 1949, Hoover forwarded a summary of Thayer's FBI "loyalty" probe to the Civil Service Commission, minus the sexual allegations. The results were disappointing; "they advised by letter that Thayer was considered 'eligible on loyalty.'" The director's attempts to persuade the Truman Justice Department to indict Thayer proved equally fruitless; in March 1950, Assistant Attorney General James M. McInerney judged that "prosecution was not warranted." The FBI's case proved no more persuasive to the State Department Loyalty Security Board. Thayer was subjected to the first of what eventually proved to be a series of formal inquisitions in October 1949, but the board "found there were no reasonable grounds to believe that he was disloyal . . . or a security risk to the Department of State." At some point, however, the State Department security division began a covert and ongoing "surveillance" of Thayer. Thwarted in the effort to oust the patrician diplomat, the bureau took steps to block what they took to be his career ambitions in other national security bureaucracies. In September 1949, Hoover provided the sexual scandal dossier on Thayer to a right-wing CIA officer who predicted that the diplomat would resign from the VOA to accept the offer of a "top job with the CIA." Hoover's ally in the agency wanted to use the security report to help "preclude any such move." Although initially foiled by the Truman administration's loyalty-security boards Hoover waited for another opportunity to deploy his compilation of sexual rumor against his target; an opportunity arose a few months later with the outpouring of unsigned letters to countersubversive senators.[10]

Anonymous snitches, some nursing ancient grudges, proliferated in the overheated atmosphere of the countersubversion and counterperversion purges. Rumors dating back ten or twenty years were deployed to settle scores. Right-wing senators, the State Department security police, the FBI, and far-Right journalists all received lists of names purporting to expose "cells" of high-level homosexuals in the State Department. In the spring of 1950, Charles Bohlen's name was included among one list of twenty-one names sent to Senator Bourke Hickenlooper, the State Department, the FBI, and the columnist Westbrook Pegler. Bohlen, the letter warned, had shown signs of homosexual tendencies by his friendliness to Ambassador William Bullitt during the first mission to Moscow in 1934–35.[11]

McCarthy and the countersubversives eagerly set out to track down the clues that their informers supplied. Within days, the senator's sleuths began seeking information from their covert allies in the FBI and the State Department. A "highly placed confidential informant within the State Department who in turn obtained his information from the Security Section of the Department under Peurifoy" encouraged the inquisitors. They learned that Charles Thayer's dossier was "a very excellent file to probe." "The facts contained in the subrosa section of this file will show clearly that Thayer is a homosexual, as well as other facts tending to show his leftist associations and leanings," claimed McCarthy's State Department spy. The counterperversion investigators fanned out to interrogate anyone they thought might implicate Thayer and his suspected homosexual associates. A "very confidential source" who had long "followed loyalty and security investigations" told them of FBI and State Department files "confirming the fact" that "Thayer and Offie [were] among the best known homosexuals in government." The informant named John Finlator as the State Department officer who "specialized in investigations of homosexuals" and who had investigated both Thayer and Carmel Offie. Furthermore, "the source confirmed the allegation that the State Department investigation of Thayer was stopped by the then Under

Secretary Mr. Lovett." Abridged copies of the State Department security documents and FBI investigative files soon made their way into the hands of the congressional pervert-hunters.[12]

With some circumspection, McCarthy and his associates sought assistance from the FBI. Referring to an "anonymous letter," a congressional inquisitor tried to confirm the existence of a "criminal record" for Offie and asked if agent G. A. Nease "could tell him whether [the bureau] had ever investigated Thayer." As part of their assault on the Truman administration, McCarthy and his associates planned to "blast the CIA" by using charges of perversion detailed in the anonymous letters. Nease recommended to his superior that the congressional pervert-hunter be "advised" that Hoover had forwarded material on Thayer and Offie to allies within the CIA—if the senator and his colleagues knew that the bureau had warned the CIA of the threat of perversion posed by Offie and Thayer, it would protect the FBI from any blame that might spill over.[13]

The Senate sleuths quickly struck pay dirt in their search for evidence of disreputable sexual practice. Avidly collecting secondhand gossip, and none too careful about evaluating the reliability of testimony supplied by Thayer's bureaucratic enemies and disgruntled former subordinates, they constructed their own dossier on Thayer and his associates. By the first week of March, they established that "Carmel Offie, the homosexual acquaintance of Thayer, was formerly secretary to Ambassador Bill Bullit[t]." Through the cooperation of Lieutenant Roy Blick, they obtained the record of Offie's September 8, 1943, arrest by the Metropolitan Police Department vice squad on charges of "disorderly conduct–investigation: pervert." Offie, a foreign service officer who had served with Thayer, Charles Bohlen, and George F. Kennan as members of William Bullitt's first embassy to the Soviets in 1934–35 and gone on to rise through the ranks of the diplomatic corps, had given his occupation as "clerk" to arresting officers. He was then "permitted to post twenty-five dollars collateral which he forfeited."[14]

McCarthy immediately exploited his discovery. Eager to divert attention from demands that he reveal the names of the accused communists in the State Department, he temporarily put Thayer's case on the back burner. Working to discredit Truman's foreign policy establishment, the crusading senator used the example of Carmel Offie. In mid-March, just as Senator Wherry was gearing up to establish as a given the proposition that Acheson's State Department harbored "three hundred to four hundred" homosexuals, McCarthy linked homosexual subversion to both the State Department and the CIA. McCarthy denounced as a homosexual a "former State Department official" identified in Washington police files, and now employed "in a most sensitive place," the CIA. He asserted that the official "spent his time hanging around the men's room in Lafayette Park." McCarthy named the official "privately" to the Senate Foreign Relations Subcommittee, fingering Carmel Offie as the guilty party. Of immigrant working-class, Italian-American background, Offie had managed to make himself valuable to many influential foreign service officers during his career. But his audacity and talented disregard for the niceties of bureaucratic rules made enemies too. Ostensibly, Offie resigned from the State Department in 1948 after his violation of currency regulations in occupied Europe eliminated him from the list for future promotions, although the State Department security investigation of his homosexuality was the more likely motive. He then became an "operator" in Frank Wisner's covert action Office of Policy Coordination, helping to organize and run clandestine covert action networks of East European ex-Nazi collaborators against the Soviets. The OPC had been established by the director of the State Department's policy planning staff, George Kennan, and was then incorporated into the new CIA. Offie's resignation was greeted with dismay by George Kennan and other high-level policymakers. But with his relocation in Washington to work in the OPC, the ambitious Offie firmly attached himself to that Georgetown subset of the larger circle of Washington's imperial patricians that included Wisner, Joseph Alsop, George F. Kennan, Charles Bohlen, Charles Thayer, and Robert Joyce.[15]

After McCarthy "outed" him, Offie was quickly forced out of the CIA. J. Edgar Hoover, alerted to Offie's homosexuality by one of the anonymous letters about Thayer, authorized a close surveillance of the former foreign service officer. FBI agents followed Offie on visits to Washington's gay bars and staked out his residence. Hoover intervened to make sure that Offie never got another government job; he continued an intermittent persecution of the former diplomat for the next two decades. The downfall of Carmel Offie was small potatoes in the larger scheme of things; he was a figure much less freighted with symbolism than was Alger Hiss. But he was socially and professionally close to a core group of the patrician imperial brotherhood. Offie's case provided another example of the recurrent demarcation of contested and unstable boundaries of political masculinity. The message was clear to his patrons, and it foreshadowed direct attacks upon them.[16]

By 1951 McCarthy shared his files on the sexual and political conspiracies surrounding Charles Thayer and the State Department with Senator Pat McCarran. McCarran and his SISS investigators pored over leaked (and incomplete) copies of FBI and State Department security dossiers. They found a slew of alarming material, although it was based almost exclusively on hostile gossip and speculation by Thayer's enemies, and premised on guilt by

association. The most lurid and specific allegations came from the report of
the State Department security "expert" on homosexuality, John Finlator,
whose report dated July 22, 1948, had been suppressed by Robert Lovett. The
State Department sex cop was also the source of the bulk of the testimony
against Thayer that appeared in the FBI's investigative dossier. Finlator had
first quizzed John Kasunich, a CIA employee and former ONI agent, who
had served as assistant naval attach at Belgrade when Thayer was chief of the
wartime OSS mission there. "K" offered evidence of Thayer's perversion by
relating "that Thayer was waited on regularly by a native Yugoslav waiter,
named Marko, who was a known homosexual." This "trustworthy, reliable,
and honest" informant further offered that while in his next OSS posting
in Vienna, Thayer had married Maria Petrucci, the daughter of an Italian
diplomat. The marriage had lasted "about two years," he reported, and "it
was his belief that she found Thayer to be homosexual and left him."[17]

Early victims of the State Department's homosexual purge offered further
evidence of association with sexual "deviants." Both Thayer and Carmel
Offie were "very close personal friends of former Ambassador Alexander Kirk
who is not now in the service but who had a very bad reputation of being a
homosexual and certainly protected a lot of homosexual people," explained
the former ONI agent. Offie's "reputation was well known," he continued.
"Offie's former secretary" became "disgusted on one occasion when Offie
took one of her boyfriends in Germany from her." Another early victim of
the purge, Ira W. Porter, seemed to link Thayer to homosexual "cells" in the
State Department. Finlator himself had extracted a "confession" from Porter
in mid-1947, and the special agent was receptive to the allegations of others
concerning the ex-employee. Finlator reported that Charles Pick, acting head
of foreign administration in the State Department, inferred Thayer's participation in Dionysian orgies from his association with Porter:

> Every time T came to town he either stayed at Porter's house or visited with
> him. Porter was asked to resign from State because he was found to be a no-
> torious homosexual who during his tenure of office brought in several other
> homosexuals who subsequently had to be weeded out. Porter often came in
> on Monday morning looking blurry eyed and invariably would say that he
> had "A terrific weekend" and that "Charlie Thayer was by to see me and we
> had a wild time." Informant advised that when he found Porter was hs [ho-
> mosexual] he felt almost sure Thayer was one also.[18]

Finlator's digging turned up evidence of sexual disorder at the Voice of
America. The Department of State's International Broadcasting Division had

from its inception proved worrisome to the provincial countersubversives as a locus of "infection" by bringing foreign ideas and people into the bureaucracy of the state. The aura of European cosmopolitanism surrounding the VOA seemed to suggest subversion, and the past political associations of many employees made them deeply suspect. Indications of homosexuality among the agency's personnel helped confirm conservative fears about conspiratorial cells of "perverted" communist sympathizers subverting the empire from within.[19]

The State Department security inquisitor placed Charles Thayer at the center of a cosmopolitan, international network of bohemian sexual and political misfits. Finlator claimed that Robert Ross of the VOA, named by others as Thayer's sexual partner, "admitted" being homosexual when interviewed, but "stated that he does not know whether Thayer is hs or not, and he denied any relations." Ross in turn identified the aristocratic Russian émigré and protégé of Charles Bohlen, Nicolas Nabokov, also of the VOA, as the inspiration for office gossip about another homosexual affair with Thayer. Thayer and Nabokov had shared an apartment for a while until the divorced Nabokov remarried, fueling rumors about the two men. The Russian composer's manner was suspicious, Ross told Finlator: "N acts and talks like a hs. . . . He waves his hands with a Continental but nevertheless an effeminate manner and he 'swishes' when he moves about." The State Department sleuth discovered that Nabokov too, had disreputable connections in his past; besides having "run around with a fast nightclub set in NY" the composer had friends and associates like "the notorious E. E. Cummings" and the Parisians Jean Cocteau and "Dishileff [Sergei Diaghilev]." Yet another informant testified that Nabokov "also associated himself with a refugee group" of "French artist[s] and musicians, among whom it was the practice for the men to sleep together." Thayer and Nabokov had aroused the suspicion of their building superintendent by briefly sheltering one French refugee artist, Jacques Brosse, "the obvious type that one calls a 'queer,'" who "drew a lot of nude pictures and read a lot of French books." Equally alarming to Finlator and the SISS countersubversives was the alert super's observation that "every person with whom they associated or brought into the apartment *not only looked foreign but also spoke with foreign accents* [emphasis in original]."[20]

The only firsthand account of any homosexual activity came from "Confidential Informant B," who claimed to be a former friend of Ira W. Porter. "B" declared that in 1946 he and Porter entered Thayer's New York apartment without knocking, only "to find Thayer in bed undressed with another officer . . . having homosexual relations." Porter, he claimed, "later told me

that Thayer 'is as queer as a $3 bill.'" "Confidential Informant B" also alleged
that in 1948 while seeking a job in the Voice of America, Porter again introduced him to Thayer, who then attempted to seduce him. SISS investigators
wondered, "Who is this B?" hoping they could confirm the damaging allegations against the high-level diplomat.[21]

Don Connors of the McCarran committee sought the identity of "B"
from the FBI. He carried to FBI headquarters a transcription of the part of
Finlator's report that purported to describe "B's" encounters with Thayer.
The senator's subaltern requested that the bureau supply the true identity of
"Confidential Informant B" as well as that of others whose anonymous allegations appeared in the various versions of the Thayer dossiers. The committee intended to dispatch inquisitors to interview everyone they could
identify. But J. Edgar Hoover, worried as always about the exposure and loss
of valuable spies ensconced within other federal agencies, denied the request.
"Tell him we cannot disclose Conf. Inf. identity," Hoover dictated. Another
senior FBI official lamented the need to exercise such caution rather than openly helping the SISS to destroy Thayer's career. "It is a shame that such a man
can remain in government service," he penciled. "I certainly concur," Hoover replied.[22]

But the McCarran committee sleuths did obtain unofficial versions of
Thayer's FBI dossier—documents that offered a bewildering and contradictory picture of Thayer. "Confidential Informant B" reappeared, this time as
Washington informant "T-6, reported by another government agency as having furnished them with extremely high reliable information." Special Agent
Edward L. Grampp summarized the same allegations that had come from
Finlator's report. But the accounts of Thayer's sexual and political predilec-
tions collected by the FBI varied wildly. Some accused Thayer of communist
sympathy but did not question his sexual morality. Others believed him politically loyal but sexually "deviant." Yet others condemned him for both
offenses. Many high-level officials—including former OSS chief William
Donovan, OPC director Frank Wisner, Harold Shantz of the National Security Council, and Robert Joyce and Llewellyn Thompson of the State Department—wholeheartedly endorsed Thayer's anticommunism, competence, and suitability for service to the state. Thayer, Thompson asserted,
represented "the ultimate in patriotism."[23]

McCarran and his associates harbored deep suspicions about Thayer. They
despised his "internationalist" politics and they resented the class privilege
and power he represented. But McCarran was more careful than the often
heedless Joe McCarthy. His SISS investigators set out to verify the accusations against Thayer. They interviewed Ira Porter, who readily described

himself as homosexual but stated that allegations of Thayer's homosexuality were "completely false." Porter then "pointed out that to the contrary, while Thayer was very much inclined to be oversexed, that such activity was always directed at the opposite sex." The inquisitors failed to confirm the testimony of "Confidential Informant B"; Porter denied stumbling upon the illicit homosexual encounter "B" had described. He questioned the motives of the security investigator, casting doubt on the solidity of the boundaries separating "perversion" and normative heterosexuality even among those designated to police them: "Mr. Porter from time to time expressed a bitterness toward John H. Finlator, investigating agent of the Department of State, pointing out that Finlator himself in appearance gave the impression that he too is homosexually inclined and that his attitude in the Thayer investigation was that of a 'sadist.' He further stated that Finlator had used 'black mailing' techniques to prove this and other homosexual cases in the Department of State." "Someone in the [State] Department was out to 'get' Thayer," suggested Porter, although "he did not know who."[24]

When McCarran's staffers quizzed Robert Ross of the International Broadcasting Division in New York about Finlator's earlier interview, "he denied that he admitted to the Agent that he, Ross, was a homosexual," or knew other homosexuals at the Voice of America. Another VOA employee "advised that Thayer was violently anti-communist" and was the first to "take steps to rid the voice of Communists and sympathizers." Don Connors of the McCarran committee then tried to verify Charles Pick's testimony to Finlator. Pick "firmly denied" having made the statement attributed to him implying a homosexual relationship between Ira Porter and Charles Thayer. Furthermore, Pick told the SISS inquisitor that "he had never met or known Thayer, and would have no basis for making such a statement."[25]

McCarran's men found and interviewed Thayer's first wife, Maria Petrucci, still living in New York. She offered them no support for the accusations of "perversion" or communist "sympathy" dogging Thayer. "Under no circumstances has she the slightest reason to feel her former husband was either communistically or homosexually inclined," they soberly reported. The reason for the divorce, Petrucci revealed, "was Thayer's violent temper." She offered the opinion that the accusations against her ex-husband "could have originated only from malicious gossip." Nonetheless, having failed to find solid evidence that the patrician diplomat was actively homosexual, McCarran did firmly link him to heterosexual "immorality," in the form of an office affair with a female VOA employee. Just as the anonymous letter to McCarthy had suggested, the SISS investigators obtained a copy of the March 19, 1948, birth certificate of a child, born to Olga Philipoff, "writer," aged thirty-five, born in Russia, and Charles W. Thayer, "radio engineer," aged thirty-eight, born in Villanova, Pennsylvania. The countersubversives also had evidence that the FBI had alerted John Peurifoy that bureau agents had run across evidence of Thayer's indiscretions in the course of an investigation of Dr. Rowe, who had been "treating Russian seamen, Amtorg employees, and members of the Soviet Consulate General in New York." Their access to the FBI and State Department security files also confirmed for them that the despised high-level patricians, Charles Bohlen and Robert Lovett, had stopped the investigation of Thayer and suppressed the reports.[26]

Although the State Department had cleared Thayer on both loyalty and security grounds in 1949, the ongoing pressure by the McCarran committee, abetted by J. Edgar Hoover, prompted the State Department security division to reopen the question of Thayer's homosexuality. The earlier inquiry had elicited assertions by some of Finlator's informants that they had been coerced by the lavender-hunter. "I know Charles Thayer is a homosexual, and so do you and I want you to make a statement to that effect," the sex cop had demanded of one. If the informant failed to do so, he "would regret his lack of cooperation," warned Finlator. Despite the repeated arguments of Thayer's elite diplomatic colleagues that the charges against him had been "trumped up" by those with a "personal dislike" for the "impulsive" diplomat, that he had "made enemies" in his career, the department's inquisitors began a series of intrusive interviews of the scandal-tainted foreign service officer. In the first round, Thayer was "thoroughly interrogated and further investigated." Summoned to Washington from Bonn for questioning, Thayer "categorically denied that he was a homosexual, that he had the reputation for being a homosexual, or that he had knowingly associated with homosexuals." Carlisle Humelsine and D. L. Nicholson of the security division then interviewed "Confidential Informant B," who gave them a story "at variance in several important respects with the information previously furnished" by Finlator. This time, "B" declared that when he and Ira Porter entered Thayer's apartment in 1946, "he was not in the bedroom, nor could he see the bedroom, and he did not see subject and the Army Lieutenant in bed." Thayer "and the Army Lieutenant were fully clothed," "B" continued. "Apparently there had been a misunderstanding" if Finlator had reported otherwise. Humelsine and Nicholson subjected "B" to "a polygraph test which showed that his statement . . . was correct."[27]

The scrutiny of Thayer continued. Carlisle Humelsine "questioned [him] at length." Again the patrician diplomat asserted "that he had never performed a homosexual act." But, in a perhaps too-eager effort to persuade the inquisitors that he was completely forthcoming, Thayer recounted an incident from his imperial adventures two decades earlier—a revelation that came back to haunt him. During the interrogation "he did volunteer that in one instance in 1934 when he had been too drunk to know what was happening, a native boy in Afghanistan may have performed an act on him." He hastened to add "that he had no way of knowing whether this act had occurred, because of his state of inebriation, but that if it had occurred, it had been through no desire of his nor willful or knowing acquiescence on his part."[28]

The pervert-hunting security agents pulled Thayer deeper into the surreal machinery of the sexual inquisition when the diplomat "consented to a polygraph test." On April 14, 1951, "after a preliminary interrogation of three or four hours," the sex cops strapped Thayer to the lie detector. "The reactions which the apparatus registered led the examiners . . . to conclude that Mr. Thayer was a homosexual." Two weeks later he was again put through the trial-by-ordeal of the polygraph, this time administered by a doctor. "The second examination was inconclusive." Distraught, "in a state of anguish, revulsion, and emotion" over the threat to his career and in reaction to the "methods employed" against him, Thayer returned to Europe. Striving to counter the damaging results of the Washington interrogations and tests, the patrician diplomat checked himself into the Neuro-psychiatric Clinic of Prefargier, in Switzerland. There, under the supervision of Dr. O. Riggenbach, chief of the clinic as well as chief of the Psychological Service of the Swiss Army, Thayer was put through "a very severe clinical examination." Over the course of five days a group of doctors spent "many hours" interviewing the patient. They "examined Mr. Thayer's nervous system." Perhaps most persuasive to the assembled psychiatric experts, the patient was subjected to "three special tests." On May 17, 1951, Dr. Pierre Bernard Schneider, "an internationally recognized authority . . . in the field of investigations to determine truth," administered the "pentothal" test. The doctors followed this with the Rorchach Test and the Szondi Test. Thayer passed with flying colors, according to Dr. Riggenbach. The panel of specialists "had not been able to discover the slightest proof or the least symptoms indicating homosexual tendencies" in the "instinctive life of Mr. Thayer." Hoping to dispel the cloud of suspicion that hovered around him, the diplomat promptly provided the State Department inquisitors with a copy of Dr. Riggenbach's "medical certificate" of absolution on "charges of abnormality."[29]

In February 1952, Carlisle Humelsine made an "administrative determination" that "no grounds existed to substantiate the allegations" of homosexuality. The deputy undersecretary notified Thayer that as a result of the inquiry "he was an employee in good standing." Humelsine's decision may have been based more upon the results of ongoing covert surveillance of the diplomat than upon the expert opinions of Swiss psychiatrists. During the period that the department's secret police spied on Thayer, they had discovered "no indication of homosexual or loose moral conduct." Despite his official status in the good graces of the department, however, Humelsine recommended that the security sex cops continue surveillance of the hapless diplomat.[30]

Pat McCarran kept a wary eye on Thayer. When the senator got wind of Thayer's possible appointment as consul general to Bavaria, in June 1952, he wrote to Carlisle Humelsine demanding "full information" regarding "the experience, qualifications, moral character, and loyalty" of the diplomat. Humelsine's response, more than a month after Thayer's appointment, included glowing excerpts and character references from Thayer's personnel file but no mention of allegations of homosexuality or communist sympathy. McCarran, McCarthy, and the countersubversive Right bided their time, waiting for a more propitious moment to attack. The moment came early the next year, after the elections that gave the Republicans the White House and a congressional majority in both houses.[31]

John Foster Dulles, the new secretary of state, placed a higher priority on remaining in office than on protecting the department from right-wing assaults. Forewarned by the example of Dean Acheson's status as a political pariah, Dulles resolved to collaborate with the congressional countersubversives. Dulles feared his own potential vulnerability to charges that he had "nominated Alger Hiss to the Carnegie Endowment after he had seen FBI reports" on Hiss. Attacks on elite State Department employees and their patrons continued with renewed fervor, but now with the tacit sanction of the new secretary. Dulles and his assistant secretary of state, Walter Bedell Smith, used the security issue to fire employees they found politically suspect or otherwise unsympathetic to their policies while placating the senatorial "primitives" who repeatedly demanded that the new administration "clean out" the State Department. These actions disturbed liberal Republicans and infuriated establishment partisans of the recently defeated Democrats, who condemned the passivity of the new president. "Eisenhower's attitude toward McCarthy is plainly one of putting his fingers in his ears and wishing to hell that McCarthy would go away," grumbled Arthur Schlesinger Jr.[32] McCarthy did not go away. Instead, in early February shortly after Eisenhower's inauguration, he renewed the attack on the State Department. The senator's investigative subcommittee took testimony from McCarthy informer John Matson, a security division file clerk, who purported to reveal the "operations of a flourishing clique of homosexuals in the State department." Senator McCarthy and his subcommittee counsel Roy Cohn painted a picture of a deeply entrenched homosexual conspiracy. "Several officials of abnormal tendencies were employed in the recruitment of employment under the Acheson regime," one right-wing newspaper reported. "The careers of sex deviates were facilitated by removing from security files all reports by security officers indicating depravity of morals." Even the lavender purge itself served as part of the establishment conspiracy, Matson's testimony implied: "When the conduct of State department sex deviates became so flagrant that the cover-up could not function, they were permitted to resign, and evidence showing the reasons for the forced resignations was deleted from the files." Equally worrisome in the eyes of the inquisitors was the self-perpetuation of homosexual "cliques" through control of hiring. "When one recruitment officer was revealed as a homosexual he was asked to resign but his replacement was eventually exposed as another man of perverted habits. Of 20 employees in the recruitment branch of the State department, three were revealed as homosexuals."[33]

Joe McCarthy targeted Charles Thayer as part of his renewed assault on the State Department and its Voice of America operation. "The situation is so bad in the New York Office of VOA," one McCarthy associate informed the FBI, "that there are secret pro-American cells." The elite diplomat had conspired to subvert the propaganda agency, he explained: "The left-wing apparatus . . . was organized by Charles Thayer, and they hope to get him before the committee." Seeing an opportunity to injure or destroy Thayer, Hoover advised that "they should certainly expose him and his present tie-in with State Dept." The pervert-hunting senator requested a "name check" of FBI files, and the bureau began preparing a "summary memorandum" on Thayer, intended for the McCarthy committee. But the complicated interagency politics of the purge proved a temporary stumbling block.[34]

Hoover had agreed to provide Deputy Attorney General William Rogers with a copy of all material "in advance of giving it to the McCarthy Committee." Supplied with the Thayer summary memo, Rogers worried about the secretary of state's reaction were he to learn that "we were feeding material to the Committee without first being tipped off." He agreed "that Thayer was no good" and argued that "Dulles would get rid of him in a hurry if he knew about it." He suggested that the bureau furnish Dulles with the scandal-filled dossier—but Hoover's subordinate Louis Nichols pointed out that the State Department already possessed "all the derogatory information." Nichols warned of serious consequences "if the memorandum got out of Dulles's possession and got into the hands of the holdovers at the State Department who were protecting people like Thayer." Instead Rogers and Nichols agreed on a compromise solution. The FBI would provide the secretary of state "with the names of the individuals" McCarthy was "checking on." Possession of the senator's blacklist would push Dulles to purge the offenders.[35]

Dulles capitulated to the demands of the "primitives" for a cleanup of Foggy Bottom by appointing Scott McLeod to head the Bureau of Security and Consular Affairs in the State Department, a new position created by the McCarran-Walter Immigration Act. McLeod, a former FBI agent and administrative assistant to Senator Styles Bridges, renewed the assault, this time from within the bastion of effete "cookie-pushing" elitism itself. He assured conservative Midwesterners "that for the first time in twenty years . . . the House Committee on Un-American Activities under Chairman Velde, the Senate Internal Security Subcommittee under Senator Jenner, and the Special Investigating Subcommittee under Senator McCarthy" would "receive the complete and unequivocal support of the State Department."[36]

The former G-man boasted of his commitment to eliminate all threats to the security of the state, including the threat of sexual disorder: "I have attempted very frankly and honestly to face the issue of sexual perversion—the practice of sodomy—in the State Department." In late March 1953, during testimony widely reported in the press, McLeod's top security assistant John Ford boasted to a House subcommittee that for the past two years the State Department had been firing "sex perverts . . . at the average rate of one every three days." But by the beginning of April, McLeod's subordinate reported even better results for the renewed homosexual purge by obtaining three "confessions" in three days: "Our batting average is now one a day."[37]

Congressional lavender-hunters continued to prod the Eisenhower administration to accelerate the purge. In late April, Senator Styles Bridges used his appropriations committee to "begin the task of ridding the State Department of homosexuals, subversives, wasters, and propagandists of international causes," as one reporter described it. McLeod appeared before the committee to disclose that during the month and a half since taking office, he had "fired 19 as homosexuals, fired 14 other payrollers because of their personal habits or private lives, . . . and accepted resignations of four others facing charges." His superior, Undersecretary of State for Administration Donold B. Lourie, signaled the department's intent to oust the "undesirables" despised by Bridges and the conservatives. The undersecretary employed a by-then-famous statistical argument to emphasize the probable dimensions of the task still facing the department's sexual inquisitors: "The [Kinsey] report, Lourie said, indicates that four to eight per cent of the population are sex deviates, and he said that would mean quite a number among the State department's 42,000 employees."[38]

As the new Republican inquisitors found their stride, McLeod's staff kept

President Eisenhower confers with Secretary of State John Foster Dulles (*center*) and State Department security chief Scott McLeod (*right*). Courtesy Dwight D. Eisenhower Library / AP/Wide World Photos.

Security chief McLeod pledged to cooperate with (*left to right*) HUAC chairman Harold Velde, SISS chairman William Jenner, and Joe McCarthy, chair of the Senate Special Investigating Subcommittee, seen here speaking to the press after a meeting with President Eisenhower in April 1953. Courtesy Cleveland Public Library / © Bettmann/CORBIS.

the press abreast of the progress of the purges. By late that year his staff informed a reporter for the Washington Post that between January 1 and September 14, 1953, 114 employees had resigned pending "morals cases," and that four applicants had been rejected on the same grounds. The security administrator kept a close eye on the numbers, quizzing a subordinate on why "the statistics for the month of October did not show any homos had been removed." McLeod wondered if the anomaly was best explained as "just 'circumstances'" or whether it signaled a worrisome lapse of zeal.[39]

The Dulles State Department pursued the purge with such vigor that McLeod was forced to hire extra "temporary" agents specializing in the detection of homosexuals to handle the caseload. The new administration publicly endorsed the purges. By late October, 1953, President Eisenhower and Attorney General Herbert Brownell boasted of the removal of 1,456 federal employees as "security risks"; evidence, they said, that the administration was aggressively "cleaning out communists in government." Senator McCarthy took partial credit for the results, when he claimed to reporters that "90 per cent [of the victims] were 'communists or perverts.'" By the spring of 1954 the sex policemen of the security division's "Miscellaneous M Unit" had a backlog of 266 "pending cases," having already fired twenty-six employees for homosexuality between January 1 and March 24.[40]

The potential targets of McLeod's lavender-hunters, almost all employees of the foreign service or State Department, might well have thought themselves subject to an arbitrary and almost surreally capricious inquisition. Prodded by their boss, the sexual inquisitors initiated investigations based on the flimsiest anonymous accusations. McLeod's snoopers began scrutinizing the sex lives of men and women because of statements by fellow employees that an associate was "probably homosexual . . . based on her [the accuser's] feminine intuition and the effeminate mannerisms" of the male coworker, including a "'jelly hand shake.'" Another might be identified as "a homosexual suspect" because he had "a feminine complexion, a peculiar girlish walk, and the witness ha[d] 'just a funny feeling about him.'" A female employee could be accused of lesbianism, thus triggering an investigation, if a coworker was disturbed by "her mannish voice, her odd-shaped lips, and her friendship" with other women, particularly if the friendship involved a pair showing an "apparent disparity in their ages and personal make-ups," one being "the older, more vigorous, and more masculine in her tone of voice and physical make-up," with the other "the gentler, softer, and more feminine type." Despite doubts the investigators might harbor about the "questionable reliability" of such informants, standard procedure dictated that "the files of the various individuals alleged against will be subjected to thorough review to determine if there is any basis whatsoever to the informant's suspicions." Such procedure frequently led to "the interview of [the suspects] as possible moral deviates."[41]

The purges were profoundly demoralizing for employees of the State Department and other government agencies. One much-remarked result was to cast suspicion of sexual or political deviance on anyone who resigned from the State Department. "All who leave the service, for whatever cause, are open to smear and innuendo," complained the president of the National Federation of Federal Employees. Joseph Alsop noted that this effect was intentional, a result of the "celebrated 'numbers game' . . . played in the State Department, under the McLeod aegis." "According to the peculiar rules of this sport, anyone who transfers to another agency or leaves the Department for whatever reason, is fair game to be tagged 'a security risk' without his knowledge—and thus the proud total is swelled," explained the columnist. In many cases, those who resigned or were released as part of the new administration's "economy measures" were unable to find jobs in academia or industry because of the stigmatizing presumption that they had been forced out of the State Department as "security risks." Some in Congress, whose constituents complained that as former department employees they were now unemployable, called unsuccessfully for the establishment of "honorable discharge" papers to certify the sexual and political orthodoxy of people leaving the Department of State.[42]

Joseph Alsop, columnist and partisan of the imperial brotherhood, deplored the damage done to the foreign policy bureaucracy by the know-nothing McLeod and his henchmen. "The professional diplomatic corps is threatened with total disintegration," bemoaned the patrician newsman. Striking at political and class enemies with ridicule, he reported that "a tremendous 'clean-up of security risks' is now going on in the Department, with flat-feet falling all over each other in the corridors." The result, he warned, was "incredible but true . . . not a single class 6 Foreign Service officer has been recruited for more than two years. This is quite literally as though the Army had become so despised that no self-respecting man would accept a second lieutenant's commission as a regular officer."[43]

With the onset of the renewed Dulles-McLeod security purges, right-wing countersubversives and agency security officers increasingly snooped into extramarital heterosexual relationships, adding to the distress of the imperial brotherhood and virile liberals generally. The more expansive definition of sexual misconduct was motivated by political expediency, for it provided conservatives another opportunity to fire politically undesirable employees. The Truman-era State Department had largely adhered to a double standard of illicit sexual behavior. In early 1953, Carlisle Humelsine had made this explicit in testimony before the Senate Foreign Relations Committee. He assured Bourke Hickenlooper and his colleagues that while "having a mistress . . . may be wrong," there was "no comparison" to the public stigma of homosexuality. The assembled senators winked and nudged one another, agreeing that although keeping a mistress might be "expensive," and the discovery of such a relationship might "get you in dutch with your wife," it would not make men vulnerable to communist blackmail. Hickenlooper endorsed this double standard of sexual morality, using language that even refused to acknowledge homosexuals as men: "I suppose people think maybe they can live down something like the keeping of a mistress . . . but the sex abnormality, or the sex deviate . . . they feel they would be forever disgraced, which often makes these sex people rather easy prey."[44]

But the new willingness of the Dulles-McLeod regime to include heterosexual affairs under the rubric of "security" offenses worried many. Vital center liberals fretted that Victorian moral standards threatened private sexual privilege; their unspoken message was anger at a threat to a core element of masculine power and pleasure. They believed that a modern, tolerant attitude toward sexual expression was a natural part of political manhood; Arthur Schlesinger Jr. had earlier demonstrated this conviction when he assured the publisher of the New York Post that he saw "no contradiction between sex and liberalism," unlike some "undergutted liberals" who still clung to prudishness.[45]

In January 1954, the columnist Anthony Lewis took up where Max Lerner had earlier left off, asserting that the "morality-security concept" represented a form of "blackmail by the Government itself." Lewis feared that carried to its "logical extreme" the purges might fill the ranks of government with people who had "no sexual impulse at all." This, of course, was a sobering prospect, in view of the popular assumption earlier reported by Lerner and shared by liberals and conservatives alike that it took "a virile man" to "meet Russian diplomacy." Lewis, too, cited psychiatric experts to argue that no proof existed that a "heterosexual who sleeps with his secretary" was intrinsically "likely to divulge government secrets." Instead, regarding homosexuals and heterosexuals alike, danger to security lay in an individual's penchant for "indiscretion."[46]

To virile establishment liberals like Schlesinger, the future assistant to President Kennedy, McLeod's appointment demonstrated the weakness of President Eisenhower and Secretary of State Dulles, highlighting their failure to live up to the heroic demands of office. By giving "McCarthy an agent in the very center of the [State] Department," Dulles showed his willingness to engage in "a program of appeasement" toward right-wing isolationists in Congress. This, Schlesinger believed, was consistent with Eisenhower's simultaneous "assault on the defense budget," another example of "expediency, shortsightedness, and cowardice." By reducing the military budget, the Eisenhower administration threatened to weaken the position of the nation in the Cold War, but, to the Cold War liberal, complicity with the purges of the State Department was "even worse." Schlesinger's friends in the agency reported that "the foreign service has never been more demoralized. Scott McLeod . . . is running wild, with no check from Dulles or Eisenhower."[47]

McLeod became a player in one of the senatorial countersubversives' most audacious and telling attacks on the establishment imperial brotherhood. Eisenhower lacked a senior diplomat in Moscow; the official temporarily in charge did not even speak Russian. George Kennan, appointed by Truman in the spring of 1952, had served briefly as ambassador, but he was declared persona non grata by the Soviet government in October after delivering a speech in Berlin comparing conditions in the Soviet Union to those in Nazi Germany. The new president nominated Charles ("Chip") Bohlen as ambassador to Moscow, sending his name to the Senate on February 27, 1953. Bohlen, Kennedy's future State Department special assistant for Soviet affairs and ambassador to France, was of impeccable social background with the best credentials of the imperial brotherhood: St. Paul's School, Harvard, Porcellian Club. He had extensive experience as a diplomat and Soviet specialist. However, Bohlen symbolized everything the "primitives" detested. His participation in Roosevelt's delegation at Yalta infuriated the senators on the Right. To them Bohlen symbolized the "weakness" of American foreign policy—a weakness explicable to the more rabid conservatives in the Senate as a by-product of treason, aristocratic "perversion," and cliques of conspiratorial elites who "whitewashed" the crimes and character defects of their peers. But the "weakness" and national "humiliation" they complained about was, at its core, a projection of their own political impotence. Eisenhower's nomination of Bohlen maddened the McCarthyites, who feared that, despite gestures like the appointment of McLeod and bellicose pronouncements by Dulles, the corporate-liberal internationalist "containment" policy already in place was unlikely to change.

The battle that ensued concealed unintended ironies. To Eisenhower, who had known Bohlen during his military career, the Soviet expert was the only logical choice for the post. No one else was available who possessed a comparable depth of experience with the Soviets. But only after the new president had decided on the nomination was it discovered that Bohlen had never been the subject of a "full-field" loyalty-security investigation. Nor, apparently, did

Eisenhower know of the "dirty laundry" security dossiers and anonymous letters circulating for years among the congressional countersubversives—dossiers that, given contemporary standards of evidence, could be used to connect the senior diplomat to "cells" of "notorious" homosexuals and suspected subversives in Washington and on two continents. Eisenhower and Dulles misjudged the virulent resentment and animosity Bohlen aroused among the congressional far Right. The rabid conservatives' sense of aggrieved exclusion drove them to provoke the internecine party strife that Dulles and Eisenhower had hoped to preclude by eager complicity with the security purges.

Bohlen appeared before the Senate Foreign Relations Committee on March 2, 1953, only three days after the president nominated him and before the FBI security check was complete. Bourke Hickenlooper, Homer Ferguson, and other conservatives quizzed Bohlen on his relationship to what they saw as the "betrayal" of U.S. interests to the Soviets at the Yalta conference. The fact that Alger Hiss had been part of the State Department contingent was of great concern to Ferguson and the conservatives. The "failure" of Yalta was connected in their minds to the presence of the patrician traitor, and they grilled Bohlen on his professional and social relationship to Hiss. While Hickenlooper tried to get the nominee to agree to the proposition that George Kennan's containment doctrine was a "policy of defeat," Ferguson hoped that he would confess that the Yalta agreements were responsible for the "enslavement" of Eastern Europe and the "loss" of China. Bohlen gave them little satisfaction, refusing to concede that the Yalta conference was at the root of U.S. foreign policy setbacks in the postwar era, or that the State Department was a haven for treasonous and weak diplomats. Bohlen's confirmation quickly took on additional urgency with the news of March 5 that Stalin had died; the new administration needed the Soviet expert to report on the transition of power within the Soviet Union.[48]

Within days Senator William Knowland warned Dulles that the nomination was "going to run into trouble." He informed the secretary that Styles Bridges planned to publicly speak against confirmation. Homer Ferguson blocked quick consideration of the nomination, and the conservatives began working to sink Bohlen. Bridges, McCarthy, and McCarran attempted to have Bohlen disqualified as a security risk by deploying sexual rumor drawn from their archive of dossiers, and by working with their agent in the State Department, Scott McLeod. They tried to smear the diplomat as a homosexual by "spreading dark and unnamed insinuations," as the liberal press soon reported it.[49]

Bohlen epitomized a cosmopolitan style of masculine privilege that offended conservative provincials in Congress. Among his establishment friends, Bohlen was celebrated for his "well-deserved reputation," before his marriage, "as one of the most successful ladies' men in Europe." Bohlen was a figure much admired by liberal internationalists of the imperial brotherhood, and by those who aspired to join the brotherhood. For them his sexual success and bureaucratic power merely added luster to his image of upperclass masculine heroism. But conservatives looked askance at Bohlen's reputation for sexual success, tainted as it was by association with Russian women and suspect men. The circulation of anonymous letters, leaked security dossiers, and rumors of aristocratic sexual "perversions" had already undermined Bohlen's position among those who disliked the politics he symbolized. And the rumors in Washington about the diplomat's early career had at least some basis in reality.[50]

Bohlen's fraternal bonds to other significant establishment figures like George Kennan and Charles Thayer had been cemented during service in the first American embassy to the Soviet Union under Ambassador William Bullitt. Bohlen and "many" others of the embassy staff had sexual affairs with Russian women. It was, one scholar argues, a period characterized by sexual license and a "carnivalesque atmosphere" crossing boundaries of "ideology, class, sexuality, rank, convention, and nationality." Bullitt, Bohlen, and Thayer experienced a "shared possession and fascination with exotic" Russian ballerinas, including the "fervent Communist Irena Charnodskaya." Writing to his friend George Kennan from Moscow in 1940, Thayer referred to the "madness of '34," the "not entirely sane existence we led before with Mrs. and mistresses all together in an alcoholic haze." He lamented the depressing obstacles that he then faced in "having to find a gal in the Russian hordes. . . . It's almost enough to turn you pansy (there are plenty of partners in the diplomatic corps)." The apparently close association of the homosexual Carmel Offie, another member of Bullitt's embassy staff, with Bohlen and his Georgetown social circle, was taken by the senatorial "primitives" as further evidence of subversive immorality.[51]

Rumors of rampant homosexuality and heterosexual impropriety among the Moscow embassy's personnel also spread widely, certainly reaching the ears of congressional countersubversives by 1953 and probably much earlier. Such rumors, too, had some basis in fact. The sexual needs of the many single males on the embassy staff presented real or potential security problems. By the early 1940s, during Ambassador Joseph E. Davies' tenure, FBI inspectors reported that "a few of the men attached to the American Embassy at Moscow refuse to associate with Soviet prostitutes but find a 'love life' among themselves." The involvement of embassy men with Russian women also presented a threat to the lax security typical of the embassy in the 1930s and 1940s. FBI reports of the time revealed that "Tatiana Alexandrovna Ilovaiskaya, an alleged OGPU agent," had established successive sexual relationships with two American code clerks.[52]

Dulles, the president, and the White House staff faced a dilemma. Dulles himself had made a very public point of the rigor he intended to impose upon the security program of the State Department by demanding "positive loyalty" from all employees. But the FBI investigation of Bohlen began only after the nomination was forwarded to the Senate. Without solid "evidence" to evaluate, Dulles and the White House staff worried that the swirling rumors about Bohlen's homosexuality might be true. On Friday, March 13, presidential aide Sherman Adams warned the secretary that they were "on very shaky grounds, from what he ha[d] heard." Dulles, too, indicated that in light of the "'moral' charges that had been aired" his commitment to the nominee was wavering. He told Adams that he "didn't want to fire anyone because of a rumor, but we must make a decision Monday," the day hearings were scheduled to resume. Dulles summoned Bohlen to ask if there was "anything" in the diplomat's "past that might be damaging." When Bohlen replied in the negative, Dulles expressed relief: "I couldn't stand another Alger Hiss."[53]

Dulles and Eisenhower bolstered their sagging resolve with encouragement supplied by character references on behalf of Bohlen. With hearings postponed for two days while Bohlen was quarantined with the measles, Dulles phoned the president to report his conversation with Douglas MacArthur II, counselor of the department (Bohlen's former position). MacArthur had assured Dulles that the "story" of Bohlen's homosexuality was "incredible." The counselor had "known him intimately for many years" and was "confident that Bohlen ha[d] a normal family life." The secretary of state telephoned Bohlen that day to give assurances that "there was no weakening of the President's determination to stand by the nomination." Dulles then extracted a promise to protect the president from embarrassment. Bohlen swore "that no matter what happened" and "regardless of the testimony," he would not simply resign in the midst of the confirmation fight. Bohlen did not know that Scott McLeod, with the ultimate sanction of Dulles, was at the time targeting his brother-in-law and old Soviet hand Charles Thayer for dismissal as a homosexual "security risk." Despite the secretary's professed support, his commitment to Bohlen was fragile. Dulles worried about the contents of the FBI report still to arrive. Also, he feared that Scott McLeod's loyalties lay outside the Department of State and might result in an attempt to sabotage the confirmation.[54]

Dulles and Eisenhower were again shaken the following day. After delivery of the FBI summary, J. Edgar Hoover "admitted" to the secretary and his brother Allen Dulles that "most of the evidence on Bohlen was suspicion." Although Hoover claimed that the FBI "did not as a usual procedure evaluate any of its reports," he could not "give Bohlen a complete clearance" because the president had asked him to confer on the case. The FBI failed to turn up any "direct evidence that Bohlen had engaged in homosexual activities," Hoover told the Dulles brothers, "but it was a fact that several of his closest friends and intimate associates were known homosexuals." Allen Dulles "suggested the lie detector" to establish Bohlen's guilt or innocence, but Hoover brushed off the suggestion, asserting that he "did not attach much credence" to the polygraph.[55]

The summary reported Bohlen's friendship and association with the sexually suspect trio of Charles Thayer, Carmel Offie, and Nicolas Nabokov, in part recapitulating the allegations from Thayer's 1948 security investigation by State Department sex cop John Finlator. The sexual character and political opinions of Carmel Offie provided the initial indictment of Bohlen's suitability. Offie had been arrested by the Washington Police vice squad in 1943 and had subsequently listed Bohlen as a character reference during a security check, the investigators asserted. During an FBI interview "Offie advised the appointee is 'an extremely intelligent and attractive fellow,' but nonetheless warned that in his professional capacity 'Bohlen followed the Harry Hopkins line'" regarding the Soviet Union. "Moscow," Offie opined, was "the last place" Bohlen should be assigned. "To send a man who prospered and who helped along the appeasement period is wrong."[56]

The FBI summary further impeached Bohlen with secondhand allegations by another homosexual who had, in 1934, served with the appointee in Moscow. George William Davis, discharged from the foreign service for homosexuality, had earlier provided information concerning Bohlen to a "representative of another Governmental agency which conducts personnel and intelligence investigations." Bohlen, Davis revealed, "walks, acts, and talks like a homosexual." Although the ex–foreign service informer "admitted that he has had no relations with Bohlen," he claimed to possess a "sixth sense" that allowed him to "separate the 'queer' from the men."[57]

The sexual allegations continued: the "Department of State [had] an index card" to the effect that "Bohlen was associated with sexual perverts." FBI gumshoes solemnly recounted that a female secretary had testified that "there [was] a definite shading in his conversation and in his manner of speech which indicate[d] effeminacy." Worthy of note, too, was her observation that "the appointee had a habit of running his tongue over his lip in the manner utilized by a woman." Furthermore, she revealed, the diplomat's "tone of conversation in speaking to Thayer was not the normal tone used in conversations with others . . . [Bohlen] sounded effeminate, and was 'quite girlish.'" Nonetheless, despite the insubstantial evidence against Bohlen, the bureau director still refused "to give him full security clearance."[58]

Dismayed by Hoover's position, Dulles and his boss pondered possible scenarios for Bohlen's resignation. The secretary of state pointed out that "if Bohlen decided to resign, he obviously wouldn't do so" by admitting to be a homosexual security risk. "Then it would look purely political," Dulles fretted. Eisenhower lamely suggested "that he might do so on grounds of health, even though it would look bad too." The irritated president demanded that henceforth no nominations would be forwarded without completed security clearances.[59]

Dulles confronted the opposition of J. Edgar Hoover, the opposition of his own appointee Scott McLeod, a sixteen-page FBI summary of "derogatory material," and his own lingering doubts about the nominee. Senators McCarran and McCarthy openly and vociferously opposed the nomination, and others made similar noises. But unable to contrive a politically acceptable exit, Dulles prepared to defend Bohlen before the Senate Foreign Relations Committee while maintaining a discreet distance from the nominee. The chairman of the committee, Alexander Wiley, a Republican from Wisconsin, warned the secretary that the proliferation of "loose talk going around about Bohlen" must be answered with a "very clear" statement of support if the nomination was to succeed. Robert A. Taft, the Senate majority leader, cautioned that Bourke Hickenlooper had a "great deal" of disturbing material "on the personal angle and the general moral problem in the State Department."[60]

Dulles braced himself to do battle but feared contamination through close association with the nominee. Before the hearing began on March 18, Dulles requested from Bohlen that they travel to Capitol Hill in "different cars" and that the two of them not "be photographed together." Dulles testified first, in a closed session charged with tension that revealed the divide within the Republican party itself. At the opening of the hearing Senator Charles Tobey, a Republican from New Hampshire, rhetorically demanded to know if the "little group of willful men," "shadows" who had been "sharpshooting behind the scenes," would appear to testify against Bohlen.[61]

While the nominee cooled his heels outside the hearing room, Dulles provided the committee with his evaluation of the FBI summary. The secretary and the assembled senators approached the subject of homosexuality very gingerly, employing polite euphemisms when possible, and carefully avoiding the mention of names that would go into the record. Dulles conceded that "everybody knows there have been in the Foreign Service a very considerable number of persons who lacked the particular moral qualities we want," but he argued that Bohlen was not among them. Instead he argued that the only "derogatory" material bearing on Bohlen's fitness consisted of "slight evidence, which is entirely hearsay, of some moral weakness, which [was] based wholly upon no direct evidence at all, but upon association." The FBI had determined that the patrician diplomat had, in three cases, "been a friend of someone who probably had some moral weaknesses." Dulles revealed that two other informants claimed that Bohlen was homosexual: one woman whose conclusion was based on her observation that "he looks somewhat effeminate in his manner," and a man who "has what he calls a sixth sense, which enables him at a distance to determine the moral character of people," who had "looked from afar upon Mr. Bohlen" and had detected homosexuality.[62]

Bourke Hickenlooper was not convinced of Bohlen's innocence. He had long been privy to the "dirty laundry" dossiers circulating among his conservative colleagues. He demanded to know whether Scott McLeod had "cleared" Bohlen's "file for loyalty and security." Dulles hedged, asserting that McLeod had not "wished to take responsibility of clearance" and had "passed the matter up to" the secretary. Although the dialogue was contorted by the effort of Dulles and the senators not to voice the names of Bohlen's suspected homosexual associates, Hickenlooper clearly understood that the FBI report identified them as Carmel Offie, Nicolas Nabokov, and Charles Thayer. Hickenlooper told of the anonymous letters he received in July 1950 accusing twenty-one State Department employees of "perversion." The list included Charles Bohlen, and "one or two . . . high officers" still in the department. He informed the group that he had forwarded the list to the State Department security division; when recent events brought the issue to his attention again, he had checked with Scott McLeod on the fates of those named. The "fantastic results" of his inquiry gave him great faith in the veracity of his anonymous informer. McLeod confirmed that eighteen of those listed "were guilty of bad moral lapses." Most on the list had already been purged, except for one identified as an "undercover intelligence agent attempting to identify homosexuals and posing as a homosexual" and three who were now targeted for investigation by the incoming administration. As further endorsement of the anonymous tipster, McLeod told Hickenlooper that the information led investigators to "ten other individuals . . . resulting in confessions of homosexuality."[63]

While Dulles refused to commit himself to "100 percent" certainty that

Bohlen posed "no risk," he argued that the "derogatory" evidence was not credible. Taft suggested that in anticipation of a bitter contest on the floor of the senate, two senators be delegated to look at the FBI files and make a report. Dulles offered to make available only the summary, warning the committee that "hardly anybody of any importance" was without "derogatory information" in raw FBI reports. "The whole business" of the investigators was to "dig up . . . sources which are unfavorable," he explained. "I mean, they go to dismissed servants, and disgruntled tradesmen," revealed Dulles, perhaps inadvertently expressing a lingering class solidarity with the patrician diplomat. The secretary also urged the committee to act with dispatch in order to contain the spread of sexual rumors to the press. "If this is delayed," he cautioned, "the question will come up of homosexuality or moral turpitude." After Bohlen's testimony, the Committee voted 15–0 to send Bohlen's nomination to the full senate.[64]

McCarthy, McCarran, and their cronies girded themselves for battle. That day McCarthy went directly to J. Edgar Hoover in an attempt to find out "in complete confidence just how bad [Bohlen] was." Hoover hedged a bit, but encouraged McCarthy in his hunt for sexual scandal:

> Senator McCarthy asked whether I thought he was a homosexual and I told him I did not know; that that was a very hard thing to prove and the only way you could prove it was either by admission or arrest and forfeiture of collateral. I stated this had not occurred in his case at all as far as we know, but it is a fact, and I believed very well known, that he is associating with individuals of that type . . . and certainly normally a person did not associate with individuals of that type. I stated that he has been a very close buddy of [Charles Thayer] for many years and he is a well-known homosexual. The Senator was advised that we had no evidence to show any overt act, but he [Bohlen] had certainly used very bad judgment in associating with homosexuals.[65]

Dulles's initial doubts about McLeod's political loyalties proved well-grounded. The following day, March 19, McLeod began applying pressure to force the administration to abandon the nomination. Undersecretary of State for Administration Donold B. Lourie (Humelsine's replacement) reported that McLeod threatened to resign unless he could pursue the case against Bohlen using "procedures that would be taken in any other case under normal situations." "McLeod," Lourie warned, "is convinced that he is one of them [i.e., homosexual]." The procedure, he explained to his boss, "would include a visit to a psychiatrist, then interviews by our security people, and then a polygraph test." Lourie, a former Quaker Oats company executive, understood the political delicacy of the situation, but suggested that compliance with McLeod's demands would avoid the "bad repercussions" bound to follow from the security administrator's resignation under protest. The swirling rumors about Bohlen bothered him. "It would be good to go ahead and have it over with once and for all—if he isn't guilty let's really clear him," recommended the undersecretary. He feared that Bohlen was, in fact, homosexual: "Those who study this type of thing feel he is one of them and work on the criteria that once one, always one, and consequently a security risk."[66]

Lourie's new behind-the-scenes familiarity with the operations of the State Department purges gave him little faith in the sexual orthodoxy of the diplomatic corps. In addition to targeting the consul general in Munich, Charles Thayer, McLeod's pervert-hunters had just uncovered another closeted homosexual diplomat high in the bureaucracy of the U.S. occupation of Germany. On March 17 and 19, Samuel Reber (Groton, Harvard), deputy high commissioner of Germany, close associate and "principal adviser" of High Commissioner John J. McCloy, was subjected to "security" investigation, interviews, and the intimidation of the polygraph. The new regime marked the distinguished diplomat for "separation" from the department. Lourie warned Dulles that "Reber has made a lot of admissions and there is apparently still quite a ring [of homosexuals in the State Department]."[67]

Despite (or because of) his doubts about the nominee, Dulles worried that using the polygraph would create more political problems than it solved. The secretary remarked to his subordinate that "Hoover did not have much confidence" in the reliability of the lie detector. The president had "gone far out" on a limb in support of Bohlen, Dulles chided, "and we must think about protecting him." Thus he did not "want to take the risk of using a test" that would "not be reliable"; if it "produced confusion" (i.e., if Bohlen failed) the result would "upset the President's position." Dulles feared the power of McLeod's backers in the Senate; he instructed Lourie to make no promises to the security administrator "that would make him feel we had doublecrossed him." But he had no intention of tempting fate by subjecting his nominee to the trial-by-ordeal of the lie detector. He counseled the undersecretary not to "worry about the security risk involved." There was "no alternative," Dulles concluded, "we must take this chance."[68]

The question of who would ultimately control the purges within a divided State Department rapidly escalated into a crisis for Dulles. McLeod took his complaints outside the State Department chain of command directly to the White House. That same day McLeod confronted Dulles in a "heated encounter," protesting Dulles's testimony of the preceding day before the Foreign Relations Committee, with its implication that McLeod had acquiesced in the "clearance" of Bohlen. Dulles answered with an "ultimatum that he did not intend to abdicate his authority as state secretary to a security officer." McLeod leaked the substance of the encounter to Styles Bridges; the account then quickly traveled from McCarthy to the press. On Friday, March 20, Dulles awoke to find in the *Chicago Tribune* "a version of the confidential talk" he and McLeod had the previous morning. The conservative paper reported that Dulles had not shown "the committee a summary of the report but conveyed his own interpretation that was said to have conflicted sharply with that reached by McLeod." The article immediately went on to identify McLeod as the security chief who had "embarked on a swift clean-up that resulted in the firing of eight homosexuals from the State Department as security risks," thoughtfully providing readers with the key to decode euphemistic references to the charges against Bohlen. The *Tribune* reported "frantic efforts" by "some G.O.P leaders to hush up the whole affair."[69]

McCarthy tried to question McLeod before his investigating committee, but Dulles quickly moved to muzzle his insubordinate security administrator. Dulles and Eisenhower realized that the contest was freighted with great significance. They believed the battle over the nomination would "decide whether McCarthy, Bridges, and Jenner are dominating the Executive Branch of this Government." But Dulles and presidential aides worried that if they fired McLeod, he would "claim that we are 'covering up' for people." James Hagerty of the White House recommended that they defend themselves from such charges by pointing out in a press conference "the fact that 23 [homosexuals] have been fired and we have refused to hire 5 or 6." With a final warning from Sherman Adams to "remember relations on the Hill, the explosion that would come," Dulles drafted a letter demanding McLeod's resignation.[70]

The threat had its intended effect. With obsequious apologies, McLeod denied talking with McCarthy or McCarran, and promised to toe the line. Dulles formally instructed McLeod not to "testify before a Congressional Committee" on "confidential matters" without "specific authorization from the President or myself." If subpoenaed, McLeod was not to appear, but to refer the demand to the president. To eliminate the threat of damaging testimony before the senatorial countersubversives, Dulles had McLeod secretly whisked away to Concord, New Hampshire, out of range of McCarthy's subpoena, there to languish in silence for several days. The secretary and the White House directed Vice President Richard Nixon to bring pressure on McCarthy to drop any attempt to subpoena the security chief.[71]

But while Secretary Dulles struggled to contain the divisions within the

State Department, the nomination controversy became front-page news around the country. Pat McCarran launched a bitter attack upon Dulles in the Senate. He condemned the secretary for failing to purge John Paton Davies, and for "allowing" John Carter Vincent to "retire with honor." The Nevada senator then accused Dulles of "summarily" overriding the findings of his own security officer in the Bohlen case; in so doing he perpetuated "a clique that has in the past protected both persons who were loyalty risks and persons who were security risks, and that today is protecting persons in both categories." This conspiratorial "clique," McCarran fumed, had "gathered to itself the reins of power over a period of many years," holding "Secretaries of State virtually captive." Dulles's actions proved complicity with the conspiracy, argued the irascible senator, most recently when he had overturned McLeod's discharge of "a State Department official whose file shows by his own admission that he is unfit to serve because of a personal characteristic." Withholding the name of the targeted official, but in all probability referring to Charles Thayer, McCarran scornfully reproached Dulles: "My information is that the Secretary of State has since stated that this official has only been recalled for questioning and has indicated that the questioning concerns only a minor matter."[72]

McCarthy backed up his countersubversive ally by confirming the account of the dispute between Dulles and McLeod. He took a backhanded swipe at the nominee, telling reporters: "I know what's in Bohlen's file, and to say he is a security risk is putting it too weak." McCarthy demanded that McLeod testify before his committee the following day, and called for both Dulles and McLeod to be put under oath in order to get to the bottom of the conspiracy. Only in sworn testimony would Dulles tell the truth, implied the red-hunter, telling reporters that "he knew McLeod to be truthful."[73]

Dulles faced an increasingly difficult problem of containment. While publicly supporting the nomination for the sake of party unity, many Republican senators were troubled by uncertainty about Bohlen's sexuality. Although the Capitol Hill lavender-hunters declared that they expected to be outvoted, they worked their rumor mill to smear Bohlen, while frantically seeking the magic bullet that would destroy him. Sensing the fragility of underlying support for the diplomat, both in Congress and in the administration, once again they tried to use McLeod in a game of bluff. From seclusion in Concord, McLeod reported to the department's legal adviser that before his departure from Washington McCarthy had called about the "Bohlen matter" with the claim "that they had some information from the Police Inspector on the morals squad." When that ploy failed to intimidate, McCarthy tipped off reporters for the Post and traveled to Westminster, Maryland, to visit

Whittaker Chambers, grasping the faint hope that the homosexual ex-communist informer might reveal damaging secrets that would unmask Bohlen as a traitor. During a two-hour visit McCarthy extracted nothing helpful from Chambers. Determined to continue the charade, McCarthy dropped out of sight of reporters, encouraging speculation that he conferred all weekend with Chambers about the treasonous activities of the nominee. But Monday, as the nomination debate began in the Senate, Chambers punctured the senator's pretense by telling a reporter from the Baltimore Sun that during a brief visit he had given McCarthy no information concerning Bohlen.[74]

On yet another front, Dulles recruited his brother Allen, director of the CIA, to obtain Bohlen's acquiescence in the complicated maneuvers required to ensure confirmation. The day after Dulles extracted a promise from Bohlen not to withdraw "in any case whatsoever," Charles Thayer called his brother-in-law with the news that the State Department was asking for his resignation "to avoid preferment of charges involving his suitability for Federal Government employment." Dulles intended to throw Thayer to the congressional wolves to placate conservatives and ease the confirmation. Bohlen confronted Dulles, getting a bland affirmative to the question whether or not Thayer's case had been the contemplated "whatsoever." At John Foster's request, Allen Dulles asked Frank Wisner to read through Thayer's entire security file, and to convince Bohlen that his brother-in-law had to be sacrificed for the sake of the nomination. Wisner ruefully undertook the mission; he later recalled "both the considerable bulk and diverse contents" of Thayer's security dossier. He decided that Thayer could not fight the purge: "There [were] too many skeletons in closets, the whereabouts of which [were] known to too many people." Wisner was persuasive; Allen Dulles reported to the secretary of state that Bohlen "was spending the week end with Frank Wisner" and "that Bohlen understands about the Charlie situation and that it is no longer a real difficulty." Thayer's father-in-law, James Clement Dunn, ambassador to Spain, also was informed of the coming purge. The CIA director reported to the secretary of state that Dunn, too, "understood" the need to fire Thayer.[75]

Meanwhile Dulles worked to satisfy restive supporters of the nomination. He assured Senators Wiley and Smith of the Foreign Relations Committee that he had McLeod under discipline, and that there would be no noisy resignation undercutting the credibility of the State Department security apparatus or casting doubt on the administration's zeal for "cleaning out" homosexuals in the State Department. Senator Taft showed a sober and judicial demeanor in his public support of the nomination, but he was deeply troubled by the allegations of widespread homosexuality among the members of William Bullitt's first Moscow mission. Taft and his colleagues had heard scrambled accounts deployed by the nominee's enemies, based on purloined material from security files. Taft was especially concerned about the reputed existence of a "confession" by Carmel Offie that would, according to scuttlebutt, confirm the lurid tales of sexual perversion in the Moscow embassy. As Senate majority leader, Taft agreed to delay the vote on the nomination to give the opposition time to "assemble information." The Ohioan's offstage misgivings led Dulles to begin negotiations within the administration to arrange for Taft to view the FBI summary.[76]

The White House and the Justice Department feared that making even the summary available was fraught with danger. They understood that the battle with the congressional Right was as much about the production and control of secrets, including sexual secrets, as it was about the particular "security risk" posed by the real or imagined "deviance" of Charles Bohlen. In the context of the purge, control of the secrets meant leverage over the careers of powerful men, and, by extension, leverage over the policy decisions they made. To open the files to outside scrutiny was to open executive prerogative to public debate—from the perspective of the administration a recipe for paralysis, or for the transfer of power away from the administration into the hands of rivals. An intense struggle to obtain the sexual secrets followed. Attorney General Brownell warned Dulles that Pat McCarran had "tried every angle" to get the Bohlen files, and to do so "would be a complete triumph for him."[77]

On Monday, March 23, while Dulles finalized arrangements for Taft and Senator John Sparkman (a Democrat from Alabama) to view Bohlen's FBI summary and report to the Foreign Relations Committee, debate began in the full Senate. McCarthy again demanded that the Foreign Relations Committee call both Dulles and McLeod to testify under oath. He once again attacked the nominee as a homosexual using the coded euphemisms clear to all listeners familiar with the homosexual "panic" and purges of the preceding three years. He announced that the objections to Bohlen were "of such importance and of such a nature that we cannot discuss it on the floor of the Senate." "If the information in the files, some 16 pages of it, is correct," McCarthy warned, "Moscow is the last place in the world to which he should be sent." The lavender-hunting senator craftily challenged Bohlen to submit to a lie-detector test to disprove the allegations of homosexuality. He argued that rumor and innuendo had so damaged Bohlen's credibility that the "cloud or doubt in the minds of the American people" must be dispelled by the polygraph and by the testimony of Scott McLeod. McCarthy, though, did not acknowledge his own prominent role in the spread of the damaging rumors. Pat McCarran and other ultraconservative senators backed McCarthy's call to publicly interrogate McLeod and to air the charges against Bohlen. But Senator Taft worried that to reveal the secrets "would in a sense destroy the FBI." A strategy of political containment offered a solution to the dilemma; two senators from the Foreign Relations Committee could examine the file and report to the senate, preventing a wider circulation of the scandalous material.[78]

Ironically, while the debate raged in the Senate, the concealed workings of the purge played out in the offices of the State Department. The hapless Charles Thayer arrived unannounced that morning in Washington to face State Department officials demanding his resignation. Thayer telephoned his brother-in-law first. Bohlen instructed him to make his way to the State Department "as inconspicuously as possible," to avoid being detected by McCarthy or his minions. Thayer first stopped at an Army-Navy store to purchase a Legion of Merit lapel button, displaying proof of military honor he had earned during the Second World War. It was a gesture that he hoped "might ring a bell with the new powers that be."[79]

Bohlen told Thayer that his return had been "most unwise." A low-level State Department security officer, John Matson, had shown McCarthy the "complete file." Bohlen and Thayer understood that they were threatened by men who resented their privilege and power. Many of McCarthy's informers within the department were "the little people," as Thayer later described them: "Little people with a grudge. They were passed over for promotion once, or they got socked for incompetence or were reprimanded for carelessness or something and now they want to get even with their bosses. They're clerks with access to the files, junior officers who can screw some secretary in the archives to get the files for them. And they're everywhere."[80]

Now the disgruntled "little people" had powerful political patrons within the department itself. McLeod had tipped off the Wisconsin senator to Thayer's "contemplated resignation," Bohlen warned. Thayer realized that the department's protection had been withdrawn, that his most personal secrets were in the hands of his enemies, and that public humiliation was likely: "If [McCarthy] found out I was in town he'd doubtless subpoena me and make mince meat out of me at a public hearing on the basis of info I had myself told the Dept. in strictest confidence and which they'd let leak back to him." The lie-detector test had been his "undoing," Thayer believed, "not the test, but the doctor's report on it." Bohlen counseled that fighting the charges would be futile "with the Sec[retary] and the Pres[ident] bent on 'getting along' with McCarthy." The battle was lost when they "put his man [McLeod] in charge of security and personnel files," argued Bohlen. Control of the secrets had shifted to enemies of the imperial brotherhood. Left unstated but implicit in the discussion was the realization that Acheson, Lovett, Kennan, and others who had held great power in the State Department under Truman were gone, or on the defensive, and could no longer offer their protection. Thayer's problem was to put the best face on his resignation.[81]

When Undersecretary of State Walter Bedell Smith learned of Thayer's arrival he "cussed 'the god-damn amateurs' who'd sent for" the scandal-tainted diplomat. Smith abruptly summoned Undersecretary of State for Administration Donold Lourie from Capitol Hill, where he was testifying before Congress. Worried that Thayer's presence threatened to embarrass the department during the confirmation debate, Smith wanted to quickly "settle the resignation business" and hustle the diplomat back to Germany. Lourie appeared in Bohlen's office as the Senate debate began. Awkward negotiations ensued, punctuated by the delivery of teletype reports on the progress of deliberations in the Senate. While Bohlen monitored the news, anxiously expecting Senator McCarthy to publicly drag his brother-in-law's name through the mud, Thayer sparred with Lourie. He wanted to establish for the record that the department requested his resignation because of his illicit heterosexual escapades, not because he was considered a homosexual security risk. He knew that "other charges of another and much less savory kind were in the file." While he argued that the charges were false, they "nevertheless looked very nasty on paper."

Thayer demanded that the department "go on record that it was the 'girl charge' on which they were acting." He showed Lourie a prepared letter of resignation to that effect. Lourie was uncooperative. He squirmed and replied that the department could not publicly announce the reason for Thayer's resignation; to do so, he claimed, "would violate the security of the files." But Thayer pointed out that his predicament arose from the "Dept.'s representatives who had violated security to McC[arthy]." If the department would not "say at least unofficially that it was in fact the girl episode, everyone would conclude it was something much worse," he remonstrated.

When Lourie remained unresponsive, Thayer stepped into the outer office to seek his brother-in-law's support. Bohlen stressed the "danger of McC[arthy]'s making the charge of 'deviation' by innuendo." Both diplomats disbelieved Lourie's reply "that there would be no publicity." Bohlen observed that his wife had just phoned bearing the news that the night before Walter Winchell had announced Thayer's impending resignation. Joe Alsop knew the story too, he continued, "and was about to plow the whole thing up" in defense of his friend Thayer. Bohlen revealed that he had spent "all Saturday [afternoon] trying to get Joe not to carry a torch" for the targeted diplomat, "lest it provoke McCarthy to new slanders."

Lourie "still hesitated," perhaps because he understood that the purge of Thayer labeled as a homosexual was the price of a working accommodation with McCarthy, McCarran, and J. Edgar Hoover. Bohlen, probably wrestling with his own complicity in the betrayal of his brother-in-law, former schoolmate, and longtime colleague, became visibly infuriated with the undersecretary. "His hands and face twitched with anger," Thayer recalled. The ambassador-nominee threatened to consider himself "released" from his promise to Dulles not to withdraw from the confirmation contest if Lourie and the State Department refused to comply with Thayer's cover story. The ultimatum forced Lourie to agree that "it could be arranged to let the news of the girl leak for background purposes." Thayer drafted and signed another letter of resignation to "make the break clean," as Lourie demanded. Still, Thayer and Bohlen got little satisfaction from the undersecretary. He refused to coordinate a State Department announcement that would make the resignation "as dignified as possible," Thayer's "main reason for coming home." Lourie simply acted as if it was unnecessary to announce the resignation of the U.S. consul general in Munich. As the undersecretary left, clutching Thayer's resignation letter, the two diplomats decided that Thayer should make the announcement in Munich after the confirmation vote.[82]

Thayer lurked out of sight talking to Bohlen while arrangements for his return to Germany were completed. Seven hours after his arrival at the State Department, Thayer took a "private elevator" to the basement where a car and driver waited. Thayer concealed his face behind a newspaper as the car pulled into the street. At Washington National Airport, he got his ticket "and slunk out of the place to Idlewild." There he was greeted by an agent of the airline, who promised to keep his "name off the loudspeaker and the public passenger list." Then he "went and hid in a corner of the bar behind a paper and gratefully gulped two scotch and sodas." But his efforts at concealment nearly came to naught. A Reuters News reporter recognized him just before departure. Thayer "swept [his] tickets off the counter, jumped across the gap in the counter where they weigh the baggage . . . and headed for the inner office." He "was slipped thru the back door in the dark and onto the plane before the other passengers" by agents of the airline. The patrician diplomat "grimly" reflected on the ignominy of his humiliating departure, "sneaking away" like a "fugitive criminal": "You could imagine it of a Soviet citizen at Moscow airport but me at Idlewild?" he mused.[83]

Thayer flew to Germany, where he stayed up all night with his friend and colleague John Paton Davies, recounting his recent experiences. With prescience, Davies predicted that he "might well be next" in line to be purged, "if not Sam [Reber] himself." Davies, as it happened, lasted longer, until October 1954, when Dulles fired him after the last in a series of nine loyalty board inquiries. Probably unknown to Thayer or Davies at the time was that the sexual inquisitors had already extracted a "confession" of homosexuality from Reber, and his termination papers were already in the works.[84]

In Washington, while the State Department security division "confidentially notified" J. Edgar Hoover that Thayer had resigned, with thanks for a "recent summary memo furnished on Thayer" by the bureau that "was of considerable help . . . in forcing the issue," John Foster Dulles finalized the arrangements for Senators Taft and Sparkman to examine Bohlen's FBI security summary. Attorney General Brownell feared that allowing senators to view the document would establish a bad precedent. But he agreed with Dulles and the president that "the rumors have become so thick" that "someone on the floor of the Senate" must be allowed to "dissipate them." Dulles scrambled to strengthen the case for Bohlen. He asked Henry Cabot Lodge, the UN ambassador, to dictate by telephone a character reference to be appended to the FBI file. The patrician Lodge (Middlesex School, Harvard), a former Republican senator, assured his erstwhile colleagues that his old friend Bohlen was a spotless paragon of heterosexual propriety. "Any suggestion of there being anything wrong with his character or morals is to me utterly fantastic," Lodge testified. "He has a number of children and happy family life and he and his wife get along well together."[85]

But at the same time that Dulles was marshaling testimony on behalf of Bohlen, he worked to prevent any more nasty surprises from emerging from within the State Department. McLeod's investigators were collecting and scouring old security files in the hunt for homosexuals, and they still hoped to uncover incriminating evidence on Bohlen. Dulles lectured Lourie on the political dangers of the ongoing investigations: "It is extremely important in any continuing inquiry that we are quite sure we keep it to ourselves, if the Hill learns of it they will hold up the nomination waiting for more evidence. From a political standpoint, this is no time to do anything to upset the boat, a defeat would be a serious blow to the President and the Secretary." Dulles demanded that Lourie "guarantee that there would be real security on this one," in contrast to McLeod's earlier attempt to thwart the nomination through leaks to Congress.[86]

That afternoon Taft and Sparkman spent three hours with Dulles and Lourie examining the FBI summary and related materials. But once closeted with the report, Taft was not satisfied with the summary only. He requested access to the "raw files," arguing that only such a step would lay to rest the suspicions of the press and the public. Consulted by phone, J. Edgar Hoover "emphasized that the summary was very complete" but denied further prying by the senator. Taft complained that McCarthy had boasted of seeing "the entire file" and of comparing it to the summary. Taft was persistent, but two more phone calls to Attorney General Brownell got no better results. The answer "did not make Taft happy," but Brownell "was adamant" that the senators "content themselves with the summary, explaining what a situation it would put them in with the McCarran committee if they made such an exception." Taft reluctantly agreed to not to press the issue further.[87]

The following morning, March 25, Taft and Sparkman reported to the Foreign Relations Committee before debate resumed on the Senate floor. Taft testified to the accuracy of Dulles's earlier characterization of the file's contents. But he revealed that his inquiry had not stopped with the FBI report. Taft disclosed that he was granted access to a taped "confession" by one of Bohlen's "associates" held by the State Department. Conforming to prevailing conventions, Taft did not name the figures in question—Thayer, Offie, and Nabokov—but he did inform his colleagues that "the names are almost so well known it could hardly be regarded as secret." Taft explained that he could clear up "some of what Senator McCarthy said or implied" about Bohlen and his sexually unorthodox friends. Taft argued that two of the three were "certainly" homosexuals and that the third was too, "in all probability." Taft disclosed that in a taped "confession" taken in conjunction with a lie-detector test, Bohlen's "brother-in-law" had "denied any habitual situation." Sparkman and Taft divulged that "there were but three instances" that implicated Thayer in homosexual acts, but "only one he admitted." While Taft could hardly conceal his distaste at the thought of Thayer's long service in the State Department, he testified that Bohlen was not implicated in such sexual corruption.[88]

Taft had pursued McCarthy's troubling rumor that a taped confession contained the charge that "everybody that went to Moscow in 1933 and 1934 were homosexuals, the whole mission." But when the State Department security officer had played the tape, "it contained no such statement." The tape did "suggest there was something of the kind there," Taft continued, "and I don't think there was any question there was quite a lot." The recorded confession, however, only addressed the question of homosexuality in the embassy in its account: "Bullit[t] had asked one man, 'Have you got a girl?' And the next man, 'Have you got a girl—anybody who did not have a girl there, well, you better watch that fellow.' . . . In other words he was encouraging his unmarried men to have girl friends in Moscow, and if they did not have any, 'You better watch that fellow.'"[89]

Fortunately for the nomination, there was "not the slightest single word that would in any way reflect on Bohlen," Taft announced. The majority leader declared that he had been unable to find "any evidence that shows a friendship with or association with these people [Thayer, Offie, Nabokov] beyond a perfectly normal existence—a man with a wife and children who has people from time to time staying at his home." Skeptical of Taft's endorsement of the old Yalta hand, Homer Ferguson and Bourke Hickenlooper demanded to know the origins of the subterranean accounts of the taped confession supposedly confirming the existence of a ring of homosexuals in the Moscow embassy. The majority leader had "traced it back" to the "Washington police." The ubiquitous lavender-hunting Lieutenant Blick had apparently provided McCarthy with the story, arising out of the "close cooperation" between "the police, the CIA, [and] the State Department" in the operations of the government's purge of homosexuals.[90]

However, Thayer was finally "on his way out," Taft assured his fellow senators, although "he should have been out long ago." The bohemian Nabokov, who had formerly been with the Voice of America, met with the senator's censure too. "I would throw him out in a minute," Taft opined. The purge of the State Department was working properly, he implied; the sexually disreputable trio of Thayer, Offie, and Nabokov had been removed, clearing the way for Bohlen's confirmation.[91]

But the senators of the far Right pressed Taft. They were bothered by their knowledge that McLeod wanted to subject Bohlen to the polygraph. Both Taft and Sparkman assured them that there was absolutely "no evidence" to justify using the lie detector. Bohlen's friendship with Nabokov "was perhaps the strongest case," mused the Ohio senator, but Bohlen didn't show the patterns that marked a man as homosexual: "usually in these things, as you know, they start and they get a favorite or something, and that sticks around for a long time, and I just could not see it here." "In my opinion," Taft declared, "he is not a homosexual."[92]

That afternoon debate resumed on the Senate floor. Taft repeated his assessment of the Bohlen file for the benefit of the assembled body. He assured his colleagues that his inspection of the FBI report removed "any cloud of doubt as to Mr. Bohlen's fitness." John Sparkman concurred, asserting that the file contained "nothing which . . . would cause any reasonable person to conclude that a suspicion had been raised" against the nominee. McCarran, McCarthy, and their ultraconservative allies refused to concede the nomination, although they expected to be outvoted. McCarran fulminated about the muzzling of Scott McLeod and demanded that the FBI supply the "raw files." "I have had dozens of them in my possession and have used them for Sunday reading," boasted the indignant senator.[93]

McCarthy delivered a lengthy tirade, demanding redoubled efforts to accomplish the "task of scrubbing, flushing, and washing clean the foul mess that the Truman-Acheson crowd left in Washington." He congratulated Secretary Dulles who had "cooperated fully" with the purge of the International Information Agency. McLeod, too, deserved congratulation for "rooting out" security threats. To illustrate his own behind-the-scenes power in orchestrating the State Department purge, McCarthy publicized the names of recent victims, starting with Benjamin Buttenweiser of the High Commission of Germany, "the man in whose home Alger Hiss was harbored between his two trials involving treason." He then disclosed that "Charles Thayer, the former head of the Voice of America, whose activities as head of the Voice are well known to the Senate," had been "ordered home" and was "to be discharged."[94]

But McCarthy knew that after Taft's report his campaign of sexual rumors would not defeat Bohlen. So he castigated Bohlen as an agent (witting or unwitting) of elite conspiracy and treasonous subversion of American foreign policy. "We want no part of this 'chip' off the old block of Yalta," continued the red-hunter's harangue. Professing outrage, McCarthy declared that Bohlen and Alger Hiss, "his co-worker at Yalta," had both been "on the team that sold our allies down the river." Bohlen was unfit for service, argued the crusading senator, because he was an architect of "containment policy." That policy, McCarthy implied, was part and parcel of the upper-class establishment conspiracy he had been fighting since 1950: "Now, my friends, containment is a big word which grew out of the Groton vocabulary of the Hiss-Acheson gang."[95]

But McCarthy's posturing and intransigence sparked an open break with his Republican ally and stalwart of the China Lobby, Senator William Knowland, illustrating the increasingly bitter divisions within the party. Newspapers gleefully reported the fray. McCarthy gratuitously badgered the California senator when Knowland produced a copy of a disputed State Department letter from three distinguished former diplomats recommending the Bohlen nomination. McCarthy challenged Knowland's truthfulness, accusing him of displaying documents with phony signatures. Knowland exploded in indignation at McCarthy, infuriated that the red-hunter would "question" his "veracity . . . on the floor of the Senate." The conservative Californian blamed McCarthy for having "destroyed confidence in men who have been selected to hold high places in the government of the United States." McCar-

Career diplomat Charles E. Bohlen outside the White House, December 1954. Courtesy Dwight D. Eisenhower Library / National Park Service.

thy's presumption of treasonous conspiracy among governing officials had reached absurd proportions, proclaimed the livid Knowland: "when a nomination comes from the President of the United States and goes to the desk of the President of the Senate and bears the signature 'Dwight Eisenhower' I do not want to have to call in a handwriting expert . . . to determine whether a forgery has been committed." After five hours of contentious debate before "jam packed Senate galleries," Majority Leader Taft postponed the confirmation vote yet again.[96]

McCarthy's denunciation of Charles Thayer was picked up by the press; the patrician's desire for a resignation with "dignity" was not to be. The *Washington Post* and the *New York Times* reported that Thayer, consul general in Munich, had resigned "after a new investigation into his diplomatic career was ordered." The department spokesman asserted that the resignation was voluntary, to enable Thayer to "give his full time to writing." But the papers identified McCarthy as the agent of the patrician's downfall, quoting a "close friend of the former diplomat." After Thayer learned of "demands by the McCarthy crowd for a reopening of his entire case and a public review of it. . . . he decided the job wasn't worth being smeared," reported the *Post*.[97]

On Friday, March 27, Senate debate resumed. The ultraconservatives once again denounced Bohlen at great length, despite their knowledge that Dulles had the votes necessary to confirm the nomination. The second string of the lavender- and red-hunting senators rose to assail the manhood and patriotism of the nominee. Herman Welker, a Republican from Idaho, speculated that "perhaps all the things that have been said about him are not true" but complained that "we will be sending far from a strong man to Russia." Karl Mundt vowed to vote against Bohlen, not, he claimed, because of the "rumors in the cloakrooms and hints and innuendoes around the floor," but because of Yalta. Bohlen was simply too closely associated with "the nefarious characters who sneaked and crept across the Yalta horizon." Even if Bohlen was not a sexual conspirator, implied Mundt, he was an establishment conspirator who acted "like a member of a Chinese tong, trying to keep anybody outside the State Department clique from knowing" what had transpired at Yalta. After a parade of senators both for and against Bohlen disassociated themselves from the shame of Yalta, the legislators voted to confirm the president's nomination, 74–13.[98]

McCarthy's opponents in the press trumpeted the vote as a "significant defeat" for the "right-wing extremists in the Senate." But the reality was more complicated. Even after the confirmation, a cloud of suspicion shadowed Bohlen. Dulles told him before his departure for Moscow that "there were rumors in some of your files about immoral behavior," and that it would "look better" if Bohlen's wife and family accompanied him on the plane. In keeping with that theme, national newsmagazines reporting the Senate confirmation prominently displayed an image of heterosexual domestic propriety, a photograph of the ambassador at home with his wife and three young children.[99]

Most significantly, the purge continued unabated; Eisenhower and Dulles got Bohlen confirmed, but they remained complicit in the ongoing attack on the foreign service and the State Department. McLeod and Lourie demanded that Samuel Reber sign a letter of resignation "effective no later than May 1." Only "the polygraph technician's opinion that Reber [had] not engaged in homosexual activities with other Foreign Service personnel" spared him more demands "to further identify his accomplices." The use of the sexual inquisition in the termination of Reber's career sent an intimidating message to opponents of the congressional red-hunters, as was intended. More or less accurate accounts of Reber's dismissal spread widely within the ranks of the establishment. Arthur Schlesinger Jr. voiced his alarm to Adlai Stevenson, former presidential candidate and Kennedy's future UN ambassador: "People are being fired or forced to resign on the most extreme, tenuous and unsupported charges, whether political or sexual. The most eminent recent victim is, of all people, Sam Reber, who apparently is being forced out on a vague homosexual allegation, fifteen years old. And the thing is reaching the point where, as John Davies told me, the very fact of accusation makes a man, in the eyes of these thugs, a future risk. . . . As some one said, we have passed beyond the Kafka phase and are moving into Dostoievsky."[100]

Far from regarding themselves as thugs operating as agents of a Kafkaesque regime of political terror, the security officers saw themselves as enlightened pillars of rectitude and guardians of civilization. Their skill and sensitivity, they told themselves, led to ongoing "informant development among dismissed homosexuals," that is, some victims of the purge willingly returned to name names for the blacklist: "Our sympathetic and understanding treatment of homosexuals continues to pay dividends. For example, this morning [a] former Foreign Service Staff Officer, who had been interrogated some months ago and confessed, came into the office requesting advice and offered his cooperation in ferreting out three other employees of the Department whom he had good reason to believe were homosexuals. He admitted a homosexual act with one of the three people mentioned." The sexual policemen of the security division even asserted that the purge provided a kind of corrective therapy for its targets. "The interrogation of homosexual suspects," claimed John Ford, director of security, was "similar to interrogations made by psychiatrists." The officers were "proud of the assistance they have afforded in straightening out the lives of these unfortunate people." The victims appreciated their enforced rehabilitation, Ford told new inquisitor-trainees, citing "examples of letters of praise, and gratitude which SY [the security division] had received from confessed homosexuals who had been separated from the Department."[101]

For purge victims of old-stock patrician background like Charles Thayer, the inquisition was explicable in part as a product of alien ideologies, imported class resentments, and transplanted political hatreds. His persecutors were, he believed, ethnic immigrants or the descendants of immigrants who had "brought over to America their age-old hatreds and fears, their jealousies and insecurities." The security officers believed themselves to be patriotically rooting out dangerous sexual and political conspiracies that threatened the integrity of the state. Thayer, however, saw a different conspiratorial dynamic at the root of the "witch-hunt," but one also originating in an infiltration of "un-American" ideas into the state bureaucracy. The patrician diplomat abhorred the "two little security agents with their devilish polygraph who had so arrogantly set themselves up as his judges." The Irish-Catholic or Eastern European immigrant background of most of the investigators and their patrons went far to explain the inquisition, he later mused: "Their fore-fathers had doubtless come over a century or more before, fleeing from the potato famine. . . . Had they now succumbed to the virus of the newer arriv-als? . . . What had persuaded them to abandon the old Anglo-Saxon stan-dards of justice and ethics and replace them by a system of terror modeled on the European dictators, of the Gestapo and GPU?"[102]

Thayer continued to fear that he was vulnerable to McCarthy and his allies in the State Department security division and the FBI. The disgraced ex-diplomat and his family took refuge on the island of Mallorca, in part to stay out of the range of the inquisition's subpoenas, and in part to live cheaply (with only a minimum staff of servants) while he attempted to learn how to make a living as a magazine writer and novelist. He was demoralized by his new condition as an "outsider," stripped of the position that supplied "that armor which had distinguished him and his colleagues from less-dedicated and less fortunate men," a condition that excluded him from the power of the imperial brotherhood. Too, he faced more mundane worries about his family's straitened finances. Thayer had spent his inheritance "getting ahead" in his career, and had since consumed as much as he earned, "on the theory that a pension would one day come along to represent my savings." With his dismissal, the pension had "gone up in thin smoke." By late spring, examin-ing his bank book and finding "a balance of $19.64," the unemployed patri-cian confessed in his diary, "I'm really up against it." Beyond the embar-rassment of borrowing from his wealthy father-in-law was the discomfort he felt at having to turn his attention to sordid money matters. Thayer's elite patrician identity was formed out of ideals of "service" and the drama of statecraft. "I can't seem to convince myself that in these days of peril and change it is worthwhile giving time and thought to such selfish and narrow aims as money-making," he mused.[103]

Toward the end of April, Thayer was horrified to learn that Donold Lourie had been publicly interrogated by McCarthy, thus completing the former diplomat's humiliation. The undersecretary of state testified at a Senate ap-propriations hearing that "the Department is dropping an average of one employee every two days on grounds of homosexuality." The *New York Times,* the *Washington Post,* and other papers reported that McCarthy had charged that a State Department press release indicating that Thayer had voluntarily resigned was "completely false"; he had then extracted a bum-bling admission from Lourie that Thayer "was separated on a basis of morals charges—I don't believe that was the wording. I'm groping for the word-ing—and he resigned." A week later McCarthy again made news when he summoned Lincoln White, State Department press officer, to browbeat him about the "false" statements concerning Thayer's moral fitness. Thayer interpreted Lourie's statement as "a complete violation" of a "promise" made in Bohlen's office. Professing outrage, he consulted with friends and lawyers about suing the undersecretary for libel, before acquiescing in their suggestion that a suit would merely provoke another round of "mudslinging" by his enemies and prolong the public's awareness of his fall.[104]

Sam Reber, too, suffered from the loss of power, prestige, and exclusion from the imperial brotherhood of high diplomacy. One of his relatives, an acquaintance of Mamie Eisenhower, even wrote to the first lady with a vain plea for the president to intervene in the case. "Dreadfully blue" and "terribly upset" by his humiliating ordeal, Reber temporarily took refuge on Mallorca during the month of July, 1953, staying in the Thayer home. Carmel Offie, too, visited in August, and Reber returned again in September, after having "been 'out in the world' for several weeks getting used to his new status."[105]

Charles Thayer's "case [became] a *cause celebre* of those foreign service officials who had known and worked with" him, as the director of State Department security later put it. Thayer remained closely connected to the social life of his imperial brothers, although excluded from the corridors and councils of power. He served as a constant reminder to them of the perils that awaited those who ran afoul of the inquisition. He bitterly joked to visiting foreign service friends that "under Stalin you went to Siberia, under Hitler to Dachau or Buchenwald but under McCarthy to Mallorca, which counts as progress."[106]

For Thayer, his imperial brothers, and for the countersubversive lavender-hunters who had so doggedly pursued him, forced ejection from the government did not end the affair. The State Department and the FBI continued to keep tabs on Thayer. When several opportunities for employment evaporated, for example, as a magazine correspondent or in "a research job" for MIT's Institute of International Studies, the ex-diplomat not unreasonably assumed that the "Security boys have thrown a roadblock." In this assumption Thayer apparently missed the behind-the-scenes manipulations of J. Edgar Hoover, who, it seems likely, bore more responsibility than the State Department for black-balling the former foreign service officer.[107]

Thayer spent the next ten years trying to clear his name of the stigma of homosexuality. He enlisted the aid of his influential father-in-law, Ambassador James Clement Dunn, as well as his brother-in-law, Charles Bohlen. They pressured Lourie's replacement, Charles Saltzman, demanding that Thayer's personnel "Form FS-349 be amended to read: 'Resigned when advised by the Under Secretary of State for Administration that he would be charged with misconduct arising from his admission of an affair, while married, with another woman.'" Dunn "lost faith in the Department of State because of the way it had treated" his son-in-law, the security director reported, and as an act of protest he refused appointment as ambassador to Brazil. To the dismay of the department's security cops, after a barrage of correspondence from the two elite foreign service officers, the new deputy undersecretary agreed to retroactively change the purge victim's paperwork to specify heterosexual impropriety as the cause of dismissal. To officially justify the firing of a foreign service officer "on the grounds of adultery" threatened the legitimacy of the purge itself, causing alarm among the officers of the inquisition. Operative security policy and doctrine had categorized homosexual relations as a security risk while illicit heterosexuality largely remained a "private" matter outside the purview of the inquisition. To attribute Thayer's removal to an adulterous affair buttressed the argument among some of his colleagues that the purge was a political witch-hunt rather than a rigorous security program. "Many foreign service officers would be saying 'I told you so,'" lamented the security division director.[108]

Thayer continued making efforts to retroactively rehabilitate his reputation. In 1960, he enlisted the help of the Democratic senator from Pennsylvania, Joseph H. Clark. On behalf of the ex-diplomat, the senator submitted to the FBI the Swiss psychiatrist's 1951 "medical certificate" attesting to Thayer's sexual orthodoxy. His constituent had "no intention of re-opening his case or attempting to get back into the Foreign Service," Clark assured J. Edgar Hoover, but merely wanted the document "made part of his permanent FBI record." In 1963, the same urge to clear his name prompted Thayer to produce the manuscript of the "autobiographical novel" An Officer and Gentleman, a thinly disguised tale of his fall at the hands of Joe McCarthy.[109]

The prospect of dredging up memories of the countersubversion and counterperversion inquisitions of the McCarthy era horrified some of his imperial brothers, who warned him of the dangers that still lingered ten years after the purges. Frank Wisner, asked to comment on the manuscript, "advised Mr. Thayer orally and in the strongest terms that he should under no circumstances publish this book in anything like its present form, either at the present time or in the foreseeable future." "The book is altogether too recognizably autobiographic," cautioned the former CIA executive,

> not only in its main theme, but in numerous descriptive references and episodes. Thus many persons in the Washington area and elsewhere who are knowledgeable—and many of whom are unfriendly toward Mr. Thayer— would spot the verisimilitude of the story; and certain of these would interpret it as an attack upon themselves and take it as a challenge to respond,

either in kind or by some other means which could be very harmful to Mr. Thayer. (Although J. F. D. [Dulles] has gone to his reward and I doubt that "Peanuts" Lowry [Lourie] would be bright enough to bite back, others might well do so with a vengeance.) The whole thing could result in much unhappiness to himself and his family. . . . there are better and wiser ways of exposing and denouncing an oppressive tyranny [McCarthyism] than by setting fire to one's own gasoline saturated garments.

After such advice, Thayer decided against publication of the novel.[110]

McCarthy and his ultraconservative allies managed to destroy the careers of Thayer, Reber, Davies, and other prominent officials. But McCarthy became the focus of divisions within the Republican Party, cracks that had first become apparent with the Bohlen nomination controversy. The Eisenhower administration attempted to use the sexual inquisition for its own political ends, but found itself embroiled in a bitter internecine party battle—a struggle over the possession and deployment of sexual secrets produced by the inquisition—that was at the same time a struggle over control of foreign policy. As McCarthy's hubris and bullying became an increasing liability to the Republican Party, the Wisconsin senator found himself the target of a growing number of enemies who employed sexual rumor, scandal, and innuendo in their arsenal. McCarthy was to learn that Max Lerner was correct when he warned the congressional lavender-hunters that the homosexual "panic" could be a sword that cut in both directions.

·SIX·

LAVENDER-BAITING AND THE PERSISTENCE

OF THE SEXUAL INQUISITION

Joe McCarthy is a bachelor of 43 years. He seldom dates girls and if he does he laughingly describes it as window dressing. . . . The persons in Nevada who listened to McCarthy's radio talk thought he had the queerest laugh. He has. He is.

Hank Greenspun, "Where I Stand," *Las Vegas Sun,* October 25, 1952

Hoping so desperately to "stop McCarthy," the Kremlin Commandos and their American stooges have resorted to charges of immorality against Senator McCarthy, his wife, and several staffers.

*National Republic: A Magazine of
Fundamental Americanism,* August 1954

SENATOR Joe McCarthy didn't confine himself to blackmailing John J. McCloy's former proconsular officials. Eventually he turned on McCloy himself. McCloy—a former Wall Street lawyer, assistant secretary of war, head of the World Bank, and high commissioner of Germany who was then head of the Chase National Bank of New York—had also recently been named president of the Council on Foreign Relations. He made a perfect target, symbolic of the "establishment," connected as he was to the world of international finance and high imperial politics. McCarthy publicly accused McCloy of once issuing an order for "the destruction of all Army Intelligence files on Communists." The senator finally began to over-reach himself with explicit attacks on the "whining, whimpering appease-ment" of the Eisenhower administration, which, he asserted, continued "to send perfumed notes, following the style of the Truman-Acheson regime," rather than making unilateral demands on U.S. allies for compliance with a U.S. blockade of China. He accused the administration of weakness for refusing to fire John Paton Davies, a China hand who had also served with George Kennan in the State Department's policy planning staff and in Germany with McCloy. As we have seen, Dulles, always eager to placate the countersubversives, did soon afterward fire Davies. But McCarthy was unwise to attack McCloy, George C. Marshall, and other icons of bipartisan U.S. imperial internationalism. The attacks on the establishment figures of the Eisenhower administration and on the U.S. Army finally prodded the reluctant Eisenhower to orchestrate a successful counterattack on McCarthy and Roy Cohn. The senator's enemies worked to discredit him and his associates using thinly veiled assaults on their masculinity, made plausible to many by rumors about McCarthy's sexuality circulated by his opponents.[1]

In the ugly political climate of the period, McCarthy and the right-wing countersubversives were not the only players to lavender-bait their opponents. McCarthy, who made many enemies during his heedless campaign of smear and slander, was himself subjected to accusations of communism, "perversion," and the presumption of guilt by association. Two enemies in the press, columnist Drew Pearson and Las Vegas newspaperman Hank Greenspun, collaborated to spread assertions that McCarthy, a "bachelor of 43 years . . . has often engaged in homosexual activities."[2]

Beginning soon after the Wheeling speech, Pearson had repeatedly attacked McCarthy in his column, including the assertion that the red-hunting senator employed a "sexual pervert" on his staff. In December 1950, McCarthy responded by physically attacking the columnist, kicking Pearson and knocking him to the ground at the Sulgrave Club in Washington. In subsequent efforts to dig up anything that would discredit the senator, Pearson collected questionable affidavits by men who claimed to have had sexual encounters with McCarthy, as well as other "evidence" of sexual disorder among his senate staff. McCarthy's enemies in the Senate, including William Benton and Millard Tydings, Democrats from Connecticut and Maryland, covertly provided Pearson with damaging accusations, including "an amazing letter which a young army lt. wrote to Senator Bill Benton of Connecticut telling how McCarthy performed an act of sodomy on him after picking him up in the Wardman Park Bar." However, the syndicated writer cautiously avoided putting in print direct accusations of "sexual deviance" against his enemy. Instead Pearson relied primarily on the Washington rumor mill, and on printed innuendo.[3]

In 1952, Hank Greenspun, embroiled in a political feud with both McCarthy and Nevada senator Pat McCarran, eagerly aired charges originating in Pearson's file on McCarthy. The publisher of the Las Vegas Sun gleefully exploited the Pearson material to tar McCarthy with the same brush the senator used when making the "reckless charge that the department [of State] was honeycombed with homosexuals." Greenspun named William McMahon, a Wisconsin Young Republican, as an "illicit" sexual partner of McCarthy. He claimed that McCarthy was known as homosexual among the patrons of a Milwaukee gay bar. He truthfully asserted that the senator's chief investigator, Don Surine, had been dismissed from the FBI for engaging in sexual relations with a prostitute while on a "white slavery" case. He accurately reported that McCarthy had employed Charles Davis, a homosexual ex-communist, as an agent provocateur in an attempt to entrap "our minister to Sweden" (the former China hand John Carter Vincent) by obtaining proof that the diplomat "was either a Red or a sexual pervert." Lieutenant Blick's list came back to haunt McCarthy; Greenspun repeated Pearson's revelation that McCarthy had formerly employed an assistant, Ed Babcock, convicted of a "District of Columbia charge for soliciting another man to engage in unnatural sexual acts."[4]

In his editorial column, Greenspun dubbed McCarthy "the queer that made Milwaukee famous." By 1953, rumors of McCarthy's homosexuality circulated freely in Washington, and were widely believed by his enemies. "There was a lot of time spent investigating" allegations of homosexuality targeting the senator, according to newspaperman Ben Bradlee, "although no one came close to proving it." McCarthy knew the "homo story" damaged him but feared that publicity surrounding a libel suit against Greenspun would add fuel to the fire. Stung by the scuttlebutt floating around Washington, McCarthy worked outside the courts to contain such allegations. In the autumn of 1953, he married his secretary, Jean Kerr, to help quash the rumors.[5]

True to form, McCarthy and McCarran tried to unearth evidence of scandal to damage Greenspun, relentlessly employing every means at their disposal. The two senators used their staff investigators, FBI files, professional informers including the self-confessed perjurer Harvey Matusow, and red-hunting journalists in the attempt to tar him as a traitor, gangster, communist, or adulterer. They attempted to interest the IRS in auditing his tax returns. Ironically, lavender-baiting enemies of the foreign service such as right-wing columnists Westbrook Pegler and George Sokolsky expressed outrage that McCarthy and his staff had been subject to "filthy smears" that cast doubt on their "personal morals."[6]

Such concern was not misplaced. Ironically, it was the questionable relationship between McCarthy's favorite inquisitorial collaborator, Roy Cohn, and Cohn's rich, handsome, and dim companion G. David Schine that precipitated the collapse of McCarthy's power in the Senate. Before he joined the senator's staff, Roy Cohn's impeccable credentials as a communist hunter

included work on anticommunist prosecutions in New York City, a significant role in the prosecution and conviction of Ethel and Julius Rosenberg,
and the patronage of Pat McCarran and J. Edgar Hoover. The anticommunist credentials of G. David Schine, taken up by Cohn as friend, traveling
companion, and unpaid staffer for McCarthy, consisted of the authorship of
a juvenile six-page pamphlet entitled *The Definition of Communism* and the
friendship of Irving Saypol, Cohn's former boss during the prosecution of
the Rosenbergs. When Schine, who had successfully avoided the military
draft since 1945, was about to be inducted into the army, Cohn appealed to
Walter Bedell Smith, a former CIA director, for a commission in the CIA for
his friend, making veiled threats of a future investigation of the agency. After
Schine was drafted, Cohn exerted all the influence at his disposal trying to
get special privileges, an officer's commission, and extra leave for the new
private.[7]

By mid-February 1954, McCarthy's public humiliation of high-ranking
army officers during investigative hearings prodded the Eisenhower administration to begin leaking material to anti-McCarthy newspapermen like Joseph Alsop and Drew Pearson, detailing Cohn's efforts to gain favors for
Schine. In his column, Drew Pearson slyly alluded to rumors of a homosexual relationship between the two men, while publicizing Cohn's abuse of
power. He revealed that McCarthy and Cohn had pressured military officials
to provide special favors for "the handsome dreamy-eyed young" draftee
Schine. The army's failure to respond fully to the demands on behalf of the
"dream boy" "brought a howl of protest from his pal and partner, Roy
Cohn," Pearson wrote. Such insinuations played into the hands of McCarthy's increasingly restive opponents within the Eisenhower administration.
Roy Cohn was, in fact, a closeted homosexual, although that was not publicly revealed until after his death from AIDS in the 1980s following a long
and checkered career. Cohn's biographer argues that while evidence indicates
that Cohn was an active homosexual during the McCarthy years, a sexual
relationship between Cohn and Schine was unlikely.[8]

McCarthy's fatal mistake lay in using his countersubversion and counterperversion investigations to attack the Republicans who had nurtured him
when he was politically useful. The Cohn and Schine relationship offered
the chance to silence him. When on March 11 the White House released a
chronology of intimidating demands by Cohn and McCarthy on behalf of
Schine, the administration set the stage to undermine McCarthy during his
investigation of communist penetration of the army. The so-called Adams
chronology proved a coup for McCarthy's opponents. Not only did it disclose Cohn's extraordinary concern for Schine and his petulant threats to

"expose" and "wreck" the army if his conditions were not met, it also revealed that McCarthy had supported Cohn's demands, while in his absence referring to Schine as "a pest" and "a nuisance." McCarthy and Cohn responded to the charges by fabricating a series of phony backdated memorandums purporting to reveal the army's threats to use Schine as a "hostage" to force the inquisitors to curb their investigation. Cohn also accused the army representatives of offering to provide information about "an Air Force base" where the presence of "a number of sex deviates" would provide fodder for "excellent hearings"—proffered as a reward for discontinuing the army probe. McCarthy's old allies like Pat McCarran began trying to distance themselves from association with Schine, and the subcommittee running the investigation of the army resolved to hear the army's charges against McCarthy.[9]

Before the hearings began McCarthy and the counsel for the army used reciprocal blackmail to reach a private understanding to avoid certain sensitive issues. Joseph Welch discovered that Roy Cohn had never served in the military. Cohn had apparently manipulated the system to avoid the draft during both wartime and peacetime and thus escaped service in World War II or Korea. In the atmosphere of the time, this could be read as evidence of questionable "manliness" and as a kind of substantiation of the rumors about Cohn and Schine. Welch made it clear to Cohn that he might well make the issue public during the hearings. Welch knew that McCarthy and Cohn were armed with the information that one of his second assistants, Fred Fisher, had once belonged to the National Lawyer's Guild, listed as a "communist front" organization. Although Fisher had already been relieved of duty, to preempt red-baiting, Welch still feared an attempt to smear the young lawyer. Before the hearings began, he and Cohn made a deal: no mention of Cohn's draft-dodging in return for no red-baiting of Fred Fisher. McCarthy understood the arrangement as a promise that Welch would not refer to the widespread rumors of a homosexual relationship between Cohn and Schine.[10]

For thirty-six days during May and June 1954 the television networks broadcast the army-McCarthy hearings. Before millions of American viewers the counsel for the army made McCarthy appear as an evasive, dishonest bully, with a penchant for faking evidence. As public support for the Wisconsin senator eroded, Welch lavender-baited the red-hunters. The Boston lawyer badgered a McCarthy staffer about the origins of a "doctored" photograph of Schine and the secretary of the army. "Did you think this came from a pixie?" Welch inquired. When Senator McCarthy demanded the definition of a pixie, Welch replied, "I should say, Mr. Senator, that a pixie is a close relative of a fairy." Struggling to contain public discussion of the sexual morality of his assistants, Schine, Cohn, and his unsavory investigator Don

McCarthy aides Roy Cohn (*left*) and G. David Schine on their return from a 1953 European inspection tour of State Department overseas libraries. Courtesy Cleveland Public Library / AP/Wide World Photos.

Surine, McCarthy believed Welch had broken the earlier "gentleman's" agreement. When Cohn took the stand, subcommittee counsel Ray Jenkins quizzed him about the possibility of homosexual ties as a motivation for the favors demanded on Schine's behalf.[11]

As McCarthy's support crumbled, other enemies used homosexual innuendo to attack the beleaguered senator. On June 1, Senator Ralph Flanders called upon the Senate to probe the "personal relationship" linking McCarthy, Cohn, and Schine. He rhetorically wondered why Cohn seemed "to have an almost *passionate* anxiety to retain Schine as a staff collaborator." Professing to puzzle over McCarthy's support of Cohn, he speculated that "the assistant has some hold on the Senator." Four days later, Drew Pearson related episodes from the European trip Cohn and Schine took shortly after the Bohlen nomination controversy, ostensibly to inspect the State Department overseas libraries for subversive literature. With a veiled allusion to the purge of Deputy High Commissioner Samuel Reber, the newspaper columnist implied that the zealous pursuit of "perverts" by Cohn and Schine was a cover for their own illicit sexual relationship: "The two McCarthy gumshoes seemed unusually preoccupied with investigating alleged homosexuals, including one very prominent United States official. The pair also made a show of registering for separate hotel rooms, remarking loudly that they didn't work for the State Department."[12]

Goaded by the "homo" innuendo, and enraged by his inability to control the course of the hearings, "Tail-Gunner Joe" McCarthy reacted with a characteristically imprudent attack. By red-baiting the hapless (and absent) Fred Fisher, McCarthy provided the opening for Welch to condemn such "reckless cruelty." The army counsel uttered the dramatic question that both signified and further precipitated the collapse of McCarthy's support in Congress and among American voters: "Have you no decency, sir, at long last? Have you left no sense of decency?"[13]

The army-McCarthy hearings, which marked the end of the Wisconsin senator's individual power of intimidation, also terminated the most visible excesses of congressional red- and-lavender-hunting.[14] Yet countersubversion

Senator Ralph Flanders confronts an angry Joe McCarthy during the Army-McCarthy hearings, June 1954. Courtesy Cleveland Public Library / AP/Wide World Photos.

and counterperversion remained strong forces in Washington politics. The initiative shifted from the legislative back to the executive branch. America's hardy perennial secret policeman of morality and subversion, J. Edgar Hoover, continued his long-standing vigil against political and sexual disorder. Hoover's position as head of the FBI made him a powerful player in the Washington politics of counterperversion; his actions strongly shaped the gender politics of the Cold War.

"Sex Deviates" and the Secret Police

During McCarthy's ascendance J. Edgar Hoover regularly leaked information from the copious FBI files to McCarthy and other congressional inquisitors. The relentless and interminable hounding of Owen Lattimore, to take just one instance, was fueled by enormous bureau resources lavished on the investigation of the Asian scholar, as well as by the tenacious obsessions of Pat McCarran, Joe McCarthy, and the China Lobby. McCarthy's staff was liberally larded with ex-FBI agents. In cooperation with Hoover and his men, they devised ingenious stratagems to covertly pipe information from bureau files into McCarthy's office "so that a theft of government property with respect to the information contained in the report could not be proved." Members of military secret police agencies that hunted homosexuals, such as the Office of Naval Intelligence, occasionally pitched in to help the congressional inquisitors flush out subversives and "sex perverts."[15]

By 1951, Hoover was eager to further systematize the collection and organization of material resulting from sexual slander, gossip, and spying. While such sexual espionage had long been a tradition in the FBI, the new popularity of the "homosexuals in government" issue spurred an innovation that allowed the laboriously collected "information" to be more easily exploited. Hoover instituted a central "Sex Deviates" file that housed dossiers dating from 1937 onward identifying alleged homosexuals. As one indication of the extent of the FBI's intrusion into the sexual lives of Americans, the sex deviates file contained over three hundred thousand pages before it was destroyed in 1977, five years after Hoover's death. Always a canny bureaucrat, Hoover's official policy guidelines specified that sexual blackmail be used for the advantage of the bureau and to achieve the political goals of the director. While the purge of homosexual federal employees was officially sanctioned by Hoover's nominal superiors and thus bureaucratically "safe," the potential consequences of intervention in other U.S. institutions demanded consideration of costs and benefits: "In appropriate instances where the best interests of the Bureau is served, information concerning sex deviates employed either by institutions of higher learning or law enforcement agencies is disseminated to proper officials of such organizations."[16]

In practice, however, the FBI often withheld information from other federal agencies concerning the presence of "sex deviates." Instead, if in the course of background investigations the FBI discovered a closeted homosexual who "occupied a strategic position" in the organization, agents would use the threat of exposure and dismissal to force the victim to spy for the bureau. Rather than impartially and automatically reporting the presence of homosexual "security risks," the director of the bureau opportunistically used the mandated employee investigations to honeycomb the federal government with FBI informers. Sexual blackmail was one method Hoover employed to ensure that each federal agency, department, or bureau "had one or more informants in it, usually *a lot* more," as one high-level aide described the extent of the network.[17]

Hoover was thorough and systematic in the collection of sexual slander. He paid particular attention to allegations regarding important political figures that he might later deploy to personal and bureaucratic advantage. Liberal Democrat Adlai Stevenson (Choate School, Princeton, and future ambassador to the UN from 1961 to 1965) became a potential presidential contender in March 1952, when Truman announced that he would not run for reelection. By mid-April Stevenson was listed in Hoover's files: "Stevenson, Adlai Ewing; Governor of Illinois; Sex Deviate." Hoover sat at the apex of an "information" gathering pyramid that reached into local police agencies and vice squads throughout the nation.[18] The report that earned Adlai Stevenson the label of "sex deviate" originated with two Bradley University athletes under indictment for fixing basketball games. "They advised" a New York district attorney's detective returning them for trial "that the two best known *homosexuals* in the state were [Bradley University] President [David] Owen and Governor Stevenson, and that Stevenson was known as 'Adeline.'" The helpful detective provided this important news to the New York FBI special agent Edward Scheidt, who in turn promptly forwarded it to Hoover.[19]

Perhaps driven by dismay at Stevenson's announcement that he would allow his name to be placed in nomination at the Democratic convention, Hoover's myrmidons catalogued the candidate's sexual and political offenses. Beyond being referred to as "Adeline" by corrupt college basketball players, Hoover's underlings noted an ominous link with Alger Hiss. Stevenson had met Hiss in 1933 at the beginning of service in the New Deal bureaucracy, "had contacts with Hiss during Hiss's service with the United Nations," and, perhaps most damning, Stevenson had provided a deposition "on behalf of Hiss's good character" during the perjury trial. "The name of Stevenson also appeared in several documents of the Institute of Pacific Relations (IPR)," linking the candidate, at least tenuously, to Owen Lattimore, bête noir of the China conspiracy theorists. Judging the Illinois Democrat unsuitable for the presidency, Hoover abetted a Republican smear of the presidential candidate. The director ordered FBI agents to be overheard in public places like the Mayflower Hotel's Town and Country Room loudly discussing Stevenson's alleged homosexuality and the existence of an extensive bureau "sex deviates" dossier on the former governor. Even ex-FBI men were soon trying to retail the sexual scandal to the author hired by the Republican National Committee to write the official Republican biography of Stevenson, including allegations from Hoover's file that "some years ago . . . Stevenson was arrested on a morals charge [in New York City], put up bond, and elected to forfeit." Word of the rumors got back to members of the Democratic National Committee, who believed that Guy Hottel, head of the Washington field office, was actively "spreading word that Stevenson was a 'queer'; that the FBI had a file on him." When challenged about the investigation of the candidate, Hoover resorted to semantic subterfuge. The summary memoranda that reported Stevenson's alleged "deviance" were never entered into the central records system of the FBI, nor were they labeled "files" or "investigative reports." Relying on such distinctions, Hoover denied maintaining an "investigative file" on the presidential candidate.[20]

Hoover kept a wary eye on moderate establishment Republicans too. Henry Cabot Lodge (Middlesex School, Harvard), namesake of his famous grandfather and future ambassador to South Vietnam during the Kennedy and Johnson administrations, came under suspicion in 1952. The occasion was a security check instigated upon his nomination to the post of U.S. ambassador to the UN, after the loss of his Senate seat to John F. Kennedy. Hoover's agents learned from operatives of Army G-2 (military intelligence) that Lodge had been named by a "self-admitted pervert" as a homosexual, and that he had consorted with a "social contact of Dean Acheson," an "alleged Communist Party member." Adding to the murky thirdhand allegations was a Counterintelligence Corps (CIC) report suggesting that an illicit sexual partner of Lodge's was a "former page boy in the United States Senate." Perhaps luckily for the nominee, Hoover's agents determined that the army's informer was "unreliable"; the most substantial black marks against the ex-senator were two-year-old newspaper stories reporting his opposition to "public loyalty probes" and an arrest for public intoxication on October 28, 1922, while a Harvard undergraduate. Hoover decided not to antagonize the staff of the new president by any mention of the allegations of homosexuality in the security report forwarded to the White House.[21]

Ironically, when a rare incidence of attempted Soviet blackmail of a prominent patrician homosexual did come to the attention of Hoover, the outcome
did not conform to countersubversive expectations. During journalist Joseph
Alsop's first and only excursion to the Soviet Union in January 1957, the
Soviet secret police attempted to entrap the closeted homosexual by pho-
tographing him during a sexual act with a male Soviet agent provocateur.
When confronted with the photographs by the NKVD, however, Alsop refused to capitulate to their demands that he act as a spy for the USSR.[22] It
seems reasonable to argue that Alsop's refusal to "appease" the blackmailers demonstrates the strength of patrician male socialization based on the
boarding-school/imperial-identity narrative of stoicism and service; certainly
Alsop's response refuted the then-current gender ideologies and cultural assumptions about the moral "weakness" of homosexuals and the "security
risks" they posed.[23]

Alsop drew upon the support of his fellows in the imperial brotherhood
of the foreign policy establishment. He was spirited out of the country by
his close friend and Porcellian Club "brother," Ambassador Charles Bohlen,
and he immediately sought the advice of Frank Wisner of the CIA, another
close friend and member of his Georgetown social/political circle. Wisner
directed Alsop to prepare a detailed narrative of the Moscow blackmail attempt and a history of his sex life, "standard" counterintelligence procedure
under such circumstances. A copy of the document went to the FBI, prompt-
ing a response from Hoover.[24]

Consistently vindictive and opportunistic, Hoover used his privileged access to sexual secrets to settle scores and attempt to ingratiate himself with
superiors in the administration. Hoover immediately referred to his files to
assess Alsop's sexual and political deviance. As in other cases, Alsop's ties to
others hinted at subversive possibilities. Although an early security check
(1943) had "developed" "nothing derogatory . . . it was determined that both
Joseph and his brother, Stewart, are cousins of Eleanor Roosevelt." Even
more serious, but perhaps explicable by his family connections, Alsop had
"frequently been critical of the FBI and the efforts being made by the FBI in
the discharge of its responsibility." And true to countersubversive expectations, the FBI's system of sexual and political informers based on its own
systematic blackmail provided one more instance confirming the "liberal"
establishment–State Department–homosexual connection. FBI records revealed that in 1954, "a confidential informant, formerly employed in the Foreign Service of the Department of State," a "confessed" homosexual, provided reports of Alsop's sexual indiscretions during a trip to Germany.[25]

While Hoover could contribute nothing to this incident to improve "national security," it provided him with more bureaucratic leverage in Washington's subterranean sexual politics. Hoover soon took it upon himself to personally inform Sherman Adams and Attorney General William Rogers of Alsop's "perversion." The White House staff apparently received the news with considerable satisfaction. Alsop's repeated attacks on Eisenhower's cheese-paring defense budget, his shrill warnings of a "missile gap," and his ill-concealed disdain for the plodding businessmen at the helm of the ship of state had angered the administration. Two years later, irritated by Alsop's repeated criticism of administration policy, Attorney General Rogers requested that Hoover again provide an account of the "incident in Russia wherein Alsop admitted to certain acts of homosexuality." Rogers promised to spread the report of "Alsop's propensities" to the "President, Secretary of Defense McElroy, Under Secretary of State Herter, [White House aide] General Persons, and Secretary to the Cabinet Gray."[26]

Hoover, of course, understood that rumors of his own sexual "deviance" could endanger his position of power; he knew too, that he was frequently the target of such gossip. Hoover never married. He lived with his mother until her death. Afterward his closest emotional bond seems to have been with his lifelong inseparable companion Clyde Tolson, associate director of the FBI. Whether or not Hoover had a sexual relationship with Tolson remains unclear. Nonetheless, one prominent biographer of Hoover argues that the bonds between the two men were "so close, so enduring, and so affectionate that it took the place of marriage for both bachelors."[27]

Hoover strove to limit the proliferation of sexual gossip concerning him. He used the full weight of his secret police bureaucracy to contain such rumors, a response unavailable to State Department employees and other targets of counterperversion during the Cold War. FBI agents and other employees reported any allegation that came to their attention, however vague, on pain of reprimand by the director. Hoover regarded the failure of a field agent to promptly report sexual rumor directed at him as a "most serious dereliction," deserving "drastic disciplinary action."[28]

When such reports arrived, Hoover dispatched teams of agents to confront and intimidate perpetrators of these outrages against his reputation. The campaign of vigilance against "direct attack on the character of the director" included, but was not limited to, people involved in Washington politics. No "scurrilous remark" was too insignificant to ignore; his minions reported rumors overheard in places as far afield as women's bridge parties in Ohio or vice squad headquarters in Louisville, Kentucky. In all cases Hoover dispatched agents to intimidate and silence offenders against his good name. A 1951 report from a woman employed in the FBI records section spurred

Hoover into action. When he learned from his faithful clerk that the owner of a local beauty salon and her employees had asserted that Hoover was corrupt, "queer," and a disgrace to the Masonic fraternal order to which he belonged, Hoover sent an assistant director and another agent to "advise" the beautician "in no uncertain terms . . . that such statements would not be countenanced" and to threaten her with an appearance before a grand jury. In cases where the author of the allegations possessed more political influence and thus posed a potentially greater threat, Hoover's men might coerce from the offender a written and signed repudiation of his "slander."[29]

The Bundy Brothers and the Inquisition

The malignant politics of the intertwined Red and Lavender Scares left scars on several junior members of the imperial brotherhood. All saw the effects of the sex security purge on the careers of prominent men like Charles Thayer and Samuel Reber, as well as the role of the anticommunist loyalty inquisitors in ousting John Paton Davies, John Stewart Service, John Carter Vincent, and other foreign service officers. But many younger men who would become bureaucrats of the Kennedy and Johnson administrations also had direct brushes with the inquisition.

One such figure was William P. Bundy, future assistant secretary of defense for international affairs under Kennedy, and assistant secretary of state for Far Eastern affairs under Johnson. Even in 1953 Bundy had extensive ties to the American imperial project. His father, Harvey, had been a close associate and protégé of Henry Stimson. William Bundy, a product of Groton School, Yale, and Harvard Law, had married Dean Acheson's daughter Mary Eleanor. He had worked as a lawyer with Covington and Burling, Acheson's law firm, after graduation from Harvard Law in 1947. William's brother McGeorge had helped Stimson write his memoirs, worked on the Marshall Plan, and was, in 1953, appointed dean of the faculty at Harvard. William Bundy worked on the Ultra code-breaking project with the OSS during the Second World War, and he joined the CIA in 1951. Bundy aroused McCarthy's ire when the red-hunter discovered, in FBI security files supplied by Hoover, that Bundy had donated four hundred dollars to the Alger Hiss defense fund in 1948 and 1949 before joining the CIA. In 1951 an internal CIA loyalty board had quizzed him in detail about his contribution to Hiss. He was subjected to a polygraph examination that included inquiries about his sexual practices. Passed by the security inquisitors, Bundy worked for the agency for two years before the Wisconsin red-hunter publicly broached the issue.[30]

Bundy had already become an object of scrutiny and intense suspicion

CIA director Allen Dulles (*second from left*) with Senators Karl Mundt, Joe McCarthy, and Charles Potter of the Senate Investigating Subcommittee, July 1953. Dulles refused to allow the subcommittee to grill CIA employee William Bundy about his 1948 contribution to the Alger Hiss defense fund. Courtesy Cleveland Public Library / © Bettmann/CORBIS.

among senatorial countersubversives; an SISS staffer's analysis of Bundy's 1951 FBI security investigation reports seemed to offer evidence of "interlocking" conspiracy within the U.S. foreign policy bureaucracy. The SISS investigator accused the FBI of deliberately failing to pursue a thorough inquiry, at the behest of the elite intelligence agency. "Obviously the CIA has authority to restrict the FBI where CIA employees are concerned, and dictate scope of investigation," complained the incensed SISS staff member. Links to political and class enemies in the Truman administration seemed to provide further ominous evidence for the power of a dark cabal to protect subversive conspirators from exposure. He believed that the bureau's report made "an effort to mislead, by dissociating Bundy as much as possible from the law firm of Acheson," and had taken pains to "conceal the fact that Bundy's wife is Acheson's daughter, or that a brother (probably) works for State." Mistaking two unrelated State department employees with the surname Bundy as brothers of the object of their investigation (names found in the State Department telephone directory), the SISS inquisitor found support for his fears that the U.S. foreign policy bureaucracy was honeycombed by an incestuous elite of dubious loyalty. The family and class connections that boosted Bundy's career carried sinister implications in the eyes of congressional loyalty crusaders, leading to flights of conspiratorial fancy. The SISS sleuth speculated that Bundy was unable to find a place in the State Department because the agency was "afraid to hire another Hiss devotee from the Acheson clan just now, and so a potential candidate for State employment was taken care of by CIA." Bundy's involvement in the supersecret Ultra code-breaking project during the war left an alarming blank in his history, fueling countersubversive suspicions. The FBI reported testimony about his "fine war record," but the red-hunter worried about the "silence as to what his work was—in 'Intelligence' or 'Security'?" This Boston "Brahmin" offered an "illuminating example of the types of people employed by Central 'Intelligence,'" sneered the SISS inquisitor. Poorly suppressed resentment of upper-class solidarity and privilege animated his conclusions. Treason lurked behind such class loyalty:

> How interesting that this lawyer, several years a member of a prominent law firm, who graduated "summa cum laude" from Harvard Law School, and a Phi Beta Kappa at the top of his graduating class in Yale, when he turned his brilliant mind in the direction of Alger Hiss, whose record in testimony before the HCUA was already replete with glaring contradictions, evasions, and self-serving loopholes, was moved to contribute to the defense of Hiss— and not once but twice and in two different years—perhaps more than twice. Since this cannot be blamed on stupidity, what reason but disloyalty?[31]

More cautious than "Tail-Gunner Joe" McCarthy, SISS leaders Pat McCarran and William Jenner held fire on the "Bundy case" despite their suspicions. But in July 1953, in possession of the FBI file passed to him by Hoover, McCarthy denounced Bundy in a speech before the Senate and threatened to issue a subpoena to compel the patrician to testify before the Senate Committee on Government Operations. Joseph Alsop condemned the speech as "evidence of the elaborate espionage system—the large private Gestapo" used by McCarthy in his countersubversive crusade. Allen Dulles, director of the CIA, resented the penetration of the CIA by McCarthy's informers and refused to allow Bundy to testify, promising instead that Bundy would undergo another CIA security review. The White House remained quietly in the background but resolved the standoff by delegating Vice President Richard Nixon and Attorney General Herbert Brownell to undercut McCarthy's committee support for the subpoena. Outmaneuvered, the Wisconsin senator blustered but soon let the matter drop. Several months later, however, Bundy was forced to undergo another "painful day" of grilling before the loyalty board, including another lie-detector exam (yielding an inconclusive result) and yet another "suitability" review, before Dulles completely and unequivocally reinstated the Brahmin bureaucrat.[32]

William's younger brother McGeorge Bundy, dean of Harvard and future national security advisor under Kennedy and Johnson, was compromised by complicity with the countersubversion and counterperversion crusades of the era. His actions reveal that the establishment reflex to protect institutional self-interest often quietly superseded lofty denunciations of McCarthyism. When Bundy accepted the appointment as dean in 1953, the Harvard administration and board of governors understood that their institution, one central to the reproduction of "establishment" privilege, was under attack by McCarthy and under scrutiny by FBI red-hunters. The Harvard administration had been quietly collaborating with the FBI for several years in the crusade to rid the nation of "reducators."[33]

Publicly, Bundy and Harvard professed a principled defense of academic freedom. When two Harvard ex-communists, Wendell Furry and Leon H. Kamin, were dragged before television cameras in Senate hearings and browbeaten by McCarthy over their refusal to name former political associates or to take the Fifth Amendment, Dean Bundy refused to fire them. Bundy was on record opposing McCarthyism and the loyalty purges: "the national security is not served when the security program becomes an instrument of insecurity and mistrust."[34]

Public declarations aside, expediency dictated different course of action. Bundy and the Harvard administration undertook a quiet preemptive purge of politically suspect untenured employees and graduate students who refused to name names. Kamin and another untenured assistant professor, Helen Deane Markham, were subsequently ejected from Harvard when their contracts were not renewed. Sigmund Diamond, a newly minted Harvard Ph.D. and research fellow with a part-time administrative job at the university, was fingered by the FBI in April 1954 as a former member of the Communist Party. Soon after an initial confrontation between Hoover's agents and Diamond, Dean Bundy summoned the new Ph.D. to his office. There he urged Diamond to name his former party associates to the FBI, warning that failure to comply might jeopardize a joint administrative/teaching appointment Bundy had already promised to the young scholar. Diamond refused to inform on his former associates, arguing that none had engaged in illegal activity and that naming them would cost them their livelihoods and privacy. He did agree to submit to two intimidating bureau interrogations in which he spoke only about his own political activities. That, however, was not enough to satisfy Bundy, who believed that "Harvard had only a limited capital of good will with the public, and could not afford to spend it" on insufficiently repentant ex-communists. Diamond was not fired, but his 1953–54 academic year appointment was allowed to expire quietly, and the position promised him was withdrawn.

Bundy thus helped administer a policy of covert liaison and cooperation with the countersubversive secret police, designed to protect Harvard from the more overt and potentially destructive interference of congressional countersubversives. Bundy later explained: "In 1954 Harvard was indeed embattled with Senator McCarthy, and precisely because it was engaged in defending its academic freedoms it was under an obligation not to behave foolishly in its administrative appointments." Nothing became public that contradicted Harvard's image as a bastion of intellectual freedom.[35]

The narrative logic of Cold War counterperversion was present even within the ivy-draped walls of Harvard University. Robert N. Bellah, an advanced doctoral candidate in sociology, ran afoul of the FBI and Dean Bundy much as Diamond had. Bellah was summoned before Bundy in the summer of 1954, identified as a Party member for two years during his undergraduate career and as one who had been active in the John Reed Club. The patrician Dean pressed him to confess his past political sins and to name his former associates "to the FBI or to any duly authorized body." A week later, FBI agents "picked up" Bellah on the street and took him to the Boston office for interrogation. Bellah, too, although threatened with the loss of his fellowship and the withdrawal of an instructorship for the following year, refused to name names. Bundy though, had no control over the fellowship, and Bellah finished the term at Harvard. The following year, when Bellah came up for appointment as an instructor, the Dean again pressed him to inform on his former comrades, and again the young sociologist refused. Bundy then arranged for Bellah to visit "an official at the Harvard Health Service." Perhaps not fully conversant with contemporary presumptions linking "perversion" and "subversion," Bellah regarded his interview as the "strangest event in this strange story." The Health Service official "began after a few pleasantries with a story about someone who worked for the State Department who decorated his apartment with pictures of naked women to hide the fact that he was homosexual. I listened in amazement wondering what this had to do with me. He became less indirect and began asking me whether I had ever engaged in sexual acts for which I could be blackmailed."[36] Bellah apparently passed the Harvard sexual inquisition. Bundy, perhaps reacting to the apparent reduction of pressure on Harvard following the fall of McCarthy, recommended appointment. But the Harvard Corporation made the position contingent—only if Bellah named names would he get the job. He refused, and left Harvard for another university. Just as Bundy's affinal relation and model of heroic statesmanship, Secretary of State Dean Acheson, had dispensed with John Stewart Service and O. Edmund Clubb when a "duly authorized body" had indicated the political wisdom of such a purge, Dean Bundy found that the demands of power sometimes required compromise with one's professed principles, and, however reluctantly, discreetly dispensed with Diamond, Kamin, and Markham.[37]

Effects of the Sexual Inquisition

As the foregoing discussion shows, the politics of gender and sexuality played a central part in political contests for position and power among governing elites. Despite an apparent Cold War ideological consensus about the nature of "manliness" and political legitimacy, the homosexual purge masked a bitter contest over institutional power. Political foes struggled to eliminate opponents by enforcing conformity to sexual and ideological norms. The fear of subversive conspiracies that dominated the political discourse of the McCarthy era found expression in a state-mandated sexual inquisition designed to certify respectable masculinity and sexual orthodoxy as the basis for political legitimacy and participation in the agencies of government. Many whose real or imagined sexual "deviance" put them outside the boundaries of legitimate manhood were targeted and purged. Linking homosexuality to fears of a conspiratorial "state within a state" was not new to the United States of the Cold War—conspiracy theories of sexual subversion often recur in the history of Western politics. But a particular confluence of events helped give the Cold War "pervert" panic its special shape and institutionalized virulence.[38]

Both McCarthy's supporters and his establishment enemies believed their respective opponents to be engaged in conspiracies subversive of basic democratic values. In part the overheated fears of conspiracy were rooted in the emergence of a vast foreign policy underworld beyond the scrutiny of Congress, dedicated to the production and control of secrets. A paradox shaped this civil war between elite groups. In the face of communist power the contending groups each conceded (or even embraced) the new necessity for the regime of secrecy, although it fundamentally violated the tenets of republican democracy. But the new culture of official secrecy was powerfully corrosive of civility, civil liberty, due process, and open debate. The model of freedom and representative government subsumed under the term "democracy" was held up to justify an antidemocratic regimentation of American society and government—depicted as vital to a defense against Stalinist subversion.

Who, precisely, possessed the masculine republican virtue required to guard the secrets and act upon them became a central issue in the struggle for power between patricians and primitives. Each side in the domestic battle acted under a cloak of secrecy while attributing malign and subversive intentions to the similar actions of rivals and enemies. Sexual secrets became especially favored weapons in the conflict. The National Security Act of 1947 codified the new secrecy regime; the creation of the CIA, for example, produced a huge agency dedicated to covert operations—in effect, secret conspiracies—on behalf of "national security" and anticommunism.

For the provincial red- and-lavender hunters, the patrician establishment that largely controlled the U.S. national security bureaucracy was naturally suspect—an outgrowth of long-standing resentment over the political and economic power held by eastern bankers, Wall Street lawyers, and liberal internationalists. As conservative isolationist countersubversives in Congress and in federal secret police agencies took the offensive after World War II, they attempted to wrest control of foreign policy (and other aspects of government) from this deeply resented imperial brotherhood. McCarthy, McCarran, and powerful allies such as J. Edgar Hoover were convinced they had the evidence to confirm their conspiracy theories. The perjury conviction of Alger Hiss provided evidence of communist espionage in the heart of the State Department. The solidarity of the imperial brotherhood behind Hiss seemed, in the minds of the red-hunters, to confirm the real or potential treason of the patrician establishment as a whole. Undersecretary of State Robert Lovett's suppression of Charles Thayer's State Department and FBI security investigations again provided apparent proof of elite sexual conspiracies in the heart of the foreign policy bureaucracy. Ironically, whatever the sexual proclivities of individual members of the imperial brotherhood, they were committed anticommunists. Thayer, Kennan, Wisner, Davies, and their associates in the Office of Policy Coordination and the State Department's policy planning staff did engage in conspiracies of a sort. Their large-scale covert recruitment of ex-Nazis and Eastern European Nazi collaborators for espionage and paramilitary operations against the Soviet Union, to take one instance, was not ratified by the citizenry or by their elected representatives after public debate.[39] High-level officials like Lovett and Bohlen did protect their own from scrutiny by the right-wing countersubversives as long as they could by suppressing bureaucratically legitimate security investigations that threatened to turn up damaging evidence of sexual scandal.

To the imperial brotherhood, lavender-hunters like McCarthy, McCarran, and Hoover conspired to unearth (or to manufacture) sexual secrets of the brotherhood by fair means or foul. In so doing they created, with the collusion of both the Truman and Eisenhower administrations, an institutional inquisition and purge that faintly mirrored some features of Stalinism. While Stalin's purges were vastly more brutal, the American purge did push some of the victims to suicide. Charles Thayer's acerbic joke comparing "exile" under Hitler, Stalin, and McCarthy contained enough truth that his former colleagues in the foreign service surely felt its sting. Both McCarthy's network of spies and informers within the State Department and the FBI leakage of the sexual secrets of the elite seemed to violate the legitimate operations of the bureaucracy and to confirm the existence of a right-wing conspiracy.

Ironically, while the loudly proclaimed rationale for the purge was the presumed vulnerability of homosexual men to blackmail by Stalinist agents, the only unequivocally successful blackmail to compel espionage occurred when J. Edgar Hoover threatened to expose homosexual bureaucrats unless they became a part of his secret network of FBI informers. But for many in Washington, the forced resignation of hundreds of homosexual or "suspected" homosexual employees of the State Department and many hundreds more in other government agencies seemed to validate the deductive premise that homosexual employees were vulnerable to pressure from foreign agents. Although no successful cases of communist blackmail emerged, the fact that the lavender-hunters could force men to resign under threat of exposure seemed to justify the purge.

Establishment figures assaulted for "weakness," "appeasement," or "perversion" were automatically defensive. They were bound by a neo-stoic, patrician ideology of masculinity and the constraints of popular cultural assumptions about sexuality, virtue, and political legitimacy. The purges struck at the heart of their identities. To become a victim of the purges was to lose a place in the arena of public power; it meant the loss of the chance to "make history," to win glory in contest with other men. For some it meant relative hardship, a loss of livelihood, but for all it meant an ejection from the system that gave significance to the internalized story of their lives. Dean Acheson later described the personal consequences for those whose identities were tied to the power of the state bureaucracy: "I know of no one who on returning from public life to private life—not always a matter of free choice—has not felt flat and empty. . . . Vital powers no longer seem stretched to the limit; no longer is the direction of excellence so clear." To be tagged as red or lavender could mean the end of public life, thwarting their deepest aspirations.

These lessons encouraged the growth of a self-protective cult of bureau-cratic "toughness."[40]

Long-term consequences for American foreign policy followed from the purge; scholars, journalists, and former bureaucrats have long remarked on the damage done to U.S.-Asia policy by the elimination of the China experts.[41] The sex-security purge of Russian and European experts like Charles Thayer and Samuel Reber has largely gone unmentioned, perhaps because historians have failed to see a systematic connection between the politics of the homosexual panic and the high politics of the anticommunist crusade. But the effect on the State Department of both the red and lavender purges was noted by Arthur Schlesinger Jr., in a 1961 memo to President Kennedy: "Dulles's punitive action against the men, especially in the Russia and China Services (Chip Bohlen, George Kennan, Charles Thayer, John Davies, etc.) who had been most consistently independent and outspoken, indicated to the others what a great mistake it was ever to go out on a limb. The Department is still suffering from the hangover of the Dulles period."[42]

The chilling effect of the loss of the Russia and China hands spilled beyond the State Department. By managing to link appeasement and subversion to homosexuality, the countersubversives succeeded in destroying the careers of many prominent diplomats. The counterperversion purge left psychic scars on individuals; more significantly perhaps, McCarthy and his cronies used the sexual witch-hunt in a campaign to redraw the boundaries of permissible political debate and policy. The purge strongly encouraged adherence to a hard-line imperial anticommunism devoid of nuance. The subterranean politics of countersubversion and counterperversion touched, in some way, nearly all of the men who later became prominent national security policymakers and functionaries in the Kennedy and Johnson administrations. The memory remained fresh in the minds of the imperial patricians, as journalist Stewart Alsop's comment of 1962 illustrates: "ten years ago at the height of the McCarthy era . . . a lot of people honestly imagined that the State Department was crawling with perverts and traitors." The lessons learned during the purges of the Red Scare profoundly shaped the way these men calculated the possible personal and political costs and benefits of foreign policy "options" they later faced.[43]

·SEVEN·

JOHN F. KENNEDY AND THE DOMESTIC
POLITICS OF FOREIGN POLICY

We are, I am afraid, in danger of losing something solid at the core. We are losing that Pilgrim and pioneer spirit of initiative and independence—that old-fashioned Spartan devotion to "duty, honor, and country." We don't need that spirit now, we think. Now we have cars to drive and buttons to push and TV to watch—and pre-cooked meals and pre-fab houses. We stick to the orthodox, to the easy way and the organization man. We take for granted our security, our liberty, and our future—when we cannot take any one of them for granted at all. . . .

I do not say that we have all weakened. There was, in Korea, a young prisoner of war who was singled out of the line-up upon capture and asked his opinion of General Marshall. "General George C. Marshall," he replied, "is a great American soldier." Promptly a rifle butt knocked him to the ground. Then he was stood up again to face his captors—and again he was asked: "What do you think of General Marshall?" And again he gave the same steadfast reply—only this time there was no rifle butt, no punishment at all. They had tested his will, his courage to resist, his manhood—and now they knew where to classify him.

Senator John F. Kennedy, January 1, 1960

JOHN F. KENNEDY'S career was premised on an "ideology of masculinity"; he used this ideology to justify his claim to presidential power. Employing culturally resonant images, Kennedy constructed an aristocratic persona embodying the virtues of the stoic warrior-intellectual. He projected an image of youth, "vigor," moral courage, and "toughness." Kennedy both shared and exploited popular fears that equated a perceived "crisis" of American masculinity with the decline of American power abroad, using them to frame his presidential campaign and his programs while in office. The United States, Kennedy asserted, had "gone soft—

physically, mentally, spiritually soft." During eight years of Republican rule the power of the nation had been crippled by "the slow corrosion of luxury—the slow erosion of our courage." He campaigned for office promising to halt America's decline into a flabbiness and impotence that had left the country vulnerable to the threat of a "ruthless" and expanding Soviet empire.[1]

In keeping with his campaign rhetoric, Kennedy surrounded himself with a staff and cabinet composed of exemplars of masculine virtue. Out of the publicity surrounding the recruitment of administration personnel emerged a composite picture of the ideal "New Frontiersman": one who had performed brilliantly as a scholar and athlete at an Ivy League university, who had been decorated for bravery during service as a junior officer in the Second World War, and who had gone on to serve the nation through a brilliant "establishment" career in government, academia, law, or banking. Many in Kennedy's administration matched the image.[2]

Kennedy's new foreign policy bureaucracy came with establishment credentials. Many were products of boarding-school culture, Ivy League universities, and elite fraternal societies. Elite, volunteer military service testified to the manly patriotism of most. Patron-protégé networks certified those of less socially exalted origins who had proved their mettle by meritorious performance in establishment institutions and by a demonstrated assimilation to patrician internationalist values. All had been shaped by the institutional prescriptions and ordeals of elite manhood, and by the proscriptive lessons of the Red Scare. They embarked upon what they conceived as a new period of heroic leadership in the executive branch, animated by the ideals of service, sacrifice, and republican virtue. Central to the self-definition of Kennedy's stoic warrior-intellectual foreign policy administrators was a commitment to struggle, engagement, and relentless competition with America's imperial rivals, the Communist "bloc."[3]

On the offensive after eight years of Republican rule, Kennedy and his allies in the liberal establishment deployed a rhetoric of polarized opposites against political opponents: manly strength and feminized weakness, youth and age, stoic austerity and debilitating luxury. They tied their claims to political legitimacy to cultural narratives of the 1950s that decried a creeping "softness" and infantilization of American manhood and American society. Intellectuals and cultural commentators of many persuasions argued, in essence, that a return to neo-stoic republican virtue was vital to assure the preeminence and security of the United States and its special postcolonial empire. John F. Kennedy and his court of warrior-bureaucrats grounded their rhetoric and their reason in the assumptions of this pervasive discourse of politics and gender.

The "Organization Man" and the Decline of Empire

The most dramatic manifestations of the congressional antisubversive crusade ended with Senator McCarthy's censure in 1954. Yet, United States political and cultural discourse in the second half of the 1950s still displayed a deep concern with the relationship between gender and the political, economic, and social order. Political intellectuals and pundits of other sorts commented anxiously on the "decline" of masculinity, pointing to worrisome changes in the relations between the sexes. Arthur Schlesinger Jr. lamented: "Women seem an expanding, aggressive force, seizing new domains like a conquering army, while men, more and more on the defensive, are hardly able to hold their own and gratefully accept assignments from their new rulers." For Schlesinger, such changes explained the disturbing "sexual ambiguity" of the age. It was "no accident," he argued, "that homosexuality . . . should be enjoying a cultural boom new in our history."[4]

Commentators linked changes in the American economy to these unsettling threats to masculinity. They bemoaned the emergence of a new breed of feminized, conformist "organization men" and the growth of a debilitating consumerism sapping the American will to resist communist encroachment around the world. In this view, the rugged individualism of America's pioneer heritage had been replaced by "other-directed" white-collar, middle-class men—ensconced in secure but unchallenging slots in large corporations and other bureaucracies—pushing paper rather than hewing an empire from the wilderness.[5]

While sociologists bewailed the "softness" of men setting their compass by the collective whims and demands of bureaucratic life, many journalists, psychiatrists, and cultural commentators identified another (and perhaps related) source of trouble: smothering "Moms" as agents of feminizing weakness and decline. Philip Wylie's wartime characterization of "Moms" as parasitic creatures infantilizing America with their economic and emotional demands became part of the narrative iconography of the fifties.[6] Represented as powerful figures controlling a "matriarchy," women, in the shape of "Moms," were held responsible for a variety of evils besetting American men and American society, including (but not limited to) immaturity, impotence, homosexuality, unfitness for the military draft, isolationism, materialism, consumerism, and susceptibility to various forms of totalitarianism.[7]

Overtly or covertly these postwar cultural critics harked back to America's neo-stoic republican ideological heritage. The problem of virtue, the central term of republican discourse, lay at the heart of the new jeremiads.[8] Critics as diverse as David Riesman, William Whyte, Arthur Schlesinger Jr., Vance

Packard, and even Betty Friedan lamented the declension of American society from earlier values of frugality, individualism, self-denial, and struggle on behalf of society. Plaints about Momism, the organization man, and "sexual ambiguity" revolved around fears of infantile regression in a society under threat from external enemies and internal weakness. Just as the Revolutionary forefathers had lamented the "elegance, luxury, and effeminacy" that threatened the "great, manly, and warlike virtues" of the new republican society, so the best-selling Vance Packard warned of "such traits as pleasure-mindedness, self-indulgence, materialism, and passivity" eroding the national character. The "trend to hedonism," Packard declared, "represents regress."[9]

Kennedy and the "vital center" liberals promised to combat these ominous trends toward regression, to defend imperial and domestic boundaries. Schlesinger's manifesto of the late 1940s set the tone for liberal claims to manly political legitimacy. *The Vital Center* placed the "new virility" of liberal anti-communism at the heart of his narrative of political heroism. Sometimes allied with a "tougher breed" of aristocrat, the manly pragmatic liberal avoided the appeasement and the "emasculate[d] political energies" of the ruling "plutocracy" (of businessmen and new entrepreneurial wealth), on the one hand, and the utopian sentimentality of left-wing progressives on the other.[10]

By the late 1950s, Schlesinger was warning that the regressive trend toward consumption and "materialism" had weakened America in its "grim and unending contest with communism." The feminized and infantilized culture of the United States could be identified by its pervasive "self-absorption." "The symptomatic drug of our age is the tranquilizer," worried Schlesinger. The self-indulgent Moms and organization men threatened the U.S. imperial project by their diversion of American strength into luxury consumption: "By the early '60s the Soviet Union . . . will have a superiority in the thrust of its missiles and in the penetration of outer space." The luxurious abundance of American consumer goods for individual gratification came at the expense of public resources for defense, and had ominous implications, Schlesinger warned. "Let no one forget that through history this condition has led to the fall of empires."[11]

Popular fears of a feminized, luxury-loving, and declining American "manhood" intersected with fears of the waning of American hegemony over the "developing nations." These anxieties were clearly expressed in the best-selling novel of 1958, *The Ugly American,* and in its enthusiastic public reception. The novel, by William Lederer, a naval officer, and Eugene Burdick, a political scientist, has been compared to *Uncle Tom's Cabin* and *The Jungle* in its importance as a catalyst of American political debate. A jeremiad endorsed by Lederer's friend Philip Wylie, *The Ugly American* warned that masculine republican virtue was the first line of defense against communist subversion around the world. Serialized in the *Saturday Evening Post* and a Book-of-the-Month Club selection, it achieved immediate and widespread popularity. The novel remained on best-seller lists for seventy-eight weeks and sold nearly five million copies.[12]

Lederer and Burdick harbored ambitions to influence then current "foreign aid debates" that they believed made a "perfect backdrop" for the release of the novel. They rushed the completion of *The Ugly American* to get the serialization "on the stands a month or two after congress reconvene[d]." Deliberately controversial, the book provoked widespread alarm about the U.S. foreign aid program. Its prescriptions helped shape both the rhetoric and the legislation of many congressmen. By early 1959, Lederer boasted to his former commander that there were "twenty-one pieces of legislation being introduced into the Congress which include the words 'The Ugly American.'"[13]

In the Senate, John F. Kennedy found *The Ugly American* congruent with his calls for a tougher, smarter policy of confrontation with the communists in postcolonial regions. As an aspiring presidential candidate, Kennedy valued the popular book's ideological buttress to his political exhortations. He had a copy sent to each member of the Senate. It offered a "script" celebrating masculine heroism and struggle that Kennedy found congenial, loosely based on the adventures of American imperial operatives like the CIA's Edward Lansdale, navy doctor Lieutenant Tom Dooley, and William Lederer himself.

Lederer and Burdick drew upon and further promoted Lansdale's carefully constructed mythic reputation as a covert miracle worker fighting Asian communism. By borrowing from the lives of Lansdale, Dooley, and other recognizable figures, they made individually heroic solutions in America's contest with communism seem plausible. Lederer saw himself as a friend and ally of Lansdale "in harmony" with the CIA operative: "our job in Asia is not a matter of money or hordes of people. It only requires a small number of highly trained or skilled guys." An admirer of Lansdale, Lederer also saw himself as one of the adventurous imperial operatives defending American interests in Southeast Asia. Admiral Felix Stump, commander of the Pacific fleet, had given Lederer a variety of political assignments in the region, including the 1954 loan of the captain's services to Allen Dulles of the CIA "in connection with [a] special project" in Indochina. Lederer once boasted to a friend that his tasks involved "some of the blinkingest cloak and dagger stuff." "The adventures," he confided, were "hazardous enough to be exhilarating and exciting," but the "state of sloth" of overseas U.S. personnel "depressed the hell" out of him.[14]

Lederer believed that his experience made him an expert in counterinsurgency, psychological warfare, and "nation building." *The Ugly American* was a mass-market expression of Lederer's thwarted ambition to join the ranks of counterinsurgency defense intellectuals at CIA-sponsored think tanks like MIT's Center for International Studies (CENIS) to help in "developing a system of mass producing a crowd of 'poor men's Lansdales.'"[15] *The Ugly American* helped shape Kennedy's campaign rhetoric, and its themes were reflected in the foreign policy of his administration with programs like the U.S. Army Special Forces, "counterinsurgency" doctrine, covert warfare against Cuba, and the Peace Corps.

The Ugly American consisted of a series of fictional cautionary tales warning of defeat in "bits and fragments" facing the United States in Asian confrontations with the Soviets. Lederer and Burdick portrayed arrogant overseas American diplomats and foreign aid bureaucrats as soft, lazy, and ignorant of the local languages, huddling in their enclaves enjoying a comfortable lifestyle of colonial privilege, vulnerable to the seductions of the Orient. All the while, wily and tough communists were out in the villages of Southeast Asia winning converts to their cause and prevailing in anticolonial "brushfire wars." Salvation lay in the few hard, bright, committed American men who, sacrificing ease and complacency, could beat the communists at their own game.

The heroes of *The Ugly American* represented two aspects of American masculinity. Two of them—"Colonel Hillandale," a buccaneering CIA psywarrior (he is an idealized but thinly disguised depiction of the real Edward Lansdale), and "Tex Wolchek," a decorated paratrooper wise in the ways of guerrilla warfare—represented the incarnation of middle-class martial virtue and initiative. Two others—"Father Finian," who resembles the real Dr. Tom Dooley (a Catholic anticommunist humanitarian and occasional functionary for the CIA), and the eponymous "ugly" American "Homer Atkins," an engineer, inventor, and self-made millionaire bringing the blessings of Yankee technology to the natives—together represented the "tough" spirituality and productive generosity of American manhood on a mission into the wilderness.[16] All were distinguished by their frontier skills, their fluency in the indigenous languages, and their willingness and ability to undergo the rigors of working and fighting alongside the natives far from the decadent enclaves of the American embassies and colonial administrations.

"Gilbert MacWhite," a Princeton educated, "hard and muscular," "tough-minded" eastern patrician diplomat, tied together these two aspects of America's special imperial mission in Asia. Inspired by establishment figures like Charles E. Bohlen and George Kennan, the fictional Ambassador MacWhite was an exception to the political hacks and conformist bureaucrats that otherwise represented the overseas foreign service.[17] His character represented a *manly* bureaucrat: tough, intelligent, and not bound by tradition or enfeebled by luxury; and by virtue of his office positioned to recognize and lead the "tiny handful of effective men" he encountered in Southeast Asia. Burdick and Lederer suggested that militarized middle-class American heroism in the persons of Hillandale and Wolchek, allied with the austere service and sacrifice of Father Finian and Homer Atkins, all under the orchestration of a virile aristocratic establishment bureaucrat like MacWhite, could mount formidable obstacles to communist encroachments in the Third World.

Chastened by his own brief lapse of vigilance early in his tenure as ambassador to the fictional nation of "Sarkhan," MacWhite forsook the comfort of the embassy and sought hands-on lessons in Third World counterinsurgency and economic development. He traveled to the Philippines, scene of a recent "victory" over communist insurgents, to consult with national hero Ramón Magsaysay (protégé of "Hillandale"/Lansdale). He ventured to the front lines in Vietnam. There MacWhite prepared to parachute into the besieged French stronghold of Dien Bien Phu for firsthand lessons in anticommunist warfare. Only the last-minute news of the defeat of the French garrison prevented MacWhite from making the drop. There, on the tarmac, he met Major Wolchek, an American military observer assigned to a French unit. Wolchek, battle-scarred son of Lithuanian immigrants, discovered that MacWhite "understood tactics and fighting." Together, the patrician and the first-generation Texan turned the guerrilla war doctrines of Mao against the Viet Minh, demonstrating to a skeptical and tradition-bound French officer the virtues of guerrilla-style counterinsurgency operations.

From Colonel Hillandale, MacWhite learned that to succeed in the struggle for the hearts and minds of Southeast Asians, Americans must understand and manipulate the cultural belief systems of the contested populations: "Every person and every nation has a key which will open their hearts. If you use the right key, you can maneuver any person or any nation any way you want." For the nation of Sarkhan, Hillandale told MacWhite, the key was "astrology and palmistry." The war with the communists required guile, intelligence, and unorthodox methods. For Lederer and Burdick, forging the new American imperial masculinity demanded fieldwork. Through a renunciation of Western colonial privilege and European contempt for other cultures, one might discover the "key" to American influence over Southeast Asian politics.[18]

From Homer Atkins, MacWhite learned the value of small-scale, hands-on economic development work. Atkins showed that large-scale aid pro-

jects—military highways, dams, and industrial infrastructure—didn't improve the lives of Southeast Asian peasants; they merely were tools of self-
aggrandizing and feminized bureaucratic elites. Such projects represented
foolish and wasteful foreign aid spending. The homespun manliness of Atkins, who attended high-level embassy meetings dressed in "a rough khaki
shirt, khaki pants, and old Marine field boots," with "the smell of the jungle
about him," contrasted with the effete "Vietnamese, French, or American"
bureaucrats, all of whom "smelled of aftershave lotion." MacWhite rescued
Atkins from the hostility and indifference of the foreign aid bureaucrats, putting him to work in Sarkhan tutoring the natives in the blessings of Yankee
inventiveness and small-scale free-enterprise capitalism.

It was feminine (or feminized) bureaucratic weakness that undermined
the effectiveness of MacWhite and his alliance of "tough and hard" Americans. The flawed Americans of *The Ugly American* posed a threat to U.S.
interests in Asia. One danger lay in the physical, intellectual, and spiritual
mediocrity of characters like "Louis Sears," "Joe Bing," and "George Swift."
Lederer and Burdick portrayed these pathetic villains as "fat," "ostentatious,"
"inside dopester" organization men of the foreign policy bureaucracies, infantilized by luxury and colonial privilege, unwilling and unable to perform
the feats of will, courage, and vigilance demanded by the threat of communist subversion in Asia, and unable even to perceive the "silent desperation"
of the conflict. Obstructing the "effective men" at every turn, they presided
over a system so removed from austere masculine virtue that it would recruit
for overseas duty a twenty-eight year old "girl" like the character "Marie Mac-
Intosh." Echoing the 1950s-era "Momism" representation of women as
agents of debilitating consumerism and luxury, the authors depicted Marie
MacIntosh as a sexually frustrated, "drab" woman "who needed a husband"
and led a dull cheeseparing life as a stenographer in Washington. By joining
the foreign service she compensated for the lack of a husband to provide her
with luxury commodities. At her post at a Southeast Asian embassy, she rev-
eled in the luxury and "incestuous" social privilege provided by the U.S. government: personal servants, duty-free goods and liquor, subsidized housing,
an unceasing round of parties for which, despite her former "drabness," she
was in demand.

Women's sexuality too, threatened America's imperial interests. Even men
who prided themselves on their "tough-mindedness" might fail to properly
defend boundaries when debilitated by the seductive sexual machinations of
the (communist) female Other. The character "Captain Boning" stood as a
cautionary figure, to show that good intentions and a superficial adherence
to masculine austerity fell short in the desperate struggle against a protean,

engulfing enemy. "A man to whom physical fitness was important," Captain Boning was assigned an important part in delicate negotiations between Southeast Asian nations and the United States; the United States wanted permission to place nuclear weapons on the soil of its Asian allies. The captain's task required the utmost alertness, concentration, and tact. He initially adhered to a spartan regime, avoiding the cheap distractions of cocktail parties and formal dinners. But an "organization man" of the American delegation introduced Boning to "Dr. Ruby Tsung," who, unbeknownst to him, was a Moscow-trained communist agent. Soon, his latent flaws stood revealed. Captain Boning, a short man married to a "tall stately woman" whose "personal fortune had been a great help to Boning in his career," eagerly capitulated to the subtle seductions of the "extraordinarily pleasing" "small body" of Ruby Tsung. Exhausted by his repeated nightlong sexual exertions, Captain Boning fell asleep during the negotiations and botched his assignment by offending the Asian delegates; they refused to allow the United States to use their territory for the containment of communism by nuclear threat. Thus, Lederer and Burdick warned, women could subvert the imperial project from two directions: from within, as indulgent luxury-loving "Moms," and from without, as alien sexual temptresses.

The authors depicted the patrician MacWhite and his "tough and hard" middle-class allies struggling bravely but, in the end, vainly against the complacency of the bureaucrats. MacWhite attempted to remake the American presence in Sarkhan to match an ideal of masculine rigor and austerity, eliminating the debilitating corruptions of luxury, "softness," and mediocrity. Lederer and Burdick ended their jeremiad on an alarming note. Ambassador MacWhite resigned out of principle (he couldn't conform to the demands of a business-as-usual State Department), only to be replaced by a particularly loathsome "organization man."

As John Hellmann has argued, *The Ugly American* was enormously popular in part because it was a reworking of American frontier myth, full of the archetypes of self-reliant pioneers bringing civilization to a "wilderness," in competition with both savages and corrupt European colonialism. The ideological appropriation of myth and archetype to legitimate "aristocratic" leadership has a long history in American politics; Theodore Roosevelt provides perhaps the most obvious example. Through the manipulation of cultural symbols and ideologies of gender, aristocrats like Roosevelt, and later Kennedy, "sought to affirm an organic and legitimating connection between their own privileged state of wealth, power, and knowledge and an original 'democracy' in which such privilege was unknown."[19]

The images of *The Ugly American* were serviceable and attractive to Kennedy in the effort to establish such a legitimating connection, meshing as they did with his self presentation as youthful war hero and defender of America's new postcolonial empire. *The Ugly American* expressed a range of idealized identity narratives for the generation of middle- and upper-class American men who came of age as junior officers during World War II. It depicted an anticommunist alliance of heroic American men bound together by virtue across old divisions of class and ethnicity. With the ghosts of the American "success" against the Huks in the Philippines, and that of the British against a communist insurgency in Malaya hovering over the narrative, *The Ugly American* also popularized notions about development and counterinsurgency current in the academic think-tanks of the 1950s. Perhaps this partly accounts for its favorable reception by some groups of Washington policymakers, despite its marked shortcomings as literature. The pervasive influence of the book, made into a Hollywood movie in 1963, reinforced Kennedy's call to mobilize men's bodies for strenuous engagement in global struggle.[20]

The example of the *Ugly American* reveals, too, how such a masculine imperial narrative was entwined with political power and the operations of foreign policy, the actions of self-aggrandizing agents of empire, and the representation of foreign policy to domestic audiences. The men who inspired and created the novel—Lansdale, Dooley, and Lederer—also created larger public personas, narratives exemplifying the virtues represented in the immensely popular imperial tale. They acted overtly as propagandists and covertly as adventurer/operatives in efforts to shape the political destiny of Southeast Asia. John F. Kennedy's political use of *The Ugly American* cannot be examined in isolation from this context of imperial adventure and its multifaceted representation to domestic audiences. Kennedy became personally acquainted with Dooley, and both appeared as speakers in support of the Diem regime at a 1956 conference organized by a lobbying and public relations organization, the American Friends of Vietnam. The AFV itself was, as was the Diem regime, or even Tom Dooley's heroic persona, partly a creation of Edward Lansdale.[21]

Lederer and Burdick's crudely crafted tales encapsulated widespread cultural fears that American men were becoming feminized and "soft" and that imperial decline must inevitably follow. Kennedy both shared such fears and exploited them politically. During the campaign, *The Ugly American* provided Kennedy with a ready-made popular critique of Eisenhower-era Third World foreign policy, coded in gender and class terms. After the election, it reflected and embodied ideas about foreign aid and counterinsurgency current with Kennedy and many of his advisers, and, in some sense, validated the orchestration of Kennedy's postcolonial imperial foreign policy. While William Lederer never remotely approached a role as a member of Kennedy's inner circle of advisers, some among Kennedy's staff cultivated the author. During the first year of the new administration, Arthur Schlesinger Jr. flattered him with the prediction that Lederer's latest book (*A Nation of Sheep*) "should have an atomic effect" at the White House. Schlesinger invited him to the White House and introduced him to the president. Lederer sent memos to Kennedy's assistant in which he outlined strategies for counterinsurgency programs in Southeast Asia.[22]

Kennedy and the Rhetoric of Empire

Kennedy's upper-class and "aristocratic" identity narrative differed in many respects from the middle-class masculine ideal of the 1950s, with its emphasis on "maturity," sexual "containment" within marriage, and the role of men as toiling breadwinners for the family. Kennedy was equipped with an elite ideology of masculinity, focused on heroic deeds of masculine will and courage in the "public" sphere, and masculine sexual privilege and power in the "private" sphere. He imagined the ideal as one resembling a kind of classical Greek masculinity: "full use of your powers along lines of excellence," an *agon* of physical, mental, spiritual striving. Despite his "aristocratic" imagination of masculinity, because of his role as a public political figure he responded defensively to popular gender norms. Kennedy married at age thirty-seven, only because, as he told one of his Senate staffers, "I was thirty-seven years old, I wasn't married, and people would think I was queer if I weren't married."[23]

Kennedy used his presentation of self, his political speech and acts, to mediate ideological contradictions between upper-class and middle-class constructions of masculinity. He constructed a politically useful heroic narrative fashioned from the elements common to the upper-class imagination of manhood, yet resonant with the cultural "texts" shared by the mass of American voters. Kennedy used the language of republicanism, with its emphasis on manly civic virtue, sacrifice, and repudiation of the infantilizing and feminizing corruptions of luxury that threatened the ability of the United States to defend itself from external threats.

In political speeches Kennedy repeatedly invoked the names of aristocratic statesmen and soldiers, from Thomas Jefferson and John Quincy Adams to Theodore Roosevelt and Winston Churchill. Each was represented as an exemplar of will, intellect, courage, and strength in defense of "freedom." Kennedy rhetorically joined a central myth of American history and character, the "Pilgrim and pioneer spirit of initiative and independence" with the patrician boarding-school worship of stoic service to the state, "that old-fashioned Spartan devotion to 'duty, honor, and country.'" With frequent allusions to imperial Athens, Rome, and Britain, Kennedy displayed a boarding-school erudition and identified himself with a tradition of heroic aristocrats struggling to preserve empire against decline. He claimed a special "historical view of the United States and of its relations through the world" that suited him to lead a twentieth-century democratic postcolonial empire.[24]

Kennedy shared cultural anxieties about the feminization of middle-class, white-collar manhood, seeing in it one aspect of a general threat to America's global dominance. He politically exploited such fears. Kennedy's campaign rhetoric linked the Eisenhower administration to a supposed alarming decline of American prestige and power in the world, without directly attacking the fatherly and still popular figure of the president. Kennedy depicted the Eisenhower administration as a cumbersome bureaucracy, staffed by short-sighted, bean-counting businessmen who were apathetic or hostile to service in the government and eagerly "awaiting their own return to private industry." The years since 1953 had been years of "drift and impotency," "the years the locusts have eaten" Kennedy asserted, using a phrase of Winston Churchill's to establish a parallel between the imperial fortunes of the United States, then facing the Soviets, and those of Britain facing Nazi Germany before the second World War: "And these too, were precious years, vital years, to the greatness of our nation, as the thirties were to Great Britain. For on the other side of the globe another great power was not standing still and she was not looking back and she was not drifting in doubt. The Soviet Union needed these years to catch up with us, to surpass us, to take away from us our prestige and our influence and even our power in the world community."[25]

In his presidential campaign speeches he cast Richard Nixon as a stand-in for Eisenhower, an example of the organization man "experienced in policies of retreat, defeat, and weakness," who had "presided . . . over the decline of our national security." Nixon, Kennedy argued, had revealed the impotence of a feminized luxury-worship during his famous confrontation with the Soviet Premier: "And in the Soviet Union, he argued with Mr. Khrushchev in the kitchen, pointing out that while we might be behind in space, we were certainly ahead in color television. Mr. Nixon may be very experienced in kitchen debates. So are a great many other married men I know. But does anyone think for one moment that Mr. Khrushchev's determination to 'bury' us was slowed down one iota by all these arguments and debates?" In this way, Kennedy implicitly condemned his opponent's culturally and ideologically inappropriate association of masculine public power with the private sphere of women. Kennedy managed to construe Nixon as an emasculated husband espousing the consumerism of "Moms," and doing so from within the kitchen, a woman's space. While Nixon had attempted to portray the abundance of American consumer appliances as symbols of national strength and prosperity, Kennedy implied that such indulgence made the United States more vulnerable to the militarized regimentation and discipline of the Soviets. Kennedy offered a contrasting picture of his own commitment to manly austerity and potency: "I would rather take my television black and white and have the largest rockets in the world."[26]

With Democrats still smarting from Republican political attacks on Truman's foreign policy, Kennedy used similar tactics against the Eisenhower administration. He charged Republicans with the failure to avert a threatening "missile gap" relative to the Soviets. He held Eisenhower and Nixon responsible for the "loss" of Cuba to communism. He argued that administration policy had left the United States unable to confront the Soviets on the contested margins of the stalemated Cold War by an excessive (and not credible) reliance on the threat of nuclear war, a threat that could not "prevent the Communists from nibbling away at the fringe of the Free World's territory and strength" with "'brush-fire' peripheral wars."[27]

Kennedy subscribed to cyclical and organic theories of national power: nations grew strong in their youth and declined with age, just as men's bodies did. Influenced in his youth by Oswald Spengler and Homer Lea, among others, Kennedy retained the conviction that the European empires were degenerate and declining, and that Asia represented a threatening "wave of the future." Global contest in a bipolar world required the United States to "demonstrate to a watching world that we are on the march, that we have not passed our peak, . . . that the Communist system is old and tired, that the Communist system is on the way down, that here in the United States we are still experiencing high noon."[28]

As a corollary to the proposition that nations and empires were like men's bodies in their life cycles of growth and decay, Kennedy held the conviction that men's bodies represent the incarnation of the state. The president-elect issued an exhortation to the strenuous life in December 1960 in the pages of *Sports Illustrated,* paraphrasing British public-school imperial mythology for "democratic" consumption in the United States:

> The harsh fact of the matter is that there is also an increasingly large number of young Americans who are neglecting their bodies—whose physical fitness is not what it should be—who are getting soft. And such softness on the

President Kennedy at the helm of a Coast Guard yacht, publicly displaying "the vigor we need," August 1962. Courtesy John Fitzgerald Kennedy Library.

part of individual citizens can help to strip and destroy the vitality of a nation. . . . Throughout our history we have been challenged to armed conflict by nations which sought to destroy our independence or threaten our freedom. The young men of America have risen to such occasions giving themselves freely to the rigors and hardships of warfare. But the stamina and strength which the defense of liberty requires are not the product of a few weeks' basic training or a month's conditioning. These only come from bodies which have been conditioned by a lifetime of participation in sports and interest in physical activity. Our struggles against aggressors throughout our history have been won on the playgrounds and corner lots and fields of America. Thus in a very real and immediate sense, our growing softness, our increasing lack of physical fitness, is a menace to our security.[29]

As president, Kennedy identified his own body with the state. Paradoxically, his severe, crippling health problems made it impossible to fully act out the cultural script dictated by his own ideology of masculinity. He compensated with a variety of strategies. Publicly, Kennedy created a fictive narrative of athletic and war injuries to explain what were actually congenital maladies. Privately, as a senator, and then within a White House circle of those "in the know," Kennedy expressed masculine privilege and power with an exaggerated campaign of sexual conquest; this was perhaps in part a compensation for the failure of his body to support other expressions of male prowess demanded by his own ideals of manhood. As president, Kennedy always cast himself as the embodiment of a national struggle against the Soviets who, in this drama, were embodied in Nikita Khrushchev. For the one-on-one contest with Khrushchev at the Vienna Summit in 1961, while suffering severe pain from an aggravation of his chronic back problem Kennedy resorted to a drug-induced manly vigor by receiving, in addition to his regular procaine treatments, injections of "amphetamines, steroids, hormones, and animal organ cells," administered by Max ("Dr. Feelgood") Jacobson.[30]

A larger strategy employed by Kennedy was to mobilize and display other men's bodies as surrogates for his own in the political drama. This answered both to his own prescriptions about masculine leadership and to proscriptive accusations of weakness in foreign policy. White House "style" encouraged admiring members of the press corps to scrutinize the bodies of virile bureaucrats like Robert McNamara, McGeorge Bundy, or Robert Kennedy and to celebrate their physical vigor. In just one example taken from a journalistic mini-industry in New Frontier profiles, the *Saturday Evening Post* touted Bundy as a brilliant young Brahmin who played a mean game of tennis. Bundy, the reporter stressed, was a tough guy, not an egghead: "Below his lean face and his spectacles there is a barrel chest, a flat belly, and sinewy legs."[31]

As president, Kennedy repeatedly created scenarios for the ritual enactment of physical ordeals as tests of manhood. This was evident in ritualized fifty-mile hikes instigated by the president in February 1963 as a "test of commitment to the New Frontier." Kennedy mobilized U.S. marines and White House staffers, cabinet members and Supreme Court justices, his relatives and close friends. Following these public examples of ritual "sacrifice," "around the country citizens started off on fifty-mile walks of their own," presumably gratifying Kennedy with the success of his dramatization of physical ordeal.[32] Other programs of the Kennedy administration, such as the Green Berets or the Peace Corps, replicated on a grander scale a pattern of upper-class ritual ordeals (for example, boarding-school and university athletics, elite military service, adventurous struggle against nature) that Kennedy and others of his class systematically used to construct and validate manhood. Kennedy's counterinsurgency initiatives and the new Peace Corps agency provided a public forum for the display of male bodies in action and struggle. In addition to everything else that they were, these programs served a ritual ideological function, illustrating a congruence of the power of the state with the power of male bodies. In his calls to mobilize men's bodies for service to the state, Kennedy drew upon cultural materials that were consonant with his "aristocratic" ideology of masculinity and which meshed with the anxieties of a national constituency.

The Bureaucrat as Warrior-Intellectual

From the earliest days of the Kennedy administration, the president began a paradoxical attempt to incorporate individual antibureaucratic masculine heroism into the structure of the foreign policy bureaucracy through the development of a counterinsurgency doctrine and apparatus. Kennedy surrounded himself with "tough" patrician bureaucrats—erstwhile guerrillas and junior officers of World War II now in the roles of foreign policy advisers and functionaries—and a few favored heroic generals. Galvanized by the heroic revolutionary counternarratives of Mao, Lin Piao, Che Guevara, and Khrushchev, Kennedy charged his men with finding a way to make American power credible and effective in Third World hot spots like Laos, Vietnam, and Cuba.[33]

Kennedy blamed Republicans for the "loss of Cuba," but he inherited from Eisenhower a half-baked secret CIA operation to invade Cuba and overthrow Fidel Castro. The new president gave the go-ahead for the "covert" assault, revealingly labeled "Operation Castration" by his in-house adviser Arthur Schlesinger Jr.[34] The invasion failed dismally in the glare of worldwide publicity. The "humiliation" of the failed Bay of Pigs invasion was closely followed by a bruising encounter with Khrushchev at the Vienna Summit in June 1961. After these setbacks, the president felt the need to demonstrate his "guts" to the Soviet leader, and to the American electorate. Kennedy created the Special Group (Counterinsurgency) and the Special Group (Augmented), bureaucratic committees formed to mobilize men's bodies for heroic combat against subversion around the world. He assigned his brother Robert, the attorney general, to the committees as a spur to action. The Special Groups recapitulated the ideological relations of class and masculinity limned in *The Ugly American*. "Tough" patrician bureaucrats like McGeorge Bundy, Roswell Gilpatric, or Averell Harriman orchestrated the strategic functioning of the professional middle-class operatives and functionaries. This was clearly exemplified in the assignment of Edward Lansdale (model for the Colonel Hillandale of the novel) to counterinsurgency planning in Vietnam, and his appointment in late 1961 to head a program of covert warfare, sabotage, and attempted assassination directed at Cuba and Fidel Castro, code-named "Operation MONGOOSE." This apparent interplay of life and art was, perhaps, founded less on the spellbinding prose of Lederer and Burdick than on the intersection of Kennedy's heroic masculine identity narrative, the proscriptive imperatives of the domestic politics of foreign policy, and the glamorous quasi-public legend surrounding the adventures of Edward Lansdale.[35]

MONGOOSE operated in secret, with a domestic political payoff awaiting a successful result from the actions of Lansdale's swashbuckling guerrilla-spy-gangster myrmidons: the murder of Castro, or the collapse of his regime. More publicly, Kennedy embraced the heroism of the "man with the rifle" as part of the counterinsurgency-development dialectic. One widely publicized Kennedy innovation that signaled a reinvigoration of national purpose and resolve was his resurrection of the U.S. Army Special Forces. Through his patronage, President Kennedy became closely identified with the Green Berets, depicted as young American supermen possessed of hard bodies and tough minds. The Green Berets were intended as a big part of Kennedy's answer to Khrushchev's provocative endorsement of "wars of colonial liberation." The Green Berets were elite volunteers, "Harvard Ph.D.'s of the Special Warfare Art" supposedly versed in "special weapons," in the guerrilla war doctrines of Mao, in foreign languages and medical skills; they were warriors able to challenge communist guerrillas anywhere in the world on their own terms. Kennedy devoted close attention to the new counterinsurgency warriors he had conjured up by personally supervising the selection of new military equipment used to arm them: canvas sneakers with steel plates to protect against bamboo spikes, lighter field radios, new rifles, more helicopters.[36]

Roger Hilsman, another guerrilla hero, became a favorite counterinsurgency strategist of Kennedy's. Hilsman lacked the legendary reputation cultivated by Lansdale, but he embodied the narrative elements of masculine heroism and possessed institutional credentials as a warrior-intellectual.[37] First as director of the State Department's Bureau of Intelligence and Research, then as assistant secretary of state for Far Eastern affairs, Hilsman became a "player" in policy toward Vietnam by trading on his experience and reputation as an OSS guerrilla leader in Burma during the Second World War. Hilsman attracted the president's favor with his calls for counterguerrilla squads led by "men of courage and great skill" based on his wartime adventures in Burma. After Kennedy read Hilsman's speech "Internal War: The New Communist Tactic" in the *Marine Corps Gazette*, Hilsman's influence grew. Kennedy was sufficiently impressed to request that Hilsman make the rounds to "brief" high-level national security advisers. Hilsman became one of the architects of the "strategic hamlet" program. After its demonstrated failure, he became a strong proponent of the U.S.-sponsored coup that toppled the Diem government in 1963.[38]

With the president's urging, the cult of counterinsurgency proliferated. A string of National Security Action Memoranda issued forth from the meetings of Kennedy's high-level antiguerrilla theorists, designed to prod recalcitrant military and civilian bureaucrats into compliance with the new doctrines of personalized, one-on-one heroism. The air force and the navy, attached to traditions of massive high-technology firepower, got on the bandwagon with the Air Commandos and Sea, Air, Land Teams (SEALs). In early 1962 the president authorized NSAM 131, mandating the creation of counterinsurgency courses in the war colleges and throughout the military and civilian foreign policy bureaucracies. As the "capstone of the educational pyramid," the foreign service established an ongoing "Interdepartmental Seminar" in which antiguerrilla luminaries like Edward Lansdale, Walt W. Rostow, and Robert Kennedy sermonized high-level diplomats. The Kennedy administration took special pains to inculcate masculine martial competence and vigilance in that bastion of effete pomposity, the State Department. New Frontier diplomats were emphatically not going to be "cookie pushers," as George Ball, Kennedy's undersecretary of state, later explained. "There was a time when every Ambassador about to go abroad . . . even if he were to go to the Court of St. James's . . . was supposed to spend three months going to counter-insurgency school—just in case some activity developed in Green Park."[39]

The image of the heroic "unconventional warrior" fit Kennedy's deeply held ideal of masculine competence, strength, and courage. His commitment to counterinsurgency was also politically expedient. It offered domestic constituencies an aggressive response to communist subversion of U.S. client governments without the apparent costs or dangers of using a conscript army for full-scale conventional warfare in tropical jungles. In combination with the kind of psychological warfare and economic development efforts popularized by *The Ugly American,* counterinsurgency implicitly promised to bring the U.S. mission to Vietnam into conformity with mythic ideals of republican manhood deeply rooted in elite American political culture. Counterinsurgency became a kind of bureaucratic cult in the Kennedy administration, serving as an institutional expression of the masculine ideals embraced by the president and many members of his national security staff.

This idealized narrative had profound foreign policy consequences. Kennedy vastly increased the commitment of American military advisers to Vietnam during his term (from approximately seven hundred to more than sixteen thousand by November 1963), predicated on the utility of counterinsurgency as a component of "nation building."

Exemplary Masculinity: Shriver and the Peace Corps

The development side of the counterinsurgency-development dialectic came to be symbolized in the eyes of the domestic constituency by another Kennedy administration innovation to mobilize men's bodies in service to U.S. global interests, the Peace Corps. Kennedy adopted the "Peace Corps" proposal in the waning days of the 1960 presidential campaign, partly as an act of political opportunism but also as another way to boost American effort and sacrifice in the global contest with Soviet communism. Americans, Kennedy argued, "have marveled at the selfless example of Tom Dooley" and

President Kennedy greeting Peace Corps Volunteers on the White House lawn, August 1962. Courtesy John Fitzgerald Kennedy Library.

"shuddered at the examples in 'The Ugly American.'" For U.S. world power to "survive the modern techniques of conquest," our overseas personnel "must do a better job."

> On the other side of the globe, diplomats skilled in the languages and customs of the nation to whom they are accredited—teachers, doctors, technicians, and experts desperately needed in a dozen fields by underdeveloped nations—are pouring forth from Moscow to advance the cause of world communism. . . . Already Asia has more of these Soviet than American technicians—and Africa may by this time. Russian diplomats are the first to arrive, the first to offer aid. . . . They know the country, they speak the language—and in Guinea, Ghana, Laos and all over the globe they are working fast and effectively. Missiles and arms cannot stop them—neither can American dollars. They can only be countered by Americans equally skilled and equally dedicated.[40]

The Peace Corps proposal was politically opportunistic because Kennedy had little real interest in it. A "peace corps" did not really fit Kennedy's imagination of masculine heroism, focused as it was on the existential drama of life and death in confrontation with other men. More pragmatically, Kennedy was reluctant to be too closely associated with risky "liberal" initiatives that might make him vulnerable to attacks from the Right. The Peace Corps offered some tangible political benefits, however. The idea was popular with the Adlai Stevenson wing of the Democratic Party and presented a way to mend fences. After the election Kennedy appointed his brother-in-law, Sargent Shriver, as head of the new agency, and left him to fend for himself in the legislative campaign to extract permanent funding from Congress.

Shriver faced ambivalence, or, at best, benign neglect, from his patron in the White House. To convince Congress to make the agency permanent, Shriver mobilized a public relations campaign to capitalize on the heroic "New Frontier" image associated with President Kennedy. Eugene Burdick's endorsement of the Peace Corps proposal had been reported on newspaper wire services shortly before election day. Shriver promoted the Peace Corps by using arguments and images much like those employed by Lederer and Burdick in *The Ugly American* to criticize the U.S. foreign policy bureaucracy. Shriver and the men around him represented their new agency as a kind of "antibureaucracy," staffed by vigorous, decisive men, circumventing the tradition-bound red tape of Washington to create a dynamic volunteer organization to wage peace around the world and to rehabilitate America's shaky image in the "underdeveloped" nations. Shriver needed to sell the

Peace Corps to JFK, to the American public, and to many conservative congressmen who looked on it with suspicion as a potential haven for "beatniks and draft dodgers."[41]

Shriver was himself a product of eastern boarding schools (Canterbury, a Catholic version), Yale and Yale Law School, and military service in an elite unit during World War II. He shared with Kennedy many of the prescriptive assumptions about masculinity common to the eastern establishment. Shriver exhibited the Kennedy concern with "toughness." For example, Shriver always wore his submarine service pin on his lapel as public proof of courage in war.[42] Given the militarized political culture of the Cold War, with virtually all political actors of both parties striving to demonstrate "strength" against foreign and domestic enemies, Shriver carefully deployed a Kennedy-style ideology of masculinity to promote the Peace Corps. Additionally, attaching an image of unrelenting manly vigor and engagement to the new agency was as important to internal administration politics as it was to more public efforts to garner support. Within some inner circles of the White House staff, Shriver was derisively known as "the boy scout" or the Kennedy "family communist" because of his idealistic liberalism. Shriver's experience as a talent scout for the president-elect had provided a lesson in Kennedy's preference for "toughness" in administration personnel. He understood that for the Peace Corps to succeed, he needed to defend its conformity to Cold War masculine ideals on two fronts: public opinion, to win the approval of Congress and the voters; and the White House, to gain the patronage of the president and his staff.[43]

Conceived by its proponents as "the moral equivalent of war," the Peace Corps provided a public theater of masculinity for left-leaning liberal internationalists in the Democratic administration. Occasionally it served as a theater of last resort for liberals squeezed out of the White House foreign policy apparatus. Dick Goodwin, removed from proximity to the president in 1962, resolved that he was not "going to let them cut off [his] balls" and was welcomed into the Peace Corps as personal assistant to Sargent Shriver, closely replicating his former relation to Kennedy.[44]

Women, of course, did serve in significant numbers as Peace Corps volunteers. But their very presence in the organization was a matter of controversy among many members of the overwhelmingly male Washington staff. Women's sexuality was seen as a potentially dangerous and disruptive influence on men in remote outposts, causing projects to fail "because of the romantic temptations involved." The pregnancy of one unmarried volunteer led a Washington staffer to suggest, during an "emergency meeting" called to discuss the issue, that they "'can' women Volunteers altogether."[45]

Nonetheless, as a liberal and professedly inclusive program (at least on the basis of merit), the Peace Corps found a place for women in roles deemed appropriate for their sex, as nurses, teachers, or as "instructors of home economics and other domestic arts." Official policy discouraged the recruitment of married couples as volunteers. The wives of overseas staff were carefully instructed in the presentation of an image of republican austerity and female virtue, to avoid the taint of "Momism" by association with the luxurious indulgence of neo-imperial privilege. The lack of ostentation by Peace Corps wives was intended as a visible contrast with the social life of the embassies and foreign aid bureaucracies.[46]

Despite the sometimes uneasy presence of women in the organization, Shriver and the Washington staff represented the Peace Corps as a bastion of masculine virtues and modern pioneer spirit. They publicized the Peace Corps as an elite volunteer unit like the Green Berets, with standards so high that only 10 percent of applicants were accepted. The rigorous selection process continued; 22 percent of the initial recruits were rejected during training. Even this restrictive acceptance rate seemed high to the director, who reported that he first "thought we needed 100 trainees for every PCV selected." Shriver promised that danger, adventure, and sacrifice awaited volunteers. Nor would the Peace Corps provide comfort or refuge for draft evaders: "This won't be a moonlight cruise on the Amazon. The military life may not only be more glamorous, but it could be safer."[47]

The bodies of the recruits were hardened, and their resolve tested, by ritual ordeal at one of two jungle "boot camps" in Puerto Rico. Shriver and his staff created the camps with the help of consultants from the British Outward Bound schools, whose principles, according to one student of their origins, were derived "from Plato, Sparta in its heyday, from Lord Baden-Powell, the founder of the Boy Scouts, and from the British public school system." Volunteers at the training camps were roused at 5:00 A.M. to a round of calisthenics. They ran through obstacle courses, jogged, and rappelled down the face of a dam. They were bound hand and foot and tossed into rivers or "grubby pools" as lessons in "drownproofing." Visiting Peace Corps staffers were expected to undergo these rigors alongside the volunteer trainees. Their exertions provided inspirational newspaper copy. One story reported that in December 1961, Peace Corps general counsel Bill Delano "dropped his law books" and temporarily "took charge" of the island training camp. Tirelessly, "he scaled rocky cliffs, went on jungle hikes with the volunteers, and kept up camp bookwork at night." William Sloane Coffin, former Yale chaplain and director of the first of the camps, justified compulsory immersion in the strenuous life with words that might have come from the lips of Theodore

Roosevelt: "We will use physical training as a vehicle to measure a man's stamina, courage, and resourcefulness."[48]

The volunteers received special training in the language and customs of their assigned destinations. They were to serve an overseas tour of two years, living austerely in villages and barrios. The Peace Corps provided another opportunity to toughen the youth of the nation and rebuild republican virtue by sacrificing the effeminate luxury of American material consumption in a global struggle for hearts and minds. Shriver spelled this out in a draft article submitted to *Foreign Affairs:*

> Our own Peace Corps Volunteers are being changed in other ways than in the acquisition of languages and expertise. They will be coming home augmented in maturity and reoriented in outlook toward life and work. Like many other Americans, I have wondered whether our contemporary society, with its emphasis on the organizational man and the easy life, can continue to produce the self-reliance, initiative and independence we consider our heritage. We have been in danger of losing ourselves among the motorized toothbrushes, tranquilizers and television commercials. Will Durant once observed that nations are born stoic and die epicurean; we have been in danger of this happening to us. The Peace Corps is truly a new frontier in the sense that it provides the challenge to self-reliance and independent action which the vanished frontier once provided on our own continent. Sharing in other countries' progress helps us to re-discover ourselves at home.[49]

The selection of volunteers who were to embody these stoic virtues was a sensitive political issue. Shriver had a prominent psychologist (with experience selecting naval pilots during World War II) prepare a screening test to weed out undesirable recruits at the outset. Lyndon Johnson, collaring Shriver to offer advice on the selection process, recommended: "Do it like I did the Texas Youth Conservation Corps. Keep out the three Cs. . . . The communists, the consumptives, and the cocksuckers." Homosexuality, linked with subversion, communism, and disease in the political discourse of the day, was incompatible with the masculine ideology deployed to legitimate the Peace Corps in the eyes of hawkish critics. In the first batch of trainees at Iowa State University a "confessed" homosexual was rooted out by the FBI and, in the euphemism favored by the administration, "deselected." Shriver had his overseas and Washington staff vetted by the FBI to prevent vulnerability on the "security" issue.[50]

In his zeal to protect the Peace Corps from conservatives in Congress, Shriver eagerly accepted the FBI's offer to conduct "full-field investigations" on every volunteer during the "'pilot program' period." The problem, as the new director described it to the president, was to "balance the possible unfavorable reaction in public and campus opinion and among cooperating groups such as the American Friends Service Committee against the firm reports we have that communist youth groups intend to infiltrate the Peace Corps." Publicity regarding successful "infiltration" would have meant political disaster. Shriver struggled to keep the support of conservative Southern Democrats in the Senate along with "eight Republicans" to stave off Senator Bourke Hickenlooper's attempt to cut the new organization's appropriations authorization from $40 million to $25 million. The House and Senate finally agreed on a bill including a provision that all Peace Corps volunteers swear a loyalty oath affirming that "they do not advocate the overthrow" of the United States, a condition that Shriver gladly accepted with the full $40 million appropriation.[51]

Shriver recruited Peace Corps administrators with care. He used them in the campaign to sell the Peace Corps to the public, and to President Kennedy. They, too, were exemplars of masculinity. Shriver churned out press releases announcing each new acquisition. They were young, successful, and athletic, with commendable (and much touted) war records. Some were clearly liberals, but the kind of virile red-blooded liberal who could go six rounds with Sugar Ray Robinson and coach the University of Michigan boxing team, or who could speak Nepali and walk 360 miles across Kashmir on an expedition to climb K2. They were depicted as men committed to service and sacrifice, abandoning lucrative careers for long hours and low pay, compensated by the challenge and creative ferment of the Peace Corps.[52]

Shriver's relentless public relations efforts portrayed the Peace Corps as a place of meritocratic excellence, open to those of any background, as long as they could measure up to the organization's standards of manly vigor, brains and commitment: "A special kind of person is attracted to the this kind of operation. They came at the beginning and they continue to come: mountain climbers, ex-boxers, ex-smugglers, members of the Football Hall of Fame, Ph.D.s, M.D.s, high school graduates with a lift to their personality, businessmen, reporters, and a few deadbeats. The latter we got rid of—pretty darned fast. When we make mistakes in personnel, we move to rectify them equal speed."[53] Shriver boasted of his recruitment of members of aristocratic and politically prominent American families like William Saltonstall, William R. Wister, John D. Rockefeller IV, and Robert A. Taft II; in the Peace Corps they rolled up their sleeves (at least metaphorically) to work alongside the bright and accomplished sons of the working class. He depicted former Yale and Princeton men working in harmony with university-educated sons of immigrants, farmers, small town businessmen. This alliance of those of different class and ethnic origins illustrated the resurgence of a modern secular social gospel, an overseas settlement house movement; now the sons (and daughters) of immigrants were ready to take their place alongside old-stock Americans in a mission to uplift the world's downtrodden masses. This collective gift of the self served, as Shriver put it, to reaffirm "a fundamental premise of American democracy—that hard-headed realistic, practical programs are consistent with the highest ideals and the noblest of motives." Service in the Peace Corps also demonstrated the success and legitimacy of American democracy to imperial rivals. It showed that potentially everyone in America could perform the volunteer service that historically had been the province of the upper classes, thus affirming the idealism, power, prosperity, and justice of the United States.[54]

Accusations by communist Cold War rivals that America was a segregated, racially oppressive society proved a sore point for Shriver and the Peace Corps in its overtures to Third World (especially African) nations. Such "propaganda" could be answered, it was hoped, by a visible policy of racial inclusion in the Peace Corps. Initial results were disappointing. Out of the first 185 trainees, "only 4 [were] Negroes." Shriver offered the president "one explanation. . . . American Negro youth are now preoccupied with struggle and the potentiality for advancement and status here." Demands from the foreign minister of Nigeria, who "strongly desired a representative portion of American Negroes" among the volunteers sent to his country, highlighted the need to recruit blacks. Shriver enlisted the aid of Urban League and NAACP officials, and sent emissaries to "Negro colleges." Their efforts brought only modest success—by the time significant numbers of volunteers were being sent overseas, only 4.2 percent were black. In the short term, the Peace Corps relied on a public relations gesture to demonstrate their commitment to racial equality before African audiences. Much as Shriver had advertised the masculine charisma of his Washington staff to sell the organization in Washington, he enlisted the "famous Negro decathlon champion," Rafer Johnson, to "stop in Nigeria, visit the Volunteers and talk with Nigerian students," then "do the same for us in Ghana." Perhaps the athletic star power of the Olympic record holder diverted attention from the absence of black volunteers in African projects.[55]

Despite the overwhelmingly white, male composition of the Peace Corps staff in Washington, Shriver recruited exemplary African-American men when they were encountered.[56] Robert Kennedy met one such model of masculine virtue during a touch football game between teams from the Labor and Justice Departments. Jesse Arnelle, the son of poor but hardworking parents (his father had come north from rural Georgia and married a Jamaican immigrant), had been an All-American college basketball star, and had put himself through law school playing semi-pro basketball before becoming a Labor Department lawyer. Kennedy arranged an interview for the athletic Arnelle with the vigorous director of the Peace Corps. Arnelle recounts his experience upon being ushered into Shriver's office by an assistant: "He says, 'Sarge, this is Jesse Arnelle.' Sarge says, 'Yes, I know.' And he throws a football to me all the way across the damn office. As the ball is coming over, he says, 'How would you like to work for the Peace Corps?' I catch the ball and he says, 'You're hired!' . . . I went to Turkey."[57] Recruiting an African-American who possessed such an attractive mixture of athletic prowess and self-made professional success helped Shriver demonstrate to critics that the Peace Corps's commitment to masculine merit and strength of character transcended racial categories.

Sensitive to accusations that theirs was an organization of "fuzzy-minded visionaries" or "Boy Scouts," Shriver and his antibureaucratic bureaucrats responded by representing themselves as steely pragmatists. To ensure that Peace Corps programs were truly "effective," Shriver created a system to recruit temporary outside "evaluators" of overseas projects. Here again the ubiquitous influence of Lederer and Burdick, propagandists of austere masculine struggle, became directly visible.[58]

In early 1962, consistent with their ambitions and reputation as Cold War foreign aid experts, Lederer and Burdick volunteered their services as evaluators of Peace Corps projects. Lederer later recalled that before offering his services to Shriver, he had "just walked all over the Philippines," where he saw the failure of early Peace Corps programs. Imperial privilege, luxury, and ignorance again threatened to subvert U.S. efforts. American volunteers "were not used to having two or three servants." Their presence was wasteful because "they didn't speak the dialect" and "all they were doing was teaching English" rather than getting their hands dirty with small-scale economic development.[59] Shriver and his Associate Director William Haddad gladly employed the famous authors, seeking answers "to the challenges posed by *The Ugly American*." Shriver's system of oversight was designed to maintain the appearance and (ideally) the substance of "efficiency" and austerity.[60]

Lederer enthusiastically plunged into his role as both consultant to the Peace Corps and foreign aid pundit, hoping to help shape American foreign policy. He suggested a role for the Peace Corps in American Samoa to anticipate and undercut resentment caused by the vast militarized U.S. presence in the region: "There is considerable evidence that America's role in the Pacific will become more and more crucial and exposed to much sharper scrutiny in the next few years. The complaints range from a sincere doubt as to our moral justification in moving into some islands for nuclear testing to the more routine ideological complaints that we are 'imperialistic.'" As in *The Ugly American,* Lederer prescribed "the development of cottage industries" and other small, hands-on projects under the tutelage of Peace Corps volunteers.[61]

Lederer remained ever mindful of the potential role of the Peace Corps in the Cold War. During a stint evaluating the effectiveness of a training program at Hilo, Hawaii, Lederer trotted out his counterinsurgency and psychological warfare expertise for the benefit of volunteer trainees bound for the Philippines. Drawing on his familiarity with the works of Mao and Lenin and with other revolutionary doctrine, the old Asia hand "put on a demonstration of how a Communist would answer the questions of a group of PC volunteers which was extremely impressive." The performance, Lederer asserted, "seemed to have an electrifying effect on the trainees." He recommended that the Peace Corps "build such discussion into the program, with however, the cautionary note added that it takes an extremely skillful person to handle the role of the Communist." Lederer's tutelage of the volunteers included morale-building "lectures on trade unions, Soviet International politics and Soviet Internal Politics." He apparently believed that his work for the Peace Corps offered another small way to act on his old ambition of "mass producing a crowd of 'poor men's Lansdales'" to fight communism in Asia.[62]

Shriver used Lederer and Burdick's reputation as hard-headed foreign aid experts to lend legitimacy to his new organization, but he didn't stop there. His office peppered the president with missives and press clippings illustrating the Peace Corps's visible conformity to elite masculine ideals of "toughness" and its success in publicizing that message. "How's this for carrying out your instructions to create a New Frontier image abroad?" Shriver inquired, as he forwarded a newspaper report of the near success a Yale-educated volunteer had in a recent "Thai-style boxing" charity match, by fighting his Thai opponent to a draw.[63] "Peace Corps' Honor Upheld in Fifty Mile Hike," boasted a "weekly summary of Peace Corps activities" sent to the president: "Volunteers Darrell Young of Kingsville, Texas, and John Bennett of Baxter Springs, Kansas, have told us they decided to 'uphold the Peace Corps' honor and image' in Colombia by walking fifty miles on a rest day." The exemplary toughness of the volunteers went beyond extraordinary feats of pugilism and peregrination. Shriver boasted to his boss of the willing self-denial practiced by the volunteers, a ritual asceticism congenial to the tastes of one bred on the manly boarding-school ideology of service and sacrifice:

"They're sleeping on cots, eating the food—3 times a day—at a cost of 5 pesos (75 cents). They are in towns where *no* North Americans are living or have lived."[64]

Kennedy embraced the Peace Corps as its political success became evident, making public appearances in the Rose Garden to send off volunteers on overseas assignments. In speeches he began to assert for the Peace Corps a role in the management of America's unique postcolonial empire. It would help solve problems identified in *The Ugly American.* Former volunteers could provide an experienced pool of talent for the foreign service, untainted by the arrogant and hidebound traditions of the "striped pants diplomat." The president encouraged the infusion of vigorous youth into stuffy, slow-to-change foreign relations bureaucracies with Executive Order 11103 of April 1963, which mandated the "non-competitive appointment" of former volunteers.[65]

Shriver and his associates encouraged Kennedy and the public to see the Peace Corps as a new and uniquely effective tool of policy in the global contest with the Soviets. The Peace Corps operated with "freedom and energy of autonomy" independent of the ossified foreign aid bureaucracies. Shriver courted neutralist or "pro-Soviet" heads of state in Africa and Indonesia with offers of Peace Corps projects. After a meeting with Sekou Touré of Guinea, Shriver apprised the president of the potential utility of the Peace Corps as a weapon in his Third World rivalry with Khrushchev: "Here we have an opportunity to move a country from an apparently clear Bloc orientation to a position of neutrality or even of orientation to the West. This is the first such opportunity I know of in the underdeveloped world. The consequences of success in terms of our relations with countries like Mali or Ghana, or even Iraq or the United Arab Republic could be very good indeed."[66]

The Peace Corps, Shriver told Kennedy, represented "the point of the lance" in the struggle against Latin American communism. "Time is running out," he warned, "especially in Peru." Nation building by Peace Corps volunteers could stem the tide, Shriver counseled: "Communist agents are boring into the villages; it is in these same villages that the Peace Corps must help the campesinos in fundamental community development tasks." During a trip to South America, Shriver reported the return from Moscow of "the leading Commie in Colombia . . . accompanied by 280 Colombian students." He counseled the president that to counter this subversive influence the Peace Corps should plan to expand the number of Volunteers to five hundred. Doing so would place volunteers in at least half of the twelve hundred Colombian towns with a population between three and ten thousand;

jet lag perhaps accounted for his questionable arithmetic. Later, with a ploy reminiscent of Edward Lansdale's cross-cultural proselytizing, Shriver claimed credit for new policy openings to Southeast Asia. By sending Peace Corps volunteers as "athletic instructors" to Sukarno's Indonesia, where "athletics is a matter of national pride and importance," Shriver hoped to woo the Indonesian leader away from his "pro-Soviet" stance. He boasted to the president, and later the press, that Sukarno invited the Peace Corps to become the first "operating agency of the U.S. Government to start work" in Indonesia since Kennedy had become president.[67]

Despite Shriver's eagerness to illustrate the Peace Corps's value in the overarching ideological contest between American "freedom" and Soviet communism, he refused to let the agency become a crudely wielded tool of direct American imperialism. He believed that the example of the volunteers' altruism, hardihood, and manly engagement in practical day-to-day struggle on behalf of the world's poor would answer the question "Is America qualified to lead the free world?" with a ringing affirmative. He saw danger to the new agency in any attempt by the United States to insert Peace Corps personnel and programs anywhere in the world without a wholehearted invitation from the host country. Therefore, Shriver took pains to ensure that the Peace Corps would maintain its "independence of strategic concerns." Anyone tainted by association with the CIA was persona non grata. Shriver used his privileged access to the president to prevent the CIA from surreptitiously "trying to stick fellows into the Peace Corps" as trainees.[68] Secretary of State Dean Rusk issued directives barring overseas personnel from attempts to recruit volunteers for intelligence functions, or any employment on behalf of the agencies controlled by the U.S. embassies: "The Peace Corps is not an instrument *of* foreign policy because to make it so would rob it of its contribution *to* foreign policy. . . . The Peace Corps is an opportunity for the nations of the world to learn what America is all about."[69]

The hard-boiled cold warriors in the national security apparatus usually did not find this proscription too onerous, because of the small size and (in their eyes) relative insignificance of the new agency. Nonetheless, some of Kennedy's bureaucratic warriors occasionally resented the Peace Corps's partial sequestration from the great game of empire. For them, the seemingly quixotic renunciation of any advantage, however small, in the global rivalry with communism was *foolish* idealism, a weakness that showed a deplorable lack of team spirit. "Shouldn't we quash this nonsense that PC [is] independent of US policy interest?" one national security staff bureaucrat tersely complained to his boss McGeorge Bundy. "Both AID and State want *Peace*

Corps in Algeria," he asserted, asking Bundy to apply pressure to the unresponsive agency director by arguing that the issue personally concerned the president. "Shriver needs a gentle straightening out," he counseled.⁷⁰

Bundy agreed that a large American presence in newly independent Algeria was desirable and that Peace Corps assistance on AID projects would further that end. He urged Shriver to forswear an aversion to "nasty international political considerations" and pitch in to advance U.S. strategic goals in Africa. An "entirely accidental benefit," Bundy added, was the "mildly irritating" effect the Peace Corps presence in Algeria would have on "some of those in Europe who are giving us the most trouble at the moment," referring to the de Gaulle government.⁷¹

Shriver remained obdurate. In the absence of an Algerian request for Peace Corps assistance he refused to impose the Peace Corps upon an unwilling or indifferent Algerian government. He retained his original conviction that his agency could best serve America's global mission by its public example of moral and physical strenuousness. Shriver saw challenges to the legitimacy of U.S. "leadership" from rivals abroad, and a feminized and decadent culture of consumption at home, as threats that must be answered. "Nikita Khrushchev is not alone in doubting the fibre of modern Americans," Shriver warned. "This is a question asked all around the world."⁷² For Kennedy's Peace Corps director, the political uses of highly visible masculine virtue—the example of American "stamina" and "sacrifice" in service to altruistic ideals—outweighed the marginal benefits of the *realpolitik* skullduggery favored by the national security bureaucrats.

The Kennedy administration politically exploited widespread elite fears of creeping "luxury" and "softness" among American men, seen as debilitating weaknesses in the grim national struggle with global communism. In his rhetoric and in his policy, Kennedy cast himself as one of a "tougher breed" of natural aristocrats dedicated to preserving U.S. power in the world. He rhetorically linked his counterinsurgency and foreign assistance policy initiatives with the prescriptions of *The Ugly American,* sharing its vision of reinvigorated masculine virtue as a bulwark against the decline of empire. Such narratives tied fashionable ideas about counterinsurgency and modernization theory to central American myths of manly republican virtue.

Kennedy's heroic new initiatives were a response to domestic political challenges, as well as to the perceived challenge of "world communism." They represented an effort to link administration policy to unquestionable and "natural" American male virtues: physical strength, force of will, adventurous bravery, technical competence, and frontier independence. Counterinsurgency and the Green Berets promised an aggressive response to the perceived threat of Soviet-inspired "wars of liberation" around the periphery of the empire. By fighting "brushfire wars" in places like South Vietnam or by sponsoring covert schemes to overthrow or assassinate Fidel Castro, Kennedy tried to answer his domestic critics who challenged his political legitimacy by labeling him a "weak sister."[73] Such risky confrontations also stemmed from his own concerns that powerful foreign rivals like Soviet premier Khrushchev be convinced of his "guts" and his willingness to defend the boundaries of "the free world." To answer liberal critics, the Peace Corps provided a counterpoint to Kennedy's emphasis on military confrontation. It offered Americans a crucible in which idealistic youth would forge manhood in service to progressive, anticommunist, postcolonial "nation building." The Peace Corps promised to advance American interests by example of virtue rather than costly large-scale foreign aid.

Counterinsurgency, the Peace Corps, and even the President's Council on Physical Fitness served the ideological needs of Kennedy and his staff while fitting their own identity narratives of elite masculinity. These programs symbolically linked the stoic manly values of the boarding-school ideology of masculinity with the frontier virtues that presumably made America powerful. Kennedy identified the strength of male bodies with the strength of the state. His programs offered solutions to a perceived crisis of masculinity at home and to the threatening encroachments of a rival empire abroad.

· EIGHT ·

MANHOOD, THE IMPERIAL BROTHERHOOD,

AND THE VIETNAM WAR

LBJ: I'm a prize fighter up against Jack Dempsey. Bob McNamara on the one hand & then Dean Rusk on the other. They still think there's a possibility that we'll quit.
Fulbright: Just why this particular area?
LBJ: Every expert you have confirmed holds "to retreat from stated objective would involve us in greater danger later."

McGeorge Bundy, notes from a meeting, July 28, 1965

I knew that Harry Truman and Dean Acheson had lost their effectiveness from the day that the Communists took over in China. I believed that the loss of China had played a large role in the rise of Joe McCarthy. And I knew that all these problems, taken together, were chickenshit compared with what might happen if we lost Vietnam. For this time there would be Robert Kennedy . . . telling everyone that I had betrayed John Kennedy's commitment to South Vietnam. . . . That I was a coward. An unmanly man. A man without a spine.

Lyndon Baines Johnson

P RESIDENTS Kennedy and Johnson each inherited the crisis of Vietnam from their predecessors. The South Vietnamese state, essentially a creation of the United States in the wake of the defeat of French colonialism in 1954, faced a long-term nationalist insurgency largely organized by Vietnamese communists. Each president believed he had only a very restricted set of permissible "options" available to attempt to rectify the problem. Each president took office amid dire predictions from their advisers that barring immediate action to forestall collapse, they could expect the imminent "loss" of the South Vietnamese client regime. Such a collapse fell outside the range of politically acceptable outcomes. The two Democratic presidents clearly remembered the lessons of the "loss" of China, and the political turmoil and damage done by right-wing Republicans who exploited the issue to discredit the Truman administration. Nor did either Kennedy or Johnson wish to be tarred by the label of "appeaser." In the peculiar imperial logic of containment, the collapse of the U.S.-created regime in South Vietnam would render U.S. leaders vulnerable to the charge of appeasement. The Munich analogy, however inappropriate, provided the primary historical model used to justify American involvement in Southeast Asia.[1]

The maintenance and defense of the South Vietnamese client state was complicated for U.S. national security strategists by a series of confusions about the precise nature of the imperial undertaking that underlay the U.S. involvement. The U.S. national security managers sought to maintain imperial influence in Southeast Asia, but did so without a conceptual language that acknowledged the existence of an American empire. The lack of such an explicit recognition of the imperial project largely precluded a systematic analysis of the measurable economic and strategic costs and benefits at stake in Vietnam. Policymakers were thrown back instead on a metaphorical and totalizing language of manly "strength" or "credibility" in defense of the "free world."

The warrior-intellectual identity narrative and the experience of a lifetime of contests for power, in boarding schools, in military service in the Second World War, and during the McCarthy-era Red and Lavender Scares provided a context that demanded the reflexive defense of boundaries and the rejection of "appeasement." The construction of political manhood itself precluded serious consideration of removal of U.S. forces from the contested territory. In the perpetual and recurrent memoranda outlining "options" for U.S. policy toward Vietnam, churned out by the national security advisers over the course of years, one theme remained constant: "Negotiated withdrawal: This would be recognized by our enemies and friends alike as total, ignominious, political and military defeat; a cowardly betrayal of our allies; and an abandonment of any American claim to honor or morality."[2] On the rare occasions when arguments against further expenditure of blood and treasure were broached, the elite masculine social reason of the imperial brotherhood placed them outside the realm of legitimate consideration.

In practice, the personal attributes of toughness and courage so valued by the imperial brotherhood meant conformity to Cold War orthodoxy and willingness to direct acts of violence against unseen foreigners. Their rhetoric celebrated those who possessed the courage to "make hard decisions," but those decisions never included options for peace which might have left the brotherhood vulnerable to hard-line domestic opponents. The result was an incremental escalation of force leading the United States inexorably into a war that devastated much of Southeast Asia, and that, in the words of one of its major architects, "caused terrible damage to America."[3]

John F. Kennedy's War

At the outset of his presidency, Kennedy was prodded to act to contain communism in Southeast Asia. Long a supporter of the Ngo Dinh Diem regime through the American Friends of Vietnam, in 1956 Kennedy identified South Vietnam as "our offspring" and asserted "that we cannot abandon it."[4] Within a week of assuming office, Kennedy met with Edward Lansdale (a covert "sire" of the Diem regime). Lansdale delivered a report on the situation in Vietnam and a plan for counterinsurgency based on a recent visit. Lansdale counseled renewed effort to beef up the military capacity of the Diem government; he lauded the enthusiasm and dedication of the Military Assistance Group in Saigon and disparaged the "defeatism" of the embassy staff and foreign service people in the imperial outpost. Kennedy, who had embraced the fictive imperial narrative of Lederer and Burdick's Colonel Hillandale, welcomed the suggestions of the real Edward Lansdale with enthusiasm, even prodding his assembled warrior-bureaucrats to go on the offensive. Not only did he want to buttress the training and armament of Diem's soldiers, he sought to have them initiate guerrilla attacks in North Vietnam.[5]

Kennedy periodically dispatched other favorite warrior-intellectuals to Vietnam to survey conditions and submit "options" for action to forestall the collapse of the South Vietnamese state. In November 1961, General Maxwell Taylor and Walt W. Rostow recommended the introduction of eight thousand American troops under guise of "flood relief" to begin fighting the insurgents. While Kennedy did not approve the immediate deployment of such a large contingent of American soldiers, he did authorize a steady buildup of "advisers" that reached nearly seventeen thousand by the end of 1963. A hoped-for solution lay in Roger Hilsman's plan to employ heroic antiguerrilla leaders and to implement a "strategic hamlet" program to cut off the insurgents from the support of Vietnamese villagers. "Brave and determined professionals," in short supply in the South Vietnamese Army, could be supplied by "American experts, Philippine veterans of the Huk campaign, and successful field officers from Malaya," Hilsman suggested. "The use of U.S. or SEATO personnel for critical jobs of forming and leading such groups and training indigenous leaders in Vietnam or abroad may afford results beyond the proportion first apparent from the numbers and costs involved."[6]

As we have seen, the individual heroism of the antiguerrilla soldier appealed to Kennedy. Counterinsurgency planning and doctrine proliferated.[7] The United States financed the other prong of Hilsman's plan, the strategic hamlet program, that fell under the control of Ngo Dinh Diem's brother Nhu. South Vietnamese peasants were uprooted from their ancestral villages and moved into fortified camps (constructed with their own forced labor) where, national security planners hoped, they could "defend themselves" against the Viet Cong. Communist "sympathizers" among the peasants could be more easily monitored and thus prevented from offering food and support to the insurgents. The Kennedy administration hoped to forestall the collapse of the Diem government without a massive intervention of U.S. ground troops. Besides the creation of strategic hamlets, other attempted solutions included counterinsurgency training for Diem's army, the use of American warplanes and aviators, and the aerial spraying of defoliant poisons in a campaign to destroy the crops and forest cover used by the elusive guerrillas.[8]

Saving Diem was imperative. Kennedy confided to Walt Rostow that a "communist takeover" in Vietnam would have the most dire domestic and foreign political consequences. Such domestic turmoil could threaten America's leadership of the imperial coalition; such a collapse of boundaries might set off a chain of disastrous events. The President told Rostow that the "loss" of Vietnam would

> produce a debate in the United States more acute than that over the loss of China. . . . The upshot would be a rise of left- and right-wing isolationism that would affect commitments in Europe as well as in Asia. Loss in confidence in the U.S. would be worldwide. Under these circumstances, Khrushchev and Mao could not refrain from acting to exploit the apparent shift in the balance of power. If Burma fell, Chinese power would be on the Indian frontier: the stability of all Asia, not merely Southeast Asia was involved. When the communist leaders had moved—after they were committed—the United States would then react. We would come plunging back to retrieve the situation. And a much more dangerous crisis would result, quite possibly a nuclear crisis.[9]

The efforts of the Kennedy administration to prevent the collapse of their imperial client were considerably impeded by the contradiction between U.S. development theory and doctrine and the political ambitions of the

tribute-taking dynastic regime of the Ngo family. A program of liberal developmentalism and liberal political reform underlay the economic development vital to "nation building" that U.S. elites presumed necessary to win
the allegiance of the peasantry. The counterinsurgency "concepts" articulated
by Lansdale, Hilsman, and others were predicated on remaking the political
economy of South Vietnam in the image of an idealized republican small-
producer democracy, such as supposedly formed the "traditional American
way." While the power of Diem and the Ngo family was very much the "offspring" of covert and overt U.S. intervention, Diem never proved very pli-
able.[10] Beginning with the creation of the South Vietnamese state, U.S.
officials repeatedly and largely without success urged Diem to institute land
reform and allow legitimate (liberal) political opposition. These pleas fell on
deaf ears. Diem's brother Ngo Dinh Nhu, head of the secret police, used brutal
repression to crush any political opposition to Diem, communist or not.[11]

Hilsman, National Security Council staffer Michael V. Forrestal, Undersecretary of State Averell Harriman, Undersecretary of State George Ball, and
others in the administration became progressively disenchanted with Diem
as the "strategic hamlet" program failed and the regime showed ominous
signs of instability. "We put Diem in power and he has doublecrossed us,"
Harriman declared. "Diem and his followers have betrayed us. . . . We had
made a mistake working with Nhu on the strategic hamlet plan."[12] It had
become apparent that Diem and Nhu used the program to line their pockets
and those of elite supporters and to better extract taxes and forced labor from
the peasantry. The Diem regime, one group in the Kennedy administration
came to believe, amounted to a "medieval, Oriental despotism of the classic
family type." Henry Cabot Lodge, the newly appointed U.S. ambassador to
Saigon, reported that the Kennedy administration had in effect nourished a
viper in its bosom: "it is clear that the U.S. has provided the weapons, training and money" to provided the despised Nhu with his own private army,
unconstrained by any U.S. control.[13]

During the summer and continuing into the fall of 1963, Diem's brutal
repression of Buddhist protest against his rule proved a public relations
nightmare for the Kennedy administration. The spectacle of the self-
immolation of protesting Buddhist bonzes caused public and congressional
revulsion toward Diem.[14] Roger Hilsman found himself in the position of
defending American support of the Diem regime to the "vital center" liberals'
favorite Cold War theologian, Reinhold Niebuhr. Hilsman countered
charges that the United States supported "the herding of many of Viet-Nam's
people into concentration camps called 'strategic hamlets,'" "that the U.S.
was engaged in the 'immoral spraying of crop-destroying chemicals,'" and

that the United States supported "'South Vietnam's religious persecution of Buddhists,'" by arguing that they were based on misinformation. The repression of the Buddhists didn't really amount to "religious persecution," Hilsman asserted. Strategic hamlets and defoliation were necessary to the "grim and often paradoxical internal terrorist warfare instigated covertly by the communists under the fiction of civil war"; both were "designed to advance the security of the Vietnamese peasant from Communist assault."[15]

While publicly defending U.S. support of Diem, the Kennedy national security bureaucrats understood that they faced a severe "operational" problem. The refusal of Diem to implement the liberal developmentalism desired by U.S. patrons and the prospect of the regime's collapse did not lead to a fundamental rethinking of U.S. goals. Nor did Kennedy's men make a realistic assessment of chances for U.S. success, given the absence of popular support for Diem or any other U.S. client government in Vietnam. They focused on the short-term actions required to maintain the fight against the communist insurgency, and thus to prevent the politically unacceptable "loss" of Vietnam. Kennedy's imperial managers split on the question of how best to maintain Vietnam as a bulwark of containment in the East. But they did not disagree on the wisdom or necessity of using U.S. power to that end. The Harriman-Hilsman-Forrestal faction particularly saw the "oriental despotism" of Diem and Nhu as an insuperable obstacle to the effective prosecution of a campaign of counterinsurgency. They first placed their hopes on the removal from power of "Brother Nhu" and Madame Nhu. The two were treated as symbols of the devious, inscrutable "Oriental mind."[16] This imperial narrative cast Madame Nhu as the beautiful but dangerous and malevolent Dragon Lady who used her sexual power to manipulate the chaste and unworldly (and thus weak and effeminate) Diem. Her intemperate public remarks claiming satisfaction with the "barbecue" of the bonzes infuriated U.S. national security managers, who became frantic to silence her.[17] "Brother Nhu" was depicted as an unstable, opium-addicted "Machiavellian" éminence grise possessed of hypnotic power over Diem. Together the two were blamed for the South Vietnamese government's political repression and arrogant independence from U.S. tutelage. The Kennedy administration tried to pressure Diem into ridding himself of his brother by suspending certain kinds of American aid to South Vietnam, but their leverage was limited by their desire not to damage the cherished counterinsurgency effort. Particularly alarming in the game of bluff between imperial patron and client were the noises that Nhu made concerning the possibility of ejecting the Americans altogether, and reaching some accommodation with Hanoi.[18] U.S. national security managers began to seriously consider ways to rid

Vice President Lyndon B. Johnson calls on Ngo Dinh Diem and Madame Ngo Dinh Nhu during his vist to South Vietnam in May 1961. Johnson lauded President Diem as "the Winston Churchill of Southeast Asia." Courtesy LBJ Library / Photo by USIA.

LBJ inspects South Vietnamese troops, May 1961. Courtesy LBJ Library / Photo by USIA.

themselves of their uncooperative client. Hilsman counseled Ambassador Lodge: "US Government cannot tolerate situation in which power lies in Nhu's hands. Diem must be given chance to rid himself of Nhu and his coterie and replace them with the best military and political personalities available. If in spite of all your efforts, Diem remains obdurate and refuses, then we must face the possibility that Diem himself cannot be preserved."[19]

There was the rub, from the perspective of the other faction of the Kennedy bureaucrats, including McNamara, Rusk, CIA director John McCone, former ambassador Frederick Nolting, Vice President Lyndon Johnson, and others. While unhappy with the "brutal methods" of Nhu's "secret police," they were skeptical that other, better proxies could be found to provide "a base for the fight against the Viet Cong."[20] Despite his faults, Diem, in their view, still represented the best available strongman to prosecute U.S. interests. Dean Rusk "recommended that Ambassador Lodge be told to tell Diem to start acting like the President of Vietnam and get on with the war." A motley collection of South Vietnamese generals, trained by the French colonial army, provided the only likely candidates to replace Diem. They lacked "the guts of Diem or Nhu," Nolting warned.[21]

Diem proved intractable. He refused to loosen his own autocratic grip on power in Vietnam through the removal of his brother Nhu and the apparatus of terror Nhu controlled. Hilsman and his allies in the administration repeatedly expressed the belief that "we cannot win the war unless Diem is removed." In late August, a divided Kennedy administration covertly gave official sanction to a group of generals plotting the overthrow of Diem.[22] But Kennedy soon had second thoughts about the wisdom of a coup.

The bad publicity surrounding Diem's repression of political opponents imperiled the administration's continuing ability to prop up an anticommunist client in the South. The president understood that he faced "a crisis of confidence in the Vietnamese Government on the part of the American public and more especially the American Congress" that threatened the flow of money to the proxy regime. Deposing Diem, it was hoped, would eliminate that danger. Nonetheless, given the uncertain reliability of the cabal of plotting generals, a coup was fraught with unforeseen hazards. Kennedy cabled Lodge, reserving the "contingent right to change course and reverse previous instructions" that had approved a coup, "until the very moment of the go signal for the operation by the Generals."[23]

The revulsion by Americans against the repressive Diem government could have offered an opportunity for the Kennedy administration to disentangle itself from its unsatisfactory imperial proxy. Paul Kattenburg, one of the few remaining State Department officials with training and experience in the history and culture of Vietnam, warned of looming disaster for the United States and counseled against deeper involvement in Vietnam. Kattenburg expressed his fears at a National Security Council meeting on August 31, 1963, carefully couching them in the masculine language of "honor." But the reflexive response by high-level imperial managers was to ridicule his suggestion for disengagement. The imperatives of political masculinity precluded serious consideration of the "withdrawal" option that Kattenburg tendered:

> I finally and imprudently for such meetings blurted out that I thought we should consider "withdrawal with honor." Dean Rusk and Lyndon Johnson's responses, cavalier dismissals of this thought, were indicative precisely of what I felt: that these men were leading themselves down a garden path to tragedy. We could not consider thoughts of withdrawal because of our "will to see it through," a euphemism once more hiding the fear of our top leadership that it might look weak—to Congress and the US public even more than to the Soviets.[24]

Ultimately, Diem's unresponsiveness to American pressure sealed his fate. Up to the last moment he ignored U.S. complaints that "we do not wish to be put in the extremely embarrassing position of condoning totalitarian acts which are against our traditions and ideals."[25] Facing such recalcitrance, Kennedy waffled, but never repudiated the idea of a coup. In early November 1963, the generals acted, deposing and murdering Diem and Nhu.

Perhaps the coup did not mesh well with the best "traditions and ideals" of American political culture, but nonetheless the Kennedy administration rushed to recognize the junta of the generals. Kennedy's men fervently hoped that by clearing away the obstructive Ngo dynasty, they could effectively defend the boundaries of the "free world" in Southeast Asia. Among themselves, U.S. imperial managers expressed desire for "a semblance of constitutionalism" in the new military regime. They hoped to preclude damaging "press speculation with respect to U.S. involvement in the coup." "Plausible denial" was possible: it could "truthfully be said that the U.S. was not privy to this coup planning." The important question, all agreed in meetings with the president, "was how to get on with the war in Vietnam against the Viet Cong."[26]

The coup ushered in a series of even more unstable "revolving door" juntas with no indigenous political legitimacy, utterly dependent on the United States for survival. Kennedy himself was assassinated three weeks later. The new president, Lyndon Johnson, inherited the problem of a chaotic and unstable proxy in the struggle to contain Asian revolution, made worse by the American-sanctioned coup.[27]

Lyndon Johnson and the Politics of Imperial Manhood

President Johnson deplored the coup and the murder of Diem. He, too, held the fixed conviction that the United States (and by extension his political fortunes) could not afford the "loss" of South Vietnam to communism. Johnson, a masterful operator in the Senate before his term as vice president, demanded absolute "loyalty" and consensus within his inner circle of national security managers. He inherited Kennedy's foreign policy personnel along with the Vietnamese crisis. His relationship with the "Harvards," as he labeled the Kennedy holdovers, was often uneasy, colored by his fear that their primary allegiance went to Robert Kennedy. Johnson wanted the prestige in foreign affairs that seemed to come with members of the Kennedy team, but he resented the enveloping aura of class privilege they carried.

Sensitive about comparisons between their Ivy League credentials and his education at San Marcos State Teacher's College, Johnson acted to establish dominance and test the loyalty of his privileged subordinates. This sometimes took the form of verbal challenges to their masculinity. In other cases it involved attempts to humiliate or embarrass them through calculated displays of his own body in ways appropriate, perhaps, to the rough-hewn male culture of the Texas hill country, but deliberately inappropriate to eastern establishment bureaucrats. For example, the Brahmin national security adviser McGeorge Bundy was "one of the delicate Kennedyites" Johnson targeted. "You are such a sissy," Johnson declared when Bundy indicated his preference for tennis over an invitation for golf with the president. "What do you want to run out here and play a girl's game for?" President Johnson occasionally conducted business with subordinates while perched upon the toilet "in an attempt to uncover, [to] heighten, the vulnerability of other men," as Richard Goodwin, himself subject to such treatment, later recalled. Unlike Goodwin, McGeorge Bundy failed the test, according to Johnson's account. Bundy, the president claimed:

> came into the bathroom with me and then found it utterly impossible to look at me while I sat there on the toilet. You'd think he had never seen those parts of the body before. For there he was, standing as far away from me as he possibly could, keeping his back toward me the whole time, trying to carry on a conversation. I could barely hear a word he said. I kept straining my ears and then finally I asked him to come a little closer to me. Then be-

gan the most ludicrous scene I had ever witnessed. Instead of turning around and walking over to me, he kept his face away from me and walked backwards, one rickety step at a time. For a moment there I thought he was going to fall into my lap. It certainly made me wonder how that man had made it so far in the world.[28]

Whatever his personal doubts about the manhood and loyalty of the Kennedy team, Johnson had opposed the coup that toppled Diem and worried that the factionalism that contributed to it was dangerous to the presidency. Nor did the new president fully appreciate the nuances of the counterinsurgency and development theories that so entranced the Kennedy bureaucrats. In one of the first meetings of the new administration the president directed that the bureaucracy stop the "bickering and any person that did not conform to policy should be removed." Johnson indicated a preference for directly forceful means to maintain the Saigon regime, as John McCone noted for the record: "he was anxious to get along, win the war—he didn't want as much effort placed on so-called social reforms."[29]

Johnson's national security managers were faced with conflicting imperatives. The South Vietnamese regime had to be preserved, even though it amounted to little more than small groups of feuding elites incapable of organizing and running a viable government. Devoid of indigenous political legitimacy, the tottering state of South Vietnam merely provided a fig leaf for the U.S. imperial presence. A massive military intervention was politically undesirable in an election year. So, too, was the prospect of the loss of Vietnam. The solution was to quietly conduct a holding operation—to "maintain the status quo" until the 1964 presidential election, while preparing for escalating levels of force afterward. The warrior-intellectual identity narrative demanded some kind of action, even when the warriors estimated such action had only limited potential for significant effect.[30]

In January 1964, McNamara, Rusk, McCone, and Bundy had Johnson approve a new campaign of "covert operations" against North Vietnam. An expansion of U.S. electronic intelligence gathering, U.S. overflights, and psychological warfare was crowned with OPLAN 34-A: "intensified sabotage operations in North Vietnam by Vietnamese personnel" run by the CIA. It was not the intent of 34-A to have a significant material impact on the North Vietnamese capacity to support the southern insurgency, which, as Secretary Rusk pointed out, was largely indigenous: "98% of the problem is in South Vietnam and not in cross-border operations." Instead, the hoped-for effect was psychological—a message of stoic resolve and "toughness" delivered to enemies—to "persuade Hanoi that we have no intention of quitting." The self-imposed imperative to demonstrate such vigorous and warlike determination demanded reasoning that contradicted their incipient understanding, based on empirical evidence, that the insurgency had strong indigenous nationalist roots. The undeclared war against the north would somehow, the virile bureaucrats argued, "put muscle behind our argument that the trouble comes from the north and that when that trouble stops, our presence in South Vietnam can become unnecessary."[31] Despite the hopes pinned on OPLAN 34-A, Johnson agreed with others outside the inner circle of advisers that "long-range over there, the odds are certainly against us." The ability to articulate one set of propositions about the nature of the problem, and then to recommend actions that logically contradict those propositions, evident here, is a recurrent pattern in the reams of paper expended on policy "options" by the national security managers. The imperative to do so was intimately connected to the maintenance of their identities as active, powerful men relentlessly defending boundaries against enemies, and tied also to the maintenance of political legitimacy and power.[32]

With the palpable failure of the government of South Vietnam to achieve stability and the strength to "pacify" its insurgent populace, U.S. policymakers stepped up contingency planning for an increase of "pressure" on the North Vietnamese state. The heroic and successful confrontation with the Soviets over missiles in Cuba provided the operational model for the war planners. They presumed that a campaign of graduated application of "pain" would induce the North Vietnamese government to see reason and to direct their instruments in the south to renounce the ambition and effort to unite Vietnam. The imperial brotherhood saw the alternative, "a bugout in Southeast Asia," as worrisome and unpalatable.[33]

By May 1964 national security planners had developed schemes for a "major stiffening" of U.S. "effort in South Vietnam, essentially by marrying Americans to Vietnamese at every level," as McGeorge Bundy's gendered metaphor described it. Bundy's language expressed a central aspect of the imperial, masculine identity narrative shared by the foreign policy bureaucrats. This narrative cast the South Vietnamese as weak supplicants, unable to defend themselves against a ruthless enemy without heroic U.S. efforts. "The object of this exercise is to provide what Khanh [then the South Vietnamese dictator du jour] has repeatedly asked for: the tall American at every point of stress and strain."[34]

Despite the implicitly imperial and orientalizing tropes employed by Johnson's national security bureaucrats, they vehemently denied the imputation that meaningful parallels could be drawn between the United States and the French empire thrown out of Vietnam in 1954. Charles Bohlen, ambassador to France, was dispatched to persuade the French leader General Charles de Gaulle to drop his advocacy of "neutralization" of Vietnam, and to line up behind U.S. policy. During the discussion Bohlen dismissed the Frenchman's assertion that the American predicament displayed remarkable similarity to the French imperial experience:

> General de Gaulle said that France did not agree with the U.S. in its analysis of the situation in that it did not consider that there was any real government in Vietnam. . . . He said that the war in essence was the same one that the French had been fighting since the end of the World War II: that the Vietnamese had no taste for this war and that the anti-Communist forces in Vietnam were not up to the task. I interrupted him to tell him . . . it was quite different, one was a colonial war which came out as colonial wars always do and the other was war against aggression directed and maintained from without.[35]

The clear warnings of European allies fell on deaf ears. Domestic politics helped propel the Johnson administration closer to full-scale intervention. A set of related incidents from the spring and summer of 1964 helps illustrate the pervasive politics of masculinity surrounding issues of national security and foreign policy decision making. Lyndon Johnson had learned well the political lessons of the "loss" of China during his tenure in the Senate. He and his high-level foreign policy advisers understood the political vulnerability of the Democratic Party to charges of weakness and "treason" based on the history of the countersubversion and counterperversion crusades of the 1950s.[36] His greatest political apprehensions concerning American policy toward Vietnam focused on the Right; he feared being blamed for the "loss" of Vietnam. His top advisers, inherited from Kennedy, reinforced these impulses. South Vietnam, counseled McGeorge Bundy, was "both a test of U.S. firmness and specifically a test of U.S. capacity to deal with 'wars of national liberation.'"[37]

Although some prominent journalists questioned the wisdom of deeper military involvement, other strident voices in the press seemed to confirm LBJ's estimation of the political risks inherent in a negotiated settlement. Bundy's friend Joseph Alsop, the Washington columnist, issued repeated shrill warnings of "catastrophe" to befall the empire if the president "duck[ed] the challenges in Viet-Nam." McGeorge Bundy kept Johnson appraised of Alsop's increasing bellicosity. He served as a middleman in his old friend's efforts to apply pressure for more military force, while advising the president how to keep the columnist's support: "Joe Alsop is back [from Sai-

gon] breathing absolute fire and sulfur about the need for war in South Vietnam. I'm going to see him this afternoon and find out just how alarmed he
is . . . I have a feeling that the best way to keep him on the reservation is for
you to have a few words."[38]

After a long career as an establishment pundit and journalist, Alsop considered his own foreign policy expertise equal to that of anyone in the Johnson administration. His frequent trips to South Vietnam convinced him that
without "direct American military pressure on the communist side" a U.S.
"defeat in Southeast Asia" loomed. The dominoes would topple and the
American imperium would crumble, he cautioned in May. After the loss of
the entire Pacific, including Japan and America's chain of island military
bases, "no sane man would bet a nickel on the future of the present regime
in India or would expect the eventual stabilization in Africa," he lectured.
"Even the American position as an Atlantic power would be gravely undermined. For this kind of staggering failure on one side of the globe never
passes unnoticed on the other side." Rather than accept defeat, Alsop prescribed a campaign of aerial bombing "to inflict enough damage on North
Vietnam to persuade Ho Chi Minh and his colleagues to abide by the Ge-
neva Treaties."[39]

Alsop's goal was to shape policy, not merely to analyze it. To that end, he
cast Johnson's holding operation as a "passive more-of-the-same policy."
Only "the more timid Washington policymakers" harbored doubts about the
wisdom of escalation, he asserted. Alsop pushed LBJ toward war—represented as the only action that would assure his presidency a heroic place in
history. A "neutralist government in the South," Alsop declared, was really
"a thinly concealed surrender." The columnist invoked the legacy of the recently martyred president: "for Lyndon B. Johnson, Viet-Nam is what the
second Cuban crisis was for John F. Kennedy." To lose the tiny Southeast
Asian client, Alsop asserted, meant political doom, just as the loss of China
had meant ruin for the Democratic administration a decade earlier: "As President Truman did in China, President Johnson now faces a situation in which
taking action will be bad politics now, whereas inaction will be worse politics
later." Alsop carefully cast the president's choices as stark polarities. To "neu-
tralize" Indochina and thus allow the Vietnamese to decide their own fate
revealed weakness, timidity and surrender; to launch America's powerful
technology of death against the (apparently) overmatched North Vietnamese
demonstrated strength, heroic leadership, and the realization of the nation's
imperial destiny. Alsop's unsolicited advice amounted to the conventional
wisdom of the imperial brotherhood, similar in essence to the recommendations of his close advisers. Nonetheless, LBJ came to deeply resent Alsop's

unrelenting public demands for war, believing such stridency circumscribed his choices. The journalist's repeated equation of negotiation with cowardice reduced the administration's room for maneuver because Alsop so effectively summarized Johnson's own view of the diplomatic and domestic consequences of "weakness."[40]

But despite recurrent calls to expand the war, President Johnson and some of his political cronies and erstwhile congressional colleagues were deeply pessimistic about the likely outcome of U.S. escalation. At the end of May, when the president sought his opinion, Senator Richard Russell warned his former protégé: "It's a tragic situation. It's just one of those places where you can't win. Anything you do is wrong." The senator from Georgia cautioned that U.S. military intervention would not work: "it would be a Korea on a much bigger scale and a worse scale. . . . If you go from Laos and Cambodia and Vietnam and bring North Vietnam into it too, it is the damnedest mess on earth. The French report that they lost 250,000 men and spent a couple of billion of their money and two billion of ours down there and just got the hell whipped out of them." When Johnson broached his war managers' proposal to bomb infiltration routes or "oil plants" in the North, Russell, bluntly, but with considerable prescience, dismissed an air war as a feasible solution to the dilemma:

> Oh, hell! That ain't worth a hoot. That's just impossible. . . . We tried it in
> Korea. We even got a lot of old B-29s to increase the bomb load and sent
> 'em over there and just dropped millions and millions of bombs, day and
> night, . . . they would knock the road at night and in the morning the
> damn people would be back traveling over it. We never could interdict all
> their lines of communication although we had absolute control of the seas
> and the air, and we never did stop them. And you ain't gonna stop these
> people either.[41]

Russell regarded Vietnam as a dangerous entanglement, not worth the profound risks of military intervention. Johnson asked him directly, "How important is it to us?" "It is isn't important a damn bit," Russell replied forcefully, "with all these new missile systems." American military security was not tied to any strategic imperative to hold Vietnam. Johnson was slightly taken aback: "Well, I guess it it's important to us—." "From a psychological standpoint," interjected Russell.[42]

Johnson confided to Russell that he too, had profound doubts about the wisdom of intervention in Vietnam. "I've got a little old sergeant that works for me over at the house and he's got six children and I just put him up as the United States Army, Air Force and Navy every time I think about making this decision and think about sending that father of those six kids in there. And what the hell are we going to get out of his doing it? And it just makes the chills run up my back. . . . I just haven't got the nerve to do it, and I don't see any other way out of it." But Johnson plaintively voiced bigger worries about the domestic political consequences if he failed to enlarge the war in Southeast Asia and thus "lost" territory to communism. "Well, they'd impeach a President though that would run out, wouldn't they? . . . outside of [Senator Wayne] Morse, everybody I talk to says you got to go in, including Hickenlooper, including all the Republicans."[43] Russell warned the president that while intervention "with all the troops" might look "pretty good right now" as a domestic and international political gesture, "it'll be the most expensive venture this country ever went into."[44]

Within minutes of the conclusion of his phone conversation with Richard Russell, LBJ consulted McGeorge Bundy. LBJ confessed that Vietnam "worried the hell out" of him—"I don't think it's worth fighting for and I don't think we can get out. . . . What the hell is Vietnam worth to me? What is Laos worth to me? What is it worth to this country?" Although he understood Vietnam or Laos to be of little intrinsic significance compared to the potential costs of war, the potential psychological effects of "softness" worried him deeply. "Of course, if you start running from the Communists, they may just chase you into your own kitchen." "That's the dilemma," Bundy agreed, "that is what the rest of that half of the world is going to think if this thing comes apart on us." LBJ wavered between his fear of appearing weak to domestic and foreign audiences and the apparent wisdom of those who counseled against escalation, simultaneously endorsing caution and disparaging the unmanly weakness of those who urged it. "Everybody I talk to that's got any sense in there says, 'Oh my God, ple-e-ease give this thought.' Of course, I was reading [Senator Mike] Mansfield's stuff this morning and it's just milquetoast as it can be. He got no spine at all. But this is a terrible thing we're getting ready to do." Bundy prodded Johnson toward a controlled toughness, to be expressed with bombs against North Vietnam: "We really need to do some target folder work, Mr. President, that shows precisely what we do and don't mean here. The main object is to kill as few people as possible while creating an environment in which the incentive to react is a low as possible."[45]

Sensing the president's hesitation to use force, Bundy tentatively ventured a suggestion that might take the political sting out of sending conscripts to fight an unpopular Asian war. The solution to the problem of "saying to a guy, 'You go to Vietnam and you fight in the rice paddies'" was to invoke the imperial brotherhood's tradition of volunteer heroism in war. "What would happen," Bundy mused, if the president were to say in a speech, "'And from now on, nobody goes to this task who doesn't volunteer.' I think we might turn around the atmosphere of our own people out there if it were a volunteer's enterprise." Johnson was skeptical, worried that volunteers would not materialize, fearing that the prospect of war was broadly unpopular. "I don't think it it's just [Senators] Morse and Russell and Gruening." Accepting LBJ's diagnosis, Bundy agreed: "I know it isn't, Mr. President. It's 90 percent of the people who don't want any part of this." The heroic burden of leadership, Bundy implied, must be borne by elites willing to ignore the reluctance of the populace to make the sacrifices required by duty.[46]

Johnson continued the circular and strangely schizophrenic behind-the-scenes discourse with his political cronies. In June LBJ again consulted Senator Richard Russell. Yet again he outlined his assessment of the political and military dilemma he faced: "I don't believe that the American people ever want me to run [from Vietnam]. . . . At the same time, I don't want to commit us to a war." Russell, chairman of the Armed Services Committee, agreed that there were no attractive alternatives: "We're just like the damn cow over a fence out there in Vietnam." The president fished for a commitment to intervention, recounting the pugnacious advice to defend boundaries given him by A. W. Moursund, a political crony from Johnson City, Texas.

> "Goddamn [Moursund said] there's not anything that'll destroy you as quick as pulling out, pulling up stakes and running. America wants, by God, prestige and power." I said, "Yeah, but I don't want to kill these folks." He said, "I don't give a damn. I didn't want to kill them in Korea, but if you don't stand up for America, there's nothing that a fellow in Johnson City"—or Georgia or any other place—"they'll forgive you for anything except being weak." Goldwater and all of 'em are raising hell about . . . hot pursuit and let's go in an bomb 'em.[47]

Without hesitation, Russell warned the president of the bloody stalemate he envisioned: "It'd take a half million men. They'd be bogged down there for ten years." But fear of the domestic political consequences of "weakness" gripped the southern senator too, despite his clairvoyance about the contemplated escalation. The "American inclination," Russell believed, was to "shoot back" when U.S. power was challenged. Russell offered equivocal advice to LBJ; the politics of manliness dictated continuing engagement in a losing battle, but the foreseeable damage to the national interest resulting from growing military intervention demanded withdrawal. Russell again outlined the double bind facing Johnson: "I don't know what the hell to do. I didn't ever want to get messed up down there. I do not agree with those brain trusters who say that this thing has got tremendous strategic and economic value and that we'll lose everything in Southeast Asia if we lose Vietnam. . . . But as a practical matter, we're in there and I don't know how you can tell the American people you're coming out. . . . They'll think that you've just been whipped, you've been ruined, you're scared. It'd be disastrous."[48]

LBJ seized upon the part of the senator's counsel that supported his own inclination to use force, proposing his own justification for escalation: "I think that I've got to say that I didn't get you in here, but we're in here by treaty and our national honor is at stake. And if this treaty's [SEATO] no good, none of 'em are any good. Therefore we're there. And being there, we've got to conduct ourselves like men." Johnson and Russell continued tracing circles, hoping to hit upon a politically acceptable solution to the Vietnam crisis. Johnson suggested that a "proposal . . . like Eisenhower worked out in Korea" could offer a way out. Russell then offered another assessment of the political psychology of the American electorate, at odds with his earlier estimate: "I think the people, if you get some sort of agreement all the way around, would understand it. . . . I don't think they'd be opposed to coming out. I don't think the American people want to stay in there. They've got enough sense that it's just a matter of face, that we can't just walk off and leave those people down there."[49]

Despite his very real doubts, LBJ saw no "honorable" alternative to force. The Gulf of Tonkin incidents of August 2 and 4, 1964, provided Johnson with an occasion to rally Congress around the flag by asking their support for an immediate military response to "aggression." Calculations about the domestic political value of a demonstration of military power also entered the equation. Immediately after the second of the real (August 2) and imagined (August 4) North Vietnamese attacks on the destroyers *Maddox* and *Turner Joy,* the Democratic president summoned the congressional leadership to confer with him.[50] Johnson entered the meeting with his resolve bolstered by political advice from friends that he should "make it look like a very firm stand." Barry Goldwater, Republican nominee for president, posed a special threat to Johnson's ability to project a convincing image of political manliness, they warned. "You're gonna be running against a man who's a wild man," fellow Texan and former treasury secretary Robert Anderson counseled; "if he can show any lack of firmness . . . this fella's gonna play all the angles." LBJ sought approval to bomb North Vietnam from conservative Republicans Bourke Hickenlooper, Charles Halleck, and Everett Dirksen, and from Democrats William Fulbright, Mike Mansfield, and Richard Russell. He posed the problem in terms designed to stir the patriotic impulse to defend boundaries. "We can tuck our tails and run, but if we do these countries will feel all they have to do to scare us is to shoot the American flag."[51]

The congressional leaders responded as the president wished, and he unleashed the waiting bombers to strike North Vietnam. The Gulf of Tonkin resolution subsequently passed by Congress at the president's request gave the executive branch carte blanche for future military action. Johnson's maneuvering was designed, in part, to outflank Goldwater, his presidential rival, and the Republican Right during an election year, by actions designed to seem at once tough but moderate. The "measured" bombing of North Vietnam made Johnson seem to respond strongly to "aggression" without reawakening domestic fears of another Korean-style "ground war in Asia" involving large numbers of American troops. He offered a studied contrast in masculine leadership, an image of reasoned strength, compared to Goldwater's militantly apocalyptic pronouncements.[52]

The Arizona senator was, as Johnson's director of the State Department's Bureau of Intelligence and Research later put it, "not your ordinary civilian presidential candidate." Goldwater projected a formidable image as a manly cold warrior. He was a major general in the air force, the "commander of a reserve unit on Capitol Hill called the 9999th Air Force Reserve Unit." Goldwater political advertisements displayed photographs of the candidate in the cockpit of a military jet aircraft dressed in flight gear, adjacent to the caption "He's a Space-Age Man with a Victory Plan!" In other photographs he appeared in his dress uniform standing at the Berlin Wall, or in a cowboy hat posed against the Arizona landscape. Goldwater's handlers sold him as a "Fighting Man," a "Courageous Man," an "All-American Man . . . THE MAN for President of the United States." The senator's publicists invoked his wartime service: despite a "knee injury" the senator had demanded active duty, and through the "intervention of both Arizona senators" spent World War II flying "multi-engine cargo planes over the China-Burma-India Hump." Goldwater, they boasted, had by then "logged 7,500 air hours as a military pilot." Goldwater's election-year speeches accused the president of "backdownsmanship" in relations with the communists. The Republican candidate taunted Johnson and his advisers as "architects of defeat." Against such an opponent, Lyndon Johnson worked to protect himself in the game of political manliness.[53] Domestically, Johnson used the retaliatory bombing to foreclose opportunities for Goldwater to bait him for "weakness" toward Asian communism. The president played down the likelihood of war during the campaign. He undertook no major initiatives in Vietnam, despite the perilous condition of the U.S. client state.

Johnson played a waiting game during the election season, urging his foreign policy officials to find an answer to the "internal feuding" of the South Vietnamese government, enmeshed in a seemingly endless series of coups and revolving-door juntas. The U.S. proxies in Saigon, however, refused to buckle down and effectively prosecute the war against the insurgents. The national security bureaucrats anticipated the need for "tough decisions" based on the "messed up situation" within the chaotic government of South Vietnam. As collapse in South Vietnam seemed imminent, the frenetic contingency planning began to include more radical solutions. By the end of August, McGeorge Bundy counseled the president that to prevent the loss of their Southeast Asian client, the United States should consider the introduction of ground troops: "A still more drastic possibility which no one is discussing is the use of substantial U.S. armed forces in operations against the Viet Cong. I myself believe that before we let this country go we should have a hard look at this grim alternative, and I do not at all think that it is a repetition of Korea. It seems to me at least possible that a couple of brigade-size units put in to do specific jobs about six weeks from now might be good medicine everywhere."[54]

Johnson, however, did not intend to introduce ground troops during the election campaign. The president, a Texan who claimed descent from ancestors who died at San Jacinto, was caught between the conflicts apparent from the counsel of his warrior-bureaucrats, the saber-rattling of his presidential rival Barry Goldwater, the anticipation of the political unpopularity of an Asian land war, and his own firmly entrenched abhorrence of "appeasement." The counsel of the patrician neo-stoic Bundy may well have struck a chord with him.[55] But his first priority was to win the 1964 election; he strove to position himself as a reasonable but firm leader.

Picking a way through the political dangers on each side led to contradictions between secret government policy and planning and political pronouncements for public consumption. A pattern of deception resulted. LBJ was careful to present an image of controlled power to the American public. The Texan assured midwestern audiences that while the United States would not retreat from South Vietnam, he "was not about to send American boys 9 or 10,000 miles from home to do what Asian boys ought to be doing for themselves."[56] "In Asia," Johnson declared, "we face an ambitious and aggressive China." But the United States was the "mightiest nation in the world," he continued, and such "great power cannot be put into the hands of those who would use it either impulsively or carelessly." Barry Goldwater was a man of the sort who "rattle their rockets some," and who "bluff about their bombs"; just the type of man, he implied, who would "seek a wider war. . . .

There are those that say you ought to go north and drop bombs, to try to wipe out the supply lines, and they think that would escalate the war. . . . We don't want to get involved in a nation with 700 million people and get tied down in a land war in Asia."[57] Under Johnson's leadership the United States was not about to "break our treaties" or "walk off and leave people who are searching for freedom," he declared. The solution to the threat to South Vietnam posed by Chinese communism was to "continue to make those people more effective and more efficient and do our best to resolve that situation where the aggressors will leave their neighbors alone. . . . We will not permit the independent nations of the East to be swallowed up by Communist conquest."[58]

In mid-October, less than three weeks before the election, the Republicans opened another salient in the political struggle, guaranteed to revive the Democrats' worst memories of the Red Scare and the politics of countersubversion and counterperversion. Walter Jenkins, Johnson's close and trusted aide for twenty-five years (and, ironically, White House liaison to the FBI), was arrested October 7 in the basement men's room of the YMCA near the White House, a place known as "a gathering spot for homosexuals." Jenkins forfeited the fifty-dollar bond and said nothing to the president or other White House officials.[59]

Alarm bells began ringing in the White House on the morning of October 14, when a local reporter asked Lady Bird Johnson's press secretary to comment on the arrest. It was soon determined that Jenkins had in fact been arrested, and the forfeiture of bond was, as we have seen, considered "proof" of guilt. The White House quickly dispatched lawyers Clark Clifford (a "wise man" and the future secretary of defense) and Abe Fortas (another "wise man" and a close adviser on Vietnam and other issues) in an attempt to contain the story. Fortas and Clifford made the rounds of the editorial offices of the Washington *Star*, the *Daily News,* and the *Post,* using their influence to delay the breaking of the story until Jenkins could be hustled into a guarded hospital room and shielded from the press. Dean Burch, chairman of the Republican National Committee, forced the issue into the open with a 6:00 P.M. statement asserting that "there is a report sweeping Washington that the White House is desperately trying to suppress a news story affecting the national security." Within a few minutes of Burch's statement, wire services reported Jenkins's hospitalization.[60]

The president "wavered between despair and anger." Johnson rightly feared that the Goldwater campaign would seize upon the presence of a homosexual presidential aide in an attempt to orchestrate a reprise of the Lavender Scare politics of the McCarthy era. Johnson himself shared stereotyped assumptions about homosexuals and threats to "security" in the State Department, perhaps adding to his distress over the potential political damage of the Jenkins scandal. Just a few months earlier in conversation with aides, LBJ had attributed newspaper leaks to homosexuals in the State Department: "McCarthy said about the State Department that they have to give these things because of sex or some other reason to these papers. And I'm beginning to believe that. 'Cause whenever they give to the papers—*regularly*—*systematically*—important things before even the President even decides them, somebody's got something on 'em."[61]

Johnson immediately and ruthlessly cut his losses and looked for a way to block Goldwater's use of the issue. When apprised of the situation he threatened to immediately fire Jenkins, but was persuaded to allow the devoted aide to proffer his resignation. Johnson refused to appear at a scheduled campaign event that evening until he was notified that Jenkins had resigned. The president put as much distance between himself and his scandal-tainted ex-employee as he could. Clifford later asserted that LBJ "never spoke of Walter Jenkins again: his faithful retainer became a nonperson."[62]

Johnson issued a statement the next day to announce that he had "requested and received Mr. Jenkins' resignation." He disavowed any prior knowledge of "questions with respect to [Jenkins's] personal conduct." To demonstrate his vigilance and resolve and to outflank the Republicans on the homosexuals-in-government issue, Johnson boasted of his decisiveness: "Within moments after being notified last night, I ordered Director J. Edgar Hoover of the FBI to make an immediate and comprehensive inquiry and report promptly to the American people."[63]

Despite the administration's efforts at containment, newspapers across the country gave front-page play to the story of Jenkins's arrest and resignation when the story appeared on October 15. Prominently displayed coverage of the scandal continued until election day. "Lyndon Aide Quits in Morals Case," blared a banner headline in the *Chicago Tribune;* the front pages of the *Washington Post* and the *New York Times* also carried the story. But potentially most damaging to Johnson and his presidential election campaign was the news reported by both the *Times* and the *Tribune* that police vice squad records revealed a previous arrest of Jenkins, five years earlier in the same YMCA men's room on charges of "disorderly conduct (pervert)."[64]

Pundits and commentators predicted that the homosexual scandal "was bound to be seriously detrimental to President Johnson's campaign." The case raised "questions of state," they argued. "There can be no place on the White House staff or in the upper echelons of government for a person of markedly deviant behavior," pronounced the editor of the *New York Times*.

At best, Johnson's relationship with Jenkins could be explained as a worri-some lapse of "security"; at worst, as the *Chicago Tribune* declared, it proved that a "cover-up [was] underway." Jenkins, the editors solemnly intoned, had "been installed at the President's elbow, privy to every secret of state and national security." They trotted out the old arguments linking communism, espionage, and "perversion" to condemn LBJ: "It is established Russian tac-tics to seize every opportunity of homosexuality, drunkenness, and loose character as means of blackmail to obtain secret information." The *Tribune* pronounced it a sex scandal as serious as the recent Profumo Affair that had brought down the British minister of war and badly damaged the Conserva-tive government.[65]

One "stroke of luck" provided Johnson leverage to reduce the political damage. Jenkins had been a member in good standing of the 9999th Air Force Reserve Unit, abolished by McNamara the day after the Republicans nominated Goldwater for president. Johnson, familiar with the politics of sexual blacklisting and the McCarthy-era Lavender Scare from his years in the Senate, looked for something he could use to intimidate his rival. Hoping to fight sexual scandal with sexual scandal, LBJ ordered the FBI to search for "derogatory information" on members of Goldwater's staff. A check of fifteen names turned up nothing. But the White House quickly discovered that all of Jenkins's recent fitness reports had been written by his commanding offi-cer, Major General Barry Goldwater. Newspapers promptly reported the connection. Despite Goldwater's denials, the apparent association restrained the Republican candidate from fully exploiting the issue of Jenkins's homo-sexuality; both Lyndon Johnson and Barry Goldwater had been "compro-mised" by association with a "security risk." As Republicans publicized the scandal, Johnson made sure that the newspapers again reported Goldwater's connection to the former White House aide. The press disclosed that FBI agents were dispatched one morning at 6:30 A.M. to question the candidate on his knowledge of "Jenkins' personal habits." Other news, too, helped di-vert some media attention from the scandal during its first days. The October 16 revelation of Soviet premier Nikita Khrushchev's ouster by rivals in the Politburo, and reports the following day of the first atomic bomb detonation by communist China, competed for front-page attention with the White House homosexual scandal.[66]

Goldwater struck a pose as a high-minded candidate who would not men-tion the Jenkins scandal "unless he [found] that it involve[d] a question of national security." He largely limited himself to innuendo about the "curious crew" surrounding LBJ, and to general condemnations of moral decay in the White House. But while Goldwater posed on the high road, his campaign aides and Republican allies gleefully gay-baited the White House, predicting that the scandal "would probably have a 'terrific impact' on the election." Dean Burch, Republican national chairman, vice presidential candidate William E. Miller, and former vice president Richard Nixon all took up the task of keeping the homosexual scandal in the headlines. They accused LBJ of a "coverup of corruption so deep that it casts a shadow over the White House itself." When the FBI released its report announcing that Jenkins's homosexuality had caused no breach of security, Dean Burch seized on a passage in the report that suggested that Jenkins "had limited association with some individuals who are alleged to be, or who admittedly are, sex deviates." "The important, unanswered questions," pronounced Burch, were: "Who are these sex deviates? Are they also employed by the federal government? If so, where do they work? When did Mr. Jenkins have 'limited association' with these sex deviates?"[67]

The Republicans repeatedly linked the presence of a homosexual in the White House to their assaults on Johnson's "weak" foreign policy. On the campaign trail, Goldwater's running mate claimed that "no man today can say there has or has not been a security leak," worrying that "Jenkins' arrest was a public police record for everyone to see—including the Communists." Moments later he denounced the "utter confusion" of the administration's Vietnam policy. "They don't know what to do except to instruct American soldiers to do enough to die but not enough to win," Miller seethed. Representative John M. Ashbrook of the House Committee on Un-American Activities decried the presence of Jenkins on the White House staff, fretting that the former aide had "been privy to the most sensitive deliberations of the American government—to our greatest secrets." Replaying the political rhetoric of the previous decade's Lavender Scare, Ashbrook blamed the Democrats for again abetting homosexual infiltration of the State Department. Not only had Jenkins compromised U.S. security, he warned, but "in this connection I would note that the records show that almost three times as many security risks were eliminated from the state department in 1963 as there were in 1960, indicating clearly an increase in the number of those risks." Playing the numbers game, Ashbrook cited executive session testimony by State Department security officials, revealing that in the years 1960–1963 respectively, 18, 24, 24, and 27 Washington employees of the State Department had been fired for homosexuality. Furthermore, press accounts of Ashbrook's statement revealed that "60 of 152 applicants for state department jobs were rejected because they were perverts."[68]

The press corps eagerly pursued the story, largely dispensing with the coded and euphemistic references common in the homosexual panic of the

1950s. The papers named Jenkins's sexual partner arrested with him in the YMCA men's room. They published extensive investigative pieces on the policies and procedures of the Metropolitan Police vice squad, trying to determine how Jenkins slipped through several "security" checks despite his 1959 arrest. Even Lieutenant Roy Blick, recently retired from the morals division, had another fleeting moment in the limelight. The *New York Times* reported that Blick had not notified Senator Johnson of the 1959 arrest, because he had been "burned" in earlier cases involving senators and their families. Feeding the renewed interest in the "question" of "homosexuals in government" a *New York Times* reporter discovered that Jenkins had written a memo admonishing federal officials to "invoke tighter screening procedures" to prevent homosexuals from obtaining government employment. Walter Trohan of the *Chicago Tribune,* an old crony of Joe McCarthy's, reported that Jenkins had once interceded with air force officials to try to reinstate an officer discharged "for a morals offense."[69]

Despite such intense scrutiny by newspapers and the "virtual monopoly on the morality issue" held by Goldwater, public reaction confounded the expectations of Washington insiders. Goldwater supporters, initially "elated" by anticipation of political damage to the Johnson campaign, saw their hopes dashed. President Johnson's political advisers were "greatly concerned" when the story broke, but a week later were relieved to see front-page newspaper stories on voter polls that showed a small *increase* in support for their candidate. Establishment columnist Walter Lippmann expressed distaste for Goldwater's campaign of "innuendo and insinuation, of sly hints and smirks," a form of "sneak attack." Public reaction, as reported by the press, was similar. After distancing himself from Jenkins and imposing stringent new security procedures on the White House, Johnson capitalized on public fears of Goldwater's extremism. On the stump, LBJ claimed to see a "trend away from the Republican party," the result of a "smearlash." "When some people get desperate they get dangerous, and when they are dangerous they are not cautious; and when they get to smearing and fearing some of their own people do not want to go along with them." As the election neared, Johnson counterattacked, asserting that Eisenhower had confronted "a situation similar to the Walter Jenkins episode," but that he had shown a humane forbearance and refused to politically exploit the case: "We Democrats felt sorry for him [i.e., Eisenhower's homosexual appointee]; thought it was a sickness and disease." Richard Nixon and other Republicans responded with outrage and charges of a "smear." Ike blandly told reporters that he didn't recall any "'problem' similar to the Walter Jenkins episode."[70]

The reactions, in 1964, of Johnson and his advisers to "aggressive" Asian communism and to a sudden vulnerability to a homosexual scare were predicated on their memory of the politics of 1949–52. Johnson formulated his response to the related crises to protect his administration from the misfortune and eventual electoral defeat that befell Truman, buffeted by the fallout from countersubversion and counterperversion and the outbreak of the Korean War. The widely publicized Jenkins scandal embarrassed the administration and provided another chastening lesson in the politics of manliness, reinforcing the predisposition toward "toughness" in foreign policy.[71]

During the fall and winter of 1964 the national security planners worked frantically to devise schemes to prevent the fall of Saigon to the insurgents. To the foreign policy bureaucrats, the loss of the Southeast Asian bulwark of containment was almost too painful and too dangerous to contemplate. Even though all estimates predicted the likely collapse of the regime, the bureaucrats approached the need to plan for that contingency with almost pathological wariness. John McNaughton, assistant secretary of defense, asked his new assistant, Daniel Ellsberg, to explore a series of possible scenarios in which South Vietnam did collapse, and to formulate possible U.S. responses to limit the damage. Before undertaking the task, McNaughton warned Ellsberg not to discuss his task with any colleagues in the department, and not to use a secretary to type the reports. A "leak" was perceived to be so dangerous politically and personally that Ellsberg was instructed to type the documents himself. The foreign policy reason of the manly warrior-intellectuals had clear boundaries; Ellsberg stepped very near the outer edge. Even to consider the possibility that the United States might "lose Indochina" conjured up the legacy of the countersubversive purges of the previous decade. "You should be clear," McNaughton cautioned, "that you could be signing the death warrant to your career by having anything to do with calculations and decisions like these. A lot of people were ruined for less."[72]

Much more likely to be rewarded were energetic efforts to devise a winning strategy. Much labor and attention went toward formulating contingency plans for "reprisals" against the North Vietnamese. The bureaucrats believed that the application of the principles of behaviorism to international diplomacy could preserve the South Vietnamese regime. Aerial bombing seemed to offer the promise of the efficient application of American technological superiority to deliver "messages" of "pain" to the men in Hanoi who presumably controlled the insurgents in the South. It was hoped, although never predicted with confidence, that the North Vietnamese leaders would act rationally in response to the graduated campaign of death and destruction; sensing U.S. resolve, they would abandon the war.[73]

In December 1964, as President Johnson conferred with his advisers on the grave situation in Vietnam, he braced for war. All that was needed to trigger American reprisals was an act of enemy "aggression": "DRV [North Vietnam] will bomb Saigon once. Then we are off to the races. . . . Day of reckoning is coming. Want to be sure we've done everything we can." Money was no obstacle to the anticipated escalation. The feeble, feminized South Vietnamese allies must be given all the reinforcement the United States could buy, commanded Johnson. "[I do] not want to send widow woman to slap Jack Dempsey."[74]

The anticipated provocation arrived on February 7, 1965, while National Security Adviser McGeorge Bundy visited South Vietnam. Viet Cong forces attacked the helicopter base and barracks of American military "advisers" at Pleiku in the Vietnamese Central Highlands. Ten days earlier Bundy, with Robert McNamara, had warned the president of "disastrous defeat" if the United States continued to wait for a "stable government" before deploying the "enormous power of the United States." After consultation with the U.S. "Country Team," and before making an inspection visit to the base at Pleiku with its dead and wounded Americans, Bundy recommended the start of the previously planned campaign of reprisal bombings against the North. Within fourteen hours of the raid on Pleiku, the president launched 132 carrier-borne aircraft on bombing sorties over North Vietnam. Johnson directed Maxwell Taylor, ambassador to Saigon, to begin the planned evacuation of American women and children. "We will carry out our December plan for continuing action against North Vietnam with modifications up and down in tempo and scale in the light of your recommendations as Bundy reports them," cabled the president.[75]

Despite the reprisal bombing, the president still hesitated at authorizing sustained aerial bombing of the North. His advisers encouraged him to begin "Phase II" or "Rolling Thunder"—a sustained campaign of bombing designed to "take the initiative" from the communists. McGeorge Bundy cast the situation much as journalist Joseph Alsop had: "The American investment is very large. . . . There is no way of negotiating ourselves out of Vietnam which offers any serious promise at present. . . . any negotiated withdrawal today would mean surrender on the installment plan." LBJ hesitated, worried that the instability of the South Vietnamese government could not provide a reliable base for such massive escalation of U.S. military intervention. In late February, another coup abetted by Ambassador Maxwell Taylor and the U.S. mission to Saigon deposed the unreliable General Khanh. On March 2, 1965, with the apparent emergence of a more "dependable" military junta and the mass arrests of South Vietnamese civil servants who supported a negotiated peace, Johnson dispatched the first U.S. aircraft in a campaign of sustained bombing against North Vietnam.[76]

In March, President Johnson demonstrated his resolve to a group of his high-level national security bureaucrats. He promised not to "give in" to "another Munich." If the United States did not defend imperial boundaries in Vietnam, Johnson argued, "then Thailand" would become the battleground. "Come Hell or high water, we're gonna stay there." He urged his cabinet and staff to "beg borrow or steal to get a government" to support the U.S. military presence in South Vietnam. The forced inactivity of the previous year had been frustrating. "We endured this thru a campaign," Johnson griped. But he made it clear that the humiliations of passivity need no longer be tolerated. The president evoked the heroic legacy of the frontier racial war of American myth. With a scrambled metaphor he exhorted his men to war: "You gotta get some Indians under your scalp."[77]

Johnson's war managers began to take large numbers of Vietnamese "scalps" with Rolling Thunder, the ongoing bombing attacks. The onset of the air campaign quickly led to the introduction of substantial numbers of U.S. ground troops, justified by the need to "protect American boys." First, marines were deployed to protect U.S. air installations, then more troops were added to conduct offensive operations in the areas around U.S. air bases to protect soldiers stationed on them. By the summer of 1965 the Pentagon had requested an increase of a hundred thousand troops, bringing levels to between 175,000 and 200,000. They projected needs for another hundred thousand within six months. The escalation that had proceeded headlong since April paused very briefly during July, while the president held a series of meetings with his war managers to "discuss in detail" the "alternatives" facing the United States in Vietnam.

The Social Reason of the Imperial Brotherhood

During 1964 and 1965, some in Congress dissented from the general bureaucratic consensus that the collapse of the proxy regime in Vietnam would represent a crushing blow to America's position as leader of the "free world." Three Democratic senators, Wayne Morse (Oregon), Ernest Gruening (Alaska), and Frank Church (Idaho) spoke publicly against escalation. Many others were dubious, but political loyalty to the president silenced them. Senator Mike Mansfield warned Johnson of the likely course of events in Vietnam and urged him to disentangle the United States from the fruitless enterprise. "We will find ourselves engaged merely in an indecisive, bloody, and costly military involvement," Mansfield cautioned. The adventure was doomed by "the absence of sufficient national interest to justify it to our own people." Mansfield believed that the benefits of maintaining American "prestige" did not justify a war in Asia, in view of the tangible costs he foresaw. The United States had gotten itself embroiled in a futile war in Korea because "we tended to talk ourselves out on a limb with overstatements of our purpose and commitment only to discover in the end that there were not sufficient American interests to support with blood and treasure in a desperate final plunge." Johnson was not receptive. One White House aide described the president's attitude: "He hated Mike Mansfield, just despised him."[78]

Vice President Hubert Humphrey, too, angered the president in mid-February 1965 with arguments against deepening the intervention in Vietnam. As was customary among men who dissented from conventional wisdom but sought to retain "influence" in government, Humphrey prefaced his missive with obsequious oaths of fealty, swearing "loyalty, help, and support." Humphrey eschewed global "strategic" arguments in favor of domestic political ones. He argued that war would be politically unpopular, especially with Democrats, that arguments justifying the intervention were politically barren and could not generate support at home, that the failure of the South Vietnamese government further jeopardized domestic support for war, that the potential for war with China (the Korean analogy) made the war unwise politically. Finally, he suggested that 1965 was the ideal time to "cut losses." "Indeed," Humphrey averred, "it is the first year when we can face the Vietnam problem without being preoccupied with the political repercussions from the Republican right." With remarkable prescience, Humphrey predicted that the administration's "political problems are likely to come from new and different sources (Democratic liberals, independents, labor) if we pursue an enlarged military policy very long."[79]

Morse, Gruening, Mansfield, and Humphrey were outside the inner circle of executive power and decision making, and thus easily dismissed. George Ball, undersecretary of state, had grave reservations about the wisdom of U.S. intervention, and his in-house role as devil's advocate reveals much about the process of reason in the inner circle of the imperial brotherhood. While Ball had spent much of his adult life as a powerful Washington lawyer involved in national and international politics, his upbringing didn't fully conform to the central patterns of the imperial brotherhood in the foreign policy bureaucracy. Although of prosperous and upwardly mobile family origins, Ball was educated in an Illinois public high school and at Northwestern University; he lacked the credentials (elite boarding school, Ivy League, clubman) that many of his associates possessed. Ball did not share the neo-stoic aristocratic or frontier identity narrative of warrior heroism. Youthful reading of the First World War "poetry of disillusion" by Wilfred Owen, Sigfried Sassoon, Robert Graves, and others had engendered in him a distaste for the celebration of hero myth. During World War II Ball did not serve in an elite military combat or operational unit; instead he participated in the Strategic Bombing Survey, conducted to assess the effectiveness of the air campaign against Germany and Japan. His wartime experience did not leave him with a personal narrative of heroic and victorious engagement in battle. Instead, he acquired a deep skepticism about the effectiveness of aerial bombardment, even against nations with a highly developed industrial infrastructure supposedly vulnerable to the crippling effects of air power.[80]

Ball's experience in international law during the forties and fifties had been closely tied to European trade issues. He worked closely with Jean Monnet, French statesman and architect of the European Coal and Steel Community. Ball's career trajectory gave him a distinct "Atlanticist" outlook. He believed that U.S. power and influence in the world was grounded in the leadership of the Atlantic community. He disdained entanglements in peripheral, politically chaotic, and economically undeveloped Third World nations as potentially wasteful and dangerous diversions from the interests that supported American power. Ball believed that tangible and substantial economic or strategic interests should be the yardstick used to measure the necessity of U.S. involvement in the world. Indonesia, which possessed rich natural resources and a large population and where Western oil corporations did business, was a Southeast Asian nation deserving American concern, Ball argued. Vietnam lacked such significance. Once, when Zanzibar seemed threatened by a "Chinese takeover," Ball twitted his fellow national security managers over their unquenchable zeal for "containment" even in such irrelevant African backwaters with a brief memo: "God watches every sparrow that may fall, so I don't see why we have to compete in that league."[81]

Perhaps most significantly, Ball, unlike his other associates in the national security bureaucracy, had closely followed the French debacle in Indochina. His French law clients had introduced him to the military and civilian architects of the colonial war. He saw firsthand the "self-deception" of leaders "seduced by self-serving arguments" while engaged in *la guerre sale* against a Viet Minh enemy with an "irrational willingness" to "take staggering losses." Over the course of years of transatlantic shuttling, Ball saw the futility of each in a series of new French "tactical schemes—the Navarre Plan, the Salan Plan, the LeClerc Plan, and the de Lattre de Tassigny Plan—that would magically assure victory in a short period."[82]

Ball had warned Kennedy in November 1961 that the Taylor-Rostow plan for the introduction of ground troops would "be a tragic error." "Within five years," Ball predicted, "we'll have three hundred thousand men in the paddies and jungles and never find them again. That was the French experience." Kennedy abruptly cut off the conversation, and Ball pursued it no farther. But in September and October 1964, deeply concerned about the drift of U.S. policy toward major intervention, Ball secretly prepared a memo of sixty-seven single-spaced pages analyzing the costs and benefits of American involvement. He foresaw the potential for disaster, and recommended that the United States "cut its losses" and find a negotiated settlement "under the best conditions obtainable." Ball sent the memo to McNamara, Rusk, and McGeorge Bundy. Their reaction, as Ball recounts it, was not to engage in debate over the challenges raised to U.S. policy, but to regard the existence of the memo itself with some alarm, for fear of "leaks." They treated it "as an idiosyncratic diversion from the only relevant problem: how to win the war." Neither McNamara, Rusk, or Bundy sent the memo on to the president.[83]

Their efforts at bureaucratic containment were only partly successful. Other imperial bureaucrats harbored profound doubts about the likely consequences of escalation. When William Bundy got wind of Ball's argument, he responded with his own forty-two-page memorandum in which he dared to argue that the loss of South Vietnam "could be made bearable." Since the South Vietnamese "had ceased to care strongly about defending themselves," they could take the blame in the eyes of the world. Bundy went farther, openly challenging the legitimacy of the South Vietnamese state, although blaming the French for the mess: "A bad colonial heritage of long standing, totally inadequate preparation for self-government by the colonial power, a colonialist war fought in half-baked fashion and lost, a nationalist movement taken over by Communism ruling in the other half of an ethnically and historically unified country, the Communist side inheriting much the better military force and far more than its share of the talent—these are the facts that dog us today."[84] American withdrawal, with prestige intact, could be accomplished by the use of more violence, Bundy argued. With the next Viet Cong provocation, the United States should respond with large-scale reprisal attacks against North Vietnam. Because the domino theory was overdrawn, the administration could then agree to international demands for Geneva-style negotiations leading to American withdrawal. But even the solution of "shooting your way out of the saloon," as Daniel Ellsberg phrased it, aroused great alarm within and without the bureaucracy, putting William Bundy's career at risk. When on November 23, after he had sent a memo with the disengagement plan to Rusk and McNamara, they summoned him to squelch the proposal. Bundy's bureaucratic superiors instructed him that "it won't wash." Admiral Mustin of the Joint Chiefs of Staff had been outraged by Bundy's proposal too, and protested vigorously. Bundy dropped his support for Ball's negotiated peace and began planning for escalation.[85]

Ball's heresies and William Bundy's tentative endorsement of a negotiated settlement, when word leaked out, provoked discord within the imperial brotherhood; perhaps in some measure they led to the vigorous suppression of in-house dissent by McNamara and Rusk. On the morning of November 23, Joseph Alsop's column warned that the "Europe minded" George Ball, "whose knowledge of Asia could be comfortably contained in a fairly small thimble, has none the less been signing memoranda advocating a negotiated settlement with the Vietnamese Communists." The only heartening news Alsop could offer was that in contrast to the "concealed surrender" advocated by Ball, "the more courageous and able" of Johnson's chief advisers" were on the "do something side." In fact, Alsop asserted, they appeared to "favor doing something pretty drastic" to save South Vietnam. William Bundy, caught that day between the doves and hawks within the administration, wrote an angry letter to his old friend Alsop. "From the most basic of all points of view—straight patriotism—this kind of piece measurably increases the difficulty of serious discussion within the government of grave issues," scolded Bundy. Alsop shot back a "peppery" reply, asserting both his patriotism and his journalistic duty to bring such "discussion with the government" to light. Public scrutiny would "prevent our always numerous scalawags and incompetents in office from advocating cowardly courses and doing dangerous things." It was left to McGeorge Bundy to mend fences with their politically influential imperial brother.[86]

Only in late February 1965, after the reprisal bombing campaign against the North had occurred, did Johnson actually see a copy of Ball's October memo questioning the practical wisdom of aerial bombing and escalation. Johnson did not unequivocally dismiss Ball's arguments. Between March and July, Ball wrote several memos to the president questioning the premises of the justifications for further U.S. intervention. Ball argued that the political and physical "terrain" of Vietnam could not support a large-scale American effort. Using the metaphor of a diseased body, Ball suggested that they "could not be sure how far the cancer has infected the whole body politic of South Viet-Nam"; a war in support of the regime would be like "administering cobalt treatment to a terminal case." Further, contrary to the assumptions of his fellow national security managers, Ball argued that the real danger to U.S. "prestige" lay in loudly proclaiming the vital importance of maintaining a

John J. McCloy, "'Chairman' of the establishment," confers with President Johnson about Vietnam during a meeting of the "Wise Men," July 1965. Courtesy LBJ Library / Photo by Yoichi Okamoto.

Undersecreatry of State George Ball presents his arguments against military escalation in Vietnam, while Secretary of State Dean Rusk (*center*) and President Johnson listen, July 1965. Courtesy LBJ Library / Photo by Yoichi Okamoto.

minor client regime, taking on a rag-tag guerrilla army with the full weight of American power, and then encountering stalemate or defeat.[87]

Ball's "cold-blooded calculation" did not sit well with Bundy, McNamara, and Rusk. They worked to contain the spread of such alarming ideas. The president agreed, in early July, to discuss two draft papers, one arguing "Ball's preference for a negotiated withdrawal" and the other "McNamara's recommendation of a substantial increase of military strength." Bundy reported that his two colleagues in the cabinet felt "strongly that the George Ball paper should not be argued with you in front of any audience larger than yourself, Rusk, McNamara, Ball, and me." They feared the political consequences if word reached the public that "withdrawal" was even considered within the realm of the possible: "it is exceedingly dangerous to have this possibility reported in a wider circle." Bundy himself was clearly apprehensive that the president might find Ball's argument persuasive. "My personal, private opinion is that both Rusk and McNamara are too diffident and that it would help you to have a few more people in the meeting."[88]

The practical test of Ball's arguments in the larger culture of the imperial bureaucracy came in late July 1965, as Lyndon Johnson convened his high-level Vietnam advisers to ponder the grave implication of sending U.S. troops in lots of a hundred thousand to fight in Vietnam, as Robert McNamara recommended.[89] George Ball later referred to the reasoning that led to the escalation as "turning logic on its head." More accurately stated, the process reveals the way that deeply ingrained ideologies of elite masculinity, buttressed by individual experience in the competition for power at both the personal and the collective level, created a context of conceivable meanings, a "logic," that made Ball's proposed course of action quite literally unthinkable.[90]

The July meetings were conducted along formally rational lines. They were designed to resolve the president's genuine doubts about the requested escalation by bringing to light the possible costs and benefits of the projected troop increases. Johnson demanded that his assembled counselors explain "what has happened in [the] recent past that requires this decision on my part? What are the alternatives? Also, I want more discussion on what we expect to flow from this decision."[91] While he cautioned that "we must make no snap judgments," and demanded of the gathering that "we must consider carefully all our options," the very language used to preface his questioning reveals an obsession with masculine "toughness" and "honor." Framing the debate in operational terms, Johnson instinctively led the discussion toward the issue of "prestige" and the appearance of "strength" and away from the assessment of economic, or directly strategic, costs and benefits. "Have we wrung every single soldier out of every country we can? Who else can help? Are we the only defenders of freedom in the world? . . . The negotiations, the pause [in the bombing campaign], all the other approaches have all been explored. It makes us look weak—with cap in hand. We have tried."[92] The president framed the issues to place the United States, under his leadership, at the center of a heroic narrative of moral and physical strength: would the assembled men act as strong men should? Would they shoulder the painful burden that others refused to defend, the central cultural value of freedom, or would they recommend that the United States crawl abjectly to face humiliation at the bargaining table? Unstated, but understood, was the assumption that such a humiliation would not only have dire international consequences, but would also undermine domestic political power and legitimacy.

George Ball, who understood the unspoken rules of loyalty and deference as the price of power, expressed his doubts about the course to be embarked upon—but first he reassured the assembled fraternity of his reliability: "I can foresee a perilous voyage—very dangerous—great apprehensions that we can win under these conditions. But, let me be clear, if the decision is to go ahead, I'm committed." He reassured his colleagues that his objections were strictly questions of pragmatism. He did not raise them because he thought escalation represented "a bad moral position." Ball did not challenge the propriety or wisdom of conducting an interventionist policy abroad to serve American interests. The question was simply whether or not the costs of intervention outweighed the benefits. Ball argued that a massive intervention did not serve to improve U.S. power in the world. He did not broach the issue of the legitimacy of the South Vietnamese state: he merely argued that it was moribund.

Henry Cabot Lodge agreed that the South Vietnamese State was moribund; his assessment reveals the imperial impulse that animated Vietnam policymaking under the rhetorical cover of defending democratic freedoms: "There is no tradition of a national government in Saigon. There are no roots in the country. Not until there is tranquillity can you have any stability. I don't think we ought to take this government seriously. There is no one who can do anything. We have to do what we think we ought to do regardless of what the Saigon government does. As we move ahead on a new phase—it gives us the right and duty to do certain things with or without the government's approval." Lodge argued, in essence, that it had proved impossible to arrange a suitable proxy to promote the "traditions and ideals" of American neo-stoic republicanism. The only politically organized subset of South Vietnamese society capable of creating and maintaining a state was the National Liberation Front, which was by definition outside the boundaries of inclusion in the "free world." Thus the "traditions and ideals" of the imperial brotherhood must hold sway; their "right" and "duty" was to discipline the unruly and chaotic imperial periphery by force of U.S. arms. None of the assembled apostles of freedom rose to defend the right of the South Vietnamese to democratic self-determination.

Ball, however, suggested that there were several operational flaws in the McNamara plan. The mission of the new troops "would be to seek out the VC in large scale units," McNamara and the generals asserted, and by "constantly harassing them, they will have to fight somewhere." The group conceded the likelihood that if the United States "put in 100,000 men, Ho Chi Minh" would "put in another 100,000," matching escalation with escalation. This prospect seemed to cheer General Wheeler, chief of an army possessing a fearsome industrialized technology of death. He blithely predicted that "this means greater bodies of men—which will allow us to cream them." Undersecretary Ball brought up the troubling possibility that "the VC will do what they did against the French—stay away from confrontation and not accommodate us." Ball predicted a quagmire: as American losses mounted the pressure to "create a larger war would be irresistible." Johnson asked Ball: "What other road can I go?" Ball's recommendation, to "take losses—let their government fall apart—negotiate—probable takeover by Communists," was, he conceded, "disagreeable." The president, who had read and discussed Ball's proposals for several months, found such a suggestion literally unthinkable; whatever the long-term dangers of intervention, negotiated withdrawal fell outside the boundaries of conceivable outcomes. Nonetheless, the ritual deliberations continued: "You have pointed out the danger, but you haven't proposed an alternative. We haven't always been right. We have no mortgage on victory. . . . I think it is desirable to hear you out—and determine if your suggestions are sound and ready to be followed."

Later that afternoon, the meeting reconvened. Ball listed reasons to avoid large-scale military entanglement in Vietnam: the possibility of intervention by China, as in the Korean War; the likelihood of losing public support as American casualties increased; world opinion turning against the United States with a protracted war. Ball expressed doubts that an "army of westerners can fight Orientals in Asian jungles and succeed." The undersecretary also attacked the notion that a war in Vietnam would buttress U.S. "prestige" and "credibility" with allies. Ball conveyed the opinion of the ambassador to Tokyo that "Japan thinks we are propping up a lifeless government and are on a sticky wicket. Between [a] long war and cutting our losses, the Japanese would go for the latter." Ball argued that Western European allies, too, believed that Vietnam was "not relevant to their situation." They were "concerned about their own security—troops in Berlin [had] real meaning, none in VN."[93]

Johnson quizzed Ball on the costs of abandoning South Vietnam to its fate: "Wouldn't all these countries say Uncle Sam is a paper tiger—wouldn't we lose credibility breaking the word of three presidents—if we get it up as you proposed. It would seem to be an irreparable blow. . . . You are not basically troubled by what the world would say about pulling out?" Ball replied that the damaging blow would come when "the mightiest power in the world can't defeat guerrillas." His face-saving prescription was to force the South Vietnamese government to invite the United States out, by stipulating conditions for involvement that the South Vietnamese would refuse to meet. Ball asked the president and his advisers to accept "a course that is costly, but can be limited to short-term costs."[94]

Ball's proposal was unthinkable to the conclave of national security managers. McGeorge Bundy complained that such a move threatened the legacy of U.S. imperial leadership: it "would be a radical switch without evidence that it should be done. It goes in the face of all we have said and done." Henry Cabot Lodge foresaw apocalyptic consequences if the United States failed to make war when challenged: "There is a greater threat [of] World War III if we don't go in." Appeasement, he argued, was the real danger, because of the "similarity to our indolence at Munich." Dean Rusk agreed with his virile patrician colleagues in their demand for unwavering defense of boundaries everywhere: "If the Communist world finds out we will not pursue our commitment to the end, I don't know where they will stay their hand."

During the next week, the president met several more times with civilian advisers, military leaders, and senior statesmen of the Cold War (the "wise men"). Paul Nitze, secretary of the navy, another distinguished patrician cold warrior (Hotchkiss School, Harvard, and the Porcellian club), counseled a deeper investment of men to prosecute the war, even though he estimated the chances of success at "about 60/40." Such poor odds were justified by the risks to U.S. power that would follow if the president avoided war: "to acknowledge that we couldn't beat the VC, the shape of the world will change."[95] Significantly, Nitze did not bother to explain the mechanics of the transformation, or even what the new shape might be. No one demanded that he explain. His "analysis," like that of the other imperial managers, was a merely ritual invocation of the need to exert U.S. power to keep rivals from presuming to challenge its preeminence. It was the reflex of a lifetime of immersion in the world of elite male power, sanctioned by the rewards of success in that world and reinforced by the history of the countersubversive struggles of the preceding fifteen years.

Robert McNamara did make predictions about the consequences of withdrawal, trotting out the image of toppling dominoes. The effect, he predicted, would be global, threatening even the eastern NATO territory and U.S. leadership of the Atlantic community: "Laos, Cambodia, Thailand, Burma, surely affect Malaysia. In 2–3 years Communist domination would stop there, but ripple effect would be great—Japan, India. We would have to give up some bases. Ayub would move closer to China. Greece, Turkey would move to neutralist position. Communist agitation would increase in Africa."[96] He provided no details about the mechanisms involved in the alarming transformation he foresaw, and no one asked for further explication.

The military brass, too, identified grave consequences to follow from withdrawal. While "the results of bombing actions" had not "been as fruitful and productive as we anticipated," persistence was the key, they argued. National security was at stake in Vietnam, General Greene asserted: "Matter of time before we go in some place else." The United States could not simply back out. "Pledge we made. Prestige before the rest of the world." Two courses of action were possible: "get out" or "stay in and win." The general did not address the first alternative. In the course of the colloquy Johnson expressed doubt about the necessity to honor a "commitment to jump off a building" after discovering "how high it is." He asked for reassurance: "I judge though that the big problem is one of national security. Is that right?" The assembled group unanimously assented to his proposition.[97]

Johnson had McGeorge Bundy read from a prepared memo to inoculate the assembled brotherhood against criticism they would face upon the announcement of escalation. Bundy's memo outlined the arguments against intervention: "For 10 years every step we have taken has been based on a previous failure. All we have done has failed and caused us to take another step which has failed. . . . we have made excessive claims we haven't been able to realize. . . . We are about to fight a war we can't fight and win, and the country we are trying to help is quitting. . . . aren't we talking about a military solution when the solution is political?"[98]

In meetings with the "wise men" only Clark Clifford recommended avoiding escalation, seeing nothing in store "but catastrophe for my country." "If we lose 50,000+," Clifford warned, "it will ruin us." John J. McCloy disagreed: "The country is looking to getting on with the war."[99] Despite the objections of Ball and Clifford, the overwhelming weight of the "establishment" advised large-scale intervention. Johnson finalized the decision to escalate by July 28, 1965, setting the United States on precisely the course predicted by Mansfield, Ball, and Clifford: a spiraling expenditure of blood and money to achieve a higher level of stalemate. For another three years Johnson and his national security bureaucrats struggled to manage a "limited" war amid growing domestic unrest, in the process devastating large areas of Southeast Asia with napalm, high-explosives, and defoliants. Their decisions led to the deaths of millions. In the end, Johnson handed the problem to his successor, as Kennedy had done to him.

Lyndon Johnson and his advisers—Bundy, McNamara, Rusk, and others—did not, as Ball asserts, "turn logic on its head." They used a different and incommensurable logic, the political logic of neo-stoic warrior manhood. The president and his advisers had the information and the cost-benefit calculations at their disposal that would have dictated a prudent tactical withdrawal from one hardly crucial salient in the great game of empire, had they employed the "logic" that Ball preferred.

The identity narrative of the imperial brotherhood demanded relentless defense of boundaries and an utter rejection of appeasement. The president and the men of the Johnson national security bureaucracy identified manhood with militant imperial anticommunism. They obsessively managed the conduct of the war, endlessly meeting to pick bombing targets, to fine-tune the "messages" of pain and pleasure (i.e., bombing pauses) they believed they were sending the North Vietnamese.

Lyndon Johnson especially, while mobilizing other men's bodies to do the fighting, metaphorically cast himself and his advisers as combatants: "It's like a prizefight. Our right is our military power, but our left must be our peace proposals."[100] Johnson cast himself as a "prizefighter up against Jack Dempsey"—and the United States as a barroom brawler locked in a struggle with the North Vietnamese, hoping to find a way to "get our feet on their neck."[101] Johnson had a predilection for sexual metaphors that identified his body with imperial struggle; a tactical setback resulting from attempts to arrange "negotiations" might be equated with homosexual penetration: "Oh yes, a bombing halt, I'll tell you what happens when there is a bombing halt. I halt and then Ho Chi Minh shoves his trucks right up my ass. That's your bombing halt."[102] Conversely, aggressive military action against the enemy carried connotations of sexual conquest. During the spring of 1965 he reassured congressional critics that his bombing would not spark a Chinese intervention: "I'm going up her leg an inch at a time. . . . I'll get the snatch before they know

what's happening, you see." To Johnson, the Gulf of Tonkin bombing symbolized a violent, sexualized male prowess: "I didn't just screw Ho Chi Minh.
I cut his pecker off."[103]

The failure of ever increasing levels of U.S. military force to accomplish
any of the hoped-for goals of the intervention became apparent as early as
late 1965. Domestic criticism challenging the morality and rationality of the
intervention grew too, just as Bundy had predicted. Many of the national
security warrior-bureaucrats suffered physically from the contradictions between a mandatory unwavering resolve to continue the war until the other
side backed down and the palpable failure and destructiveness of that policy.
The failure of "air mobility" and aerial bombing, so central to the war strategy of the establishment, perhaps also took a toll on the self-conception of
bureaucrats as active powerful agents in the prosecution of the war. Despite
the pain inflicted on both American and Vietnamese people, and despite
the self-inflicted pain suffered by the stoic bureaucrats, they pressed on
with the war.

Some began to manifest stress symptoms, milder, but at least analogous to
those of soldiers forced to be "passive" in dangerous circumstances. Dean
Rusk's son recounts finding his father writhing in pain on the living room
floor, convulsed with chronic stomach pains that "were never diagnosed despite dozens of physical exams and the best medical advice" obtainable.
Rusk's pain began "in the months prior to the American build-up in Vietnam
in 1965." William Bundy, assistant secretary of Far Eastern affairs, developed
ulcers; nonetheless, unlike his brother McGeorge, he stayed on at his post
until President Johnson left office. Robert McNamara, who began to realize
the futility of the bombing campaign by late 1965 or early 1966, developed
"bruxism," grinding his teeth in his sleep. He stoically managed the war for
Johnson for the next two and a half years, but by 1967 he developed a propen-
sity to break into tears at public appearances and in war planning meetings.
Lyndon Johnson feared that McNamara would become "another Forrestal,"
referring to the first secretary of defense, a suicide who suffered a breakdown
and leapt from a window at Bethesda Naval Hospital. President Johnson
refused to heed his defense secretary's advice in late 1967 to stop the bombing
and begin to extricate the United States from war in Southeast Asia. It took
the Tet Offensive of February 1968 and the advice of McNamara's replacement, Clark Clifford, to push the president in that direction.[104]

AFTERWORD

THE U.S. intervention in Vietnam was the product of a long and complex history. The social construction of masculinity among the elites who managed America's postcolonial empire must be accounted for in the effort to fully understand that history. How decision makers understood threats, and which responses they considered legitimate or even conceivable, followed in significant measure from ideologies of manhood, class, and culture. Gender ideologies can be seen from a functionalist perspective as cultural mechanisms that help ensure that the material conditions of survival are met: the prescriptions of "manliness" compel men to defend their society against internal and external threat, a role necessary to permit the work of production and reproduction to continue. That manhood ideologies can become "pathological" is evident, too. The example of the American war in Vietnam provides such evidence. A lifetime of immersion in masculine competition and a culture celebrating militarized manhood gave many highly educated, privileged, and powerful men the conviction that duty and the protection of both their own power and that of the nation demanded a war.[1]

Despite the rhetoric of personal courage and "toughness" central to the self-conception of the imperial brotherhood, the practical test of toughness meant the willingness to use American military power to kill unseen foreigners. Courage meant conformity to Cold War orthodoxy, not a willingness to confront the ongoing failure of that orthodoxy in the rice paddies and hamlets of Vietnam. But a self-congratulatory institutional culture of "courage" and "toughness," one that squelched independent thought and challenges to received wisdom, damaged the nation it professed to serve. Courage was defined in very narrow and particular ways—courage was as the brotherhood did. In retrospect, these claims to virtue seem perverse. After all, these were men of privilege who, to protect their own "credibility" and political power, fought a war with the lives and bodies of working- and middle-class Americans. Those of the inner policymaking circles who most clearly saw the futility and dangers of escalation refused to break ranks and publicly oppose a bankrupt policy of counterrevolutionary "bureaucratic homicide."[2] They refused even to privately press for extrication—when warned that withdrawal "won't wash," their self-protective careerism prevailed. Another kind of courage would have been required, the individual courage to risk their positions as imperial managers.

As Karl Marx observed, "Men make their own history, but they do not make it just as they please; they do not make it under circumstances chosen by themselves, but under circumstances directly encountered, given and transmitted from the past."[3] It is undeniable that the failures and brutalities of the Vietnam era policymakers are matters of individual responsibility, but explanations for individual actions follow an understanding of the cultural and political structures that licensed those acts. The men who came to power in the Kennedy and Johnson administrations had been formed by a series of institutions which glorified empire while officially denying its existence. Boarding schools, Ivy League universities, elite men's clubs, and volunteer military service provided explicit lessons in the performance of a class-based "manliness" as means to and justification for power. The "prize of command," as Dean Acheson celebrated it, came to these men as the United States consolidated its global primacy in the wake of the Second World War; the success of the empire was construed by the brotherhood as the result of the heroic strivings of those "present at the creation" of the postwar order. The stories they told themselves and the images they projected to the electorate touted their reputations as warrior-intellectual statesmen.

But darker memories of the domestic political culture of the early Cold War also helped shape the foreign policy thinking of John Kennedy, Lyndon Johnson, and the advisers who served them. The McCarthy-era countersubversion and counterperversion crusades destroyed or damaged the careers of many prominent State Department diplomats. A newly institutionalized culture of secrecy enabled an alliance of resentful congressional conservatives, the FBI, and right-wing security agency bureaucrats to seriously challenge the political power of the imperial brotherhood. By casting homosexual men as "security risks" vulnerable to blackmail, and by institutionalizing a profoundly intrusive sexual inquisition mirroring the anticommunist witchhunt, the McCarthy-era "pervert" hunters made sexuality and sexual secrets important weapons in the struggle for power in Washington. With the homosexual purge they damaged or destroyed the careers of several prominent diplomats, lending apparent credence to McCarthy's indictment of "commies and queers" in the State Department. This stigmatizing discourse equating diplomacy, appeasement, weakness, and conspiratorial homosexuality continued to shape assumptions about manliness and political legitimacy in Washington. Thus the ideologies of masculinity internalized by the imperial brotherhood contained both prescriptive and proscriptive dimensions. The examples of the punishment inflicted on establishment figures accused of appeasement, conspiracy, and "perversion" powerfully reinforced the bureaucratic impulse toward an aggressive, boundary-defending anticommunism.

The politics of manhood crucially shaped the tragedy of Vietnam. Presidents Kennedy and Johnson, along with their national security bureaucrats, made the fateful incremental decisions for war in a political and personal double bind. While their own intelligence reports, war game models, and political assessments predicted the futility of escalating violence, to abandon the otherwise insignificant imperial client seemed to threaten, collectively and individually, their very sense of self as well as their political careers. While all harbored doubts, open dissent proved impossible, silenced by the code of the brotherhood and the memory of the fate that befell predecessors accused of foreign policy weakness. Trained to celebrate "sacrifice" in service to the state, none mustered the courage to risk the sacrifice of their own career in an effort to prevent a foreseeable disaster. The belief that the American electorate would "forgive" its leaders "anything but being weak" pushed Lyndon Johnson and his advisers into the tragic escalation of a war they feared; a war they predicted the United States could not win.

NOTES

Introduction

1. Questions about the decisions that led the United States into war in Vietnam have generated a huge literature. For a useful bibliography that emphasizes a political science approach to Vietnam decision making, see Barrett, *Uncertain Warriors.* Barrett's book is an attempt to answer a question that animates a part of this book; as he puts it, "how could a rational advisory system produce such a 'bad' war?" Barrett attempts to reconcile "structural" and "personalist" explanations for the "irrational" outcome of the foreign policy decision process under Lyndon Johnson, using traditional political science models. While "ideology" is a factor in his explanation, gender as an element shaping ideology is absent. See especially his "Afterword: On Rationality, Johnson's Worldview, and the War." Other essays that offer useful introductions to the historiography of the Vietnam war include Divine, "Vietnam Reconsidered," and the "Bibliographical Note" in VanDeMark, *Into the Quagmire.*

2. McNamara, *In Retrospect.*

3. See, for instance, the "McNamara's memoirs" thread on the H-Net H-Diplo Internet discussion group, late spring and summer 1995.

4. Johns, "Re: McNamara's Memoirs."

5. McNamara, *In Retrospect,* 203.

6. Ibid., xvi.

7. A few examples of the large literature which examines the process of Vietnam decision making include Berman, *Planning a Tragedy;* Berman, *Lyndon Johnson's War;* Gelb and Betts, *The Irony of Vietnam;* Kahin, *Intervention;* VanDeMark, *Into the Quagmire;* Burke and Greenstein, *How Presidents Test Reality.*

8. On the gendered meanings of "prestige," "credibility," "honor," etc. associated with the defense of boundaries, see Gilmore, *Manhood in the Making*.

9. Some examples include Barnet, *Roots of War;* Beschloss, *The Crisis Years;* Halberstam, *Best and Brightest;* Kearns, *Lyndon Johnson and the American Dream*. One brief pioneering essay of the 1970s attempted to explicitly link the social construction of masculinity with Vietnam policy; see Fasteau, "Vietnam and the Cult of Toughness in Foreign Policy," in *The Male Machine*.

10. Isaacson and Thomas, *Wise Men,* 26; Barnet, *Roots of War,* 48–49. On the postwar "establishment," see Hodgson, "The Establishment," 3–40. Other useful works include Bird, *The Chairman,* and Hodgson, *The Colonel.*

11. See Cumings, *Origins of the Korean War,* 23–31, on the class origins and economic interests at the root of the domestic politics of U.S. foreign policy during the early Cold War. For an introduction to the sexualized political discourse of the Cold War, see Smith, "National Security and Personal Isolation," 307–37.

12. I use a variety of sources to construct the argument that follows. Because of the relatively "private" nature of some aspects of the patterns I describe, and the large number of individuals studied, I must sometimes rely on oral history interviews, published memoirs, and the careful collation of "secondary" accounts by historians and journalists for some parts of my argument. While archival documents are often to be preferred, issues such as the particular formative experiences of boys at boarding school, or men at war, or the ways that sexuality is linked to social power and the politics of inclusion and exclusion are often not directly accessible in the archives. In the cases where helpful documents do exist, privacy restrictions by individual donors or by federal agencies often prevent access.

13. On identity narrative as the "central means by which people endow their lives with meaning across time," see Gergen and Gergen, "Autobiographies and Gendered Lives"; on narrative identity and experience of war, see Rosenberg, "Threshold of Thrill," 43. Also see Roper and Tosh, *Manful Assertions,* 14–15, on cultural representations of heroism and the construction of masculine identity narratives.

14. Cohn, "Wars, Wimps, and Women," 228; Scott, "Gender," 1069–1070.

15. Dawson, *Soldier Heroes,* 1, 22–23. The idea that constructed "narratives" are central to human experience of the world is by now quite widespread across scholarly disciplines. For instance, one can now find it even employed by evolutionary paleontologists and population geneticists; see Gould, "Speaking of Snails and Scales," 14–15; Lewontin "'Sex, Lies, and Social Science': An Exchange," 44.

16. Dawson, *Soldier Heroes,* 23. For a useful theoretical discussion of the role of narrative in the construction of gender, see Dawson, chap. 1.

17. Ibid., 23.

18. For one example, see chapter 3 on the contradictions between boarding-school ideals of manliness and the relations of power with the student peer group.

19. See D'Emilio, *Sexual Politics, Sexual Communities.*

1. The Foreign Policy "Establishment"

1. Sorensen, interview; Kennedy, *Thirteen Days*.

2. Lovett, interview, November 19, 1964, 2, 4. Henry L. Stimson (1867–1950), a prominent Wall Street lawyer, served as secretary of war, 1911–13; governor-general of the Philippines, 1928–29; secretary of state, 1929–33; and secretary of war, 1940–45.

3. Lovett, interview, November 19, 1964, 4; Hodgson, *The Colonel*, 386.

4. Stimson and Bundy, *On Active Service*, 676.

5. Quote from John J. McCloy, commencement address, Haverford College, 1965, box 72, Alsop Papers.

6. Bundy, *Pattern of Responsibility*, viii. Bundy, a Republican, had also worked under Richard Bissell, his old Yale economics professor, on the Marshall plan, and had written foreign policy speeches for Thomas Dewey in 1948. Bundy was connected to Acheson by affinal ties, too; his brother William, employed by the CIA during the fifties, was married to Acheson's daughter, Mary Eleanor.

7. On the foreign policy "establishment" that was particularly influential between 1947 and 1968, see Hodgson, "The Establishment," 3–40. Useful works that use the concept of a foreign policy "establishment" for analysis of American foreign policy include Barnet, *Roots of War;* Halberstam, *Best and Brightest;* Isaacson and Thomas, *Wise Men;* and Bird, *The Chairman*. On Stimson's role in the creation of a foreign policy establishment, see Hodgson, *The Colonel*, 367–90.

8. McCloy, commencement address. McGeorge Bundy too, later referred to the missile crisis as the "most important single event of the Kennedy Presidency," a success attributable to the heroic statesmanship of President Kennedy. See Bundy, "Presidency and the Peace," esp. 359–61.

9. McCloy, commencement address.

10. See McLachlan, *American Boarding Schools;* Ashburn, *Peabody of Groton*.

11. Hodgson, *The Colonel*, 36, 247; Bird, *Color of Truth*, 62. Both McGeorge and his brother William were Bonesmen, as was their father Harvey, one of Stimson's closest assistants during Stimson's tenure as secretary of state under Hoover, and as secretary of war under FDR.

12. See Bird, *The Chairman*, 15–20, 31–46. On the Plattsburg movement, its class composition and links to the elite men's clubs of New York and Boston, see Clifford, "Plattsburg and 'Our Kind of People,'" in *Citizen Soldiers;* and Pearlman, *To Make Democracy Safe*, who provides a rich study of the connections between class, culture, and military "preparedness." On McNamara see Shapley, *Promise and Power;* on Rusk, see Rusk, *As I Saw It*.

13. Schlesinger, *Thousand Days*, 127–33; Bird, *The Chairman*, 495–99; Alsop, *I've Seen the Best of It*, 420.

14. Baltzell, *Protestant Establishment*, 81; Hamilton, *JFK*, 208–9; Halberstam, *Best and Brightest*, 124–25. For a useful insider's account of the composition of the "old money" upper class, the "curriculum" of the American upper class, and the pattern of "ordeals" used to construct upper-class (masculine) identity, see Aldrich, *Old Money*.

15. Lovett, interview, July 20, 1964; Acheson, interview. McNamara, for example,

was offered a cabinet post largely on the recommendation of Robert Lovett, who had first encountered McNamara during World War II as part of the Army Air Corps's "Whiz Kids" (Tex Thornton's Statistical Control unit). After his appointment by the president-elect, McNamara consulted with Lovett and John J. McCloy for recommendations on staffing the Defense Department. See Shapley, *Promise and Power,* 27–37; and McNamara, *In Retrospect,* 17.

16. Alsop, *I've Seen the Best of It,* 38–39, 442–43. On Alsop's career as both reporter and shaper of U.S. foreign policy, see, Almquist, *Joseph Alsop.*

2. The Reproduction of Imperial Manhood

1. Several sociologists and historians have studied the emergence and perpetuation of an "eastern establishment" and emphasized the role of boarding schools, elite university fraternities and senior societies, and elite metropolitan men's clubs in, as C. Wright Mills put it, "transmitting the traditions of the upper social classes, and regulating the admission of new wealth and talent." This scholarship has focused on class and religious-ethnic-racial aspects of the cultural construction of the "establishment" with little analytical effort devoted to the role of gender in these sex-segregated institutions. For a succinct discussion of the "boarding school–university club" institutional system of social accreditation, see White, "The Formation of an Eastern Establishment," in *Eastern Establishment.* For two politically divergent sociological approaches see Mills, *Power Elite,* and Baltzell, *Protestant Establishment,* or Baltzell, *Philadelphia Gentlemen.*

2. Levine, "Rise of American Boarding Schools," 67, 70–71; Cookson and Persell, *Preparing for Power,* 23; Baltzell, *Protestant Establishment Revisited,* 5; Baltzell, *Philadelphia Gentlemen,* 357.

3. McLachlan, *American Boarding Schools,* 153–54, 203, 246, 254–55, 257. Of twelve of America's "leading" boarding schools, seven were founded between 1883 and 1906, and three between 1851 and 1865. Andover and Exeter academies, while founded in the late eighteenth century, did not adopt the exclusively college-prep, boarding-school model until the late 1880s. See Levine, "Rise of American Boarding Schools," 64.

4. On the "transatlantic cult of manliness" that flourished in Britain and the United States between 1850 and 1940, see Mangan and Walvin, *Manliness and Morality,* 2–5. Wister, *Roosevelt,* 66; Lears, *No Place of Grace,* 108–9; Levine, "Rise of American Boarding Schools," 68–73. Aldrich, *Old Money,* 112.

5. Cookson and Persell, *Preparing for Power,* 22–26; Goffman, "Characteristics of Total Institutions," 64.

6. Endicott Peabody, quoted in Morgan, *FDR,* 58; McLachlan, *American Boarding Schools,* 287, 293–96.

7. Philips Brooks (Episcopalian bishop of Massachusetts, 1891–93), addressing students at St. Paul's School; quoted in Saveth, "Education of an Elite." On republicanism in elite boarding schools, see Saveth, 373–77. On the gendered dimensions of republicanism see Kann, *On the Man Question.*

8. Ashburn, *Peabody of Groton,* 319–22, 404; McLachlan, *American Boarding Schools,* 296; John Train, "Letter to a Classmate," in Zahner, *Views from the Circle,* 288.

9. Dean Acheson, "Address, Prize Day 1966, Groton School," box 166, Ball Papers.

10. Ibid.

11. Henry Cabot Lodge to Endicott Peabody (headmaster of Groton), August 17, 1898, cited in McLachlan, *American Boarding Schools,* 294.

12. Christopher T. E. Rand, "The School in Time and Space," in Zahner, *Views from the Circle,* 224–25. It should be borne in mind that this was written not long after Joseph McCarthy and others had conducted a systematic attack on the prerogatives and power of the "Anglophile element," an attack that demonized FDR and Dean Acheson as symbols of "weakness," treason, etc. in American foreign policy. The gender and class dimensions of the Red Scare will be discussed in later chapters.

13. On the "purified male social order" and the importance of initiation into "male solidarity groups" for the reproduction of ideologies of male social dominance, see Sanday, *Fraternity Gang Rape,* 135–93.

14. Alsop, *I've Seen the Best of It,* 59.

15. Peabody was descended from early Puritans and wealthy Salem merchants in the China trade. He had family connections to the investment banking world of the House of Morgan, and to Lee, Higginson and Co., and he had blood ties to many prominent Boston "Brahmin" lineages. He remained as headmaster of Groton for fifty-six years, retiring in 1940. During his long career he trained several generations of prominent "establishment" figures connected to America's empire: an incomplete list includes the sons and grandsons of Theodore Roosevelt, the sons of General Leonard Wood, the son of Alfred Thayer Mahan, Franklin Roosevelt and his sons, Joseph C. Grew, Sumner Welles; among the Groton old boys of Peabody's era prominent in one capacity or another during the Kennedy administration were Averell Harriman, Dean Acheson, C. Douglas Dillon, Richard Bissell, William and McGeorge Bundy, and the influential journalists Joseph and Stewart Alsop. However, other boarding schools like Choate, Hotchkiss, St. Paul's, Milton, Kent, Middlesex, and Hill (whose alumni were represented in the Kennedy foreign policy apparatus), or even the Peddie Institute, promulgated a similar cult of manliness. See McLachlan, *American Boarding Schools,* 189–241; Baltzell, *Philadelphia Gentlemen,* 303; Ashburn, *Peabody of Groton,* 1–21. Pearlman, *To Make Democracy Safe,* 100–101.

16. Ashburn, *Peabody of Groton,* 68, 38–39, 22–29; McLachlan, *American Boarding Schools,* 154. For a useful essay on the relation between muscular Christianity and Social Darwinism in English public schools during the period of Peabody's education and the early years of Groton, see J. A. Mangan, "Social Darwinism and Upper-Class Education in Late Victorian and Edwardian England," in Mangan and Walvin, *Manliness and Morality,* 133–59.

17. Edward Thring, quoted in Hyam, *Empire and Sexuality,* 71–72. On the role of public schools in the construction of imperial upper-class masculine "gentlemen" to run the British empire, see Callaway, *Gender, Culture, and Empire,* 39–42.

18. On the cultural narrative of political legitimation which accompanied the eastern patrician's western adventures, see Green, *Dreams of Adventure,* esp. 150; and

Green, *Adventurous Male*, 151–53; White, *Eastern Establishment*, 196–200. On the role of the western adventure as the "ordeal by Nature" in the construction of the patrician identity narrative, see Aldrich, *Old Money*, 158–69. Peabody to Julius Atwood, April 13, 1882, reproduced in Ashburn, *Peabody of Groton*.

19. La Farge, *Raw Material*, 9–10. The emphasis on "manly" conformity pervaded boarding-school culture: "What is the spirit of St. Paul's? In the accepted meaning, the boy who has school spirit, the right 'attitude,' is one who conforms cheerfully to regulations and customs, . . . is energetic and enthusiastic in club athletics, is pleasant and friendly with masters and never 'two-faced' with boys, and is quite uncritical in his outlook." Pier, *St. Paul's School*, 60.

20. Cookson and Persell, *Preparing for Power*, 152–57; Morgan, *FDR*, 56; La Farge, *Raw Material*, 12; Goodwin, *Fitzgeralds and Kennedys*, 458; Martin, *A Hero for Our Time*, 29.

21. Alsop, *I've Seen the Best of It*, 60.

22. La Farge, *Raw Material*, 12. Zahner, *Views from the Circle*, 273.

23. Isaacson and Thomas, *Wise Men*, 54–55 ; Morgan, *FDR*, 56.

24. Isaacson and Thomas, *Wise Men*, 54–55; Acheson, *Morning and Noon*, 26.

25. See McLachlan, *American Boarding Schools*, 280, 285–86; Train, "Letter," in Zahner, *Views from the Circle*, 280–85, Cookson and Persell, *Preparing for Power*, 25.

26. Train, "Letter," in Zahner, *Views from the Circle*, 283; La Farge, *Raw Material*, 12; Cookson and Persell, *Preparing for Power*, 152–53.

27. Train, "Letter," in Zahner, *Views from the Circle*, 283.

28. Cookson and Persell, *Preparing for Power*, 25. For a useful discussion of abusive fraternal initiation ritual in the social construction of masculine identities, see Sanday, *Fraternity Gang Rape*.

29. Acheson, *Morning and Noon*, 26; Isaacson and Thomas, *Wise Men*, 54–56; Joseph Alsop to Nicholas Bruce, September 17, 1964, box 69, Alsop Papers; also see: Alsop to Mrs. David Bruce, November 11, 1965, box 71, Alsop Papers; Alsop to Fred L. Glimp, dean of admissions, Harvard University, March 17, 1961, box 17, Alsop Papers; La Farge, *Raw Material*, esp. 48, 106–10.

30. Baltzell, *Philadelphia Gentlemen;* Aldrich, *Old Money*.

31. See La Farge, *Raw Material;* for an English perspective on the damaging aspects of boarding school, see Connolly, *Enemies of Promise*.

32. John De Koven Alsop, "Recollections 1928–1933," in Zahner, *Views from the Circle*, 235.

33. La Farge, *Raw Material*, 52–71. Roosevelt, *For Lust of Knowing*, 24.

34. Rotundo, *American Manhood*, 223–24; Green, *Fit for America*, 242, 252; Kaplan, "Romancing the Empire," 659–90: Lears, *No Place of Grace*, 107–8; Mrozek, *Sport and American Mentality*, esp. 28–66, 189–225; Park, "Biological Thought and a 'Man of Character,'" 7–30. On Sandow's life, see Chapman, *Sandow the Magnificent*. On Social Darwinism and the games cult in the English public schools, see Mangan, "Social Darwinism and Upper-Class Education," in Mangan and Walvin, *Manliness and Morality*, 135–59.

35. Mrozek, *Sport and American Mentality*, xii–xx. On Britain, see Mangan, *Athlet-*

icism in the Victorian and Edwardian Public School, and Mangan, *Games Ethic and Imperialism;* Donald Roden offers a fascinating cross-cultural study in *Schooldays in Imperial Japan.*

36. Ashburn, *Peabody of Groton,* 71.

37. Roosevelt, *Strenuous Life,* 155–56.

38. See Sanday, *Fraternity Gang Rape,* 141–42, on ritual and consciousness.

39. La Farge, *Raw Material,* 52.

40. Hartsock, "Masculinity, Heroism." See below and the following chapter for a discussion of war heroism and the construction of elite identity narratives.

41. Biddle, *An American Artist's Story,* 67; Peabody to Walter Camp, November 23, 1909, in Ashburn, *Peabody of Groton,* 195. On the Stoic strand in Muscular Christianity see Mangan, "Social Darwinism and Upper-Class Education," in Mangan and Walvin, *Manliness and Morality,* 139, Aldrich, *Old Money,* 279, Acheson, *Morning and Noon,* 18.

42. Holmes and Lodge, in Townsend, *Manhood at Harvard,* 102–3.

43. On the use of sports as a metaphor and mechanism for war preparedness in American universities between 1914 and 1918, see Miller, *Playing Fields of American Culture,* chap. 6.

44. Davies, *Legend of Hobey Baker,* 6, and throughout; See Aldrich, *Old Money,* 100–103, on class and the moral narrative of sportsmanship.

45. Davies, *Legend of Hobey Baker,* 89.

46. Davies, *Legend of Hobey Baker,* 95–107; Aldrich, *Old Money,* 176–77.

47. President Hibben of Princeton, quoted in Davies, *Legend of Hobey Baker,* 110.

48. Al Lang, quoted in Davies, *Legend of Hobey Baker,* 114.

49. Davies, *Legend of Hobey Baker,* 113; Aldrich, *Old Money,* 173–74, Drury, quoted in Aldrich, *Old Money,* 174.

50. For examples of period narratives focused on the self-sacrifice of patrician warrior heroes, see the two memorial volumes of 1917 commemorating the lives and deaths of two founding Lafayette aviators, Victor Emmanuel Chapman (St. Paul's school, Harvard, and the Porcellian club) and Norman Prince (Groton, Harvard, and Harvard Law); Chapman, *Victor Chapman's Letters,* and Babbitt, *Norman Prince.*

51. Rickenbacker, *Fighting the Flying Circus,* chap. 20; Aldrich, *Old Money,* 180–83; Aldrich, *Tommy Hitchcock;* Isaacson and Thomas, *Wise Men,* 90–93. Paine, *First Yale Unit,* esp. 1:5–21.

52. Stimson and Bundy, *On Active Service,* 86–87; On Plattsburg as a redemptive ordeal for eastern patricians, see Pearlman, *To Make Democracy Safe,* esp. 11–121.

53. Pearlman, *To Make Democracy Safe,* 100–104.

54. Clifford, *Citizen Soldiers,* 54–69; Paine, *First Yale Unit,* 1:8–9, Aldrich, *Old Money,* 175–77. On the class and family origins of Preparedness Movement leaders, see Pearlman, *To Make Democracy Safe,* appendix table 1, 273–74. Despite the presumptively democratic nature of America's army of citizen-soldiers, war and service in the military did not preempt the ongoing construction of elite brotherhoods; Robert Lovett was initiated into the elite Yale secret society Skull and Bones while serving overseas, "at the headquarters of the navy's Northern Bombing Group be-

tween Dunkirk and Calais." The Yale unit was itself another (overlapping) elite brotherhood. See Isaacson and Thomas, *Wise Men,* 93.

55. Hamilton, *JFK,* 508.

3. Heroism, Bodies, and the Construction of Elite Masculinity

1. Schlesinger, *Thousand Days,* 86–87; Reeves, *President Kennedy,* 109; Dugger, *Politician,* 149–51.

2. See, for example, Schlesinger, "On Heroic Leadership" (1960) or "The Decline of Greatness" (1958), in *Politics of Hope;* Schlesinger, *Thousand Days,* 87. See also Mosse, *Fallen Soldiers.*

3. Hartsock, "Masculinity, Heroism."

4. Ibid.; Kann, *On the Man Question,* esp. chap. 10.

5. For useful accounts of the wartime service of Kennedy and Johnson, see Blair and Blair, *Search for JFK;* Hamilton, *JFK;* Dugger, *Politician.* The construction of these political hero-narratives will be discussed below.

6. Roosevelt, *Rough Riders,* 9, 16; see p. 60 on the Oyster Bay Polo Team contingent. On the political implications of culture and gender in the debate over the Spanish-American War, see Hoganson, *Fighting for American Manhood.*

7. Dugger, *Politician,* 133–39; Goodwin, *Lyndon Johnson,* 35; Acheson, *Morning and Noon,* 3, 9, 27–37; Schlesinger, *Robert Kennedy and His Times,* 631. Party politics in the United States have long been expressed in competing visions of masculinity, often with a strong class dimension, which have contributed to the premium placed on military heroism as a part of political legitimacy. See Edwards, *Angels in the Machinery,* esp. 27–35.

8. On the recognition of their own status as "militarized proletarians," see Leed, *No Man's Land,* 94–95, and note 56 below.

9. Dawson, "Blond Bedouin," 125. On the brutal experience of industrial warfare faced by an average infantry "grunt" (selected by ranking in the bottom half of the Army General Classification Test) in combat during World War II, see Adams, *Best War Ever,* 87, 97–108, 110–13; another indispensable account of the dehumanizing realities of battle in World War II is Fussell, "'The Real War Will Never Get in the Books,'" in *Wartime.*

10. For an example of an archetype of the patrician Morgan partner-cum-Rooseveltian statesman as promoter of American involvement in World War I, see Scott, *Robert Bacon.*

11. Alsop, *I've Seen the Best of It,* 143; Knox also commanded an ammunition train in France during World War I; see Hoopes and Brinkley, *Driven Patriot,* 128–29. On Stimson's connections to Theodore Roosevelt and traditions of strenuous manliness, see Hodgson, *The Colonel.*

12. Alsop, *I've Seen the Best of It,* 143–44, 310.

13. Ibid., 149; Stewart described the condition as "tachycardiac hypertension," see Stewart Alsop to Joseph Alsop, October 28, 1941, box 224, Alsop Papers.

14. Alsop, *I've Seen the Best of It,* 149–50. The example of Alan G. Kirk (commander of amphibious forces in the Atlantic during World War II) offers another

small illustration of the dense web of connections between the elite men who came to compose the postwar "establishment." Kirk was a longtime friend of Dean Acheson's, dating from Acheson's clerkship with Supreme Court Justice Brandeis and Kirk's command of the presidential yacht *Mayflower*. During his tenure as secretary of state, Acheson appointed Kirk first as ambassador to Belgium and then as ambassador to Moscow. McGeorge Bundy (the future national security adviser to President Kennedy and a "family friend" of Kirk) served in army intelligence as Vice Admiral Kirk's aide-de-camp during the invasion of Sicily, during the Normandy invasion, and in setting up the Admiral's Paris headquarters. (Bundy, who had passed his enlistment physical only by memorizing the eye charts, then "won" a transfer to the infantry in the Pacific for the invasion of Japan that never came.) In 1961, Bundy "persuaded Kennedy to appoint Kirk Ambassador to Taipei." See Acheson, *Present at the Creation*, 417; Beschloss, *Crisis Years*, 252.

15. Chennault had retired from the American military at the rank of captain. In 1937, beginning his role as aviation adviser to Chiang Kai Shek, Chennault adopted the title "Colonel." The creation of the AVG involved the participation of men at the highest levels of the U.S. government, including Frank Knox, Secretary of the Treasury Henry Morgenthau, Secretary of State Cordell Hull, General George C. Marshall, Lauchlin Currie, and President Roosevelt. At least one former member of the Lafayette Flying Corps, Richard Aldworth, was involved in organizing and recruiting pilots for the AVG during 1940–41. Aldworth had fought in France after the declaration of war by the United States; to make his recruiting appeals more persuasive, however, he encouraged the mistaken impression that he had flown with the legendary Lafayette Escadrille. (The Escadrille proper was the highly publicized volunteer squadron formed before the official entrance of the U.S. into the war.) See Ford, *Flying Tigers*, 7, 20–21, 41, 47–48, 59.

16. Alsop, *I've Seen the Best of It*, 153, 150; on his war experience generally, 143–261; Morgan *FDR*, 733; Merry, *Taking on the World:*, 122–45. During his absence from Washington, Alsop rented his Georgetown home to that icon of upper-class masculinity, Tommy Hitchcock (Porcellian Club "brother," former Lafayette pilot, and polo star) when Hitchcock began his World War II government service. See Aldrich, *Tommy Hitchcock*, 135–36, 268.

17. Stewart Alsop to Joseph Alsop, October 28, 1941, Alsop Papers.

18. Alsop, *I've Seen the Best of It*, 310; Joseph Alsop to "Tish and Stew" (Patricia and Stewart Alsop), 18 February [1945], box 224, Alsop Papers. On Stewart's war experiences, see Merry, *Taking on the World*, 105–21.

19. One historian of the AVG asserts that Alsop, "with his spectacles, his fussy manner, and his elevated speech, honed at Groton and Harvard and on the Washington dinner circuit" was a figure of fun to the pilots and technicians of the squadron. See Ford, *Flying Tigers*, 85.

20. Alsop, *I've Seen the Best of It*, 310–11.

21. For Alsop to do so recapitulated, in rough outline but on a less heroic scale, former Secretary of War Henry L. Stimson volunteering at age fifty to command a combat artillery unit during World War I. Stimson "did not serve with Teddy Roosevelt's Rough Riders in Cuba in 1898, an omission he regretted ever afterward," his

biographer asserts. This is not to argue that Alsop was, in any conscious way, specifically attempting to emulate Stimson. This example does suggest that the ordeal of
battle played a large part in the imagination of an idealized upper-class masculinity.
See Hodgson, *The Colonel,* 12, 83–85. While Alsop did hold Stimson in "awe," the
secretary of war apparently regarded Alsop with disdain, and resented his intervention with FDR on behalf of Chennault. In his diary Stimson referred to Alsop as
"that wretched little grandson" of Theodore Roosevelt's sister, a "little devil" who
used his influence to "poison" FDR against General Stillwell. See Alsop, *I've Seen the
Best of It,* 143; Morgan, *FDR,* 733.

22. Alsop, *I've Seen the Best of It,* 316.

23. Ibid., 316–22. Alsop's particular need to visibly conform to the manhood script
of his patrician background might have followed from his private "deviance" from
that script. Alsop was a closeted homosexual; he has been posthumously "outed" by
Edwin M. Yoder in *Joe Alsop's Cold War,* 9–10, 153–58. Alsop's sexual orientation had
been a matter of speculation at least since the early Cold War—but those of his
family and friends who knew never publicly acknowledged his homosexuality. Richard Helms, a senior official in the CIA, has independently confirmed Yoder's account
of a 1957 Soviet blackmail attempt that threatened to expose Alsop; the attempt was
"contained" by Alsop's friends in the CIA. See the *Los Angeles Times* story "U.S.
Journalist Alsop Was Soviets' Blackmail Target in '57, Book Says" (reprinted in the
Arizona Republic, November 6, 1994). The issue of Alsop's homosexuality will be
further explored in the following chapter, which places it in the context of the postwar Red Scare and the sexualized politics and homosexual purges of that period.

24. Alsop, *I've Seen the Best of It,* 62, 319.

25. Yoder, *Joe Alsop's Cold War,* 46–48.

26. There is a large biographical literature on Kennedy, with discussions of his
physical debilities (chronic back problems, digestive tract problems, Addison's disease, sexually transmitted diseases, etc.). Several examples are, Hamilton, *JFK;* Blair
and Blair, *Search for JFK;* Parmet, *Jack;* Reeves, *President Kennedy.* Compare those
accounts with Kennedy's naval medical records, now available at the John F. Kennedy
Library. Especially useful is the summary document labeled Medical Record, Lieutenant John Fitzgerald Kennedy, USN, Entire service, December 15, 1944, box 11,
Kennedy Personal Papers; it reveals a consistent and largely successful attempt to
mislead navy doctors about the origins and extent of Kennedy's many health
problems.

27. Blair and Blair, *Search for JFK,* 150–53; Hamilton, *JFK,* 515–16.

28. Inga Arvad to John F. Kennedy, February 14, 1942, Correspondence 1939–50:
Inga Arvad, Kennedy Personal Papers. Transcripts of wartime FBI wiretapping and
sexual surveillance of Kennedy and Arvad are reproduced in Theoharis, *Secret Files,*
16–34. The most detailed narrative of Kennedy's relationship with Arvad is Hamilton, *JFK,* 419–94.

29. Schlesinger, *Thousand Days,* 80, 86–87; Hamilton, *JFK,* 526, 549–50.

30. Hamilton, *JFK,* 90.

31. Ibid., 450, 459, 479, 534, 632, 646; Blair and Blair, *Search for JFK,* 322–23.
Billings later was accepted into the U.S. Navy (through the intervention of "a friend

of the family," the "captain of the Port of Baltimore") and participated in operations during the invasion of Okinawa. John Kennedy had returned home a war hero before Joe Jr. was assigned antisubmarine patrol duty flying from England into the North Atlantic. Failing to win any particular renown or distinction during his first tour, Joe Jr. volunteered for a secret and highly dangerous mission. He was supposed to pilot a heavy bomber laden with ten tons of explosives toward a purported Nazi secret weapon site, then bail out while the bomber was piloted by remote control directly into the target. The bomber exploded soon after takeoff, August 12, 1944, killing Joe Jr. and his copilot. See Hamilton, *JFK,* 658–61, and Blair and Blair, *Search for JFK,* 341–44.

32. Blair and Blair, *Search for JFK,* 156–57; Hamilton, *JFK,* 500–502.

33. White, *They Were Expendable,* 99.

34. Blair and Blair, *Search for JFK,* 156–57; Hamilton, *JFK,* 499–506, 517, 542.

35. Despite Kennedy's dramatic night swims, the message carved on a coconut shell, etc., the credit for the actual rescue of Kennedy and his crew must largely go to Lieutenant. A. R. Evans, an Australian "coast watcher," and his network of indigenous scouts operating in the central Solomon Islands. The official response of the naval hierarchy toward Kennedy's loss of PT-109 was ambivalent. While one immediate superior recommended him for the Silver Star, the navy awards board downgraded the decoration to the Navy and Marine Corps medal, and held it up for nine months. The citation was finally signed on May 19, 1944, by family friend James Forrestal during his first day in office as secretary of the navy. For detailed accounts of Kennedy's experience in the South Pacific see Blair and Blair, *Search for JFK,* and Hamilton, *JFK.*

36. Wills, *Kennedy Imprisonment,* 33; Bradlee, *Conversations with Kennedy,* 65–67, 69; Sheehan, *Bright Shining Lie,* 297–98; Blair and Blair, *Search for JFK,* 294–97; Fay, interview; Fay, *Pleasure of His Company,* 20–21, 56, 67–79, 214, 218–20. Other examples of Kennedy's appointments of war buddies and heroic acquaintances include his fellow PT-boat officer and lifelong friend Paul Fay as undersecretary of the navy, and Victor ("Brute") Krulak as special assistant for counterinsurgency to the Joint Chiefs of Staff. President Kennedy had met Krulak, his favorite Marine general, during the war when Krulak commanded a series of daring commando-style diversionary raids in the Solomons and Kennedy's PT boat came to the rescue of some of Krulak's hard-pressed soldiers. Ex-warriors were found even among the "Irish Mafia" (i.e., the Boston political operators Kennedy brought with him to the White House); Kenneth P. O'Donnell, a former Harvard football star, was "first lieutenant and war hero during the war, during which he flew thirty missions as a lead bombardier over European targets; he was shot down and wounded in a mission over Belgium, escaped and later received the Distinguished Flying Cross and the Air Medal with five clusters." Heller and Heller, *Kennedy Cabinet,* 155–56. Dave Powers, with Kennedy since the first congressional campaign, had joined the U.S. Air Corps and served in the China theater "as a base intelligence specialist with Claire Chennault's Flying Tigers." Blair and Blair, *Search for JFK,* 435.

37. Blair and Blair, *The Search for JFK,* 236.

38. Ibid., 320–22, 325–26, 333–36.

39. Ibid., 236; Reeves, *Question of Character*, 311.

40. Dugger, *Politician*, 25–46. While Dugger and Goodwin (*Lyndon Johnson*) seem to agree about the importance of courage for Johnson's self-conception, another biographer offers an unflattering assessment of the reality of Johnson's physical courage (with the exception of the military plane ride in service to his political career discussed below). See Caro, *Years of Lyndon Johnson*, 37, 46.

41. Dugger, *Politician*, 41–42, 130–51. In addition to repeatedly referring to the Texas Rangers during speeches and conversation, President Johnson wrote the introduction to Walter Prescott Webb's *The Texas Rangers*. For a useful exploration of Theodore Roosevelt's version of the frontier-hero myth see Slotkin, *Gunfighter Nation*, 33–42; for an account of Roosevelt's creation of a "ranchman" persona, see McCullough, *Mornings on Horseback*, 316–50.

42. Johnson quoted in Goodwin, *Lyndon Johnson*, 55, 95. Goodwin gives the best account of the origins of, in my terms, Johnson's "identity narrative." As president, in a public letter to Alice Longworth in January 1965, Johnson quoted Theodore Roosevelt: "The United States of America has not the option as to whether it will or will not play a great part in the world. It *must* play a great part. All that it can decide is whether it will play that part well or badly. And it can play it badly if it adopts the role either of the coward or the bully. . . . Democratic America can be true to itself, true to the great cause of freedom and justice, only if it shows itself ready and willing to resent wrong from the strong, and desirous doing generous justice to both strong and weak." *Public Papers of the Presidents, Lyndon B. Johnson*, 1:10.

43. Caro, *Years of Lyndon Johnson*, 26–34, adviser's quote, 30; Dugger, *Politician*, 136, 239–41, Johnson quote, 241. Goodwin, *Lyndon Johnson*, 94.

44. Dugger, *Politician*, 243. For a popular account of Johnson's military escapades in the South Pacific cast as an epic narrative, see Caidin and Hymoff, *Mission;* Robert Dallek offers another useful account of Johnson's brief military career, stressing the mixture of motives animating LBJ (patriotism, service, and willingness to be exposed to danger coexisting alongside self-promotion and political calculation); see Dallek, *Lone Star Rising*, 230–45.

45. Dugger, *Politician*, 248–49; Caro, *Years of Lyndon Johnson*, 44–45. Before Johnson's return to the United States, he agreed to carry a report by *Time* correspondent Robert Sherrod, who needed a high-ranking courier in order to evade military censorship by MacArthur's headquarters. The report was highly critical of MacArthur's conduct of the war. Johnson later told Sherrod that the report was "so hot I put it in the toilet"; most accounts by biographers take him at his word. But Johnson actually retained several copies and fed the critical information to FDR and Harold Ickes, who were apprehensive about MacArthur's presidential ambitions. See Schaller, *Douglas MacArthur*, 65.

46. Dugger, *Politician*, 250–53; Caro, *Years of Lyndon Johnson*, 44–52; Goodwin, *Lyndon Johnson*, 94–95. Three congressmen (including LBJ) returned to Washington after being recalled by FDR; four resigned their seats to remain in the military. One, Victor Harrington of Iowa, was killed in action. Senator Henry Cabot Lodge, of patrician Boston lineage and the future ambassador to South Vietnam under both Kennedy and Johnson, joined the army reserve in 1924. He went on "extended active

duty" as a captain on August 1, 1941, while retaining his Senate seat. He fought in North Africa with the British and was promoted to the rank of major. Recalled with the other members of Congress in July 1942, he resigned from the Senate, served in campaigns in Italy and Northern Europe, was promoted to lieutenant colonel, and was decorated with the Bronze Star and Legion of Merit. Lodge was reelected to the Senate in 1946.

Other Americans with political ambitions set out to manufacture reputations as war heroes. A significant example is "Tail Gunner Joe" McCarthy, who took a leave of absence from his Wisconsin state circuit judgeship to receive a direct commission as a first lieutenant in the Marine Corps. He served sixteen months in the South Pacific as an intelligence officer for a Marine dive-bomber squadron. The future senator managed to go along on fewer than a dozen "milk run" missions as the tail gunner of the dive bomber, out of which he constructed an elaborate (and ever changing) story of wartime heroism. He forged a citation and got the Purple Heart for a shipboard injury he received during a pratfall in a "shell-back" ceremony crossing the equator (McCarthy claimed that he had been wounded in aerial combat). He set the "record" for the most ammunition expended by a Marine during one mission (he accomplished this by shooting at coconut trees). He had himself photographed in full combat regalia, and updated his constituents at home with dramatized accounts of his exploits. At the height of his Senate career in 1952, McCarthy managed to get the Marine Corps to bestow upon him the Distinguished Flying Cross and two Air Medals by asserting his participation in 32 combat missions (in 1944 he had claimed 14, in 1947 the number had been 17). McCarthy's military career differs from that of most of the imperial brotherhood in that it seems to have been motivated by an unalloyed concern for self-promotion, in contrast to internalized notions of service and sacrifice by the patrician elite. See Thomas C. Reeves, *Life and Times,* 45–61; Oshinsky, *Conspiracy So Immense,* 29–34.

47. Johnson quoted in Beschloss, *Taking Charge,* 111.

48. See, for instance, the report by Roger Hilsman (director of the Bureau of Intelligence and Research, Department of State), "A Strategic Concept for South Vietnam," February 2, 1962, box 3, Hilsman Papers; Hilsman (assistant secretary of state for Far Eastern affairs) to Ambassador Lodge, "Action plan for Viet-Nam," n.d. [Sept. 16, 1963], box 4, Hilsman Papers. The recent account by Robert McNamara puts particular emphasis on Hilsman's role in the coup; see McNamara, *In Retrospect,* 52–87. For Hilsman's version, see his *To Move a Nation,* 482–521; another participant, George W. Ball, offers his interpretation of the coup against Diem in *Past Has Another Pattern,* 370–74.

49. Hilsman, *American Guerrilla,* xi.; Hilsman, interview, 27–28.

50. See Fussell, *Wartime,* 66–78, 267–93.

51. Dawson, *Soldier Heroes,* 174. See Showalter, "Rivers and Sassoon," 61–69, for a discussion of the often irreconcilable contradiction between gender ideologies of active, brave, cheerful warrior masculinity and the experience of the enforced passivity of warfare in the trenches of World War I; this double bind produced the condition known as "shell shock." See also Leed, *No Man's Land,* 180–86, on W. H. R. Rivers and his theory of "neuroses" created in soldiers by the immobilizing impera-

tives of trench warfare. Stanley D. Rosenberg provides an invaluable discussion of the evolution of American aviator identity narratives and their connections to psychological mechanisms for denying and repressing the violence and horrors of aerial warfare. He addresses such changes from World War II up to the Gulf War, examining the links between the construction of the language of the warrior fraternity and the development of high-technology electronically aided aircraft and weapons. He argues that air combat itself has increasingly been construed as an erotic thrill in comparison with accounts by pilots of World War II. "The pilots' culture encourages and allows a more eroticized identification with, and immersion in, the male fraternity of fliers, a culture dominated by high-tech machines, danger, and death as its central icons." See Rosenberg, "Threshold of Thrill," 43–66.

52. Hilsman, *American Guerrilla,* 1–2.

53. Ibid., 7–11, 89.

54. Ibid., 52, 59, 41–47.

55. Ibid., 82–91.

56. See Leed, *No Man's Land,* 94–95, for a discussion of the "disillusionment" of educated, middle-class volunteers with industrialized warfare (for example, Robert Graves, Sigfried Sassoon, etc.). Leed argues that their disillusionment followed from their subjection to a "militarized proletarianization"; instead of being a venue for heroic action and realization of the masculine self, industrial war demanded "resignation to meaningless, boring, endless, and dangerous jobs." The work of killing was thus the work of alienated labor. Rather than empowered warriors, they were exploited victims, who directed their "bitterness" at the "'managers' of war, the staff." Note that Hilsman's brief experience of combat in the regular army resembled in important ways the offensive component of trench warfare, that is, infantry charges against heavily fortified strongholds. See Keegan, *Face of Battle,* 285–322, on the essential similarities of battlefield experience during the first and second world wars.

57. Hilsman, *American Guerrilla,* 127.

58. On the long-standing discrepancy between traditional historical narratives of battle and the "reality" of the soldier's experience of chaos, death, dismemberment, powerlessness, and futility during industrial war, see Keegan, *Face of Battle,* esp. 1–73, 204–80, 295–324; see Fussell, *Wartime* (esp. 283–90), on the unbridgeable contradictions between the euphemism that pervaded "home front" representation of the war and the experience of soldiers who fought.

59. Hilsman, *American Guerrilla,* 100; Fussell, *Wartime,* 281–82; See also Keegan, *Face of Battle,* 270, where he argues that the desirability of a wound as a means of honorable exit from the battlefield is predicated on the availability of modern medical treatment. Keegan also discusses the self-inflicted wound, a related means to escape combat, which first appeared during World War I. He tells us that no evidence of this pattern can be found before the development of antiseptics.

60. Hilsman, *American Guerrilla,* 127.

61. Ibid., 127, 252.

62. Ibid., 127, 155, 152.

63. Ibid., 151–52.

64. For a useful discussion of the gendered political and cultural meanings attached to imperial adventure literature, see Green, *Adventurous Male,* 4, 11, 15–16, 49, 183–93.

65. Hilsman, *American Guerrilla,* 155–61.

66. It should be noted that the American fascination with the frontier rifleman as citizen soldier stretches back to the American Revolution itself. Even then, the image of the military effectiveness of westerners in buckskin hunting shirts "with their amazing hardihood, their method of living so long in the woods without carrying provisions with them," and their "dexterity in the use of the Rifle Gun," far exceeded their actual military significance. See Royster, *Revolutionary People at War,* 33–34. Hilsman revealed his fascination with men who embody adventure narrative with his discussion of the exploits of Grant-Taylor, an Englishman he encountered on a visit to the British Fourteenth Army headquarters. There Grant-Taylor provided instruction in "instinctive firing" of small arms, based upon the traditions of the quick-draw artist and Wild West gunslinger. He regaled his audiences with tales of Wild Bill Hickok as an exemplar of "instinctive firing." Hilsman's account of the adventurous Englishman shows how easily the Wild West and imperial adventure stories could be conflated. Grant-Taylor himself represented the imperial adventure hero, but drew upon the U.S. western lawman image: someone, Hilsman asserts, who had always "gravitated to where the fighting was." His exploits included a stint as the "number two man on the Shanghai police force," a tour with the Cairo police, and duty with the FBI as a gangbuster ("in fact, he had been one of those who had gunned down John Dillinger outside a movie house in Chicago in the 1930s"). His "most fabulous exploit," according to Hilsman, occurred during the early part of the Battle of Britain, when Grant-Taylor led a commando raid upon a German flying school to assassinate six elite Luftwaffe pilot instructors. See Hilsman, *American Guerrilla,* 143–46.

67. Hilsman, "Internal War," 26–27; Hilsman, *American Guerrilla,* 169, 264. It should also be noted that Hilsman's adventures "behind the lines" as a guerrilla hero resemble, in rough outline, the twentieth-century archetypal adventure narrative created around the exploits of T. E. Lawrence during and immediately after the World War I by the U.S. war-propagandist and lecturer Lowell Thomas. See Dawson, "Blond Bedouin."

68. Hilsman, "Internal War," 27; *American Guerrilla,* 204–10.

69. Hilsman, *American Guerrilla,* 186–87, 220–22, 134–40.

70. Ibid., 169–70, 164–66, 214–15; Hilsman, "Internal War," 29–30.

71. Hilsman, interview, 27–28.

72. Hilsman, *American Guerrilla,* 229–36, 252.

73. Hilsman, interview, 4.

74. Ibid., 18–19. Collier and Horowitz, *The Kennedys,* 386–87.

75. Halberstam, *Best and Brightest,* 153.

76. Rostow, interview.

77. Rostow, *Diffusion of Power,* 215.

78. Rostow, interview.

4. "Lavender Lads" and the Foreign Policy Establishment

1. On the Truman administration's exaggeration of the Soviet threat see Kofsky, *Truman and the War Scare;* on the role of Kennan, Wisner, Thayer, Bohlen and others in the recruitment of ex-Nazis and collaborators for anti-Soviet programs of destabilization and psychological warfare, see Simpson, *Blowback.* Peter Grose, in *Operation Rollback,* examines Kennan's central role in the 1948 creation of the Office of Policy Coordination, a new, secret, covert operations agency designed to destabilize and "roll back" communist power in Eastern Europe and the Soviet Union, which operated with "unvouchered funds" and immunity from congressional oversight. Grose reveals that Charles Thayer was pivotal in the conception of the OPC and its emphasis on the recruitment of anticommunist "displaced persons," right-wing émigrés, etc., for paramilitary incursions into Soviet-controlled areas.

2. The political struggle between competing political elites was fueled, in part, by class resentments grounded in material interests. Provincial conservative "isolationists" generally had economic interests rooted in small to medium-sized capitalist enterprise, protection of a domestic market, and the direct purchase of labor power. They harbored the desire to exploit Asian and Latin American markets. They exalted the values of "individualism" and feared the global financial tribute systems that grounded the interests of the class of metropolitan internationalist investment bankers and Wall Street lawyers that dominated the foreign policy establishment. See Doenecke, *Not to the Swift,* 24–27. A brief survey of the biographies of congressional countersubversives such as Senators Kenneth Wherry, Bourke Hickenlooper, Styles Bridges, Pat McCarran, Karl Mundt, and Joe McCarthy reveals that most were born in the last two decades of the nineteenth century, or the first decade of the twentieth, in rural or small-town America. Most attended public schools and the state universities where they resided. They typically entered law or other professions connected to the agricultural economy, many while engaging in some combination of farming, ranching, real estate and insurance, and merchant enterprises serving the local market. Most entered local politics and gradually worked their way up the political ladder, achieving national office around age fifty. See Biographical Directory of the United States, http://bioguide.congress.gov. Perhaps the best elucidation of the class politics of the Cold War and Red Scare is to be found in Cumings, *Origins of the Korean War,* chaps. 2–3. George Lipsitz offers a useful analysis of the economic squeeze facing conservative small capitalists during the postwar emergence of a big-business, internationalist "corporate liberal" order; see Lipsitz, *Rainbow at Midnight,* esp. 158–90. See also Jacobs, "'How about Some Meat,'" 910–41, which elucidates the economic genesis of one aspect of the postwar conservative Republican backlash against New Deal "socialism."

3. *Cong. Rec.,* 82d Cong., 1st sess., March 15, 1951, A1526. The term "cookie pusher" came from "the popular belief that our diplomats, at home and abroad, were principally engaged in attending teas and cocktail parties"; see Constantine Brown, "State Department Prestige at Lowest Ebb in History," *Sunday Star* (Washington, D.C.), March 19, 1950. Before John F. Kennedy began his gradual decade-long shift toward the "vital center," he shared many of these assumptions. On January 25, 1949, Con-

gressman Kennedy of Massachusetts placed the blame for the "loss" of China "squarely within the White House and the Department of State." "So concerned were our diplomats and their advisers, the Lattimores and the Fairbanks, with the imperfections of the democratic system of China . . . that they lost sight of our tremendous stake in a non-communist China." Quoted in Parmet, *Jack,* 209.

4. Hoopes, *Devil and John Foster Dulles,* 153–58; Shils, *Torment of Secrecy,* 85, 135–43; Bohlen, *Witness to History,* 327–35; Fried, *Nightmare in Red,* 167–68. Important scholarship on the history and cultural significance of the Lavender Scare includes D'Emilio, *Sexual Politics, Sexual Communities;* May, *Homeward Bound;* Smith, "National Security and Personal Isolation," 307–37.

5. This was, of course, part of a long countersubversive tradition in U.S. history. During the first Red Scare (1919–20), for instance, Wilson's attorney general, A. Mitchell Palmer, characterized communism as an attempt "to overthrow the decencies of private life, to usurp property . . . , to disrupt the present order of life regardless of health, sex or religious rights." Revolution, he argued, appealed to "criminals, moral perverts, [and] hysterical neurasthenic women." Quoted in Ribuffo, *Old Christian Right,* 6. For an early and influential essay on the "sex/gender system," see Rubin, "Traffic in Women," 157–210.

6. Kinsey, Pomeroy, and Martin, *Sexual Behavior in the Human Male,* 650–51; William Moore, "Senators Act to Oust State Undesirables," *Washington Times-Herald,* April 21, 1953.

7. On the sexualized political discourse of the Cold War, see Smith, "National Security and Personal Isolation," 307–37; D'Emilio, "The Bonds of Oppression: Gay Life in the 1950s," in *Sexual Politics, Sexual Communities,* or D'Emilio, "Homosexual Menace," which places the Lavender Scare of the '50s in the context of the emergence of a "gay" subculture during the '40s; and May, "Explosive Issues: Sex, Women and the Bomb," in *Homeward Bound.* For a Cold War–era articulation of the assumptions underlying the issue of homosexuality as a threat to state security, see the remarkable Senate investigative subcommittee report discussed below, *Employment of Homosexuals in Government,* esp. 3–6.

8. Memorandum, "Problem of Homosexuals and Sex Perverts in the Department of State," Carlisle H. Humelsine (deputy undersecretary of state) to Mr. Webb, June 23, 1950, White House central files, confidential files, sex perversion folder, Truman Papers. On "engendered civic virtue" and the republican tradition, see Kann, *On the Man Question.*

9. Senate, *Employment of Homosexuals in Government,* 2, 4–5. Also see Major, "New Moral Menace," 105. Espionage and homosexuality were closely associated in the Hiss-Chambers and the Burgess-MacLean spy scandals.

10. Schlesinger, *Vital Center,* 127; Schlesinger thoughtfully footnoted Marcel Proust, *Remembrance of Things Past, Cities of the Plain,* part 1. For a right-wing, low-culture contrast with Schlesinger, see Lait and Mortimer, "Garden of Pansies," and "Little Red Herrings," in *Washington Confidential,* a blunt and lurid text that links homosexuality, nonmarital heterosexuality, and communist subversion in the U.S. government. Many of the themes alluded to in Schlesinger appear there, however. "Fairies," Lait and Mortimer tell us, "recognize each other by a fifth sense immedi-

ately." Furthermore, "they have a grapevine of intercommunication as swift and sure as that in a girl's boarding school" (90).

11. Schlesinger, *Vital Center,* 151.

12. Wherry, *Report on the Infiltration of Subversives and Moral Perverts,* 10.

13. White, "Portrait of a 'Fundamentalist,'" 14. It should be noted that Wherry's self-identification as a "fundamentalist" referred to political "fundamentals," not to evangelical Protestantism.

14. Schlesinger, *Vital Center,* 35–50, 157–88, 104–5; Schlesinger, "U.S. Communist Party," 96, 85; Wherry, *Report on the Infiltration of Subversives and Moral Perverts,* 15. Senator Wherry didn't dwell on the psychological roots of "subversion and perversion," but he did assert the connection. "Moral perversion, like other crimes against society is caused by abnormal minds, which may be broadly classified as diseased." The imperial brotherhood subscribed to this general thesis—that communism appealed only to the psychologically, sexually, or socially marginal. George Kennan, director of the policy planning staff of the Department of State, in 1949, wrote a memo arguing that the "small percentage" of people attracted to communism were characterized by "jealousy, sense of inadequacy and inferiority, bitterness, and above all, escapism." "Unsuccessful and untalented" intellectuals as well as other "maladjusted groups: in our country—Jews, Negroes, immigrants—all those who feel handicapped in the framework of a national society" made up the ranks of communists, Kennan asserted. Communists were driven by "emotional rather than economic" concerns, by a "desire to win appreciation, attention and power." See memorandum, Kennan to Robert G. Hooker, October 17, 1949, *Foreign Relations of the United States, 1949,* 403–5.

15. McPartland, "Portrait," 75–76. See Lait and Mortimer, *Washington Confidential,* 100–101, for a description of the manner in which communists used sexual seduction to recruit "sex-starved government gals" and "meek male clerks" working for federal agencies.

16. McPartland, "Portrait," 75. The idea that the "weakness" of women poses a special danger to society by making them likely to enlist body and soul in service to darkness has a long history in American thought; the characterization of the postwar countersubversive crusade as a "witch-hunt" resonates at this level of sexual demonology. Puritan colonists believed that a female witch "purposefully allowed the devil to use her body . . . to recruit more witches and perform *maleficium.* . . . Witches' bodies no longer belonged to themselves; Satan could take them wherever he pleased to use as he pleased. . . . When a specter assaulted a victim in a sexual way, it was always in the shape of a woman." See Reis, "Devil, Body, and Feminine Soul," esp. 25, 31.

17. McPartland, "Portrait," 77. This argument is replicated in Lait and Mortimer, *Washington Confidential,* 102–3: "It is Communist strategy to line Negroes into the party through white gals who, to show their complete compliance and condition of servitude, are urged to give themselves to colored men. Into this specialized service they seem to wade with more than token application."

18. McPartland, "Portrait," 75–82.

19. Senator Joe McCarthy, Lincoln's Day address, Wheeling West Virginia, Febru-

ary 9, 1950, copy of speech supplied by Radio Station WWVA, p. 7, RG 59, Department of State decimal file, 1950–54, box 477, National Archives, College Park, Md.; *New York Times:* March 1, 1950, 2; March 9, 1950; March 15, 1950, 3; April 25, 1950, 8; May 22, 1950, 8; May 25 1950, 19; June 8, 1950; June 15, 1950; and especially William S. White, "Inquiry by Senate on Perverts Asked," *New York Times,* May 20, 1950, 8; and "Federal Vigilance on Perverts Asked," *New York Times,* December 16, 1950; "Object Lesson," *Time,* December 25, 1950, 10. On McCarthy, his Wheeling speech, and Republican politics of anticommunism, see Reeves, *Life and Times,* 205–33; and Oshinsky, *Conspiracy So Immense,* 89–139, 157.

20. See Max Lerner, "The Washington Sex Story No. 1—Panic on the Potomac," *New York Post,* July 10, 1950, 4.

21. *Cong. Rec.—House,* 81st Cong., 2d sess., April 19, 1950, 96:5405; Columnist John O'Donnell, quoted in Max Lerner, "Scandal in the State Department: XI—Sex and Politics," *New York Post,* July 21, 1950, 2.

22. Lerner, "Washington Sex Story," 24; Hersh, *Old Boys,* 150–52; the most detailed discussion of the high politics of the episode is Gellman, *Secret Affairs.* Lait and Mortimer illustrate the wide circulation of the story, with a pejorative retelling (without identifying Welles by name) in *Washington Confidential,* 97. Joseph Alsop deplored the firing of Welles over a "doubtful scandal involving a Pullman porter," however "disagreeable" Welles might have been, because Alsop foresaw the need for "the ablest man in the State Department" in the coming contests with the Russians over the division of Europe; Joseph Alsop to his parents, September 8, 1943, box 223, Alsop Papers.

23. Despite the "successes" of the Truman Doctrine, and despite the apparent power of the United States and its monopoly on atomic weapons, communism still claimed victories. The creation of Soviet satellite states in Eastern Europe, the confrontation in Berlin, the Soviet detonation of a fission bomb, the "loss" of China to the communists, and, finally, the June 1950 invasion of South Korea by communist forces which embroiled U.S. armed forces in a shooting war, gave plausibility to calls for ever more stringent loyalty-security programs to purge the federal government and other American institutions. On the spy cases, see Caute, *Great Fear,* 54–69; Incidents included the 1945 *Amerasia* case involving the publication of "classified" State Department documents on U.S.-China relations, leaked by John S. Service among others; the 1947–48 testimony of "the Blond Spy Queen," Elizabeth Bentley, before HUAC in which she repented her involvement as a spy courier for her Soviet lover Jacob Golos, and named high-level Roosevelt administration officials Lauchlin Currie and Harry Dexter White as conduits of secret information to the Soviets (note that Harry Dexter White and Lauchlin Currie were rumored to be homosexual, see Cumings, *Origins of the Korean War,* 111); Whittaker Chambers, another repentant homosexual ex-communist, accused Alger Hiss of espionage, and with the efforts of Congressman Richard Nixon precipitated Hiss's trial and retrial for perjury 1948–50 (during the trial, Chambers also named Harry Dexter White, who had died of a heart attack soon after giving testimony to HUAC); Judith Coplon, an employee of the Justice Department, was arrested in March 1949 during a rendezvous with Valentin Gubichev, a Soviet attaché to the UN, and was tried for espionage (she was

convicted twice, but released on a technicality with her third appeal). In early 1950 the physicist Klaus Fuchs, convicted of espionage in London, led the FBI to other members of a "Los Alamos" spy ring. Harry Gold, David Greenglass, and finally, Julius and Ethel Rosenberg were soon arrested; the case supplied an explanation for the September 1949 Soviet success in producing a fission bomb.

24. Quoted in Cumings, *Origins of the Korean War,* 110.

25. See, for instance, Griffith, *Politics of Fear,* 44–45.

26. Bundy, quoted in Bird, *Color of Truth,* 107; Cooke, *Generation on Trial,* 3–41; Hiss, *Laughing Last,* 52–122; Zeligs, *Friendship and Fratricide,* 333–42; Chambers, *Witness,* 790–94. Acheson's daughter Mary was the wife of William Bundy, McGeorge's brother; and their father, Harvey Bundy, had, like Hiss, also clerked for Oliver Wendell Holmes. The countersubversives of the Senate Internal Security Subcommittee (McCarran Committee) spent enormous time and energy trying to link Alger Hiss to other political enemies (e.g., Dean Acheson) by combing and clipping society page stories, membership lists of clubs, and political organizations linked to "establishment" institutions.

27. Senator Joe McCarthy, Lincoln's Day address, Wheeling, W. Va., February 9, 1950, WWVA transcript.

28. Chambers's FBI interview, quoted in Tanenhaus, *Whittaker Chambers,* 344–45. Tanenhaus also discusses Chambers's heterosexual affairs prior to his "underground" life, including cohabitation with "party wives" and the sexual sharing of one woman with a younger male friend during one period when all three lived together.

29. Hiss, *Laughing Last,* 2, 133; Cooke, *Generation on Trial,* 304–10; Chambers, *Witness,* 733, 790. On Chambers's homosexuality during his period in the Communist Party, see Blumenthal, "Cold War and the Closet," 112–17. Hiss's defense strategy also sought to contain the revelation of sexual scandal within his own family; his wife feared that news of an abortion prior to her marriage to Hiss would become public, and Hiss also refused to let his stepson testify to prevent public knowledge of a 1946 episode in which the stepson requested a discharge from a naval cadet program on grounds of homosexuality (Hiss managed to get the stepson admitted to St. Albans Naval Hospital and put under the care of a psychiatrist, to hush up the incident). See Hiss, *Laughing Last,* 119–20, 135–36; Tanenhaus, *Whittaker Chambers,* 393. Although the rumors of a Hiss-Chambers sexual relationship were an "underground" phenomenon, evidence of the widespread circulation of such rumors can be found in a "Tijuana Bible" (underground pornographic comics of the 1930s–1950s) titled "Chambers and Hiss in Betrayed." The author and political pornographer crudely but explicitly depicts Hiss and Chambers engaging in homosexual acts, and explains Chambers's betrayal of Hiss as a product of sexual jealousy resulting from Hiss's heterosexual activity. See it reproduced in *Tijuana Bibles: Art and Wit in America's Forbidden Funnies, 1930s–1950s* (New York: Simon and Schuster, 1997), 125.

30. Acheson, *Present at the Creation,* 354, 364, 369; Joe McCarthy, "First Speech Delivered in Senate by Senator Joe McCarthy on Communists in Government; Wheeling Speech," in *Major Speeches,* 14; Report, "Public Comment on Secretary Acheson's January 25 Remarks about Alger Hiss," January 30, 1950, RG 59, Records of the Department of State, Office of Public Opinion Studies, Reports on State De-

partment and its Policies, 1944–1963 (cited hereafter as OPS Reports), box 20, National Archives, College Park, Md.

31. Dean Acheson to Arthur Schlesinger Jr., October 27, 1948, box P-8, Arthur Schlesinger Papers; Acheson, *Present at the Creation,* 360–61, 250–51; Acheson, *Morning and Noon,* 18; Aldrich, *Old Money,* 279. It should be noted that Hiss went from being a golden boy of the establishment as head of the Carnegie Endowment for World Peace at a salary of $30,000, with commensurate social prominence, to unemployment, prison, disbarment, divorce, social ostracism, more unemployment, and the final blow to a gentleman's identity narrative, a job in commerce as a $6000 per year paper salesman.

32. Cecil Holland, "Didn't Condone Acts, He Tells Senate Group," *Washington Star,* February 28, 1950; *New York Times,* March 1, 1950, 1–2; Willard Edwards, "Didn't Mean to Condone Hiss, Acheson Says," *Washington Times Herald,* March 1, 1950; Marshall McNeill, "New State Dept. Pervert Hunt On," *Washington Daily News,* March 16, 1950; Lerner, "Washington Sex Story No. 1," *New York Post,* July 10, 1950, 4. Peurifoy's disclosure of the ongoing homosexual purge was not, strictly speaking, news to many members of Congress, but it did have the political effect of making the issue a part of public debate. In 1947 and again in 1949 Peurifoy had testified in executive session before congressional committees where he discussed the discovery and dismissal of homosexual "security risks" in the State Department. But the issue did not become a part of widespread public discussion until February 28, 1950, with Peurifoy's Senate testimony. Even after the Lavender Scare took off, some congressmen still referred to homosexuals as "the unmentionables," to avoid voicing the word in public. See *Cong. Rec.—House,* 81st Cong., 2d sess., April 19, 1950, 96:5404–5.

33. Robert C. Albright, "Bridges Wants Manhunt for 'Master Spy,'" *Washington Post,* March 28, 1950; McCarthy, *McCarthyism,* 14–15.

34. Kahn, *China Hands,* 179; *Cong. Rec.—House,* 81st Cong., 2d sess., April 19, 1950, 96:5403.

35. Oscar L. Chapman (secretary of the interior) to the president, April 12, 1950; administrative assistant to the president; Donald S. Dawson to Oscar L. Chapman, July 28, 1950; memo, "Monthly report—Pervert Elimination Campaign," February 1, 1950; all in RG 48, Department of the Interior central classified files, 1937–1953, 12–41 administrative, box 3838, National Archives, College Park, Md.

36. Wherry, *Report on the Infiltration of Subversives and Moral Perverts,* 1, 5, and throughout; *New York Times,* May 22, 1950, 8; May 25, 1950, 19; June 15, 1950.

37. Department of State memorandum of conversation between Mr. John Finlator, Mr. Fred Traband, and Lieutenant Roy Blick, March 29, 1950, White House central files, confidential files, sex perversion folder, Truman Papers. Blick's willingness to make exaggerated claims about his knowledge of homosexuals in the State Department is evident from a document of April 10, 1950, sent by J. Edgar Hoover to Truman's assistant, Rear Admiral Sidney W. Souers. Hoover forwarded a list of names of people holding "highly rated positions in Government or quasi Government agencies or with prominent organizations or groups" drawn from Metro PD Lieutenant Blick's vice squad records. Out of the sixty-six names (from a total of 393

government employees arrested since 1947) only two worked for the Department of State—one a foreign service reserve officer, one an administrative assistant. Interestingly, this contrasts with twenty-two names of professional or officer class army and navy employees, far outnumbering any other federal agencies; right-wing attacks on homosexuals never mentioned the Defense Department as a haven for homosexuality, while the State and Commerce Departments (three names on Hoover's list) came under particular scrutiny. See Hoover to Souers and attachment, April 10, 1950, FBI, subject file, president's secretary files, box 169, Truman Papers.

38. Bradlee, quoted in Kaiser, *Gay Metropolis,* 71.

39. Blick, quoted by Max Lerner, "'Scandal' in the State Dept.: VII—Blick of the Vice Squad," *New York Post,* July 18, 1950, 2.

40. Ibid

41. Max Lerner, "'Scandal' in the State Dept.: IX—They Never Appeal," *New York Post,* July 19, 1950, 38; United States Senate, executive session hearing held before the Investigations Subcommittee, Committee on Expenditures in the Executive Departments (cited hereafter as Hoey Subcommittee), 2179–80, RG 46, executive session hearings, PS1, National Archives, Washington, D.C.

42. Senate, *Employment of Homosexuals in Government,* 18; Hoey Subcommittee hearings, July 14, 1950, 2143. Judging from Civil Service Commission and Justice Department reports to the White House, it appears that the only remotely "factual" basis for Lt. Blick's estimate of 3750 homosexuals working for the federal government was a list of 192 executive branch employees with an arrest record, 125 of whom had already been "separated" from federal employ by April 10, 1950, 17 "retained" after investigation, and 50 whose fate had not been decided by September 12, 1950. The FBI responded to the demand for more names, apparently creating a "form T-2 reporting arrests for perversion" to systematize the growing blacklist. See "Report of Result of Consideration of the Arrest Records of the 192 Persons Named on the Department of Justice List of September, 12, 1950" and "Report on the *341* Persons Named on List Received from Department of Justice on September 12, 1950," n.d., White House central files, confidential files, Truman Papers.

43. Wherry, *Report on the Infiltration of Subversives and Moral Perverts,* 6.

44. S. R. 280, 81st Cong., 2d sess.

45. Lerner, "'Scandal' XI—Sex and Politics"; memorandum, David D. Lloyd to Mr. [Stephen J.] Spingarn, July 3, 1950, White House central files, confidential files, Truman Papers.

46. Memorandum, ld to Mr. Murphy, June 30, 1950, White House central files, confidential files, Truman Papers; Memorandum, Charles S. Murphy, George M. Elsey, and Stephen J. Spingarn to the president, July 11, 1950, assistant to the president file, box 13, Spingarn Papers.

47. Stephen J. Spingarn, memorandum for the Hoey Subcommittee sex pervert investigation file, July 5, 1950; memorandum, R. E. N. [Richard E. Neustadt] to Stephen J. Spingarn, July 5, 1950; handwritten notation by George Elsey on memorandum from S. J. Spingarn to Elsey, June 30, 1950; memorandum, Herbert Maletz to Spingarn, July 3, 1950; all in White House central files, confidential files, Truman Papers.

48. *Washington Times-Herald,* July 27, 1950. It should be noted that the author of this story, Willard Edwards, was a *Chicago Tribune* reporter who had helped McCarthy assemble his Wheeling speech with its fictive list of 205 names of communists in the State Department. He subsequently provided the Wisconsin senator with a House Appropriations Committee report by Robert E. Lee complaining of fifty-seven State Department communists still employed, the number that appeared in the *Congressional Record* version of the Wheeling speech. See Powers, *Not without Honor,* 239.

49. Memorandum, "Public Comment on Investigation of State Department Personnel," July 10, 1950, RG 59, Department of State OPS Reports, box 20; D. B. Eberhart to Senator Kenneth Wherry, August 28 and August 17, 1950, and Wherry to Eberhart, August 22, 1950, box 11, Kenneth Wherry Papers.

50. Lerner, "Washington Sex Story," 4.

51. Lerner, "'Scandal' XI—Sex and Politics," 2; Max Lerner, "'Scandal' in the State Dept.: IV—Kinsey in Washington," *New York Post,* July 13, 1950, 2.

52. Lerner, "Washington Sex Story"; Lerner, "'Scandal' IV—Kinsey," 26. Kinsey, of course, was red-baited as soon as his work appeared, and came under the scrutiny of the congressional red-hunters in 1956 when a House committee investigated charges that Kinsey abetted communism with research that undermined the American family. As a related aside, in 1954, Dean Rusk, the former Truman-era assistant secretary of state for Far Eastern Affairs and future secretary of state to Kennedy and Johnson, canceled funding for Kinsey's institute. Rusk was acting in his role as president of the Rockefeller Foundation. The foundation had been Kinsey's primary sponsor, but Rusk feared that continued funding for the controversial sex researcher would leave his institution open to attack by McCarthy or other lavender-baiting politicians. Kinsey was targeted by homophobes in early 1954 when the Reece Committee investigated tax-exempt foundations. Rusk's decision was in part a legacy of his State Department experience of the sexual politics of the purge. As a member of the foundation's board of trustees, John Foster Dulles strenuously opposed the 1951 renewal of Kinsey's funding for similar reasons, a factor which also entered Rusk's calculations. See Jones, *Kinsey,* 721–37, 649–51.

53. Lerner, "Washington Sex Story"; Lerner, "'Scandal' in the State Dept.: II—The Scientists Speak," *New York Post,* July 11, 1950, 5, 28; Lerner, "'Scandal' in the State Dept.: III—How Many Homosexuals?" *New York Post,* July 12, 1950, 5; Lerner, "'Scandal' IV—Kinsey," 26; "'Scandal' in the State Dept. VII—Sen. Wherry's Crusade," *New York Post,* July 17, 1950, 2, 20; "'Scandal' in the State Dept. XII—What Can Be Done about It?" *New York Post,* July 22, 1950, 20.

54. Lerner, "'Scandal' in the State Dept.: V—The Problem of Blackmail," *New York Post,* July 14, 1950, 2, 24; "'Scandal' in the State Dept.: VI—Are Homosexuals Security Risks?" *New York Post,* July 16, 1950, 2, 7. Francis Flanagan, counsel to the Hoey Subcommittee, was also unable to find "documented instances in which homosexualism had endangered security" but still remained convinced it represented a "serious security threat." See Stephen J. Spingarn, memorandum for the Hoey Subcommittee sex pervert investigation file, July 10, 1950, White House central files, confidential files, Truman Papers.

55. Lerner, "'Scandal' VI—Security Risks?" *New York Post,* July 16, 1950, 7.

56. Memorandum, Philleo Nash to Stephen J. Spingarn, July 7, 1950, with handwritten note by S. J. Spingarn dated July 8, 1950, White House central files, confidential files, Truman Papers.

57. Hoey Subcommittee, executive session hearings, July 19, 1950, 2202–3; memorandum, J. R. Ylitalo to D. L. Nicholson, "Review of 176 Closed Miscellaneous-M files," August 27, 1951, RG 59, Records of the Department of State, Bureau of Security and Consular Affairs, decimal file, box 12, National Archives, College Park, Md.

58. Memorandum, "Problem of Homosexuals and Sex Perverts," Humelsine to Webb, June 23, 1950; Department of State memorandum of conversation between Finlator, Traband, Blick; Spingarn, memorandum for the Hoey Subcommittee sex pervert investigation file, July 5, 1950; Charles Sawyer (secretary of commerce) to Donald S. Dawson [received June 23, 1950]; all in White House central files, confidential files, Truman Papers; Hoey Subcommittee hearings, July 19, 1950, 2210; Ylitalo to Nicholson, "Review of 176 Miscellaneous-M Files."

59. Max Lerner, "'Scandal' in the State Dept.: X—Homosexuals in Uniform," *New York Post,* July 20, 1950, 22. The figure came from testimony before the Hoey Subcommittee by Captain E. P. Hylant of ONI, who explained that the list "contain[ed] the names of individuals who [were] all known or alleged homosexuals and who [were] persons having had connections with such individuals." The breakdown by category: 3,285 ex-uniformed naval personnel, 156 ex-civilian employees of the navy, 1,117 members of other military services and civilian employees of other federal agencies, and 3,301 "civilians outside of the Armed Services in Government." Hoey Subcommittee hearings, July 14, 1950, 2146.

60. Memorandum, re: Files Desired by Investigations Subcommittee in Conduct of Investigation [Francis Flanagan], June 27, 1950; Harry B. Mitchell, chairman U.S. Civil Service Commission, to Senator Kenneth S. Wherry, May 16, 1950; memorandum, Lawson A. Moyer, executive director U.S. Civil Service Commission, to Donald Dawson, assistant to the president, May 8, 1950; all in White House central files, confidential files, Truman Papers. Flanagan later worked as general counsel for the Subcommittee on Permanent Investigations under Joe McCarthy, and alongside Roy Cohn, the committee's "chief counsel"; see Reeves, *Life and Times,* 462–63.

61. John Cramer, "Files on Aberrants Closed to Hill," *Washington Daily News,* July 20, 1950; memorandum, Stephen J. Spingarn to Mr. Dawson, July 21, 1950; Department of State memorandum, "Suggestions as to the objectives of the Committee and Methods of operation," n.d. [circa June 24, 1950]; Department of State memorandum, Arch K. Jean to Mr. Peurifoy, June 20, 1950; all in White House central files, confidential files, Truman Papers.

62. State Department memorandum for the record, Mr. D. L. Nicholson and Travis L. Fletcher, May 3, 1950; memorandum, "Problem of Homosexuals and Sex Perverts," Humelsine to Webb, June 23, 1950, both in White House central files, confidential files, Truman Papers; Hoey Subcommittee hearings, 2211–12.

63. Memorandum, "Problem of Homosexuals and Sex Perverts," Humelsine to Webb, June 23, 1950.

64. Hoey Subcommittee hearings, July 14, 1950, 2089–93.

65. Ibid., 2094–99.

66. Ibid., 2094–99, July 19, 1950, 2183–89.

67. Hoey Subcommittee hearings, July 26, 1950, 2299–2301, and throughout.

68. Memorandum, "Problem of Homosexuals and Sex Perverts," Humelsine to Webb, June 23, 1950, White House central files, confidential files, Truman Papers; Senate, *Employment of Homosexuals in Government;* testimony of Carlisle Humelsine in "Loyalty-Security Problems in the Department of State," February 5, 1953, *Executive Session of the Senate Foreign Relations Committee* (Historical Series), vol. 5, 83d Cong., 1st sess. (Washington, D.C.: U.S. Government Printing Office, 1977), 66, 86–87. Between January 1947 and January 1953, the Truman State Department "separated" 402 employees for homosexuality (or suspicion of homosexuality) through firings, forced resignations, etc. This compares with 244 discharged for suspicion of nonsexual political or security offenses. See the testimony of Humelsine, ibid., 72, 76. For expressions of concern by high-level patricians over the damaging effects of the purge, see "Speech—15 minute draft, Undersecretary [David] Bruce, Honor Awards Ceremony," October 31, 1952, and memorandum, Paul Nitze to the secretary [Acheson], "Possible Improvements in Security Procedures," July 19, 1951, both in RG 59, Department of State decimal file 113/10–650 to 113/12–1952, box 478.

69. Memorandum, Mr. Boykin to Mr. Humelsine, "Donald Duart MacLean and Guy Francis de Moncy Burgess," June 22, 1951, RG 59, misc. lot files, records of the Bureau of Security and Consular Affairs, 1946–53, box 1; "British Hunt 2 Missing Diplomats Ranked as High and Trusted Aides," *New York Times,* June 8, 1951; "The Missing Diplomats," *Newsweek,* June 18, 1951; "'Third Man' in Spy Case to Be Named in Commons," *Washington Post,* October 23, 1955; "MacLean and Burgess: History of Two Spies," *New York Times,* September 25, 1955; See SISS name file: Burgess, Guy, and MacLean, Donald, RG 46, Records of the U.S. Senate. On Burgess, homosexuality and the Cambridge spies, see Sommer, "Anthony Blunt and Guy Burgess."

70. Lerner, "'Scandal' XI—Sex and Politics"; Bert Wissman, "Federal Agency Spots Perverts by Lie-Detector," *Washington Times-Herald,* May 21, 1950.

71. McCarthy, "Information on Lattimore, Jessup, Service, and Hanson Cases, March 30, 1950," and "Lattimore Letter on Chinese Employed by OWI; Additional Information on Philip Jessup, June 2, 1950," and "American Foreign Policy, December 6, 1950," in *Major Speeches,* 65–145, 157; McCarthy, *McCarthyism,* 55, 56; Oshinsky, *Conspiracy So Immense,* 122–25, 136–57; Reeves, *Life and Times,* 255–56, 261–85; Newman, *Owen Lattimore,* 214–21. Newman gives a good picture of the role of the ubiquitous Alfred Kohlberg; Cumings, *Origins of the Korean War,* 92, 108–9, 115, 117, 153, locates Kohlberg (a textile manufacturer/importer dependent on cheap Chinese labor) in the economic-political world of the early Cold War United States. Kohlberg's early attacks on Hiss should be noted too; Kohlberg repeated Chambers's allegations about Hiss to J. F. Dulles of the Carnegie Endowment upon Hiss's appointment. See Weinstein, *Perjury,* 368–69. Philip Jessup, a former professor of international law, was a friend of Acheson's, a distinguished diplomat, a friend of and character witness for Alger Hiss, and an influential member of the Institute for Pacific Relations, the bête noir of Kohlberg and the China Lobby.

72. Unsigned document, "Harvard Alumni Directory 1937," *New York Times* clipping, January 23, 1949, and unsigned document "Dean Acheson," n.d., and list of "persons cited by either Miss Bentley or Mr. Chambers . . . ," n.d., all in SISS name file: Acheson, Dean G., RG 46, National Archives, Washington, D.C.

73. Laurence Burd, "GOP Pushes Campaign to Oust Acheson," *Washington Times Herald,* March 26, 1950; "Acheson Bad Security Risk and Must Go, Says Wherry," *Washington Times Herald,* March 22, 1950; Constantine Brown, "State Department Prestige at Lowest Ebb in History," *Washington Sunday Star,* March 19, 1950; Cal Alley cartoon, *Memphis Commercial Appeal,* reprinted in *Headlines and What's behind Them,* 3:1 (February 1, 1951), 4; Lait and Mortimer, *Washington Confidential,* 10; Davis, "Crusade against Acheson," 23–24.

74. Walter Lippmann, "Today and Tomorrow," *Washington Post,* March 21, 1950; Bert Wissman, "Growing Demand for Ouster of Acheson Voiced in Nation," *Washington Times Herald,* August 12 1950; David Lawrence, "Full Responsibility is Truman's," *Washington Evening Star,* July 26, 1951; "Acheson's Ouster is Urged by G.O.P.," *New York Times,* December 16, 1950; Davis, "Crusade against Acheson," 24; Hans J. Morgenthau, "John Foster Dulles," in Graebner, *Uncertain Tradition,* 293; S. R. 2, January 15, 1951, 82d Cong., 1st sess.

75. Brown, "State Department Prestige"; see also James, "Secretary Acheson: A First Year Audit," *New York Times Magazine,* January 22, 1950, 9; and report on "Public Comment on Communists in the State Department," March 7, 1950, 2, Department of State OPS Reports, box 20; John Duncan Miller, quoted in Davis, "Crusade against Acheson," 24; Acheson, "My Adventures," 27–28.

76. Kahn, *China Hands,* 222; Isaacson and Thomas, *Wise Men,* 557.

77. Wherry, quoted in *New York Times,* August 17, 1950, 1; Kahn, *China Hands,* 237–43. Also in late 1951, a similar fate befell O. Edmund Clubb, another foreign service "China hand" impugned before Congress by Whittaker Chambers.

78. Blumenthal, "Ruins of Georgetown," 228; Merry, *Taking on the World,* 362; Walter T. Ridder, "The Brothers Cassandra, Joseph and Stewart," *The Reporter,* October 21, 1954, 37.

79. Alsop and Alsop, "Why Has Washington Gone Crazy?" 21.

80. Ibid.; Bayley, *Joe McCarthy and the Press,* 161.

81. *Cong. Rec.—Senate,* 81st Cong., 2d sess., August 8 1950, 1278; Bayley, *Joe McCarthy and the Press,* 161–64; Merry, *Taking on the World,* 215–17.

82. Joseph Alsop to Arthur Schlesinger Jr., June 4, 1954; Schlesinger to Alsop, June 1, 1954, both in box P-8, Schlesinger Papers; Yoder, *Joe Alsop's Cold War,* 120. Schlesinger thought the "feebleness" of the "Western alliance" justified "despair (and desperate measures)." He objected to a "preventive showdown" not primarily because of "moral objections" but because he believed a "swift, surgical operation, laying the enemy low," was militarily unfeasible, thus "gross folly to attempt it." Instead he advocated a containment stalemate based on "pushing weapons development": "I want us to have the best radar net in the world; the most potent Strategic Air Command, the most advanced guided missiles, the most ghastly atomic weapons." See Schlesinger to Alsop, June 1, 1954.

83. Joseph Alsop, statement for the McCarran Committee, n.d. [October 18, 1951];

J. Alsop to Sen. Pat McCarran, February 29, 1952, both in SISS name file: Alsop, Joseph and Stewart, RG 46, National Archives, Washington, D.C.; Alsop, draft statement to Tydings Committee, n.d., box 5, Alsop Papers; Yoder, *Joe Alsop's Cold War*, 72–82; Merry, *Taking on the World*, 214. See also Alsop, "Strange Case," 29–33.

84. Joseph Alsop to Senator Smith [SISS], October 19, 1951; Libby [?] to Arthur [Schlesinger], n.d. [October 19, 1951], both in box P-8, Schlesinger Papers; Merry, *Taking on the World*, 219–25; Ball, *Past Has Another Pattern*, 106–9; Yoder, *Joe Alsop's Cold War*, 77–78; Newman, *Owen Lattimore*, 346–51. On Alsop, the patrician identity narrative, and the inculcation of patterns of stoic engagement in struggle and rejection of "appeasement," see the preceding two chapters.

5. The Sexual Inquisition and the Imperial Brotherhood

1. Kahn, *China Hands*, 222, 179; Powers, *Secrecy and Power*, 320–21; anonymous letter to Senator McCarthy, received February 26, 1950; letter to McCarthy signed "an American who H.O.P.E.S.," received February 14 [1950]; and copy of anonymous letter received by Senator Bridges, February 1950, all in Senate Internal Security Subcommittee, name file: Thayer, Charles W., box 259, RG 46, National Archives, Washington, D.C.; U.S. Senate, transcript of executive session hearing before the Committee on Foreign Relations, March 18, 1953, 36–46. The role of Hoover's FBI in the politics of counterperversion will be discussed below.

2. Enclosure, "Foreign Service Officer Charles Wheeler Thayer," Carlisle H. Humelsine to Senator Pat McCarran, July 11, 1952; FBI memorandum, "Charles Wheeler Thayer, Personal History," March 1953, FBI Freedom of Information Act file, Subject: Charles Wheeler Thayer (hereafter cited as Thayer FBI FOIA file).

3. Unsigned memorandum, "Thayer, Chas. W.," n.d. [1950], and anonymous letter to Senator McCarthy, received February 26, 1950, SISS name file, Thayer, Charles W. (portions hand underlined by recipient). The letter to Bridges cited above contains the same charges in a slightly different form. The author of some of the anonymous letters to McCarthy and Bridges may have been John Valentine ("Frenchy") Grombach. Grombach was a right-wing former military intelligence officer who operated as a "freelance" contractor for the CIA and corporate customers and ran a private spy network of ex-Nazis and their Eastern European collaborators. Grombach worked assiduously to collect sexual scandal on his present and former rivals in the intelligence-national security community (the same "establishment" figures despised by McCarthy) and allied himself with the congressional Right in hopes of becoming chief of the CIA. See Simpson, *Blowback*, 245–43; and Kirkpatrick, *Real CIA*, 149–53. Simpson dates Grombach's campaign of smear letters to 1952, based on an interview with Lyman Kirkpatrick of the CIA—but the documents from 1950 I cite contain information that could well have come from someone like Grombach who had contacts within the various secret intelligence-security agencies and was familiar with wartime Yugoslav politics and OSS operations. Reconstructing the exact details and cross-currents of this subterranean sexual and political blackmail is very difficult—much of the documentary material which must have once existed is either still classified for reasons of "privacy," the congressional fifty-year rule for

investigative committee materials, or was likely destroyed by participants (a speculation based on internal evidence found in the archives). Several relatively cursory accounts of this aspect of McCarthyism written during the last twenty years have been based on interviews with surviving participants—but the documents I have uncovered indicate that those accounts are often problematic. Almost all of the firsthand participants are by now dead, so resolving contradictions and omissions through interviews is now impossible.

4. Memorandum, "Thayer, Chas. W."; anonymous letter to McCarthy, received February 26, 1950. Robert A. Lovett (Hill School, Yale, Skull and Bones) was undersecretary of state from 1947 to 1949. See chapters 1 and 2 for discussion of Lovett.

5. Memorandum, "Thayer, Chas. W."; anonymous letter to McCarthy, received February 26, 1950.

6. Copy of anonymous letter, n.d.; letter to McCarthy signed "an American who H.O.P.E.S."

7. Memorandum, W. R. Glavin to Mr. Tolson, January 26, 1949; Mr. Rosen to Mr. Ladd, January 28, 1949, Thayer FBI FOIA file; Subcommittee on Foreign Relations and Investigations Subcommittee of the Committee on Expenditures in the Executive Departments, "Voice of America," S. R. 2, 81st Cong., 1st sess.

8. Rosen to Ladd; Hoover's marginal notation on Rosen to Ladd, February 2, 1949, Thayer FBI FOIA file.

9. Memorandum, Mr. Ladd to the director, FBI, April 27, 1949, with Hoover's marginal notation; memorandum, D. M. Ladd to the director, April 28, 1949; memorandum, Guy Hottel, SAC, Washington Field, to director, FBI, 4–8–49, all in Thayer FBI FOIA file. Finlator's name has been censored by the FBI, but his identity is apparent through comparison with material in Thayer's Senate Internal Security Subcommittee name file. In a review of the Thayer case ten years later (discussed below), an FBI agent determined that many of the witnesses denied making the statements Finlator attributed to them, or reported being coerced into providing the desired response, a result also obtained by SISS investigators in 1951. See Memorandum, SAC, WFO to director, FBI, July 13, 1964, and discussion of SISS inquiries.

10. Ladd to the director, April 27, 1949; Ladd to the director, April 28, 1949; J. Edgar Hoover to James E. Hatcher, Civil Service Commission, June 21 and August 19. 1949; Charles Wheeler Thayer, Loyalty of Government Employees report, May 27, 1949, p. 23; memorandum, V. P. Keay to Mr. H. B. Fletcher, September 6, 1949; unsigned memorandum for the director, March 4, 1950; memorandum, director, FBI to Alexander M. Campbell, assistant attorney general, Criminal Division, June [?], 1949; memorandum, Mr. L. L. Laughlin to Mr. A. H. Belmont, December 3, 1951; J. Edgar Hoover to Mr. Jack D. Neal, Division of Security, Department of State, August 10, 1949; SAC, WFO to director, FBI, July 13,1964; all in Thayer FBI FOIA file. Because of the heavy censorship of Thayer's FBI file, the exact dates when the surveillance began and ended are not available. In a 1964 review of State Department records of the Thayer case, however, the agent in charge of the Washington office of the FBI reported the existence of such surveillance. A reasonable guess would be that the spying began in the spring of 1950 and continued for the next three years.

11. U.S. Senate Committee on Foreign Relations, *Hearings on the Nomination of Charles E. Bohlen,* March 18 and 25, 1953, 274.

12. Unsigned memorandum, re: Charles W. Thayer, n.d. [March 1950]; unsigned memorandum, re: Charles Thayer—Carmel Offie, n.d. [March 1950]; see also memorandum, re: Charles W. Thayer, March 3, 1950; "Excerpts from FBI Reports: New York 6/8/49, Special Agent James E. Tierney"; and "Memorandum Feb. 3, 1949, for Mr. Boykin from John E. Peurifoy," all in SISS name file, Thayer, Charles W. It is likely that the "very confidential source" was "Frenchy" Grombach or perhaps Lyle Munson, a conservative CIA employee and ally of McCarthy. Lyman Kirkpatrick of the CIA, an enemy of McCarthy and his right-wing allies in the CIA, later confirmed that Offie was "one of the most notorious homosexuals in the United States at the time," surely an exaggeration but indicative of Offie's reputation in elite Washington circles. See Hersh, *Old Boys,* 294–95, 326–27.

13. G. A. Nease, memorandum for the director, March 4, 1950, Thayer FBI FOIA file. This document describes a phone conversation with a senator or his staffer, and although the names of participants and subjects other than Thayer are blacked out by FBI censors, context indicates that Carmel Offie is the CIA employed associate of Thayer's whose "criminal record" is sought.

14. District of Columbia Metropolitan Police Department arrest record for "Offie," September 8, 1943, SISS name file: Thayer, Charles W; FBI summary memorandum "Charles Eustis Bohlen," March 16, 1953, FBI FOIPA no. 419532.

15. State Department telegram 802, May 6, 1948, Marshall to Berlin; 282, May 14, 1948, Frankfurt to secretary of state; and 161, May 13, 1948, Kennan to Offie, all in RG 59, Records of the Department of State, 123 decimal file 1945–49, box 854, National Archives, College Park, Md.; Wherry, *Report on the Infiltration of Subversives and Moral Perverts,* 15, 5–6; *New York Times,* March 9 and 15, 1950; April 25, 1950; Max Lerner, "'Scandal' in the State Dept.: IX—They Never Appeal," *New York Post,* July 19, 1950, 38; Harry B. Mitchell to Senator Kenneth Wherry, May 16, 1950, White House central files, confidential files, Truman Papers; Hersh, *Old Boys,* 241–55, 441–48. Offie's State Department personnel records at the National Archives in College Park are incomplete and not especially helpful; as of this writing the FBI has not responded to my FOIA request of several years standing for their file on Offie. On Offie's role in the covert schemes of Frank Wisner's Office of Policy Coordination, see Grose, *Operation Rollback.*

16. Ibid., 294–95, 443–44.

17. Memorandum, "Subject Charles Wheeler Thayer," signed by John H. Finlator, special agent, July 22, 1948, SISS name file, Thayer, Charles W.

18. Ibid. Ira W. Porter probably met Thayer while attending the U.S. Military Academy at West Point—Thayer was class of '33, Porter was class of '32, see *Register of the Department of State 1946* (Washington, D.C., 1947).

19. Joseph McCarthy investigated the International Information Agency (VOA) in 1952–53, precipitating a large-scale purge (accomplished with the help of the State Department). A fascinating State Department security document charting the investigations of 112 VOA employees reveals that forty-one were investigated for sexual deviance or "immorality." The allegations against each employee were listed; ex-

amples included statements like "alleged to be effeminate, to use rouge and powder, and to 'swish' when he walks," "alleged to be obvious lesbian, to smoke cigars," "alleged to be pansy," or simply "allegations regarding effeminancy [*sic*]." One married employee was targeted because of the "allegation that subject is associated with known or suspected homosexuals." Thirty-two employees were investigated for political offenses related to communism, although that included accusations such as "alleged to have brought in recordings bearing emblem of the hammer and sickle" or "alleged to be friendly with Soviet appointed Archbishop of Armenian Church in New York." In only two cases were individuals accused of homosexuality *and* communism. By mid-June 1953, twenty-one of the sex/gender offenders had been "terminated," one "cleared" (ironically, the rouge and powder wearer), and the remaining cases were still "pending SY [security] morals" investigations. See SY chart on IIA investigations, June 11, 1953, RG 59, Bureau of Security and Consular Affairs decimal files, 1953–56 (hereafter cited as Bur. SCA), box 15, National Archives, College Park, Md.

20. Memorandum, "Subject Charles Wheeler Thayer," July 22, 1948; unsigned, undated copy of Finlator's report on Thayer, SISS name file, Thayer, Charles W. While Thayer was not included, Robert Ross, who worked for the Office of War Information between 1942 and 1945, was apparently one of the eighty-one cases on McCarthy's list purporting to name communists in the State Department, along with John Carter Vincent, Philip Jessup, John Stewart Service, and Owen Lattimore—another example of the complex mutation and multiplication of blacklists exchanged and deployed by countersubversives over a period of years. See Seth W. Richardson, chairman, Loyalty Review Board, U.S. Civil Service Commission, to secretary of state, April 5, 1950, and attached list, RG 59, Department of State decimal file 1950–54, 115/1–350 to 115/12 2154, box 487, National Archives. Nicolas Nabokov, a composer and cousin of the novelist Vladimir Nabokov, resigned as chief of the Russian desk of the IBD after a State Department security investigation and in 1951 became secretary-general of the Congress of Cultural Freedom in Paris, an organization largely funded by the CIA as a buttress to the noncommunist Left in postwar Europe. See Coleman, *Liberal Conspiracy*, esp. 43–44, 46–50.

21. "Subject: Charles Wheeler Thayer," June 22, 1948, and handwritten marginal notation, SISS name file, Thayer, Charles W.

22. Memorandum, Mr. L. L. Laughlin to Mr. A. H. Belmont, December 3 1951, Thayer FBI FOIA file.

23. "Excerpts from FBI Reports: New York 6/8/49, and Washington, May 27, 1949," SISS name file, Thayer, Charles W; see also Charles Wheeler Thayer—Loyalty of Government Employees report, FBI, May 27 1949, FBI-FOIA release, Subject: Charles Thayer.

24. Memorandum, Winton H. King to Dick Arens, re: Charles W. Thayer, December 10, 1951, SISS name file, Thayer, Charles W.

25. Ibid.; SAC, WFO to director, FBI, July 13, 1964, Thayer FBI FOIA file (describes State Department security branch memo of December 17, 1951 from Charles Pick).

26. New York City Department of Health, birth certificate 10808, copy dated

November 30, 1951, and SISS transcription of State Department memorandum, John E. Peurifoy to Mr. Boykin, February 3, 1949, SISS name file, Thayer, Charles W. See also memorandum, Mr. Boykin to Mr. Peurifoy, "Charles Wheeler Thayer," May 12, 1949, RG 59, Records of the Bureau of Security and Consular Affairs, 1946–53, lot 53D223, box 1, National Archives. According to FBI files on Thayer, his divorce from Maria Petrucci (on grounds of abandonment) was not finalized until May 27, 1949 Thayer indicated in his diary that he traveled to Mexico City, where on the same day he married and then divorced Olga Philipoff in order to make his child legitimate. If, as seems likely, the Mexican wedding/divorce preceded his divorce from the first Mrs. Thayer, it brings up the possibility, not mentioned in any security documents I have found, that briefly Thayer was at least technically a bigamist. See memorandum, SAC, WFO to director, FBI, July 13,1964, Thayer FBI FOIA file.

27. SAC, WFO to director, FBI, July 13,1964, Thayer FBI FOIA file, citing a letter to State Department security (February 19, 1949), a State Department memorandum (April 15, 1951), and a memorandum from Mr. Nicholson of the Office of Security (May 12, 1951).

28. Ibid., citing memorandum, Humelsine to Mr. Lourie, February 24, 1953.

29. Ibid.; translation of medical certificate by Dr. O. Riggenbach, May 19, 1951, Thayer FBI FOIA file.

30. SAC, WFO to director, FBI, July 13, 1964, Thayer FBI FOIA file.

31. Carlisle H. Humelsine to Senator Pat McCarran, July 11, 1952, and enclosure "Foreign Service Officer Charles Wheeler Thayer," SISS name file, Thayer, Charles W.

32. Morgenthau, "John Foster Dulles," in Graebner, *Uncertain Tradition,* 292–93; interview with Ambassador Charles E. Bohlen by Philip A. Crowl, 23 June 1964, John Foster Dulles Oral History Project, Princeton University Library, 13–14; Arthur Schlesinger Jr. to Adlai Stevenson, April 1, 1953, box 73, Adlai Stevenson Papers, Seely G. Mudd Library, Princeton University.

33. Willard Edwards, "Sex Deviates in State Dept. Called Clique," *Washington Times Herald,* February 6, 1953.

34. Memorandum, L. B. Nichols to Mr. Tolson, February 4, 1953, with Hoover's marginal notation; memorandum, A. H. Belmont to D. M. Ladd, February 17, 1953; "Charles Wheeler Thayer Summary," February 17, 1953, all in Thayer FBI FOIA file.

35. Memorandum, Nichols to Tolson.

36. Hoopes, *Devil and John Foster Dulles,* 153–57; Department of State press release no. 425, August 7, 1953, address by Mr. Scott McLeod before the American Legion Convention, Topeka, Kansas, White House Memoranda Series, box 8, Dulles Papers.

37. Address by Mr. Scott McLeod, American Legion Convention; "Reveals Files on State Dept. Sex Perverts," *Chicago Tribune,* March 27, 1953; "State Dept. Firing Sex Deviates," *Washington Post,* March 27, 1953; "Perverts Fired at Rate of One Every 3 Days," *Washington Times-Herald,* March 27, 1953; memorandum, Mr. Ford to Mr. McLeod, "Moral deviation cases—statistics," April 2, 1953.

38. William Moore, "Senators Act to Oust State Undesirables," *Washington Times-Herald,* April 21, 1953.

39. Memorandum, Ford to McLeod; memorandum for the files, Gwenn Lewis,

"Conversation with Mr. Murrey Marder, October 1, 1953; memorandum, Gwenn Lewis to Robert F. Cartwright, January 8, 1954, RG 59, Department of State, Bureau of Security and Consular Affairs, decimal file, box 12, National Archives, College Park, Md.

40. Memorandum, Dennis A. Flinn to Mr. McLeod, "Statistical Report—Miscellaneous M Unit," March 30, 1954; transcript of White House Press Conference with James C. Hagerty, October 23, 1953, all in RG 59, Department of State, Bureau of Security and Consular Affairs, decimal file, box 12, National Archives, College Park, Md.; William Shannon, "Sin and 'Security,'" *New York Post,* June 14, 1953; "McLeod Lists 107 State Dept. Firings in '53," *Washington Post, July 3, 1953;* Anthony Lewis, "What Does It Mean to Be a Security Risk?" *Washington Daily News,* January 6, 1954. An illustration of the way that the history of the homosexual purges has been erased can be found in Tanenhaus, *Whittaker Chambers,* 479, where he refers to the administration announcement that "more than fourteen hundred 'subversives' had been dropped from the federal payroll, according to Eisenhower's press secretary. . . . When asked how many were spies or even Party members, Hagerty acknowledged the number was few. But all were 'security risks,' a *term now transparently devoid of meaning"* (emphasis added). Tanenhaus is wrong—the term was, of course, freighted with meaning, signifying sexual "perversion" rather than political "subversion."

41. Memorandum, anonymous employee to Mr. McLeod, March 13, 1953; memorandum, Mr. McLeod to Mr. Ford, "Lesbian?" March 16, 1953; memorandum, John W. Ford to Mr. McLeod, "Anonymous Memorandum of March 13 . . . ," April 13, 1953; memorandum, Michael J. Ambrose to C. M. Dulin, "Allegations of Lesbianism, Homosexuality, and Disloyalty," April 16, 1953; memorandum, M. J. Ambrose and James E. Place to C. M. Dulin, April 20, 1953; memorandum, John W. Ford to Mr. McLeod, May 8, 1953, all in RG 59, Bureau of Security and Consular Affairs decimal file, box 12, National Archives.

42. Press release, National Federation of Federal Employees, October 15, 1954; Representative John H. Ray to Secretary of State Dulles, March 10, 1954, RG 59, Department of State decimal file, 1950–1954, box 487, National Archives, College Park, Md.; Joseph Alsop, "Foreign Service Being Wrecked," *Washington Post and Times Herald,* June 6, 1954; Assistant Secretary of State Thruston B. Morton to Representative John H. Ray, March 15, 1954, RG 59, Department of State decimal file, 1950–1954, box 479, National Archives, College Park, Md.; transcripts of White House press conferences with President Eisenhower, January 27, 1954, and February 3, 1954, RG 59, Bureau of Security and Consular Affairs decimal file, 1953–56, box 12, National Archives. The State Department decided that it could not issue "honorable discharge papers" because the procedure might lead to the inadvertent certification of "security risks" (Thruston Morton to John H. Ray, March 29, 1954).

43. Alsop, "Foreign Service Being Wrecked."

44. "Loyalty-Security Problems in the Department of State," February 5, 1953," in U.S. Senate Committee on Foreign Relations, *Executive Sessions,* 86–87.

45. Arthur Schlesinger Jr. to James Wechsler, January 23, 1950, box P-25, Schlesinger Papers. Unsurprisingly, the double standard as a matter of bureaucratic policy also hit women hardest—while official policy allowed the firing of unmarried moth-

ers, there seems to have been no corresponding policy on unmarried fathers. See memorandum, Scott McLeod to Daniel Clare, "Unmarried Mothers," October 18, 1954; Dennis A. Flinn to McLeod, "Unwed Mothers," October 14, 1954; Otto F. Otepka to Dennis A. Flinn, "Unmarried Mothers," October 8, 1954; all in RG 59, Bur. SCA, box 12.

46. Anthony Lewis, "When Does Sexual Behavior Become a Blackmail Risk?" *Washington Daily News,* January 6, 1954; Max Lerner, "'Scandal' in the State Dept.: VI—Are Homosexuals Security Risks?" *New York Post,* July 16, 1950, 7.

47. Schlesinger to Stevenson, May 26, 1953; May 11, 1953; April 1, 1953, box 73, Stevenson Papers.

48. U.S. Senate Committee on Foreign Relations, *Hearings on the Nomination of Charles E. Bohlen,* March 2 and 18, 1953, 10–11, 29–34, 37–43, 48–49; Nominations (Bohlen), March 2, 1953, in U.S. Senate Committee on Foreign Relations, *Executive Sessions,* 210–13.

49. Memorandum, telephone conversation with Senator Knowland, March 7, 1953, box 8, Dulles Papers; minutes, March 10, 1953, in U.S. Senate Committee on Foreign Relations, *Executive Sessions,* 266; "The Menace of McCarthyism," *New Republic,* April 6, 1953, 5–6; "Ike's Victory with Bohlen Reduces McCarthy Influence," *Newsweek,* April 6, 1953, 22. The press of the Christian far Right was blunter about the subterranean accusations against Bohlen; Gerald L. K. Smith in *The Cross and the Flag* of May 1953 asserted that "secret files reveal a perversion in his life," "a besetting sin which had best not be put into words." In the same coded language *The Cross and the Flag* assured its readers that "inside sources" vouched that Senator McCarthy was not "vulnerable" to the public exposure of a similar "besetting sin."

50. Alsop, *I've Seen the Best of It,* 349–50.

51. Costigliola, "'Unceasing Pressure for Penetration,'" 1315–17; Bohlen, *Witness to History,* 20–21; Charles W. Thayer to George Kennan, April 10, 1940, box 3, Charles Thayer Papers.

52. Memorandum, "Personnel Conditions Moscow Embassy," Inspector J. K. Huddle, April 17, 1937, RG 59, General Records of the Department of State, Inspection Records on Foreign Service Posts 1906–39, box 102, National Archives, College Park, Md.; FBI Special Agent Louis Beck's report, quoted in Bearse and Read, *Conspirator,* 47; digests of FBI reports August 23, 1941, January 1, 1942, September 20, 1940, found in summary of "material taken from safe of chief of FP [Division of Foreign Service Personnel] and turned over to SY [Division of Security] on date stamped below 3–23-53," Bur. SCA, decimal files 1953–56, box 15. One of the clerks, Tyler G. Kent, a down-at-the-heels Virginia patrician (Kent school, St. Alban's, Princeton) was later convicted and imprisoned in England on espionage charges when he publicly revealed secret cables between FDR and Churchill. Kent was a right-wing anti-Semite trying to prevent U.S. intervention in WW II. The case was publicized in the United States and became something of a cause célèbre for right-wing isolationist opponents of FDR in 1944. See Bearse and Read, *Conspirator.*

53. Memorandum, telephone conversation with Governor Adams, March 13, 1953, box 8, Dulles Papers; Bohlen, *Witness,* 322.

54. Memorandum, telephone conversation with the president, March 16, 1953;

memorandum, conversation with Mr. Bohlen, March 16, 1953; memorandum, conversation with Mr. Lourie, March 16, 1953; all in box 8, Dulles Papers; Bohlen, *Witness,* 323.

55. L. B. Nichols to the director, "Director's Conferences regarding Charles E. Bohlen, Ambassador to Russia," March 16, 1954, JEH O&C #38, FBI FOIPA reading room, Washington, D.C.; memorandum, telephone conversation with the president.

56. FBI summary—Charles Eustis Bohlen, March 16, 1953, FOIA request appeal no. 98–2723, Subject: Charles E. Bohlen, File Number 77–56416-99.

57. Ibid.

58. Ibid.; memorandum, telephone conversation with the president.

59. Memorandum, telephone conversation with the president.

60. Memorandum, telephone conversation with Senator Wiley, March 17, 1953; memorandum, telephone conversation with Senator Taft, March 17, 1953.

61. Bohlen, *Witness,* 324; U.S. Senate Committee on Foreign Relations, *Report of Proceedings, Nomination of Charles E. Bohlen,* 2.

62. U.S. Senate Committee on Foreign Relations, *Report of Proceedings, Nomination of Bohlen,* 34–35, 23–24. Apparently, to the FBI, the credibility of the "sixth sense" witness was based on the fact that he was a "representative of another government agency" who was himself an admitted homosexual, and who claimed that "in all of his forty-two years as a homosexual he has learned to separate the 'queer' from the men. . . . He can spot them very easily and has never made a mistake in this activity. He described it as part of a sixth sense. He admitted he had had no relations with Bohlen but strongly believes Bohlen to be a homosexual." See Mr. Ladd to Mr. Rosen, "Charles Eustis Bohlen Special Inquiry," March 16, 1953; and memorandum, "Charles Eustis Bohlen," March 16, 1953 (Doc. 4), in JEH O&C#38, FBI. Granting credibility to such testimony accords with popular stereotypes of the time—see the citation in chapter 4, note 12, to *Washington Confidential* and the claim that homosexuals recognized each other through a "fifth sense."

63. U.S. Senate Committee on Foreign Relations, *Report of Proceedings, Nomination of Bohlen,* 25, 38–40, 48; unsigned memorandum, "Analysis of FBI Report," n.d., box 8, Dulles Papers.

64. U.S. Senate Committee on Foreign Relations, *Report of Proceedings, Nomination of Bohlen,* 49, 88, 91.

65. Memorandum, J. Edgar Hoover to FBI assistant directors Clyde Tolson, D. Milton Ladd, and Louis Nichols, March 18, 1953, in Theoharis, *Secret Files,* 259.

66. Memorandum, telephone conversation with Mr. Lourie, March 19, 1953, box 8, Dulles Papers.

67. Ibid.; memorandum, Scott McLeod to Mr. Lourie, "Samuel REBER," April 9, 1953; Donold B. Lourie to Samuel Reber, April 9, 1953, both in RG 59, Bureau of Security and Consular Affairs decimal file, 1953–56, box 15, National Archives; Department of State telegram no. 2299, April 8, 1952, McCloy to secretary of state, RG 59, Department of State decimal file, 123 Reber, box 631, National Archives.

68. Memorandum, telephone conversation with Mr. Lourie.

69. Memorandum, telephone conversation re McLeod Case (White House file),

March 20, 1953; and Dulles to McLeod, March 20, 1953, both in box 8, Dulles Papers; "Bohlen Report Builds Up Feud in State Dept.," *Chicago Tribune,* March 20, 1953.

70. Memorandum, telephone conversation re McLeod Case; memorandum, telephone conversation re McLeod Case; Secretary of State Dulles to Mr. R. W. Scott McLeod, March 20, 1953, both in box 8, Dulles Papers.

71. Memorandum, Dulles to Mr. McLeod; McLeod to Dulles, March 20, 1953; memorandum, Dulles to Mr. McLeod, March 21, 1953; memorandum, telephone conversation with Attorney General Brownell, March 21, 1953, all in box 8, Dulles Papers.

72. Willard Edwards, "Rips Dulles's Cover-up on Bohlen Case," *Chicago Tribune,* March 21, 1953; "Dulles, McCarran Clash over Bohlen," *Washington Post,* March 21, 1953; *Cong. Rec.—Senate,* March 20, 1953, 83d Cong. 1st sess., 2155–57. According to Thayer's account, he was notified by the State Department that he could resign or face charges soon after Dulles extracted the promise from Bohlen not to quit "under any circumstances." It is very likely that McCarran learned that Thayer had been targeted but did not get the full details of the process of "separation." The purge of Thayer will be discussed in detail below. See entry for March 23, 1953, Diaries, Munich and Mallorca, 1953–1954, Thayer Papers (hereafter cited as Thayer Diaries).

73. "Dulles, McCarran Clash"; Edwards, "Rips Dulles's Cover-up."

74. Unsigned memorandum on letterhead of secretary of state, March 21, 1953, box 8, Dulles Papers; "Foes Concede Bohlen's Confirmation; McCarthy Visits Whittaker Chambers," *Washington Post,* March 22, 1953; Tanenhaus, *Whittaker Chambers,* 476–77.

75. Department of State Personnel Action, April 1, 1953, box 4, Thayer Papers; March 23, 1953, Thayer Diaries; Frank G. Wisner, "Notes and Reflections upon Charlie Thayer's Proposed Autobiographical Novel," December 10, 1963, box 19, Thayer Papers. Thayer married Cynthia Dunn on March 28, 1950, with whom he had a son, James D. Thayer. Thayer's unpublished novel about his experience of the purge, "An Officer and a Gentleman" (1963), provides insight into the politics of the nomination battle and his understanding of his sacrificial role in a deal between McCarthy and Dulles. The Bohlen figure in the novel describes the machinations to the Thayer character: "When Urban [i.e., McCarthy] raised objections, he and the Secretary made a deal. Urban wanted another scalp. It didn't matter much as long as it was someone important. The President wanted the nomination to go through. So the Secretary suggests presenting your scalp in return for which Urban would keep on opposing me but not enough to stop the nomination." While I have not discovered any official documents in the archives which would provide the "smoking gun" to confirm the deal, the available record is consistent with such an interpretation. Frank Wisner, who was privy to the secret machinations of the battle, vouched for the accuracy of the novel. See the Wisner memo cited above, and Thayer, "An Officer and a Gentleman," 1st draft, Thayer Papers.

76. Dulles to Senator Alexander Wiley, March 21, 1953; and memorandum, telephone conversation with Senator Smith, March 21, 1953; "Taft Agrees to Put Off Senate Action," *Chicago Tribune,* March 22, 1953; memoranda, telephone conversation with Senator Taft, March 23 and 24, 1953; memorandum, conversation with the

president, Attorney General Brownell, Mr. Dulles, March 22, 1953; memorandum, telephone conversation with Attorney General Brownell, March 23, 1953, all in box 8, Dulles Papers.

77. Memorandum, telephone conversation with Attorney General Brownell.

78. *Cong. Rec.,* 83d Cong., 1st sess., March 23, 1953, 2192, 2196.

79. March 23, 1953, Thayer Diaries.

80. Ibid.; Thayer, "An Officer and a Gentleman." It should be noted that Matson, also an informer for McCarthy, alerted the FBI to the presence of an "index card" in Bohlen's State Department file asserting that the nominee "was associated with several perverts." See Mr. Rosen to Mr. Ladd, "Charles Eustis Bohlen Special Inquiry," March 16, 1953, p. 4, JEH O&C#38, FBI; this sanitized document is part of the "raw files" upon which the FBI summary report was based.

81. March 23, 1953, Thayer Diaries. The following paragraphs also draw on this entry.

82. Ibid.

83. Ibid.; Thayer, "An Officer and a Gentleman," 2d draft, chap. 7, p. 7, Thayer Papers.

84. March 24, 1953, Thayer Diaries. The official reasons for Davies' dismissal were as follows: "his behavior activities, and associations as an officer of the Foreign Service have been such as to reflect adversely upon his judgment, discretion, and security reliability because (1) he opposed and sought to circumvent U.S. poli[c]y toward China in 1942–1945; (2) investigation reflected his close connection with reported Communist elements in the IPR, (3) information received reflected he recommended to another government agency persons of known Communist activities, (4) he associated with a number of persons reliably reported to have been active with the Communist party activities." See unsigned memorandum, "Detailed statistical analysis . . . ," n.d. [1954], RG 59, Bureau of Security and Consular Affairs, decimal files, 1953–56, box 15, National Archives.

85. Memorandum, A. H. Belmont to D. M. Ladd, March 24, 1953, Thayer FBI FOIA file; memorandum, telephone conversation with Attorney General Brownell, March 24, 1953; memorandum, telephone conversation with Senator Wiley, March 24, 1953; memorandum, telephone conversation with Henry Cabot Lodge, letterhead of secretary of state, March 24, 1953, character reference for Bohlen, dictated by Henry Cabot Lodge, March 24, 1953, all in box 8, Dulles Papers. At the same time that Dulles worked to get Bohlen confirmed, he feared political damage from his association with Alger Hiss through his service as a trustee of the Carnegie Endowment, an issue dredged up by the nomination controversy. Dulles prepared a memo for Senator H. Alexander Smith of the Foreign Relations Committee designed to refute charges that he had ever supported Hiss, and to demonstrate his zeal to remove Hiss from the presidency of the Endowment after Hiss testified before HUAC in 1948. Memorandum and cover letter, J. F. Dulles to H. Alexander Smith, March 23, 1953, box 8, Dulles Papers.

86. Summary of "material taken from safe of chief of FP and turned over to SY"; memorandum, telephone conversation with Mr. Lourie, March 24, 1953, box 8, Dulles Papers. On the day that Thayer was forced out, McLeod and his investigators

took possession of FBI reports dating from 1940 and 1941, containing long lists of names of foreign service employees accused of homosexuality, heterosexual promiscuity, and other infractions. Bohlen's name did not appear in those documents, but "Charles Thayer was reported to have 'become identified again with Russian women.'" McLeod also learned of "homosexual activities regarding ... Olaf (chauffeur for Ambassador Steinhardt and Charles Thayer)," among many others.

87. Memorandum, telephone conversation with J. Edgar Hoover and Attorney General Brownell—Bohlen Case, March 24, 1953, box 8, Dulles Papers; L. B Nichols to the director, March 16, 1954, JEH O&C#38, FBI.

88. Hearings, March 25, 1953, U.S. Senate Committee on Foreign Relations, *Executive Sessions,* 271–73.

89. Ibid., 272–74. On the "homosociality" and related sexual license of the 1934–35 Moscow mission, see Costigliola, "'Unceasing Pressure for Penetration,'" esp. 1313–23.

90. Hearings, March 25, U.S. Senate Committee on Foreign Relations, *Executive Sessions,* 275–76.

91. Ibid., 273, 275, 277.

92. Ibid., 274–75.

93. *Cong. Rec.*—Senate, March 25, 1953, 2278, 2280, 2283.

94. Ibid., 2291. In his spoken delivery McCarthy did temper his use of sexual innuendo by comparison with his written speech. In the draft, he identified Thayer as one "to be discharged" then followed by spelling out the reason: "It will be recalled that Acheson, during the campaign, made that statement that the State Department was staffed solely with 'clean living' outstanding Americans. In less than two weeks, Mr. McLeod has removed because of moral degeneracy an increasing number of Acheson's 'clean living' outstanding Americans. Thus is the promise which we made to the American people that we would clean out the State Department being fulfilled." See "Speech of Senator Joe McCarthy, United States Senate, March 25, 1953," box 8, Dulles Papers.

95. *Cong. Rec.*—Senate, March 25, 1953, 2293–95. McCarthy's invocation of the demon-figure "Hiss" was utterly reflexive—in the typescript of the speech he referred to the "Groton vocabulary of the Roosevelt-Acheson gang," both of whom actually did attend Groton School, unlike Alger Hiss.

96. "Clash Delays Vote on Bohlen," *Washington Post,* March 26, 1953; "Bitterness Marks Debate on Bohlen; Taft Defers Vote," *New York Times,* March 26, 1953. The dispute concerned the recommendations of former ambassadors Joseph C. Grew, Norman Armour, and Hugh Gibson, who had prepared a list, at the secretary's request, of suggestions for filling embassy posts, including Bohlen for the USSR (and, interesting in light of subsequent events, George Kennan for Yugoslavia and Samuel Reber for Vietnam). See memorandum with attachments, Messrs Grew, Gibson, and Armour to the secretary, January 29, 1953, and Joseph C. Grew to Sen. H. Alexander Smith, March 26, 1953, box 8, Dulles Papers.

97. "Thayer Quits as Consul in New Inquiry," *Washington Post,* March 27, 1953; "Bohlen's Relative Quits; Consul General in Munich Was Mentioned by McCarthy," *New York Times,* March 27, 1953.

98. *Cong. Rec.*, 83d Cong. 1st sess., March 27, 1953, 2375, 2391.

99. Editorial, *New York Times,* March 28, 1953; editorial, *Washington Post,* March 28, 1953; Bohlen, *Witness,* 329–26; J. F. Dulles, memorandum, telephone conversation with Mr. Bohlen, March 30, 1953, box 8, Dulles Papers; "Ambassador Is Confirmed," *Time,* April 6, 1953, 27; "Ike's Victory," *Newsweek,* April 6, 1953, 21.

100. Memorandum, Scott McLeod to Mr. Lourie, "Samuel Reber," April 9, 1953, and Donold B. Lourie to Samuel Reber, April 9, 1953, both in RG 59, Bur. SCA decimal files, 1953–56, box 15; Schlesinger to Stevenson, May 26, 1953, box 73, Stevenson Papers. Reber didn't actually formally "retire" until July 31, 1953, after he had completed thirty years of service—McLeod was apparently overruled by Walter Bedell Smith. See Walter Bedell Smith to Mary Hoyt Wiborg, June 25, 1953, RG 59, 123 decimal file, box 631, National Archives.

101. Memorandum, John W. Ford to Mr. W. Scott McLeod, May 26, 1953, RG 59, Bur. SCA decimal file, box 12; "Summary, Eighth Session, Course M-106, State Department Administration, Role of the Administrative Officer in Security," n.d. [1953], Bur. SCA miscellaneous subject files, 1951–58, box 2.

102. Charles Thayer, "Officer and a Gentleman," 2d draft, chap. 7, pp. 9–10, Thayer Papers.

103. Ibid., 16; April 23 and June 1, 1953, Thayer Diaries; Sol A. Rosenblatt to Charles Thayer, 27 May, 1953; Charles Thayer to Jimmy [James Clement Dunn], June 4, 1953, correspondence file box 12, all in Thayer Papers; SAC, WFO to director, FBI, July 13, 1964, Thayer FBI FOIA file.

104. Washington City News Service report, April 20, 1953, Thayer FBI FOIA file; "19 Lose U.S. Posts on Morals Charge," *New York Times,* April 21, 1953; "State Firing 5 a Week as Bad Risks," *Washington Post* April 21, 1953; "Aide Will Be Queried on Resignation Story," *New York Times,* April 28, 1953.

105. Walter Bedell Smith to Mary Hoyt Wiburg, June 25, 1953; Smith to Mrs. Dwight D. Eisenhower, June 25, 1953; memorandum, Scott McLeod to W. B. Smith and Donold Lourie, June 25, 1953, all in RG 59, 123 decimal file, box 631, National Archives, College Park, Md.; Charles Thayer to Avis Bohlen, June 22, 1953, correspondence file, box 1, all in Thayer Papers; July 7 and 20, August 16 and 17, September 5, 1953, Thayer Diaries.

106. Ibid.; SAC, WFO to director, FBI, July 13, 1964, citing State Department Security Director Dennis A. Flinn memorandum, January 5, 1955, Thayer FBI FOIA file.

107. Ibid.; telegram, Hoover to legal attaché, Madrid, Spain, February 26, 1954; memorandum, Mr. Belmont to Mr. Tolson, July 14, 1959; memorandum, M. A. Jones to Mr. DeLoach, March 22, 1960; memorandum, SAC, WFO to director, FBI, March 30, 1964, all in Thayer FBI FOIA file; May 23, 1953, Thayer Diaries.

108. SAC, WFO, to director, FBI, July 13, 1964, citing Flinn.

109. Senator Joseph Clark to J. Edgar Hoover, March 15, 1960; J. Egdar Hoover to Senator Clark, March 22, 1960, Thayer FBI FOIA file.

110. Thayer, "An Officer and a Gentleman"; Frank G. Wisner, "Notes and Reflections Upon Thayer's Novel," both in Thayer Papers. Note that this image of self-

immolation as political protest came on the heels of the Vietnamese Buddhist bonze's self-immolation earlier in 1963.

6. Lavender-Baiting and the Persistence of the Sexual Inquisition

1. Bird, *The Chairman*, 417–18; Reeves, *Life and Times*, 525, 540. Oshinsky, *Conspiracy So Immense*, 349–50. See also McCarthy's Senate speech "America's Retreat from Victory; the Story of Gen. George C. Marshall, June 14, 1951," *Major Speeches*, 215–309 (the speech was published as a book by Devin-Adair in 1951, and appeared as a fifty-cent paperback under the title *The Story of General George Marshall* in 1951), and McCarthy, *McCarthyism*, 67–70.

2. Typed copy of Hank Greenspun, "Where I Stand," *Las Vegas Sun*, October 25, 1952, 1, McCarran Papers; Reeves, *Life and Times*, 512; Oshinsky, *Conspiracy So Immense*, 310–11. Greenspun used the same techniques against McCarthy that McCarthy used against his targets. By 1954, Greenspun ran a series of columns in which he claimed to offer evidence that McCarthy was a "secret communist" as well as a "sex deviate" and "by his own admission a security risk on grounds of homosexuality." See, for example, Greenspun, "Where I Stand," *Las Vegas Sun*, February 1, 1954.

3. Oshinsky, *Conspiracy So Immense*, 179–81, 310–11; Pearson's January 14, 1952, diary entry, quoted in Kaiser, *Gay Metropolis*, 75; see also Gentry, *J. Edgar Hoover*, 432–34.

4. Greenspun, "Where I Stand," *Las Vegas Sun*, October 25, 1952; Oshinsky, *Conspiracy So Immense*, 179–81, 206, 310–11; Reeves, *Life and Times*, 512; See also J. Edgar Hoover to Rear Admiral Sidney W. Souers and attachment, April 10, 1950, FBI subject file, PSF, Truman Papers, which lists Babcock, "Secretary to Senator McCarthy," as one of sixty-six persons holding "highly rated" government positions arrested for homosexuality since 1947.

5. Greenspun, "Where I Stand," newspaper clipping, n.d., McCarran Papers; Oshinsky, *Conspiracy So Immense*, 310–11, 328–29; Bradlee, quoted in Kaiser, *Gay Metropolis*, 75.

6. Ed Walsh (assistant city editor, *Newark Star Ledger*) to Eva Adams, October 23, 1952; Walsh to Adams, December 29, 1952; memorandum, Jack to Eva [Adams], n.d.; Alan Jarlson, "Matusow Admits Secret Mission in Vegas for McCarran, McCarthy," newspaper clipping, n.d.; memorandum, Karl Baarslag to Senator Joe McCarthy, November 5, 1954; blind memorandum [FBI], re: Herman Milton Greenspun, with aliases, March 27, 1952; FBI fingerprint record of Herman Greenspun, March 26, 1952; unsigned memorandum, "Regarding the Income Tax of Herman Greenspun," n.d.; all in McCarran Papers; Westbrook Pegler, "About a Lenient Judge," *Washington Times Herald*, December 15, 1953; Pegler, "Blackmailers in Clover!" *Los Angeles Examiner*, March 16, 1954, 19; Pegler, "Dirty Deal for Cohn, Schine," *Washington Times Herald*, [mid] 1954.

7. Straight, "Two Roy Cohns," 14; "Statement by the Secretary of the Army Mr. Robert T. Stevens before the Senate Permanent Subcommittee on Investigations," April 22, 1954, 5–8, and throughout, box 156, Alsop Papers. Thomas Doherty plausi-

bly argues that it may have been a Drew Pearson column of July 17, 1953, on Schine's evasion of military service which prompted the Pasadena, California, draft board to demand that Shine's 4-F classification be reconsidered by the New York draft board (Shine had managed to get the Pasadena 1-A classification changed in New York). The New York board subsequently changed their earlier decision and drafted Schine. Doherty, "Pixies."

8. U.S. Senate, Permanent Subcommittee on Investigations of the Committee on Government Operations, transcripts of executive session testimony of Joseph Alsop, May 7, 1954, 4–8, box 156, Alsop Papers; Drew Pearson, "Schine Leads Charmed Life," *Washington Post*, February 15, 1954; Von Hoffman, *Citizen Cohn*, 127, 183–90. For more allusions to Greenspun's charges about McCarthy's homosexuality see Pearson's column "Backstage Factors in the Schine Case," *Washington Post*, March 17, 1954.

9. Untitled memorandum [Adams chronology], 4,6, 23, and throughout, box 156, Alsop Papers; memorandum, Julien [Sourwine] to Senator [Pat McCarran], March 17, 1954, McCarran Papers; Reeves, *Life and Times*, 575–77; Oshinsky, *Conspiracy So Immense*, 403–7. In the last-cited memo, McCarran's assistant warned that Schine had claimed to have "worked with McCarran in 1952." He counseled the senator that when questioned by army investigators to adopt a position of "calm disinterest" and to assert that Schine had no association with the committee on McCarran's authority.

10. Oshinsky, *Conspiracy So Immense*, 458–60; Powers, *Not without Honor*, 270; Thomas, *When Even Angels Wept*, 591; Reeves, *Life and Times*, 625. The exact date of the "deal" is not clear—Oshinsky's account places it on June 7, while the others place it much earlier.

11. Straight, "McCarthy Takes the Stand," 8; Powers, *Not without Honor*, 270; Oshinsky, *Conspiracy So Immense*, 427, 461–63; Reeves, *Life and Times*, 603. Senator Stuart Symington attempted to subpoena Don Surine, to publicize his dismissal from the FBI for sexual misconduct in the course of an investigation (Reeves, *Life and Times*, 633).

12. Editorial, "Nosedive for McCarthy," *Washington Post*, May 3, 1954; Oshinsky, *Conspiracy So Immense*, 451–52; Drew Pearson, "More on Cohn-Schine Jaunt," *Washington Post* and *Washington Times Herald*, June 5, 1954.

13. Oshinsky, *Conspiracy So Immense*, 460–64. On the next-to-last day of the televised hearings, McCarthy started to attack the CIA by again naming William Bundy as an example of "infiltration" of the agency. But after naming Bundy, he remembered the failure of his attack on Fred Fisher and did not pursue the accusation; see Straight, "Fanaticism of Joseph McCarthy," 6.

14. It is probably also significant that death had eliminated from the political scene two other powerful conservative animators of congressional countersubversion. Senator Kenneth Wherry had died in December 1951, and Senator Patrick McCarran died at the end of September 1954, before the Senate's vote to censure McCarthy.

15. See especially memorandum, SAC Washington Guy Hottel to FBI director, September 19, 1950, FBI 121–41668-28, and memorandum, Assistant Director D. Milton Ladd to director, October 5, 1950, FBI 121–41688-Not Recorded, reproduced in

Theoharis, *Secret Files*, 255-57; See also D'Emilio, "The Bonds of Oppression," in *Sexual Politics, Sexual Communities*, 44-46.

16. Theoharis, *Secret Files*, 357-58, and memorandum, Assistant Director Leland Boardman to director, October 28, 1954, FBI 62-93875-2503, reproduced in Theoharis, *Secret Files*, 293. In the course of his long career, Hoover used sexual espionage and blackmail to achieve his political ends in extremely malevolent and threatening ways. Perhaps the most infamous episode relates to Hoover's 1964 attempt to destroy Dr. Martin Luther King. The FBI conducted an ongoing wire-tapping and hotel-bugging operation which provided the FBI with tapes of King's extramarital sexual activity. Hoping to prevent King from receiving the Nobel Prize, perhaps to eliminate him completely, Hoover authorized an anonymous blackmail letter to the civil rights leader suggesting that suicide was the only alternative to public revelation of the sexual indiscretions. The letter and related FBI documents are reproduced in Theoharis, *Secret Files*, chap. 7. See also O'Reilly, *"Racial Matters."*

17. Gentry, *J. Edgar Hoover*, 412-13.

18. See D'Emilio, "Bonds of Oppression," 46-47, on the FBI's nationwide liaison with local police agencies for purposes of sexual surveillance and containment of homosexuality.

19. Index card, Sex deviate index card file, and informal memorandum, New York SAC Edward Scheidt to FBI director Hoover, April 17, 1952, in Theoharis, *Secret Files*, 284.

20. Informal memorandum, FBI Supervisor Milton Jones to Assistant Director Louis Nichols, July 24, 1952, in Theoharis, *Secret Files*, 285; Baker, *Stevensons*, 329-30. Theoharis, "Operation 'Adlai/Adeline,'" 635-36; Gentry, *J. Edgar Hoover*, 402-3. Baker also reports that Hoover passed on the allegations of Stevenson's homosexuality to a Kennedy "emissary" when the newly elected president was choosing a secretary of state; Baker, *Stevensons*, 406-7; Theoharis states that in 1961, Hoover told John Siegenthaler of the Justice Department that Stevenson was a "notorious homosexual."

21. Addendum, November 10, 1952, JTM: mad; re: Senator Henry Cabot Lodge Jr. information in bureau files; and memorandum, Assistant Director Alex Rosen to Assistant Director D. Milton Ladd, December 17, 1952, in Theoharis, *Secret Files*, 78-79.

22. Yoder, *Joe Alsop's Cold War*, 154.

23. See chapters 2 and 3 above for a discussion of the creation of upper-class masculine identity narratives.

24. Yoder, *Joe Alsop's Cold War*, 154-55.

25. Letterhead memorandum re Joseph Alsop and Stewart Alsop, March 29, 1957, in Theoharis, *Secret Files*, 315-16; Merry, *Taking on the World*, 362-63.

26. Yoder, *Joe Alsop's Cold War*, 155-56; memorandum, FBI director J. Edgar Hoover for personal files, April 14, 1959, in Theoharis, *Secret Files*, 316. While the Soviet blackmail incident dogged Alsop for years afterward, he never publicly emerged from the closet. The Soviet secret police apparently circulated copies of the sexual photographs among elite Washington opinion journalists as late as the nineteen seventies, but his colleagues refused to "out" him. There is no mention of the blackmail in

Alsop's memoirs, published posthumously. Alsop took on the protective coloration of a wife in 1961, when he married the recently widowed Susan Mary (Jay) Patten. Her late husband, William Patten, had been a foreign service officer, Porcellian Club brother, and Alsop's ex-roommate from his first years as a journalist in New York. Alsop proposed by mail from the Democratic Convention in Los Angeles, "When the opportunity to slip into the role of companion and father to a family I had known intimately for so many years, I eagerly volunteered." Mrs. Alsop served as an elegant hostess for "private" dinners with President Kennedy, and for Alsop's heavy social calendar. They split in 1972, although she continued to serve as his hostess. See Alsop, *I've Seen the Best of It,* 65–66, 74–75, 438–40, 469. In contrast to the Soviets, J. Edgar Hoover seems to have successfully blackmailed Alsop with the material in his files. In 1964 he implicitly or explicitly threatened disclosure of Alsop's homosexuality to persuade the journalist to be a conduit for FBI claims that the civil rights movement was riddled with communists. See Branch, *Pillar of Fire,* 293–94.

27. Powers, *Secrecy and Power,* 171. Anthony Summers has written a biography of Hoover in which he argues that Hoover was actively homosexual (and a transvestite, among other peccadilloes); as amusingly ironic as that would be, the evidence he deploys is highly questionable and impossible to corroborate. See Summers, *Official and Confidential.* For the most thorough debunking of Summers's "evidence" and the most complete discussion of Hoover's systematic use of sexual blackmail, see Theoharis, *Hoover, Sex, and Crime.*

28. See, for instance, personal and confidential letter, SAC New York E. E. Conroy to FBI director, January 21, 1944, Nichols file, and memorandum, FBI director J. Edgar Hoover to FBI Assistant Directors Clyde Tolson, Edward Tamm, D. Milton Ladd, and Alex Rosen, n.d. [ca. January 19, 1944], Nichols file, in Theoharis, *Secret Files,* 347–48.

29. Letter, SAC New York E. E. Conroy to Director J. Edgar Hoover, March 1, 1946, Nichols file; personal and confidential Do Not File memorandum, Assistant Director Robert Hendon to Assistant Director Clyde Tolson, June 30, 1943; memorandum, Assistant Director Louis Nichols to Associate Director Clyde Tolson, June 20, 1951; memorandum, Assistant Director Louis Nichols to Associate Director Clyde Tolson, June 22, 1951; Do Not File memorandum, Assistant Director Louis Nichols to Associate Director Clyde Tolson, January 24, 1944; all reproduced in Theoharis, *Secret Files,* 348–49, 353–55, 351–52.

30. Bird, *Color of Truth,* 157, 161–70.

31. Transcription of FBI security report "William P. Bundy—Appointee, Central Intelligence Agency (son-in-law of Acheson)" and attached "Wm. P. Bundy case: (Comment)," n.d. [probably late 1951 or 1952], SISS name file, Bundy, William P., RG 46, National Archives, Washington, D.C. SISS countersubversives continued to keep an eye on Bundy throughout his subsequent career; see his SISS name file cited above. The surly sloppiness of the countersubversive inquisitors is often astonishing. A simple check of the State Department's *Biographical Register* would have revealed that the two employees assumed to be Wm. Bundy's brothers were unrelated; Frederic O. Bundy, b. 1914 in Baskerville, Virginia, and Vernon Everett Bundy, b. 1892 in Blue Rapids, Kansas. For a summary of the countersubversives' conspiracy theory

and the evidence used to support it, see the report by the Senate Internal Security Subcommittee of the Committee on the Judiciary, *Interlocking Subversion in Government Departments,* 83d Cong., 1st, sess., July 30, 1953. Among its conclusions: "the Soviet international organization has carried on a successful and important penetration of the United States Government and this penetration has not been fully exposed," and "Powerful groups and individuals within the executive branch were at work obstructing and weakening the effort to eliminate Soviet agents from positions in Government."

32. Senator Joseph McCarthy to Allen W. Dulles, July 27, 1953; Allen W. Dulles to Senator Joseph McCarthy, 1 August 1953, box 58, Dulles Papers; Joseph Alsop, "McCarthy Is Beaten," *New York Herald Tribune,* July 17, 1953; Oshinsky, *Conspiracy So Immense,* 323–26. Another patrician CIA official, Cord Meyer (St. Paul's School, Yale) became the target of FBI red-hunters in late 1953 and was suspended during loyalty board hearings. Meyer was at the time married to Mary Pinchot, later a mistress of President Kennedy. For an account of Meyer's brush with the inquisition see Cord, *Facing Reality,* 72–81. On the effect of the homosexual and security purges within the CIA see Corson, *Armies of Ignorance,* 377–80.

33. On the systematic policy of Harvard and other universities to covertly cooperate with the anticommunist purge, see Diamond, *Compromised Campus;* another valuable work is Schrecker, *No Ivory Tower.*

34. Reeves, *Life and Times,* 535–34; Bundy, quoted from 1953 in *Current Biography 1962* (New York: H. H. Wilson, 1963).

35. Diamond, "Veritas at Harvard," 13–17; Bundy, "An Exchange," 42.

36. Bellah, "'Veritas' at Harvard," 38.

37. Ibid.; Bird, *Color of Truth,* 128–29. On Acheson as a model of heroic statesmanship, see Bundy, *Pattern of Responsibility.*

38. On homosexuality and its place in political and racial conspiracy theories of modern Europe, see Mosse, *Nationalism and Sexuality,* 138; and Mosse, *The Image of Man,* 68–70.

39. On the roles of Kennan, Thayer, Wisner, etc. in the secret recruitment of Nazis for covert operations, see Simpson, *Blowback.*

40. Dean Acheson, Prize Day address, 1966, Groton School, box 166, Ball Papers.

41. For a firsthand assessment of the damaging effect of the purges on the policy of the Kennedy and Johnson administrations, see McNamara, *In Retrospect,* 32–33, 116–17.

42. Arthur Schlesinger Jr., memorandum for the president, June 12, 1961, box WH-3a, Schlesinger Papers.

43. See Alsop, "Trouble with the State Department," 11–15.

7. John F. Kennedy and the Domestic Politics of Foreign Policy

1. John F. Kennedy, "Are We Up to the Task?" in *Strategy of Peace,* 200. *Freedom of Communications,* pt. 1, *Speeches of Kennedy,* 51, 54–55, 259–60, and throughout.

2. For something of the flavor of the White House publicity surrounding the staffing of the administration, see Heller and Heller, *Kennedy Cabinet.*

288 NOTES TO PAGES 170-173

3. Arthur Schlesinger Jr., court historian to the Kennedy administration, contributed to the cultural and political arguments in favor of an activist executive branch, led by a heroic man, to prevent American society from "acquiescence" in "the drift of history." See Schlesinger, "On Heroic Leadership and the Dilemma of Strong Men and Weak Peoples," in *Politics of Hope.*

4. Schlesinger, "The Crisis of American Masculinity," in *Politics of Hope,* 238.

5. Two important sociological texts forming part of this discourse on declining manhood include Riesman, *Lonely Crowd,* and Whyte, *Organization Man.*

6. For the Ur-text of the "Momism" discourse see Wylie's jeremiad "Common Women," in *Generation of Vipers,* 184–204. The "Momism" thesis took on the legitimacy of science with Strecker, *Their Mothers' Sons.*

7. Two essays from 1958 illustrate liberal-intellectual and popular-conservative variants of masculine anxiety in the 1950s, showing the influences of both the "organization man" argument and the "Momism" argument. See Schlesinger, "Crisis of American Masculinity" (a reprint of a 1958 *Esquire* article), 236–47; and Moskin, "Why Do Women Dominate Him?" (a reprint of a 1958 article in *Look*), 3–24. For a brilliant discussion of some of the meanings of "Momism" in American culture of the Cold War see Rogin, "Kiss Me Deadly: Communism, Motherhood, and Cold War Movies," in *Ronald Reagan, the Movie;* See also Ehrenreich, "Breadwinners and Losers" and "Early Rebels," in *Hearts of Men,* for a useful discussion of the gendered aspects of the terms "maturity," and "conformity" in the 1950s.

8. The etymological root of the word helps illustrate the gendered quality of republican ideology: VIRTUE, n.—ME. *vertu, virtu,* fr. OF. (= F.) *vertu,* fr. L. *virtūtem,* acc. of *virtūs,* 'virtue,' lit. 'manliness, 'manhood,' fr. *vir.* See virile. VIRILE, adj., manly; masculine.—F. *viril,* fr. L. *virīlis,* 'pertaining to a man, masculine, manly, vigorous, spirited.' Ernest Klein, *A Comprehensive Etymological Dictionary of the English Language* (Amsterdam: Elsevier, 1967), 2:1714. For a useful discussion of the intertwining of gendered republicanism with liberalism in American political thought see Kann, *On the Man Question.*

9. John Adams, quoted in Wood, *Creation of the American Republic;* Packard, *Waste Makers,* 233–34. In *The Feminine Mystique* Betty Friedan offers an interesting twist on the discourse of "Momism" and the debilitating effects of consumerism. She granted many of Wylie's assumptions about the parasitism and infantilization of American women and their effect on society, and turned them to another end. She argued that the American culture of consumption compelled women to seek fulfillment exclusively in sexuality and the fraudulent satisfactions of consumer goods. The answer to "the problem that has no name" (comparable in some ways to the problems of Wylie's "Moms") was to give women the chance to find a place in the world of work outside the home, and to end their infantilized frustration and destructive obsession with their children.

10. Schlesinger, *Vital Center,* 13–15, 25, 36–44.

11. Schlesinger, "The New Mood in American Politics" and "The Decline of Greatness," in *Politics of Hope,* 26, 31, 82–83, 86, 88–89.

12. Lederer and Burdick, *Ugly American;* Philip Wylie to the editor, W. W. Norton & Co., October 11, 1958; Wylie to William J. Lederer, April 3, 1959, Lederer

Papers; Hellmann, *American Myth,* 15. Hellmann offers a provocative and insightful reading of *The Ugly American,* focused on American literary history and the cultural myth of the frontier; his treatment omits consideration of gender and class in its account of the cultural or political significance of the book.

13. William J. Lederer to Martin Sommers, October 28, 1957; Lederer to Ivan Von Auw, January 21, 1957; Lederer to Eric Swenson and Ivan Von Auw, August 16, 1957; Lederer to Admiral Felix Stump, April 19, 1957, Lederer Papers.

14. Edward Geary Lansdale was a San Francisco advertising executive who joined the OSS during World War II and afterward worked for the CIA (presenting himself officially as a commissioned officer in the air force). Lansdale's personal legend originated with his actions in the Philippines using psychological warfare techniques to "defeat" the Huk insurgency directed at the oligarchic landlords that ruled the former U.S. colony. Lansdale's tutelage of Ramón Magsaysay—the "reformist," anticommunist secretary of national defense who then became president of the Philippines—created a pattern Lansdale again tried to follow during the American installation of Ngo Dinh Diem as head of the newly created South Vietnam in the years 1954–56. Lansdale's activity in Saigon during this period apparently provided some inspiration for the character Pyle in Graham Greene's *The Quiet American* (1955). William Lederer, a former submarine skipper, became acquainted with Lansdale, and the heroic narrative attached to his exploits, during service in the Philippines in support of Magsaysay. That heroic narrative of postcolonial imperial adventure lives on; Cecil B. Currey, Lansdale's biographer, asserts that Lansdale "richly deserved" the title of "America's latter-day T. E. Lawrence of Southeast Asia" that some used to label Lansdale early in his career. See Currey, introduction to Lansdale, *In the Midst of Wars,* xix; and Currey, *Edward Lansdale.* For an interpretation of the Huk rebellion that challenges the Cold War orthodoxy promulgated by Lansdale and most subsequent U.S. counterinsurgency theorists, and puts the putative "victory" against a "communist" insurgency in a very different light, see Kerkvliet, *Huk Rebellion.* For an interpretation of U.S.-Philippine relations that debunks the myth of Lansdale's influence, see Cullather, *Illusions of Influence,* esp. 96–122. For an exploration of the Lansdale myth, and the uses to which Lansdale and others put it, see Nashel, "Edward Lansdale." Captain W. J. Lederer to Colonel Ed Lansdale, October 28, 1957, box 38, Lansdale Papers; William J. Lederer to Eric [Swenson], Manila, October 14, 1956; and Allen Dulles to Admiral Felix Stump, May 11, 1955, Lederer Papers.

15. W. J. Lederer to Edward Lansdale, December 3, 1957; Lederer to Dr. Max F. Millikan (director of CENIS), August 13, 1954; Dulles to Stump, May 11, 1955; and Max F. Millikan to W. J. Lederer, August 11, 1955, Lederer Papers. Millikan was an assistant director of the CIA in 1951–52 and director of CENIS from 1952 to 1969; CENIS was closely but covertly associated with and funded by the CIA. See Bruce Cumings, "Boundary Displacement: Area Studies and International Studies during and after the Cold War," *Bulletin of Concerned Asian Scholars,* posted on the World Wide Web at http://csf.colorado.edu/bcas/sympos/sycuming.htm.

16. William Lederer first encountered Lieutenant (j.g.) Tom Dooley in 1955 in Haiphong. Dooley operated a clinic as part of the U.S. Navy's "Operation Passage

to Freedom," the relocation of North Vietnamese Catholics to the newly created South Vietnam under Diem. Lederer, in his capacity as public affairs aide to Admiral Felix Stump, encouraged Dooley to keep a diary of his experiences. After a nine-month period of supervising the treatment of hundreds of thousands of refugees, Dooley left on one of the last American ships out of Haiphong. Dooley was decorated by President Diem (the citation "inspired" and written by Edward Lansdale) and received the Legion of Merit from the U.S. Navy. He then joined Lederer in Hawaii for help writing the soon-to-be-famous book *Deliver Us from Evil* (1956), replete with fabricated atrocity stories illustrating the tyrannical cruelty and sadism of the godless North Vietnamese regime. The young naval hero soon became a media star, delivering his anticommunist message in a lecture tour across the United States. During this first period of fame Dooley became acquainted with Cardinal Spellman and Senator John F. Kennedy. Not long afterward, however, Dooley's navy career abruptly ended with an undesirable discharge. Dooley was homosexual, and the Office of Naval Intelligence had conducted an undercover investigation of his sex life, using paid informers in the course of the surveillance. The navy did not want to publicly reveal the "perversion" of its most famous young hero, so Dooley announced his resignation to return to Southeast Asia to continue his humanitarian anticommunist crusade; he also made propaganda appearances under the aegis of the American Friends of Vietnam and served as an informant for the CIA in Laos. The best account of Dooley's career is Fisher, *Dr. America.* See also: Shilts, *Conduct Unbecoming,* 22–27, 517–21, 735–36; Fisher, *Catholic Counterculture,* 140–83; Brownell, "Vietnam Lobby," 289–92; Dooley, *Deliver Us from Evil.*

17. Lederer met Ambassador Charles Bohlen in 1957, when Bohlen had been recalled from Moscow and assigned to Manila. Lederer wrote to a friend, "What a joy it would be to operate with somebody of his nature." See William Lederer to Roy Essoyan, August 22, 1957, Lederer Papers.

18. Edward Lansdale did, in fact, attempt to influence Southeast Asian politics by manipulating indigenous leaders' beliefs in "the effects of wizardry, prophecy, spiritualism, astrology, palmistry, phrenology, necromancy, geomancy, numerology, animistic taboos, and subtle mesmerism," inspired, it seems, by "that basic textbook in counterespionage in this [Asian] part of the world, 'Kim' by Rudyard Kipling." For example, in 1967 he recommended that the U.S. Mission in Saigon compile a list of "personal soothsayers and astrologers who service leading Vietnamese personalities" and subject the soothsayers to "certain influences" to further U.S. aims. Memorandum, Ed Lansdale to Ambassador Bunker and members, U.S. Mission Council, June 1968; and Ed Lansdale to Ambassador Bunker, May 18, 1967, box 62, Lansdale Papers.

19. Slotkin, *Gunfighter Nation,* 37–42. Hellmann, *American Myth,* 35. White, *Eastern Establishment,* 161–70.

20. Lederer and Burdick, *Ugly American;* Burdick was a political scientist at the University of California, Berkeley, and also a Rhodes Scholar and a decorated junior officer of World War II. Englund, *Ugly American;* it should be noted that the screenplay by Stewart Stern took great liberties with the (cinematically intractable) vignettes that composed the novel. The characters of Gilbert MacWhite (played by

Marlon Brando) and Homer Atkins were retained in name but were changed in ways that fundamentally altered their significance as bearers of ideological meaning.

21. See Brownell, "Vietnam Lobby," 122–33; Morgan, "Vietnam Lobby," 125–27, 186; for an extensive and useful treatment of Lansdale and his mythology in the culture of the Cold War, see Nashel, "Edward Lansdale." It should be noted that Kennedy, Arthur Schlesinger Jr., and Angier Biddle Duke (future chief of State Department protocol under Kennedy) all belonged to the AFV.

22. See William P. Bundy's introduction to Blaufarb, *Counterinsurgency Era*, x; Schlesinger, *Robert Kennedy*, 495–98; Arthur Schlesinger Jr. to W. J. Lederer, March 27, 1961; and Lederer to Schlesinger, June 20, 1961, Lederer Papers; W. J. Lederer, memorandum, "Methods for Defeating Reds in Malay," n.d. [summer 1961], box WH-3a, Schlesinger Papers. Lederer endorsed the use of troops "sent into jungles and swamps to flush out the communist guerrillas," lightly armed and "equipt [*sic*] to eat berries, ferns, nuts, fruits, birds and animals which the[y] shot." On at least one occasion Secretary of State Dean Rusk sought "information" from Lederer and Burdick on Southeast Asian politics for inclusion in a speech delivered in Bangkok; on another Schlesinger offered to introduce Lederer to Averell Harriman, the new assistant secretary of state for Far Eastern affairs. See Lederer to Schlesinger, March 22, 1961; telegram, Lederer to Schlesinger, n.d.; and Schlesinger to Lederer, December 15, 1961, Lederer Papers.

23. On "sexual containment" see May, *Homeward Bound*; presidential news conference of October 31, 1963, in *Public Papers of the Presidents, John F. Kennedy*, 830. On the "Greek" ideal see also Kennedy "Soft American," 16; and Schlesinger, *Thousand Days*, 112–13. Priscilla McMillan quote from interview on "The Kennedys," *American Experience* (PBS broadcast, 1992).

24. For example see Kennedy, *Strategy of Peace*, 45, 188, 195, 201, 216; *Freedom of Communications*, pt. 3, *Joint Appearances*, 56, 112, 149, 272, 378. *Freedom of Communications*, pt. 1, *Speeches of Kennedy*, 812. To illustrate the different identity narratives and masculine ideologies of the two candidates: Nixon made only one allusion to Winston Churchill during the campaign, and, speaking before audiences in western United States, he referred to Theodore Roosevelt as the Republican progenitor of dams and water projects. Nixon's main historical argument was that the contemporary Democratic Party had abandoned the honorable traditions of individualism and small government represented by "Jefferson, Jackson, and Wilson," only to be captured by the "radical federalists" "Galbraith, Bowles, and Schlesinger." Later in the campaign Nixon began to substitute Walter Reuther's name for Schlesinger's. See *Freedom of Communications*, pt. 2, *Speeches of Nixon*, 51, 68, 70, 267, 274, 276, 297, 303, 307, 397, 407, 469, 470, 651, 654, 970, 979, 992.

25. Kennedy, "A New Approach on Foreign Policy: A Twelve Point Agenda," in *Strategy of Peace*, p. 3 of unpaginated addendum; Kennedy, "The Years the Locusts Have Eaten," in *Strategy of Peace*, 193.

26. *Freedom of Communications*, pt. 1, *Speeches of Kennedy*, 43, 810.

27. Kennedy, "The Missile Gap," in *Strategy of Peace*, 33–45. Goodwin, *Remembering America*, 75. Kennedy, "Conventional Forces in the Atomic Age," in *Strategy of Peace*, 184.

28. John F. Kennedy to Lemoyne Billings, February 12, 1942, quoted in Hamilton, *JFK*, 459. JFK to Kathleen Kennedy, March 10, 1942, box 4a, Kennedy Personal Papers. JFK to Rip Horton, n.d., box 4b, Kennedy Personal Papers. *Freedom of Communications*, pt. 1, *Speeches of Kennedy*, 54–55.

29. Kennedy, "Soft American," 16. See the themes repeated in Kennedy, "Vigor We Need," 12.

30. On the construction of the story of Kennedy's athletic and war injuries see the extensive discussions in Blair and Blair, *Search for JFK*, and Parmet, *Jack*; both also give useful accounts of Kennedy's use of women in competition and "bonding" with other men. On Max Jacobson and Kennedy's amphetamine treatments, see Michael R. Beschloss, *The Crisis Years*, or Reeves, *President Kennedy*, 146–47, 158–59. It is interesting to compare Max Jacobson's treatment to that prescribed for William James in the late 1860s, "a compound that included an extract from bull's testicles," administered in the hope that "'courage and aggressiveness [would] replace pusillanimity.'" See Townsend, *Manhood at Harvard*, 45.

31. MacKaye, "Bundy of the White House," 84.

32. Reeves, *President Kennedy*, 471–72); Bradlee, *Conversations with Kennedy*, 150–51; Schlesinger, *Robert Kennedy and His Times*, 631; O'Donnell and Powers, *"Johnny, We Hardly Knew Ye,"* 351.

33. See Shafer, *Deadly Paradigms*, 107–10, on the narrative structure created by the revolutionary "theorists," in which they figure as the "vanguard of the people" and a catalyst for the inevitable unfolding of history as revolution.

34. Arthur Schlesinger Jr., memorandum for the president, April 10, 1961, box WH-5, Schlesinger Papers. It should be noted that the patrician liberal Democrat (and Groton old boy) Richard Bissell was in charge of the CIA planning of the invasion.

35. Beschloss, *Crisis Years*, 225, 297, 375–77; Gilpatric, interview, 8–9, 36, 99–100; Michael V. Forrestal, interview by Jean Stein, in *American Journey*, 205–7; McGeorge Bundy, memorandum for the attorney general, March 14, 1963; and Michael V. Forrestal, memorandum for W. Averell Harriman, May 20, 1963; both in box 319, Meetings and Memos, National Security Files, John F. Kennedy Library. See also memorandum of the Operation Mongoose meeting, October 4, 1962, document 1520, in *Cuban Missile Crisis, 1962;* this document reveals that Robert Kennedy expressed the president's "dissatisfaction in the sabotage field," because "nothing was moving forward"; after "a sharp exchange" with the members of the Special Group (Augmented), "General Lansdale's authority over the entire Mongoose operation" was "clarified." Kennedy was so enamored of the legend of antibureaucratic derring-do surrounding Lansdale that early in his administration he wanted Lansdale as ambassador to South Vietnam, or failing that, as chief of the Military Assistance and Advisory Group to Saigon. Lansdale's appointment was blocked by Secretary of State Rusk and Secretary of Defense McNamara (men of middle-class origin, recruited into the administration through the certification of patrician wise man Robert Lovett), who were not so taken with Lansdale's style. Because of their opposition, and despite his "empathy" with the patrician Roswell Gilpatric (deputy secretary of de-

fense), Lansdale found himself increasingly cut off from policy on Vietnam. Kennedy continued as a patron of Lansdale, who he apparently admiringly regarded as the "American counterpart of Ian Fleming's fictional character James Bond." Lansdale continued cooking up elaborate psywar schemes, sabotage and assassination plots for Operation Mongoose until the CIA official Desmond FitzGerald took over the Kennedy administration's efforts to eliminate Castro in 1963. See Robert Shaplen to Edward Lansdale, May 25 [1965], box 39, Lansdale Papers; Felix B. Stump to Lansdale, January 26, 1961, box 41, Lansdale Papers; Currey, *Edward Lansdale*, 227–30, 236–56; Halpern, "Revisiting the Cuban Missile Crisis," 21; Lansdale, memorandum to General Johnson, Subject: Illumination by Submarine, October 15, 1962; and memorandum for the record, minutes of the meeting of the Special Group (Augmented) on Operation Mongoose, October 26, 1962, Mandatory Review Case NLK-90–51, John F. Kennedy Library.

36. Kraft, "Hot Weapon," 87–91. Sorensen, *Kennedy*, 632–33. For another example of media representations of the Green Berets see. Goodman, "Unconventional Warriors." For an example of the military thinking that Kennedy favored see *The Guerrilla—And How to Fight Him: Selections from the Marine Corps Gazette*, ed. T. N. Greene (New York: Praeger, 1962). It should be noted that Edward Lansdale was intimately involved in the genesis and promotion of a series of books on counterinsurgency published by Praeger; the publisher advocated the creation of a "somewhat different American soldier and officer, frugal, tough, adjusted to tropical climate, mentally attuned to long stretches of jungle life." Frederick A. Praeger to Lansdale, July 10, 1962, box 48, Lansdale Papers. See also Frederick A. Praeger to Lansdale, March 8, July 17, and July 18, 1962; and Lansdale to Praeger, March 26 and October 22, 1962, box 6, Lansdale Papers. By 1963, Charles W. Thayer, former diplomat and victim of the homosexual purge in 1953, joined the parade of counterinsurgency pundits with his book *Guerrilla;* among those he consulted was the ubiquitous Edward Lansdale, as well as Roger Hilsman, Averell Harriman, General Victor Krulak, and General William Yarborough of the Special Forces.

37. See chapter 3 for a discussion of Hilsman and the experience of war as a central element of his identity narrative.

38. Hilsman, "Internal War," 29; Hilsman, memorandum for the president, January 13, 1962, box 98, President's Office Files; Hilsman, *American Guerrilla*, 253–80. Hilsman, interview, 18; report by Roger Hilsman (Bureau of Intelligence and Research, Department of State), "A Strategic Concept for South Vietnam," February 2, 1962, box 3, Hilsman Papers. During Hilsman's tenure in office, he favored Lansdale's approach to the problems in Vietnam (based on success against the Huk insurgency in the Philippines). Hilsman "even put his [Lansdale's] name on a list for ambassadors once." Only later did Hilsman come to "feel that he didn't really understand the problems the way I thought he had." Oral History Collection, John F. Kennedy Library, August 14, 1970, 22.

39. Memorandum for the Special Group (Counter-Insurgency), "Counterinsurgency and Related Training for Embassy Officers . . . ," January 23, 1962; memorandum for the Special Group, "Interdepartmental Review of Internal Defense

Courses," July 9, 1962, both in box 319, National Security Files, JFKL; Blaufarb, *Counterinsurgency Era*, 76–77, 71–74; Ball, interview in Stein, *American Journey*, 207–8.

40. *Freedom of Communications*, pt. 1, *Speeches of Kennedy*, 1238–39.

41. "Author Backs Kennedy Plan," UPI, November 6, 1960 (see *New York Times*, November 7, 1960, 35); Rice, *Bold Experiment*, 33, 86–87. Rice provides a serviceable institutional history of the Peace Corps. During the presidential campaign, Nixon had attacked Kennedy's Peace Corps proposal as an "escape hatch" for upper-class draft evaders; see *Freedom of Communication*, pt. 2, *Speeches of Nixon*, 1061.

42. "The Peace Corps: A U.S. Ideal Abroad," *Time*, July 5, 1963, 20–21; Braestrup, "Peace Corpsman No. 1."

43. Rice, *Bold Experiment*, 138–39. Adam Yarmolinsky, interview by Daniel Ellsberg, John F. Kennedy Library, November 11, 1964, 20.

44. "The Peace Corps: Missionary Society? Peace Army? or What?" ed. David Christensen, 1966, box 9, Bush Papers; Rice, *Bold Experiment*, 7; Goodwin, *Remembering America*, 216.

45. Wingenbach, *Peace Corps*, 64–67; Redmon, *Come As You Are*, 96–97.

46. Wingenbach, *Peace Corps*, 65; memorandum, "Orientation for Peace Corps Staff Wives," July 2, 1962; and memorandum for the president from Paul Geren, October 10, 1961, box 6, Bush Papers. This brief discussion does not begin to explore the complexity and variety of women's experience in the Peace Corps, or the ramifications of that experience to the women's movement in the later 1960s, all of which lie outside the scope of this book. However, it is worth quoting Betty Harris (founder of *Ms.* magazine) on her experience as deputy associate director of the Office of Peace Corps Volunteers: "People ask me, how did I get involved in the women's movement? I tell them: at the Peace Corps. For the first time, I had come to realize fully the very discriminatory nature of men's attitudes toward women." Redmon, *Come As You Are*, 97.

47. "Peace Corps: U.S. Ideal Abroad," 20; memorandum, Shriver to the president, July 12, 1961, box 6, Bush Papers; Shriver, "Outlook for Corpsmen," 38–39.

48. AP story, "Free Wheeling Peace Corps Causes Stir in Capital," *Honolulu Star Bulletin*, August 20, 1962, 9. Rice, *Bold Experiment*, 153–54; Wilson, *Inside Outward Bound*, 9; Redmon, *Come As You Are*, 58. Brainchild of Kurt Hahn, the founder and headmaster of the public school Gordonstoun, the Outward Bound Schools began in Britain during World War II as an effort to "re-masculinize" soft British (working-class) youth. Apparently, one intent of the schools was to expose working-class males to the kinds of neo-stoic physical and moral ordeals upper-class boys experienced in public school. See Wilson, *Inside Outward Bound*, 7–34; and Hogan, *Impelled into Experiences*.

49. Sargent Shriver, "The Peace Corps' First Two Years," draft article submitted to *Foreign Affairs*, May 14, 1963, p. 28, box 86, President's Office Files.

50. Rice, *Bold Experiment*, 142, 160. *Who's Who in the Peace Corps: Washington* [1963], 46, box 9, Bush Papers; memorandum, Bradley H. Patterson, August 10, 1961, box 6, Bush Papers. On the Cold War discourses of homosexuality, disease, and

subversion, see the preceding three chapters and Smith, "National Security and Personal Isolation," 307–37.

51. Sargent Shriver, memoranda to the president, March 23, August 29, and September 19, 1961, box 6, Bush Papers.

52. R. Sargent Shriver, memorandum to the president, December 7, 1961, box 85, President's Office Files. "Biodata" sheet on Robert Hicks Bates, box 86, President's Office Files. For a representative sample of the publicity about the staff, see *Who's Who in the Peace Corps,* box 9, Bush Papers. On standards of "service and volunteerism" see R. Sargent Shriver to overseas staff, n.d. [1961], box 85, President's Office Files.

53. Sargent Shriver, "The Best Job in Washington," draft article submitted to the *New York Times,* May 2, 1963, box 86, President's Office Files.

54. *Who's Who in the Peace Corps,* box 9, Bush Papers.

55. Sargent Shriver, memoranda for the president, July 12, June 27, August 1, August 8, November 28, November 7, 1961, box 6, Bush Papers. This strategy was consistent with the long-standing U.S. State Department policy to publicize the achievements of individual black Americans to African and other Third World audiences— "promoting successful individuals as examples of democracy at work"—to deflect attention from the oppressive conditions facing blacks in the Jim Crow South or in northern ghettos. The dark underside of this policy was the systematic discrediting or outright persecution of outspoken African-American public figures who opposed U.S. Cold War policy toward Africa and the Third World or who linked U.S. racial oppression at home with imperialism abroad, including figures like Paul Robeson, W. E. B. Dubois, and even Josephine Baker. See Von Eschen, "Who's the Real Ambassador?" and Dudziak, "Josephine Baker, Racial Protest, and the Cold War."

56. According to *Who's Who in the Peace Corps* [1963], 33, one African-American (male) held a position of major responsibility on the Washington staff.

57. Arnelle, quoted in Nicholas Von Hoffman, "Corridors of Power: Crossing the White Shoe Line," *New Yorker,* May 10, 1993, 56.

58. Rice, *Bold Experiment,* 155, 195, 207,

59. William J. Lederer to William Haddad, January 14 and February 3, 1962, Lederer Papers; William J. Lederer, telephone interview by author, January 29, 1997.

60. William F. Haddad to William J. Lederer, July 12 and June 26, 1962; William J. Lederer to William Haddad, January 14 and February 3, 1962, Lederer Papers; *Honolulu Star Bulletin,* August 20, 1962, 9.

61. Memorandum, William J. Lederer and Eugene Burdick to Sargent Shriver, April 24, 1962, Lederer papers. Although Lederer persuaded William Haddad of the wisdom of a Samoan Peace Corps project, the rest of the Washington staff had no desire to intrude upon "the Interior Department's bailiwick." Haddad to Lederer, July 5, 1962, Lederer Papers.

62. William Lederer, rough draft, *Evaluation Report on Philippines VIII Project at Hilo, Hawaii,* n.d.; W. J. Lederer to Colonel E. G. Lansdale, December 3, 1957, Lederer Papers.

63. RSS [Shriver] to the president, June 7, 1962, box 86, President's Office Files;

clipping, AP story, dateline June 6, 1962, "Thai Boxer Held to Draw by U.S. Peace Corpsman," box 86, President's Office Files.

64. Memorandum, Bill D. Moyers, acting director to the president, March 12, 1963, box 284, National Security Files, John F. Kennedy Library; Shriver to the president, October 27, 1961, box 85, President's Office Files.

65. Kennedy-Shriver conversation on the Peace Corps, April 2, 1963, belt 17B, p.2, presidential recordings transcripts, President's Office Files; John F. Kennedy, "Remarks of the President at Peace Corps Meeting in the Chamber of Commerce Auditorium," Washington, D.C., June 14, 1961, box 86, President's Office Files; Rice, *Bold Experiment,* 292–93.

66. Memorandum, Sargent Shriver to the president, June 20, 1961, cited in Rice, *Bold Experiment,* 264.

67. Sargent Shriver, memorandum for the president, November 21, 1961, box 6, Bush Papers. Harris Wofford, memorandum to the president, May 25, 1961, box 85; R. Sargent Shriver to the president, October 27, 1961, box 85; R. Sargent Shriver to Eunice Shriver, n.d. [1962], box 86; clipping, "The Secrets of its Success: the Hearst Panel interview with Sargent Shriver," box 86; all in President's Office Files.

68. Transcript, Kennedy-Shriver conversation on the Peace Corps, April 2, 1963, belt 17A, p.1, President's Office Files.

69. Sargent Shriver, commencement address, University of Notre Dame, June 4, 1961, box 284; memorandum, HHS [Harold Saunders] to McGB [Bundy], January 18, 1963, box 284; Dean Rusk, airgram to overseas missions, March 25, 1963, box 284; all in National Security Files, John F. Kennedy Library.

70. Memorandum, HHS to McGB, emphasis in original.

71. Memorandum, McGeorge Bundy to Shriver, January 19, 1963, box 284, National Security Files, John F. Kennedy Library.

72. Shriver, commencement address.

73. E. M. Dealy, editor of *Dallas Morning News,* quoted in Beschloss, *Crisis Years,* 327.

8. Manhood, the Imperial Brotherhood, and the Vietnam War

1. The "Munich analogy" was ubiquitous in the arguments for U.S. intervention in Vietnam; it was frequently deployed in high-level national security meetings and was a mainstay of the effort to persuade the American public of the need for war. For example, see President Johnson's assertion to his assembled national security staff that to "give in" on Vietnam would equal "another Munich. If not here, then Thailand." Meeting notes, March 10, 1965, box 1, Bundy Papers. For representations to the public, see the U.S. Defense Department film *Why Viet-Nam? (1965)* which opens with images of Adolf Hitler.

2. Unsigned memorandum, "United States Policy Options in Vietnam: A Synopsis," n.d. [ca. late 1964], box 24, Thomson Papers.

3. McNamara, *In Retrospect,* xvi.

4. Kennedy, "America's Stake in Vietnam," 617–19.

5. Summary record of a meeting, The White House, Washington, January 28,

1961; memorandum, president's deputy special assistant for national security affairs (Rostow) to president's special assistant for national security affairs (Bundy), January 30, 1961; paper prepared by the Country Team Staff Committee: "Basic Counter-insurgency Plan for Viet-Nam," January 4, 1961, in *Foreign Relations of the United States, 1961–1963*, 1:13–19, 1–12 (hereafter *FRUS Vietnam 1961–1963*).

6. Memorandum, director of intelligence and research (Hilsman) to secretary of state, November 16, 1961, *FRUS Vietnam 1961–1963*, 1:623. See also Edward Lansdale, memorandum for General Taylor, "Unconventional Warfare," October 23, 1961, box 203, National Security Files, John F. Kennedy Library (JFKL).

7. See, for instance, National Security Action Memorandum No. 124, subject: establishment of the Special Group (Counter-Insurgency), January 18, 1962, box 333, National Security Files, JFKL; and Maxwell Taylor, memorandum for Mr. Bundy, subject: counterinsurgency doctrine, 13 August, 1962, and attached "U.S. Overseas Internal Defense Policy," NSC Meetings and Memoranda (hereafter M&M), boxes 338–39, National Security Files, JFKL.

8. Roger Hilsman, "A Strategic Concept for Vietnam," February 2, 1962, box 3, Hilsman Papers; memorandum, secretary of state to the president, "Defoliant Operations in Viet-Nam," November 24, 1961, *FRUS Vietnam 1961–1963*, 1:663–64. U.S. officials were, of course, aware of the abusive nature of the strategic hamlet program. The problem, as they saw it, was one of public relations. In April 1962 the Special Group (CI) was warned "that poor handling of implementation of the strategic hamlet concept could result in a propaganda loss for the United States. The uprooting of families from their homes and resettlement in strategic hamlets, if not handled with considerable sensitivity could give the U.S. a black eye." The U.S. embassy received instructions that "groups of Americans should not be present during resettlement movements," presumably to avoid identifying the United States government as an architect of the peasants' forced relocation. Minutes of meeting of Special Group (CI), April 3, 1962, M&M, box 319, National Security Files, JFKL.

9. Rostow, *Diffusion of Power*, 270.

10. See, for instance, Roger Hilsman, memorandum for the president, "A Report on South Vietnam," and the attached "Eyes Only Annex: Performance of U.S. Mission," n.d., box 3, Hilsman Papers. American officials had long hoped to persuade Diem to ease his oppression of the peasantry, moderate his repressive police apparatus, and "democratize" his rule; Diem ignored these pleadings. See Eldridge Durbrow, telegram, embassy in Vietnam to the Department of State, March 16, 1961; telegram, consulate in Switzerland to the Department of State, October 13, 1961, *FRUS Vietnam 1961–1963*, 1:47–51, 363–64.

11. Secretary of defense's deputy assistant for special operations (Lansdale) to President Diem, January 30, 1961, *FRUS Vietnam 1961–1963*, 1:20–23; While exhorting Diem to liberalize his rule on the model of "freedom and democracy," Lansdale's letter also demonstrates his conscious complicity in the ongoing campaign of secret police terror orchestrated by Nhu. See Kahin, *Intervention*, on the Diem government.

12. Memorandum of conference with the president, subject: Vietnam, August 28, 1963, M&M, box 316, National Security Files, JFKL.

13. Henry Cabot Lodge, telegram from the embassy in Vietnam to the Department of State, September 5, 1963, *FRUS Vietnam 1961–1963,* 4:110; cable, to [Department of] State from Lodge, Saigon 652, October 7, 1963, box 204, National Security Files—Countries, Vietnam, JFKL. Michael Forrestal (Exeter, Princeton, Harvard Law) was the son of James V. Forrestal, first secretary of defense, and had worked as an aide to Averell Harriman on Marshall Plan affairs from 1948 to 1950.

14. See, for example, telegram, consulate at Hue to the Department of State, May 10, 1963; telegram, embassy in Vietnam to the Department of State, May 31, 1963; telegram, Department of State to embassy in Vietnam, June 11, 1963; telegram, Department of State to embassy in Vietnam, June 14, 1963, *FRUS Vietnam 1961–1963,* vol. 3.

15. Draft letter, Roger Hilsman to Reinhold Niebuhr and Bishop Pike, n.d. [ca. early July 1963], box 24, Thomson Papers. See also the justification of the strategic hamlet program Hilsman promised to include: research memorandum, deputy director of the Bureau of Intelligence and Research (Denney) to the acting secretary of state, July 1, 1963, reproduced in *FRUS Vietnam 1961–1963,* vol. 3.

16. Several national security bureaucrats invoked the "oriental mind" as an explanation for their failure to successfully implement their schemes for the transformation of Vietnamese politics and society. See, for instance, Gilpatric, interview, 24; Hilsman, interview, 22.

17. Memorandum, conference with the president, subject: Vietnam, September 11, 1963, NSF (M&M), box 317, National Security Files, JFKL. The image held by Kennedy administration policymakers, that of Madame Nhu as a malign influence holding Diem in thrall to her sexual power, persists to this day. See McNamara, *In Retrospect,* 42, for a description of her as "bright, forceful, and beautiful, but also diabolical and scheming—a true sorceress."

18. Memorandum to the secretary of state from INR, Thomas L. Hughes, subject: the problem of Nhu, September 15, 1963; and Central Intelligence Agency memorandum: possibility of a GVN deal with North Vietnam, September 14, 1963, M&M, box 317, National Security Files, JFKL; cable, State to Amembassy Saigon: 534, October 5, 1963; and cable, Lodge to State, Saigon 652, October 7, 1963, Countries-Vietnam, box 204, National Security Files, JFKL.

19. Telegram, Hilsman to Ambassador Lodge, August 24, 1963, M&M, box 316, National Security Files, JFKL. See also research memorandum, director of the Bureau of Intelligence and Research (Hughes) to the Secretary of State, June 21, 1963; memorandum, director of the Vietnam Working Group (Kattenburg) to the assistant secretary of state for Far Eastern affairs (Hilsman), July 24, 1963, *FRUS Vietnam 1961–1963,* 3:405–8, 527–28.

20. Memorandum, conference with the president, subject: Vietnam, August 27, 1963; memorandum, meeting at the State Department, subject: Vietnam, August 31, 1963, M&M, box 316, National Security Files, JFKL.

21. Memoranda, conferences with the president, September 11, August 27, 1963, M&M, box 316, National Security Files, JFKL.

22. Memorandum, conference with the president, August 28, 1963, M&M, box

316, National Security Files, JFKL; George Ball, telegram, Department of State to the embassy in Vietnam, August 24, 1963, *FRUS Vietnam 1961–1963*, 3:628–29.

23. Unsigned planning document draft, "Part A, Phase I: Lodge's approach to Diem," n.d. [ca. early September 1963], M&M, box 317, National Security Files, JFKL; cable draft, personal for the ambassador from the president: No Other Distribution Whatever, August 29, 1963, M&M, box 316, National Security Files, JFKL.

24. Kattenburg, *Vietnam Trauma*, 120.

25. Henry Cabot Lodge, report of meeting with Diem on October 27, 1963; cable, Amembassy Saigon to RUEPCR/OSD 805, October 29, 1963, Countries-Vietnam, box 204; see also cable draft, Eyes Only for Ambassador Saigon, October 29, 1963, and Eyes Only for Ambassador Lodge from McG. Bundy, White House, October 30, 1963, Countries-Vietnam, box 204, National Security Files, JFKL.

26. Memorandum, conference with the president, subject: Vietnam, November 1, 1963; memorandum, conference with the president, November 2, 1963; White House memorandum, checklist for 4 P.M. meeting, October 29, 1963, M&M, box 317, National Security Files, JFKL.

27. Almost as soon as the magnitude of the disaster of U.S. intervention became apparent, partisans and admirers of John F. Kennedy began asserting that had he lived, he would have forsworn escalation and, following reelection in 1964, extricated the United States from Vietnam. Roger Hilsman, Arthur Schlesinger Jr., Kenneth O'Donnell, Mike Mansfield, and later Oliver Stone and John M. Newman advanced one version or another of this claim. The most recent effort along these lines is Logevall, *Choosing War*. Despite the many other virtues of that book, his "counterfactual" argument is unpersuasive. Leaving aside the deep epistemological problems in making assertions about the future intentions and capacities of dead presidents, had they only survived, Logevall's argument is at it root similar to that of his predecessors—a mixture of wishful thinking and hero worship, animated by a distaste for Lyndon Johnson. The only evidence of Kennedy's intention to disengage after the election consists of secondhand reports of private conversations where he expressed unease with U.S. involvement and hints that he might have more freedom of action after the election. We have, however, much evidence of what Kennedy *did:* send ever increasing numbers of military "advisers," escalate levels of combat, and finally encourage and sanction the overthrow and murder of Diem and Nhu with the intent to replace them with more cooperative figureheads willing to prosecute the war more vigorously. To argue that Kennedy would have let Vietnam "go communist," sparing the United States a bloody and futile war, strikes me as a form of historical wish-fulfillment. Logevall's case rests on the supposed contrast between LBJ's character and Kennedy's purportedly greater sophistication, flexibility, and self-confidence in his own judgment. Interestingly, Logevall ultimately places great interpretive weight on LBJ's machismo, "his haunting fear that he would be judged insufficiently manly for the job." Thus the "war as a test of his own manliness" was a primary cause of the decision to escalate. By comparison, "though himself imbued with a good dose of *machismo,* [Kennedy] was less prone to extending it to the nation, to the complex world of foreign policy." This, of course, is much too simple. Despite the centrality

of gender to Logevall's ranking of causes for escalation, he devotes no systematic attention to cultural constructions of masculinity, or to the role of manhood ideologies in the U.S. domestic politics of the era, and thus misses the deep assumptions about "manliness" held by Kennedy and his advisers. Instead, he argues, the choice for war was a product of LBJ's idiosyncratic machismo, and thus almost entirely a matter of individual choice and responsibility rather than a product of deep underlying historical structures or processes.

28. Conversation with McGeorge Bundy, May 2, 1964, transcribed in Beschloss, *Taking Charge*, 341; Goodwin, *Remembering America*, 258.

29. Memorandum for the record, subject: South Vietnam situation, 25 November, 1963, box 1, Meeting Notes File, Lyndon B. Johnson Library.

30. Transcript of telephone conversation, LBJ and McGeorge Bundy, Monday March 2, 1964, in Beschloss, *Taking Charge*.

31. Memorandum, president's special assistant for national security affairs (Bundy) to the president, January 7, 1964; memorandum, Joint Chiefs of Staff to the secretary of defense (McNamara), May 19, 1964, *Foreign Relations of the United States, 1964–1968: Vietnam 1964* (hereafter *FRUS: Vietnam 1964*).

32. Transcript of telephone conversation, LBJ and John S. Knight, Monday Feb. 3, 1964, in Beschloss, *Taking Charge*, 213.

33. Memorandum, Michael V. Forrestal to the president's special assistant for national security affairs (Bundy), March 18, 1964; memorandum, secretary of defense (McNamara) to the president, March 16, 1964, *FRUS: Vietnam 1964*.

34. Memorandum, McGeorge Bundy to the president, May 22, 1964, Memos to the President, box 1, National Security Files, Lyndon B. Johnson Library (LBJL); see also draft memorandum for the president prepared by the Department of Defense, subject: scenario for strikes on North Vietnam, May 24, 1964, *FRUS: Vietnam 1964*.

35. Message from the ambassador in France (Bohlen) to the president, April 2, 1964, *FRUS: Vietnam 1964*. Also see Logevall, *Choosing War*, on de Gaulle and his recognition of the nationalist roots of the conflict in Vietnam.

36. See chapter 4 above.

37. Memorandum, Senator Mike Mansfield to President Johnson, January 6, 1964; memorandum, McGeorge Bundy to the president, January 9, 1964, Memos to the President, McGeorge Bundy, box 1, folder vol. 1, National Security Files, LBJL; draft memorandum to the president, comment on memoranda by Senator Mansfield, July 1, 1964, Memos to the President, folder vol. 2, National Security Files, LBJL; Thomas Hughes statement in Gittinger, *Johnson Years*, 12–13.

38. Transcripts of telephone conversations, LBJ and McGeorge Bundy, March 2, May 15, 1964, in Beschloss, *Taking Charge*, 262, 356;

39. Joseph Alsop, "President Johnson's Choice," *Washington Post*, May 22, 1964.

40. See this chapter's epigraph in which Johnson expresses fear of being seen as "a coward, an unmanly man, a man without a spine" (quoted in Kearns, *Lyndon Johnson and the American Dream*, 253). Halberstam, *Best and Brightest*, 605–6; Merry, *Taking on the World*, 414–16; Joseph Alsop, "Harsh Test for Johnson," *Washington Post*, September 2, 1964; Alsop, "Johnson's Cuba II," *Washington Post*, December 30, 1964; Alsop, "The World He Never Made," *Washington Post*, November 30, 1964.

41. Transcript of telephone conversation, LBJ and Senator Richard Russell, May 27, 1964, in Beschloss, *Taking Charge,* 367, 369.

42. Ibid.

43. Ibid., 369.

44. Ibid.

45. Ibid., 370–71.

46. Ibid., 371–72.

47. Transcript of telephone conversation, LBJ with Richard Russell, June 11, 1964, in Beschloss, *Taking Charge,* 401–3.

48. Ibid.

49. Ibid.

50. The destroyer attacked on August 2, 1964, was in proximity to a U.S.-supported commando assault on North Vietnamese coastal installations, part of the secret OPLAN 34-A, not revealed to Congress or the public. See Kahin, *Intervention,* 219–25; or, for a discussion of Tonkin Gulf by some of the principals involved, see Gittinger, *Johnson Years,* 17–38. For a thorough treatment of OPLAN 34-A operations, the Tonkin Gulf incidents, and the reprisal air attacks, see Moise, *Tonkin Gulf.*

51. LBJ phone call with Robert Anderson, August 3, 1964, Cit. 4631–32, audiotape WH6408.03; notes taken at leadership meeting on August 4, 1964 (McNamara's and Rusk's statements not included), box 1, Meeting Notes File.

52. Hughes statement, 45.

53. Hughes statement, 44–45; advertisements, California Goldwater for President Committee and Goldwater for President Committee, Santa Clara County [1964], in author's possession; Goldwater quotes in Logevall, *Choosing War,* 195.

54. McGeorge Bundy, memorandum for the record, meeting on South Vietnam, September 9, 1964, box 1, Meeting Notes File; summary notes of the 541st meeting of the National Security Council, August 25, 1964, *FRUS: Vietnam 1964;* memorandum from the president's special assistant for national security affairs (Bundy) to the president, August 31, 1964, *FRUS: Vietnam 1964.*

55. Gittinger, *Johnson Years,* 41; See chapter 3 above for a discussion of Johnson's use of cultural narratives of war heroism.

56. *Public Papers of the Presidents: Lyndon B. Johnson,* 1387–1393.

57. Ibid., 1126.

58. Ibid., 1390–91.

59. Morton Mintz, "Jenkins, Aide to LBJ, Resigns after Arrest," *Washington Post,* October 15, 1964; Max Frankel, "President's Aide Quits on Report of Morals Case," *New York Times,* October 15, 1964; Clifford, *Counsel,* 399–402; Kalman, *Abe Fortas,* 234–35. An analysis of 1960s counterperversion discourse centered on the Walter Jenkins episode can be found in Edelman, "Tearooms and Sympathy."

60. O'Donnell, interview, 79; Clifford, *Counsel,* 400–402.

61. Transcript of taped office conversation, February 20, 1964, in Beschloss, *Taking Charge,* 248.

62. Clifford, *Counsel,* 401–2; DeLoach, *Hoover's FBI,* 384–87.

63. Press release, Office of the White House Press Secretary, statement of the president, October 15, 1964, Jenkins, box 11, Aides Files.

64. "Lyndon Aid[e] Quits in Morals Case," *Chicago Tribune,* October 15, 1964; Mintz, "Jenkins"; Frankel, "President's Aide Quits."

65. "Lyndon Aid[e]"; Mintz, "Jenkins"; Frankel, "President's Aide Quits"; James Reston, "Setback for Johnson," *New York Times,* October 15, 1964; "The Jenkins Case," *New York Times,* October 16, 1964; "White House Morality," *Chicago Tribune,* October 16, 1964; editorial, "The Security Sieve," *New York Times,* October 18, 1964; Arthur Krock, "The Jenkins Case: The Issue of National Security Is Raising Some Vital Questions," *New York Times,* October 18, 1964.

66. See Hughes statement, 45. Senator Lyndon B. Johnson to the State Department, January 27, 1953; and Assistant Secretary of State Thruston B. Morton to Senator Johnson, February 18, 1953, both in RG 59, Department of State decimal file, 1950–54, box 479, National Archives, College Park, Md.; Gentry, *J. Edgar Hoover,* 579; Joseph Hearst, "Barry Reveals Early Morning Quiz by FBI," *Chicago Tribune,* October 20, 1964; E. W. Kenworthy, "Goldwater Asks F.B.I. to Explain Check on Jenkins," *New York Times,* October 20, 1964. Hughes (head of State Department Intelligence and Research in 1964) actually argues that the discovery of Goldwater's efficiency reports on Jenkins was a "stroke of luck" that "quashed" the issue. But an examination of the *Chicago Tribune, Washington Post,* and *New York Times* from October 15 to November 2, 1964, reveals that the issue was not "quashed"; it played a prominent role in coverage of the election, and continued to get front-page headlines despite the October 16 news that Nikita Khrushchev had been deposed in the USSR, and the October 17 revelation of the first successful atomic bomb test in communist China.

67. Richard L. Lyons, "Goldwater Bars Jenkins Issue but for Security," *Washington Post,* October 16, 1964; Charles Mohr, "Goldwater to Shun Jenkins Case but Not Its Aspects of Security," *New York Times,* October 16, 1964; Roland Evans and Robert Novak, "The Jenkins Affair," *Washington Post,* October 16, 1964; Robert E. Baker, "Barry Assails 'Curious Crew' in White House," *Washington Post,* October 25, 1964; "G.O.P. Aide Sees Strong Impact on Campaign in Jenkins Case," *New York Times,* October 15, 1964; "Jenkins Report Sought By Nixon," *New York Times,* October 16, 1964; "White House Cloud Darker, Miller Holds," *Chicago Tribune,* October 22, 1964; "Miller Urges: Demand Full Jenkins Story," *Chicago Tribune,* October 24, 1964: Laurence Stern, " FBI Finds No Security Breach: Blackmail Indications Missing," *Washington Post,* October 23, 1964; "Finds Jenkins Report Vague," *Chicago Tribune,* October 24, 1964.

68. "Miller Urges"; Philip Warden, "Calls for Tightened Security Screening," *Chicago Tribune,* October 20, 1964.

69. Tom Wicker, "Secret Service Had Jenkins File," *New York Times,* October 17, 1964; Walter Trohan, "Fought to Get Pervert Reinstated," *Chicago Tribune,* October 24, 1964; "FBI Files Jenkins Report," *Chicago Tribune,* October 23, 1964.

70. John D. Morris, "Democrats Calm on Jenkins Case," *New York Times,* October 17, 1964; Austin C. Wehrwein, "Global Events Seen Overshadowing Jenkins Case in Midwest," *New York Times,* October 19, 1964; Charles Mohr, "Campaign Issues—V," October 29, 1964; "Johnson Up 2% in Poll Taken after Jenkins Case, Red Crisis," *Washington Post,* October 23, 1964; Walter Lippmann, "His Last Ploy" October 29,

1964; Fendall W. Yerxa, "Johnson Finds 'Smearlash' Costing Goldwater Votes," *New York Times,* October 22, 1964; "Ike Also Faced a 'Jenkins Case' Johnson Says," *Washington Post,* October 29, 1964; "Ike Doesn't Recall 'Jenkins Problem' during His Terms," *Washington Post,* October 29, 1964; "Nixon Says Johnson Smeared Ike's Aides," *Washington Post,* October 31, 1964. It is clear from a sanitized FBI memorandum that the Eisenhower White House was directly touched by the homosexual purges, although details are still classified. When Hoover reported the attempted Soviet sexual blackmail of journalist Joseph Alsop to presidential aide Sherman Adams, he justified deploying the sexual secrets because "one of the employees in the White House who was involved in homosexual acts admitted he had seen a report in the Executive Office referring to [one or more words deleted] being in the same category. [2 lines deleted] In view of this I told Mr. Rogers I felt the Governor should be aware of the Alsop matter." John Edgar Hoover, memorandum for Mr. Tolson, Mr. Boardman, Mr. Belmont, Mr. Nichols, April 17, 1957, JEH O&C#26, FBI Freedom of Information Act request.

71. Memorandum to the president, January 9, 1964, Memos to President, box 1, National Security Files, LBJL.

72. Ellsberg, "Quagmire Myth," 90–91. James C. Thomson, too, testified to White House strictures against producing a paper trail connected to deliberations on negotiated withdrawal: "the very concept of negotiation was, for a while, so anathema that any concept of turning down an escalatory track and turning away from it was considered so subversive that Mac Bundy would tell Chet Cooper under no circumstances to put anything on possible peace negotiations in a typewriter, but instead to put it in handwriting, so that there would be no copy." This was "because such issues were regarded as so potentially explosive both upward and outward." Thomson, interview, 24.

73. See for example, paper prepared by the National Security Council Working Group: Summary, Courses of Action in Southeast Asia, November 21, 1964; telegram from the commander in chief, Pacific (Sharp) to the chairman of the Joint Chiefs of Staff (Wheeler), November 22, 1964; memorandum from the Joint Chiefs of Staff to the secretary of defense (McNamara), November 23, 1964; memorandum of the meeting of the Executive Committee, Washington, November 24, 1964; paper prepared by the Executive Committee: Position Paper on Southeast Asia, December 2, 1964; all in *FRUS: Vietnam 1964.*

74. [Handwritten] meeting notes, Cabinet Room—ExCom (SVN), December 1, 1964, box 1, Meeting Notes File.

75. McGeorge Bundy, memorandum for the president, re: basic policy in Vietnam, January 27, 1965; telegram, Department of State, for Ambassador Taylor from the president, February 8, 1965, Bundy, box 2, Aides Files.

76. Bundy's report to the president February 7, 1965, quoted in Bird, *Color of Truth,* 307. The best account of the complexities of U.S.–South Vietnamese politics surrounding the bombing is Kahin, *Intervention,* 286–305.

77. Meeting notes, March 10, 1965, box 1, Bundy Papers.

78. Logevall, *Choosing War,* 136–39; Mike Mansfield to the president, February 1, 1964; Mike Mansfield to the president, January 6, 1964; see also Mike Mansfield to

the president, December 7, 1963, Memos to the President, box 1, National Security Files, LBJL; O'Donnell, interview, 109.

79. Hubert Humphrey, memorandum to President Johnson, February 15, 1965, reprinted in Gittinger, *Johnson Years,* 156–58.

80. DiLeo, *George Ball,* 11–12; George Ball, *The Past Has Another Pattern.*

81. DiLeo, *George Ball,* 72, 73; Ball, quoted in Stein, *American Journey,* 208; On Ball's position on the "margins of power" in the Kennedy administration because of his "second tier" educational background, his skepticism about Third World development schemes and counterinsurgency, and his "Eurocentrism," see DiLeo, *George Ball,* 38–43.

82. Ball, *Past Has Another Pattern,* 153.

83. Ibid., 380–84.

84. William Bundy, memorandum for Secretary Rusk, Secretary McNamara, Mr. Ball, Mr. McGeorge Bundy, "Attached Think-Piece on Our Choices in Southeast Asia," October 19, 1964, quoted in Bird, *Color of Truth,* 291–92.

85. Bird, *Color of Truth,* 294–96.

86. Joseph Alsop, "The Deceptive Calm," *Washington Post,* November 23, 1964; William Bundy to Joseph Alsop, November 23, 1964; Alsop to Wm. Bundy, n.d. [late November 1964]; McGeorge Bundy to Alsop, Saturday [probably November 28, 1964]; Alsop to McGeorge Bundy, n.d. [end of November 1964]; all in box 69, Alsop Papers.

87. Ball, *Past Has Another Pattern,* 395–98.

88. McGeorge Bundy, memorandum for the president, subject: meeting Friday morning on Vietnam, July 1, 1965, Memos to the President, box 4, National Security Files, LBJL.

89. Extensive accounts of the July 1965 meetings and decisions can be found in Ball, *Past Has Another Pattern;* Berman, *Planning a Tragedy;* Kahin, *Intervention;* Van-DeMark, *Into the Quagmire;* Barrett, *Uncertain Warriors.*

90. Ball, *Past Has Another Pattern,* 383, 389.

91. Notes, Cabinet Room, Wednesday, July 21, 1965, subject: Vietnam, box 1, Meeting Notes File. Present at this meeting were: McNamara, Rusk, [Cyrus] Vance, [McGeorge] Bundy, General Wheeler, George Ball, Bill Bundy, Len Unger, [Richard] Helms, Admiral Raborn, [Henry Cabot] Lodge, [Carl] Rowan, [John] Mc-Naughton, [Bill] Moyers, [Jack] Valenti.

92. Notes of meeting, July 21 1965, 10:40 A.M., Meeting Notes File. Quotations in the paragraphs that follow are from this source.

93. Meeting notes, July 21, 1965, resume same meeting at 2:45 P.M., box 1, National Security Files, LBJL. Throughout 1964 U.S. allies, with the exception of Australia, had expressed profound doubts or outright opposition to U.S. escalation of the war. See Logevall, *Choosing War,* esp. 130–33, 222–28

94. Notes of meeting, July 21, 1965, Meeting Notes File.

95. Notes of meeting, Cabinet Room, July 22, 1965, box 1, Meeting Notes File. Present were: the president, McNamara, Vance, General Wheeler, General Johnson, Secretary Resor, General McConnell, General Greene, Admiral McDonald, [Clark] Clifford, Nitze, Secretary Zuchert, Secretary Brown, [McGeorge] Bundy.

96. Notes of meeting, July 22, 1965, 12 noon, Meeting Notes File.

97. Ibid.

98. Ibid.

99. Notes of meeting, Camp David, Aspen Lodge, July 25, 1965, 5:00 P.M.; Cabinet Room, July 22, 1965, 3:00 P.M.; both in box 1, Meeting Notes File.

100. Notes of meeting, July 22, 1965, 3:00 P.M.

101. Notes of meetings, July 28 and April 1, 1965, box 1, Bundy Papers.

102. Johnson, quoted in DiLeo, *George Ball,* 132.

103. Johnson, quoted in Emerson, *Winners and Losers,* 377; Johnson, quoted in Halberstam, *Best and Brightest,* 414.

104. Rusk, *As I Saw It,* 418; Isaacson and Thomas, *Wise Men,* 657; Shapley, *Promise and Power,* 426, 434–35; Clifford, *Counsel,* 456–57.

Afterword

1. For such a functionalist argument see Gilmore, *Manhood in the Making.* For a sophisticated analysis of the relationship of ideology to "structural power," See Wolf, *Envisioning Power.*

2. Appy, *Working-Class War;* on "bureaucratic homicide," see Barnet, *Roots Of War.*

3. Karl Marx, *The Eighteenth Brumaire of Louis Bonaparte* (New York: International Publishers, 1969), 15.

REFERENCES

Acheson, Dean. "My Adventures among the Senators." *Saturday Evening Post,* April 1, 1961.

———. Interview by Lucius D. Battle, April 27, 1964. John F. Kennedy Library, Boston, Mass.

———. *Morning and Noon.* Boston: Houghton Mifflin, 1965.

———. *Present at the Creation: My Years in the State Department.* New York: W. W. Norton, 1969.

Adams, Michael C. C. *The Best War Ever: America and World War II.* Baltimore: Johns Hopkins University Press, 1994.

Aides Files. Lyndon Baines Johnson Library, Austin, Tex.

Aldrich, Nelson W., Jr. *Tommy Hitchcock: An American Hero.* Fleet Street Corporation, 1984.

———. *Old Money: The Mythology of America's Upper Class.* New York: Alfred A. Knopf, 1988.

Almquist, Leann Grabavoy. *Joseph Alsop and American Foreign Policy: The Journalist as Advocate.* Lanham, Md.: University Press of America, 1993.

Alsop, Joseph W. Papers. Library of Congress.

———. "The Strange Case of Louis Budenz." *Atlantic Monthly,* April 1952.

———. *I've Seen the Best of It: The Memoirs of Joseph W. Alsop.* New York: Norton, 1992.

Alsop, Joseph W., and Stewart Alsop. "Why Has Washington Gone Crazy?" *Saturday Evening Post,* July 29, 1950.

Alsop, Stewart. "The Trouble with the State Department." *Saturday Evening Post,* March 3, 1962.

Appy, Christian G. *Working-Class War: American Combat Soldiers and Vietnam.* Chapel Hill: University of North Carolina Press, 1993.

Ashburn, Frank D. *Peabody of Groton: A Portrait.* New York: Coward McCann, 1944.

Babbitt, George. *Norman Prince: A Volunteer Who Died for the Cause He Loved.* Boston: Houghton Mifflin, 1917.

Baker, Jean. *The Stevensons: A Biography of an American Family.* New York: W. W. Norton, 1996.

Ball, George W. Papers. Seely G. Mudd Manuscript Library, Princeton University, Princeton, N.J.

——. *The Past Has Another Pattern: Memoirs.* New York: W. W. Norton, 1982.

Baltzell, E. Digby. *Philadelphia Gentlemen: The Making of a National Upper Class.* Glencoe, Ill.: Free Press, 1958.

——. *The Protestant Establishment: Aristocracy and Caste in America.* New York: Random House, 1964.

——. *The Protestant Establishment Revisited.* New Brunswick: Transaction Publishers, 1991.

Barnet, Richard J. *Roots of War: The Men and Institutions behind U.S. Foreign Policy.* New York: Random House, 1972.

Barrett, David M. *Uncertain Warriors: Lyndon Johnson and His Vietnam Advisors.* Lawrence, Kans.: University Press of Kansas, 1993.

Bayley, Edwin R. *Joe McCarthy and the Press.* Madison: University of Wisconsin Press, 1981.

Bearse, Ray, and Anthony Read. *Conspirator: The Untold Story of Tyler Kent.* New York: Doubleday, 1991.

Bellah, Robert N. "'Veritas' at Harvard: Another Exchange." Letter to the editors. *New York Review of Books,* July 14, 1977.

Berman, Larry. *Planning a Tragedy: The Americanization of the War in Vietnam.* New York: W. W. Norton, 1982.

——. *Lyndon Johnson's War.* New York: W. W. Norton, 1989.

Berube, Alan. *Coming Out under Fire: The History of Gay Men and Women in World War II.* New York: Free Press, 1990.

Beschloss, Michael. *The Crisis Years: Kennedy and Khrushchev, 1960–1963.* New York: HarperCollins, 1991.

——, ed. *Taking Charge: The Johnson White House Tapes, 1963–1964.* New York: Simon and Schuster, 1997.

Biddle, George. *An American Artist's Story.* Boston: Little, Brown, 1939.

Bird, Kai. *The Chairman: John J. McCloy, the Making of the American Establishment.* New York: Simon and Schuster, 1992.

——. *The Color of Truth: McGeorge Bundy and William Bundy: Brothers in Arms.* New York: Simon and Schuster, 1998.

Blair, Joan, and Clay Blair Jr. *The Search for JFK.* New York: Berkley, 1976.

Blaufarb, Douglas S. *The Counterinsurgency Era: U.S. Doctrine and Performance, 1950 to the Present.* New York: Free Press, 1977.

Blumenthal, Sidney. "The Ruins of Georgetown." *New Yorker,* October 21 & 28, 1996.

——. "The Cold War and the Closet: The True Legacy of Whittaker Chambers." *New Yorker,* March 17, 1997.

Bohlen, Charles E. *Witness to History, 1929–1969.* New York: W. W. Norton, 1973.

Bradlee, Benjamin C. *Conversations with Kennedy.* New York: W. W. Norton, 1975.

Braestrup, Peter. "Peace Corpsman No. 1—a Progress Report." *New York Times Magazine,* December 17, 1961.

Branch, Taylor. *Pillar of Fire: America in the King Years 1963–65.* New York: Simon and Schuster, 1998.

Brownell, Will. "The Vietnam Lobby: The Americans Who Lobbied for a Free and Independent South Vietnam in the 1940s and 1950s." Ph.D. diss., Columbia University, 1993.

Bundy, McGeorge. Papers. Lyndon Baines Johnson Library, Austin, Tex.

——. "The Battlefields of Power and the Searchlights of the Academy." In *The Dimensions of Diplomacy,* edited by E. A. Johnson. Baltimore: Johns Hopkins Press, 1964.

——. "The Presidency and the Peace." *Foreign Affairs* 42, no. 3 (April 1964).

——. "An Exchange on 'Veritas at Harvard.'" Letter to the editors. *New York Review of Books,* May 26, 1977.

——, ed. *The Pattern of Responsibility.* Boston: Houghton Mifflin, 1952.

Burke, John P., and Fred I. Greenstein. *How Presidents Test Reality: Decisions in Vietnam, 1954 & 1965.* New York: Russel Sage Foundation, 1989.

Bush, Gerald W. Papers. John F. Kennedy Library, Boston, Mass.

Caidin, Martin, and Edward Hymoff. *The Mission.* Philadelphia: J. B. Lippincott, 1964.

Callaway, Helen. *Gender, Culture, and Empire: European Women in Colonial Nigeria.* Houndmills, England: Macmillan, 1987.

Caro, Robert A. *The Years of Lyndon Johnson: The Means of Ascent.* Vol. 2. New York: Alfred A. Knopf, 1990.

Caute, David. *The Great Fear: The Anti-communist Purge under Truman and Eisenhower.* New York: Simon and Schuster, 1978.

Chambers, Whittaker. *Witness.* New York: Random House, 1952.

Chapman, David L. *Sandow the Magnificent: Eugen Sandow and the Beginnings of Bodybuilding.* Urbana: University of Illinois Press, 1994.

Chapman, John Jay. *Victor Chapman's Letters from France.* New York: Macmillan, 1917.

Clifford, John Garry. *The Citizen Soldiers: The Plattsburg Training Camp Movement, 1913–1920.* Lexington: University Press of Kentucky, 1972.

Clifford, Clark, with Richard Holbrooke. *Counsel to the President: A Memoir.* New York: Random House, 1991.

Cohn, Carol. "Wars, Wimps, and Women: Talking Gender and Thinking War." In *Gendering War Talk,* edited by Miriam Cooke and Angela Woolacott. Princeton, N.J.: Princeton University Press, 1993.

Coleman, Peter. *The Liberal Conspiracy: The Congress of Cultural Freedom and the Struggle for the Mind of Postwar Europe.* New York: Free Press, 1989.

Collier, Peter, and David Horowitz. *The Kennedys: An American Drama.* New York: Summit Books, 1984.

Connolly, Cyril. *Enemies of Promise.* New York: Macmillan, 1948.

Cooke, Alastair. *A Generation on Trial: U.S.A. v. Alger Hiss.* New York: Alfred A. Knopf, 1950.

Cookson, Peter W., Jr., and Caroline Hodges Persell, *Preparing for Power: America's Elite Boarding Schools.* New York: Basic Books, 1985.

Corson, William R. *The Armies of Ignorance: The Rise of the American Intelligence Empire.* New York: Dial, 1977.

Costello, John. *Virtue under Fire: How World War II Changed Our Social and Sexual Attitudes.* Boston: Little, Brown, 1985.

Costigliola, Frank. "'Unceasing Pressure for Penetration': Gender, Pathology, and Emotion in George Kennan's Formation of the Cold War." *Journal of American History* 83, no. 2 (March 1997).

The Cuban Missile Crisis, 1962. Alexandria, Va.: Chadwyck-Healy, 1990.

Cullather, Nick. *Illusions of Influence: The Political Economy of United States–Philippines Relations, 1942–1960.* Stanford: Stanford University Press, 1994.

Cumings, Bruce. *The Origins of the Korean War.* Vol. 2, *The Roaring of the Cataract 1947–1950.* Princeton, N.J.: Princeton University Press, 1990.

Current Biography 1962. New York: H. H. Wilson, 1963.

Currey, Cecil B. *Edward Lansdale: The Unquiet American.* Boston: Houghton Mifflin, 1988.

Dallek, Robert. *Lone Star Rising: Lyndon Johnson and His Times, 1908–1960.* New York: Oxford University Press, 1991.

Davies, John. *The Legend of Hobey Baker.* Boston: Little, Brown, 1966.

Davis, Elmer. "The Crusade against Acheson." *Harper's Magazine,* March 1951.

Dawson, Graham. "The Blond Bedouin: Lawrence of Arabia, Imperial Adventure and the Imagining of English-British Masculinity." In *Manful Assertions: Masculinities in Britain since 1800.* London: Routledge, 1991.

———. *Soldier Heroes: British Adventure, Empire, and the Imagining of Masculinities.* London: Routledge, 1994.

DeLoach, Cartha. *Hoover's FBI: The Inside Story by Hoover's Trusted Lieutenant.* Washington, D.C.: Regnery Publishing, 1995.

D'Emilio, John. *Sexual Politics, Sexual Communities: The Making of a Homosexual Minority in the United States, 1940–1970.* Chicago: University of Chicago Press, 1983.

———. "The Homosexual Menace: The Politics of Sexuality in Cold War America." In *Making Trouble: Essays on Gay History, Politics, and the University.* New York: Routledge, 1992.

DiLeo, David L. *George Ball, Vietnam, and the Rethinking of Containment.* Chapel Hill: University of North Carolina Press, 1991.

Diamond, Sigmund. "Veritas at Harvard." *New York Review of Books,* April 28, 1977.

———. *Compromised Campus: The Collaboration of Universities with the Intelligence Community, 1945–1955.* New York: Oxford University Press, 1992.

Divine, Robert A. "Vietnam Reconsidered." *Diplomatic History* 12, no. 1 (1988).

Doenecke, Justus D. *Not to the Swift: The Old Isolationists in the Cold War Era.* Lewisburg, Pa.: Bucknell University Press, 1979.

Doherty, Thomas. "Pixies: Homosexuality, Anti-communism, and the Army-McCarthy Hearings." Paper delivered at the annual meeting of the American Studies Association, 1995.

Dooley, Dr. Tom. *Deliver Us from Evil.* New York: Farrar, Straus and Giroux, 1956.

Dudziak, Mary L. "Josephine Baker, Racial Protest, and the Cold War," *Journal of American History* 81, no. 2 (September 1994).

Dugger, Ronnie. *The Politician: The Life and Times of Lyndon Johnson; The Drive for Power from the Frontier to Master of the Senate.* New York: W. W. Norton, 1982.

Dulles, Allen W. Papers. Seely G. Mudd Manuscript Library, Princeton University, Princeton, N.J.

Dulles, John Foster. Papers. White House Memoranda Series. Dwight D. Eisenhower Library, Abilene, Kans.

Edelman, Lee. "Tearooms and Sympathy, or, the Epistemology of the Water Closet." In *Nationalisms and Sexualities,* edited by Andrew Parker et al. New York: Routledge, 1992.

Edwards, Rebecca. *Angels in the Machinery: Gender in American Party Politics from the Civil War to the Progressive Era.* New York: Oxford University Press, 1997.

Ehrenreich, Barbara. *Hearts of Men: The American Dream and the Flight from Commitment.* Garden City, N.Y.: Doubleday, 1983.

Ellsberg, Daniel. "The Quagmire Myth and the Stalemate Machine." In *Papers on the War.* New York: Simon and Schuster, 1972.

Emerson, Gloria. *Winners and Losers: Battles, Retreats, Gains, Losses, and Ruins from a Long War.* New York: Random House, 1976.

Englund, George, dir. *The Ugly American.* Screenplay by Stewart Stern. Universal Pictures, 1963.

Fasteau, Marc Feigen. "Vietnam and the Cult of Toughness in Foreign Policy." In *The Male Machine.* New York: McGraw-Hill, 1974.

Fay, Paul B. *The Pleasure of His Company.* New York: Harper and Row, 1966.

——. Interview by James A. Oesterle, November 9–10, 1970. John F. Kennedy Library, Boston, Mass.

Fisher, James Terrence. *The Catholic Counterculture in America, 1933–1962.* Chapel Hill: University of North Carolina Press, 1989.

——. *Dr. America: The Lives of Thomas A. Dooley, 1927–1961.* Amherst: University of Massachusetts Press, 1997.

Ford, Daniel. *Flying Tigers: Claire Chennault and the American Volunteer Group.* Washington: Smithsonian Institution Press, 1991.

Foreign Relations of the United States, 1949. Vol. 1. Washington, D.C.; U.S. Government Printing Office, 1976.

Foreign Relations of the United States, 1961–1963: Vietnam. 4 Vols. Washington, D.C.: U.S. Government Printing Office, 1988.

Foreign Relations of the United States, 1964–1968: Vietnam 1964. Vol. 1. Washington, D.C.: U.S. Government Printing Office, 1992.

Freedom of Communications: Final Report of the Committee on Commerce, United

States Senate. Part 1, *The Speeches, Remarks, Press Conferences, and Statements of Senator John F. Kennedy, August 1 through November 7, 1960.* Washington, D.C.: U.S. Government Printing Office, 1961.

Freedom of Communications: Final Report of the Committee on Commerce, United States Senate. Part 2, *The Speeches, Remarks, Press Conferences, and Study Papers of Vice President Richard M. Nixon, August 1 through November 7, 1960.* Washington, D.C.: U.S. Government Printing Office, 1961.

Freedom of Communications: Final Report of the Committee on Commerce, United States Senate. Part 3, *The Joint Appearances of Senator John F. Kennedy and Vice President Richard M. Nixon and other 1960 Campaign Presentations.* Washington, D.C.: U.S. Government Printing Office, 1961.

Freeland, Richard M. *The Truman Doctrine and the Origins of McCarthyism: Foreign Policy, Domestic Politics, and Internal Security, 1946–1948.* New York: Alfred A. Knopf, 1972.

Fried, Richard. *Nightmare in Red: The McCarthy Era in Perspective.* New York: Oxford University Press.

Friedan, Betty. *The Feminine Mystique.* New York: W. W. Norton, 1963.

Fussell, Paul. *Wartime: Understanding and Behavior in the Second World War.* New York: Oxford University Press, 1989.

Gabler, Neal. *An Empire of Their Own: How the Jews Invented Hollywood.* New York: Crown Publishers, 1988.

Gelb, Leslie, and Richard Betts. *The Irony of Vietnam: The System Worked.* Washington, D.C.: Brookings Institution, 1979.

Gellman, Irwin F. *Secret Affairs: Franklin Roosevelt, Cordell Hull, and Sumner Welles.* Baltimore: Johns Hopkins University Press, 1995.

Gentry, Curt. *J. Edgar Hoover: The Man and the Secrets.* New York: W. W. Norton, 1991.

Gergen, Mary M., and Kenneth J. Gergen, "Autobiographies and the Shaping of Gendered Lives." In *Discourse and Lifespan Identity,* edited by Nikolas Coupland and Jon F. Nussbaum. Newbury Park, Calif.: Sage, 1993.

Gilmore, David D. *Manhood in the Making: Cultural Concepts of Masculinity.* New Haven: Yale University Press, 1990.

Gilpatric, Roswell. Interview by Dennis J. O'Brien, May 5, 1970. John F. Kennedy Library, Boston, Mass.

Gittinger, Ted, ed., *The Johnson Years: A Vietnam Roundtable.* Austin, Tex.: Lyndon B. Johnson School of Public Affairs, 1993.

Goffman, Erving. "The Characteristics of Total Institutions." In *Complex Organizations: A Sociological Reader,* edited by Amitai Etzioni. New York: Holt, Rinehart and Winston, 1966.

Goodman, George W. "The Unconventional Warriors." *Esquire,* November 1961.

Goodwin, Doris Kearns. *The Fitzgeralds and the Kennedys.* New York: Simon and Schuster, 1987.

———. *Lyndon Johnson and the American Dream.* New York: St. Martin's, 1991.

Goodwin, Richard N. *Remembering America: A Voice from the Sixties.* Boston: Little, Brown, 1988.

Gould, Stephen Jay. "Speaking of Snails and Scales." *Natural History,* May 1995.

Graebner, Norman A. *An Uncertain Tradition: American Secretaries of State in the Twentieth Century.* New York: McGraw-Hill, 1961.

Green, Harvey. *Fit for America: Health, Fitness, Sport, and American Society.* New York: Pantheon Books, 1986.

Green, Martin. *Dreams of Adventure, Deeds of Empire.* New York: Basic Books, 1979.

———. *The Adventurous Male: Chapters in the History of the White Male Mind.* University Park: Pennsylvania State University Press, 1993.

Greene, Graham. *The Quiet American.* London: W. Heinemann, 1955.

Griffith, Robert. *The Politics of Fear: Joseph R. McCarthy and the Senate.* 2d ed. Amherst: University of Massachusetts Press, 1987.

Griffith, Robert, and Athan Theoharis, eds. *The Specter: Original Essays on the Cold War and the Origins of McCarthyism.* New York: Franklin Watts, 1974.

Grose, Peter. *Operation Rollback: America's Secret War behind the Iron Curtain.* Boston: Houghton Mifflin, 2000.

Halberstam, David. *The Best and the Brightest.* New York: Random House, 1972.

Halpern, Samuel. "Revisiting the Cuban Missile Crisis." *Society for Historians of American Foreign Relations Newsletter* 25, no. 1 (March 1994).

Hamilton, Nigel. *JFK: Reckless Youth.* New York: Random House, 1992.

Hartsock, Nancy C. M. "Masculinity, Heroism, and the Making of War." In *Rocking the Ship of State: Toward a Feminist Peace Politics,* edited by Adrienne Harris and Ynestra King. Boulder, Colo.: Westview, 1989.

Heller, Deane, and David Heller. *The Kennedy Cabinet.* Freeport, N.Y.: Books for Libraries Press, 1961.

Hellmann, John. *American Myth and the Legacy of Vietnam.* New York: Columbia University Press, 1986.

Hersh, Burton. *The Old Boys: The American Elite and the Origins of the CIA.* New York: Charles Scribner's Sons, 1992.

Hilsman, Roger. Papers. John F. Kennedy Library, Boston, Mass.

———. "Internal War: The New Communist Tactic." In *The Guerrilla—and How to Fight Him,* edited by T. N. Greene. New York: Praeger, 1962.

———. *To Move a Nation: The Politics of Foreign Policy in the Administration of John F. Kennedy.* New York: Doubleday, 1967.

———. Interview by Dennis J. O'Brien, August 14, 1970. John F. Kennedy Library, Boston, Mass.

———. *American Guerrilla: My War behind Japanese Lines.* Washington, D.C.: Brassey's, 1990.

Hiss, Tony. *Laughing Last.* Boston: Houghton Mifflin, 1977.

Hodgson, Godfrey. "The Establishment." *Foreign Policy,* no. 10 (spring 1973).

———. *The Colonel: The Life and Wars of Henry Stimson, 1867–1950.* New York: Alfred A. Knopf, 1990.

Hogan, J. M. *Impelled into Experiences: The Story of the Outward Bound Schools.* Wakefield, England: Educational Productions, 1968.

Hoganson, Kristin L. *Fighting for American Manhood: How Gender Politics Provoked the Spanish-American and Philippine-American Wars.* New Haven: Yale University Press, 1998.

Hoopes, Townsend. *The Devil and John Foster Dulles.* Boston: Little, Brown, 1973.

Hoopes, Townsend, and Douglas Brinkley. *Driven Patriot: The Life and Times of James Forrestal.* New York: Alfred A. Knopf, 1992.

Hyam, Ronald. *Empire and Sexuality: The British Experience.* Manchester: Manchester University Press, 1990.

Isaacson, Walter, and Evan Thomas. *The Wise Men: Six Friends and the World They Made.* New York: Simon and Schuster, 1986.

Jacobs, Meg. "'How about Some Meat': The Office of Price Administration, Consumption Politics, and State Building from the Bottom Up, 1941–1946," *Journal of American History* 84, no. 3 (December 1997).

Johns, Andrew L. "Re: McNamara's Memoirs." Electronic posting, H-Net, Diplomatic history discussion group (H-Diplo), June 8, 1995.

Jones, James H., *Alfred C. Kinsey: A Public/Private Life.* New York: W. W. Norton, 1997.

Kahin, George McT. *Intervention: How America Became Involved in Vietnam.* New York: Alfred A. Knopf, 1986.

Kahn, E. J., Jr. *The China Hands: America's Foreign Service Officers and What Befell Them.* New York: Viking Press, 1972.

Kaiser, Charles. *The Gay Metropolis, 1940–1996.* Boston: Houghton Mifflin, 1997.

Kalman, Laura. *Abe Fortas: A Biography.* New Haven: Yale University Press, 1990.

Kann, Mark E. *On the Man Question: Gender and Civic Virtue in America.* Philadelphia: Temple University Press, 1991.

Kaplan, Amy. "Romancing the Empire: The Embodiment of American Masculinity in the Popular Historical Novel of the 1890s." *American Literary History* 2, no. 4 (winter 1990).

Kattenburg, Paul. *The Vietnam Trauma in American Foreign Policy, 1945–75.* New Brunswick, N.J.: Transaction Books, 1980.

Keegan, John. *The Face of Battle.* New York: Viking Press, 1976.

Kennedy, John F. Personal Papers. John F. Kennedy Library, Boston, Mass.

——. "America's Stake in Vietnam." *Vital Speeches,* August 1, 1956.

——. *The Strategy of Peace.* New York: Harper, 1960.

——. "The Soft American." *Sports Illustrated,* December 26, 1960.

——. "The Vigor We Need." *Sports Illustrated,* July 16, 1962.

Kennedy, Robert F. *Thirteen Days: A Memoir of the Cuban Missile Crisis.* New York: W. W. Norton, 1971.

Kerkvliet, Benedict J. *The Huk Rebellion: A Study of Peasant Revolt in the Philippines.* Berkeley: University of California Press, 1977.

Kinsey, Alfred C., Wardell B. Pomeroy, and Clyde E. Martin. *Sexual Behavior in the Human Male.* Philadelphia: W. B. Saunders, 1948.

Kirkpatrick, Lyman B., Jr. *The Real CIA.* New York: Macmillan, 1968.

Kofsky, Frank. *Harry S. Truman and the War Scare of 1948: A Successful Campaign to Deceive the Nation.* New York: St. Martin's, 1993.

Kovel, Joel. *Red Hunting in the Promised Land: Anticommunism and the Making of America.* New York: Basic Books, 1994.

Kraft, Joseph. "Hot Weapon in the Cold War." *Saturday Evening Post,* April 28 1962.

La Farge, Oliver. *Raw Material.* Boston: Houghton Mifflin, 1945.

Lait, Jack, and Lee Mortimer. *Washington Confidential.* New York: Crown Publishers, 1951.

Lansdale, Edward G. Papers. Hoover Institution Archives, Stanford University, Stanford, Calif.

——. *In the Midst of Wars: An American's Mission to Southeast Asia.* New York: Fordham University Press, 1991.

Lears, T. J. Jackson. *No Place of Grace: Antimodernism and the Transformation of American Culture 1880–1920.* New York: Pantheon, 1981.

Lederer, William J. Papers. Special Collections and Archives, W. E. B. Du Bois Library, University of Massachusetts, Amherst.

Lederer, William J., and Eugene Burdick. *The Ugly American.* New York: W. W. Norton, 1958.

Leed, Eric J. *No Man's Land: Combat and Identity in World War I.* New York: Cambridge University Press, 1979.

Levine, Steven B. "The Rise of American Boarding Schools and the Development of a National Upper Class." *Social Problems* 28, no. 1 (October 1980).

Lewontin, R. C. "'Sex, Lies, and Social Science,' An Exchange." *New York Review of Books,* May 25, 1995.

Lipsitz, George. *Rainbow at Midnight: Labor and Culture in the 1940s.* Urbana: University of Illinois Press, 1994.

Logevall, Fredrik. *Choosing War: The Lost Chance for Peace and the Escalation of War in Vietnam.* Berkeley: University of California Press, 1999.

Lovett, Robert A. Interview by Dorothy Fosdick, July 20, 1964. John F. Kennedy Library, Boston, Mass.

——. Interview by Dorothy Fosdick, November 19, 1964. John F. Kennedy Library, Boston, Mass.

MacKaye, Milton. "Bundy of the White House." *Saturday Evening Post,* March 10, 1962.

Major, Ralph H. "New Moral Menace to Our Youth." *Coronet,* September 1950.

Mangan, J. A. *Athleticism in the Victorian and Edwardian Public School: The Emergence and Consolidation of an Educational Ideal.* Cambridge: Cambridge University Press, 1981.

——. *The Games Ethic and Imperialism: Aspects of the Diffusion of an Ideal.* Harmondsworth, England: Penguin, 1986.

Mangan, J. A., and James Walvin, eds. *Manliness and Morality: Middle-Class Masculinity in Britain and America 1800–1940.* Manchester: Manchester University Press, 1986.

Martin, Ralph. *A Hero for Our Time: An Intimate Story of the Kennedy Years.* New York: Macmillan, 1983.

May, Elaine Tyler. *Homeward Bound: American Families in the Cold War Era.* New York: Basic Books, 1988.

McCarran, Pat. Papers. Eva Adams Collection, University of Reno Library, Reno, Nevada.

McCarthy, Joe. *Major Speeches and Debates of Senator Joe McCarthy Delivered in the United States Senate 1950–1951.* Washington, D.C.: U.S. Government Printing Office, n.d.

——. *McCarthyism, the Fight for America: Documented Answers to Questions Asked by Friend and Foe.* New York: Devin-Adair, 1952.

McCullough, David. *Mornings on Horseback.* New York: Simon and Schuster, 1981.

McLachlan, James. *American Boarding Schools: A Historical Study.* New York: Charles Scribner's Sons, 1970.

McNamara, Robert S., with Brian VanDeMark. *In Retrospect: The Tragedy and Lessons of Vietnam.* New York: Times Books, 1995.

McPartland, John. "Portrait of an American Communist." *Life,* January 5, 1948.

Meeting Notes File. Lyndon Baines Johnson Library, Austin, Tex.

Merry, Robert W. *Taking on the World: Joseph and Stewart Alsop—Guardians of the American Century.* New York: Viking, 1996.

Meyer, Cord. *Facing Reality: From World Federalism to the CIA.* New York: Harper and Row, 1980.

Miller, Patrick B. *The Playing Fields of American Culture: Athletics and Higher Education, 1850–1945.* New York: Oxford University Press, forthcoming.

Mills, C. Wright. *The Power Elite.* New York: Oxford University Press, 1956.

Moise, Edwin E. *Tonkin Gulf and the Escalation of the Vietnam War.* Chapel Hill: University of North Carolina Press, 1996.

Morgan, Joseph Gerard. "The Vietnam Lobby: The American Friends of Vietnam, 1955–1975." Ph.D. diss., Georgetown University, 1993.

Morgan, Ted. *FDR: A Biography.* New York: Simon and Schuster, 1985

Moskin, J. Robert. "Why Do Women Dominate Him?" In *The Decline of the American Male,* edited by the editors of *Look.* New York: Random House, 1958.

Mosse, George L. *Nationalism and Sexuality: Middle Class Morality and Sexual Norms in Modern Europe.* Madison: University of Wisconsin Press, 1988.

——. *Fallen Soldiers: Reshaping the Memory of the World Wars.* New York: Oxford University Press, 1990.

——. *The Image of Man: The Creation of Modern Masculinity.* New York: Oxford University Press, 1996.

Mrozek, Donald J. *Sport and American Mentality, 1880–1910.* Knoxville: University of Kentucky Press, 1983.

Murphy, Lawrence R. "The House on Pacific Street: Homosexuality, Intrigue, and Politics during World War II." *Journal of Homosexuality* 12, no. 1 (fall 1985).

Nashel, Jonathan D. "Edward Lansdale and the American Attempt to Remake Southeast Asia, 1945–1965." Ph.D. diss., Rutgers University, 1994.

National Security Files. John F. Kennedy Library. , Boston, Mass.

National Security Files. Lyndon Baines Johnson Library, Austin, Tex.

Newman, Robert P. *Owen Lattimore and the "Loss" of China.* Berkeley: University of California Press, 1992.

O'Donnell, Kenneth. Interview by Paige E. Mulhollan, July 23, 1969. Lyndon Baines Johnson Library, Austin, Tex.

O'Donnell, Kenneth P., and David F. Powers with Joe McCarthy. *"Johnny, We Hardly Knew Ye": Memories of John Fitzgerald Kennedy*. Boston: Little, Brown, 1972.

O'Reilly, Kenneth. *"Racial Matters": The FBI's Secret File on Black America, 1960–1972*. New York: Free Press, 1989.

Oshinsky, David M. *A Conspiracy So Immense: The World of Joe McCarthy*. New York: Free Press, 1983.

Packard, Vance. *The Waste Makers*. New York: David McKay, 1960.

Paine, Ralph D. *The First Yale Unit: A Story of Naval Aviation, 1916–1919*. 2 Vols. Cambridge, Mass.: Riverside Press, 1925.

Park, Roberta J. "Biological Thought, Athletics and the Formation of a 'Man of Character': 1830–1900." In *Manliness and Morality: Middle-Class Masculinity in Britain and America 1800–1940,* edited by J. A. Mangan and James Walvin. Manchester: Manchester University Press, 1986.

Parmet, Herbert S. *Jack: The Struggles of John F. Kennedy*. New York: Dial Press, 1980.

Pearlman, Michael. *To Make Democracy Safe for America: Patricians and Preparedness in the Progressive Era*. Urbana: University of Illinois Press, 1984.

Pier, Arthur Stanwood. *St. Paul's School 1885–1934*. New York: Charles Scribner's Sons, 1934.

Powers, Richard Gid. *Secrecy and Power: The Life of J. Edgar Hoover*. New York: Free Press, 1987.

——. *Not without Honor: The History of American Anticommunism*. New York: Free Press, 1995.

President's Office Files. John F. Kennedy Library, Boston, Mass.

Public Papers of the Presidents of the United States: John F. Kennedy: Containing the Public Messages, Speeches, and Statements of the President, January 1 to November 22, 1963. Washington, D.C.: U.S. Government Printing Office, 1964.

Public Papers of the Presidents of the United States: Lyndon B. Johnson: Containing the Public Messages, Speeches and Statements of the President, 1963–1964. Book 2. Washington, D.C.: U.S. Government Printing Office, 1965.

Redmon, Coates. *Come As You Are: The Peace Corps Story*. San Diego: Harcourt Brace Jovanovich, 1986.

Reeves, Richard. *President Kennedy: Profile of Power*. New York: Simon & Schuster, 1993.

Reeves, Thomas C. *The Life and Times of Joe McCarthy: A Biography*. New York: Stein and Day, 1982.

——. *A Question of Character: A Life of John F. Kennedy*. New York: Free Press, 1991.

Reis, Elizabeth. "The Devil, the Body, and the Feminine Soul in Puritan New England." *Journal of American History* 82, no. 1 (June 1995).

Ribuffo, Leo P. *The Old Christian Right: The Protestant Far Right from the Great Depression to the Cold War*. Philadelphia: Temple University Press, 1983.

Rice, Gerard T. *The Bold Experiment: JFK's Peace Corps*. Notre Dame, Ind.: University of Notre Dame Press, 1985.

Rickenbacker, Eddie. *Fighting the Flying Circus*. New York: Frederick A. Stokes, 1919.

Riesman, David. *The Lonely Crowd*. New Haven: Yale University Press, 1950.

Roden, Donald. *Schooldays in Imperial Japan: A Study in the Culture of a Student Elite*. Berkeley: University of California Press, 1980.

Rogin, Michael Paul. *The Intellectuals and McCarthy: The Radical Specter*. Cambridge: MIT Press, 1967.

——. *Ronald Reagan, The Movie and Other Episodes in Political Demonology*. Berkeley: University of California Press, 1987.

Roosevelt, Archibald B. *For Lust of Knowing: Memoirs of an Intelligence Officer*. Boston: Little, Brown, 1988.

Roosevelt, Theodore. *The Strenuous Life: Essays and Addresses*. New York: Century, 1902.

——. *The Rough Riders*. In *Theodore Roosevelt: Memorial Edition*. New York: Charles Scribner's Sons, 1924.

Roper, Michael, and John Tosh, eds. *Manful Assertions: Masculinities in Britain since 1800*. London: Routledge, 1991.

Rosenberg, Stanley D. "The Threshold of Thrill: Life Stories in the Skies over Southeast Asia." In *Gendering War Talk*. Princeton, N.J.: Princeton University Press, 1993.

Rostow, W. W. *The Diffusion of Power: An Essay in Recent History*. New York: Macmillan, 1972.

——. Interview by author, Austin, Tex., July 21, 1992.

Rotundo, E. Anthony. *American Manhood: Transformations in Masculinity from the Revolution to the Modern Era*. New York: Basic Books, 1993.

Royster, Charles. *A Revolutionary People at War: The Continental Army and the American Character, 1775–1783*. Chapel Hill: University of North Carolina Press, 1979.

Rubin, Gayle. "The Traffic in Women: Notes on the 'Political Economy' of Sex." In *Toward an Anthropology of Women*, edited by Rayna R. Reiter. New York: Monthly Review Press, 1975.

Rusk, Dean, as told to Richard Rusk. *As I Saw It*. Edited by Daniel S. Papp. New York: W. W. Norton, 1990.

Sanday, Peggy Reeves. *Fraternity Gang Rape: Sex, Brotherhood, and Privilege on Campus*. New York: New York University Press, 1990.

Saveth, Edward N. "The Education of an Elite." *History of Education Quarterly* 28, no. 3 (fall 1988).

Schaller, Michael. *Douglas MacArthur: The Far Eastern General*. New York: Oxford University Press, 1988.

Schlesinger, Arthur M., Jr. Papers. John F. Kennedy Library, Boston, Mass.

——. "The U.S. Communist Party." *Life,* July 29, 1946.

——. *The Vital Center: The Politics of Freedom*. Boston: Houghton Mifflin, 1949.

——. *The Politics of Hope*. Boston: Houghton Mifflin, 1963.

——. *A Thousand Days: John F. Kennedy in the White House*. Boston: Houghton Mifflin, 1965.

——. *Robert Kennedy and His Times*. Boston: Houghton Mifflin, 1978.

Schrecker, Ellen. *No Ivory Tower: McCarthyism and the Universities.* New York: Oxford University Press, 1986.

——. *Many Are the Crimes: McCarthyism in America.* Boston: Little, Brown, 1998.

Scott, James Brown. *Robert Bacon: Life and Letters.* New York: Doubleday, Page, 1923.

Scott, Joan W. "Gender: A Useful Category of Historical Analysis." *American Historical Review,* December 1986.

Shafer, Michael D. *Deadly Paradigms: The Failure of U.S. Counterinsurgency Policy.* Princeton, N.J.: Princeton University Press, 1988.

Shapley, Deborah. *Promise and Power: The Life and Times of Robert McNamara.* Boston: Little, Brown, 1993.

Sheehan, Neil. *A Bright Shining Lie: John Paul Vann and America in Vietnam.* New York: Random House, 1988.

Shils, Edward A. *The Torment of Secrecy: The Background and Consequences of American Security Policy,* Chicago: Ivan R. Dee, 1996.

Shilts, Randy. *Conduct Unbecoming: Gays and Lesbians in the U.S. Military.* New York: St. Martin's Press, 1993.

Showalter, Elaine. "Rivers and Sassoon: The Inscription of Male Gender Anxieties." In *Behind the Lines: Gender and the Two World Wars,* edited by Margaret Randolf Higonnet et al. New Haven: Yale University Press, 1987.

Shriver, Sargent. "Outlook for Corpsmen: Army Could Be Better." *Life,* March 17, 1961, 38–39.

Simpson, Christopher. *Blowback: America's Recruitment of Nazis and Its Effect on the Cold War.* New York: Collier Books, 1988.

Slotkin, Richard. *Gunfighter Nation: The Myth of the Frontier in Twentieth-Century America.* New York: Atheneum, 1992.

Smith, Geoffrey. "National Security and Personal Isolation: Sex, Gender, and Disease in the Cold-War United States." *International History Review* 14, no. 2 (May 1992).

Sommer, Fred. "Anthony Blunt and Guy Burgess, Gay Spies." In *Gay Men and the Sexual History of the Political Left,* edited by Gert Hekma, Harry Oosterhuis, and James Steakley. New York: Haworth, 1995.

Sorensen, Theodore. Interview by Carl Kaysen, April 6, 1964. John F. Kennedy Library, Boston, Mass.

——. *Kennedy.* New York: Harper and Row, 1965.

Spingarn, Stephen J. Papers. Assistant to the President File, Harry S. Truman Library, Independence, Mo.

Stein, Jean. *American Journey: The Times of Robert Kennedy.* Edited by George Plimpton. New York: Harcourt Brace Jovanovich, 1970.

Stimson, Henry L., and McGeorge Bundy. *On Active Service in Peace and War.* New York: Harper & Brothers, 1948.

Straight, Michael. "Trial by Television—II: McCarthy Takes the Stand," *New Republic,* May 17, 1954.

——. "Trial by Television—V: The Two Roy Cohns," *New Republic,* June 14, 1954.

——. "Trial by Television—VII: The Fanaticism of Joseph McCarthy," *New Republic,* June 28, 1954.

Strecker, Edward A. *Their Mothers' Sons: The Psychiatrist Examines an American Problem.* Philadelphia: J. B. Lippincott, 1946.

Summers, Anthony. *Official and Confidential: The Secret Life of J. Edgar Hoover.* New York: G. P. Putnam's Sons, 1993.

Tanenhaus, Sam. *Whittaker Chambers: A Biography.* New York: Random House, 1997.

Thayer, Charles W. Papers. Harry S. Truman Library, Independence, Mo.

———. *Guerrilla.* New York: Harper and Row, 1963.

Theoharis, Athan G. *Seeds of Repression: Harry S. Truman and the Origins of McCarthyism.* Chicago: Quadrangle Books, 1971.

———. "Operation 'Adlai/Adeline': How the FBI Gaybaited Stevenson." *Nation,* May 7, 1990.

———. *J. Edgar Hoover, Sex, and Crime.* Chicago: Ivan R. Dee, 1995.

———, ed. *Beyond the Hiss Case: The FBI, Congress, and the Cold War.* Philadelphia: Temple University Press, 1982.

———. *From the Secret Files of J. Edgar Hoover.* Chicago: Ivan R. Dee, 1993.

Thomas, Lately. *When Even Angels Wept: The Senator Joseph McCarthy Affair—a Story without a Hero.* New York: William Morrow, 1973.

Thomson, James C. Papers. John F. Kennedy Library, Boston, Mass.

———. Interview by Paige E. Mulhollan, July 22, 1971. Lyndon Baines Johnson Library, Austin, Tex.

Townsend, Kim. *Manhood at Harvard: William James and Others.* New York: W. W. Norton, 1996.

Truman, Harry S. Papers. White House Central Files, Harry S. Truman Library, Independence, Mo.

U.S. Senate. *Employment of Homosexuals and Other Sex Perverts in Government: Interim Report Submitted to the Committee on Expenditures in the Executive Department.* . . . 81st Congress, 2d sess., S. Doc. 241. Washington, D.C.: U.S. Government Printing Office, 1950.

U.S. Senate Committee on Foreign Relations. *Hearings on the Nomination of Charles E. Bohlen,* 83d Cong., 1st sess. Washington, D.C.: U.S. Government Printing Office, 1953.

———. *Report of Proceedings, Nomination of Charles E. Bohlen,* 83d Cong., executive sess., March 18, 1953.

———. *Executive Sessions of the Senate Foreign Relations Committee (Historical Series),* vol. 5, 83d Cong., 1st sess. Washington, D.C.: U.S. Government Printing Office, 1977.

U.S. Senate Judiciary Committee. Senate Internal Security Subcommittee. Records, 1951–1975, RG 46. National Archives, Washington, D.C.

VanDeMark, Brian. *Into the Quagmire: Lyndon Johnson and the Escalation of the Vietnam War.* New York: Oxford University Press, 1991.

Von Eschen, Penny M. "Who's the Real Ambassador? Exploding Cold War Racial Ideology." In *Cold War Constructions: The Political Culture of United States Imperialism, 1945–1966,* edited by Christian G. Appy. Amherst: University of Massachusetts Press, 2000.

von Hoffman, Nicholas. *Citizen Cohn.* New York: Doubleday, 1988.

———. "Crossing the White-Shoe Line." *New Yorker,* May 10 1993.

Webb, Walter Prescott. *The Texas Rangers.* Austin: University of Texas Press, 1965.

Weinstein, Allen. *Perjury: The Hiss-Chambers Case.* New York: Alfred A. Knopf, 1978.

Wherry, Kenneth. Papers. Nebraska State Historical Society Archives, Lincoln, Nebraska.

———. *Report of the Investigations of the Junior Senator of Nebraska . . . on the Infiltration of Subversives and Moral Perverts into the Executive Branch of the United States Government.* Senate Committee Print S4179, 81st Cong., 2d sess., May 1950.

White, G. Edward. *The Eastern Establishment and the Western Experience: The West of Frederic Remington, Theodore Roosevelt, and Owen Wister.* New Haven: Yale University Press, 1968.

White, W. L. *They Were Expendable.* New York: Harcourt, Brace, 1942.

White, William S. "Portrait of a 'Fundamentalist.'" *New York Times Magazine,* January 15, 1950.

Whyte, William W. *The Organization Man.* New York: Simon and Schuster, 1956.

Wills, Garry. *The Kennedy Imprisonment: A Meditation on Power.* Boston: Little, Brown, 1982.

Wilson, Renate. *Inside Outward Bound.* Charlotte, N.C.: Fast and McMillan, 1981.

Wingenbach, Charles E. *The Peace Corps—Who, How, and Where.* New York: John Day, 1963.

Wister, Owen. *Roosevelt: The Story of a Friendship, 1880–1919.* New York: Macmillan, 1930.

Wolf, Eric R. *Envisioning Power: Ideologies of Crisis and Dominance.* Berkeley: University of California Press, 1999.

Wood, Gordon S. *The Creation of the American Republic: 1776–1787.* Chapel Hill: University of North Carolina Press, 1969.

Wylie, Philip. *Generation of Vipers.* New York: Farrar & Rinehart, 1942.

Yarmolinsky, Adam. Papers. John F. Kennedy Library, Boston, Mass.

Yoder, Edwin M. *Joe Alsop's Cold War: A Study of Journalistic Influence and Intrigue.* Chapel Hill: University of North Carolina Press, 1995.

Zahner, Louis, ed. *Views from the Circle: Seventy-Five Years of Groton School.* Groton, Mass.: Trustees of Groton School, 1960.

Zeligs, Meyer A. *Friendship and Fratricide: An Analysis of Whittaker Chambers and Alger Hiss.* New York: Viking, 1967.

INDEX

ROBERT DEAN is assistant professor of history at Eastern Washington University. He studied Fine Art at the University of Colorado and received his Ph.D. in history from the University of Arizona. He is married with two children and lives in Spokane, Washington, and Tucson, Arizona.

ISBN 1-55849-414-6

90000

9 781558 494145